# In the Saddle with the Texans

## Day-by-Day with Parsons's Cavalry Brigade, 1862-1865

edited by
Anne J. Bailey

McWhiney Foundation Press
McMurry University
Abilene, Texas

**Support for this project was provided by the Summerfield G. Roberts Foundation, the Summerlee Foundation, and the Nicholas P. Sims Library in Waxahachie, Texas.**

**Library of Congress Cataloging-in-Publication Data**

In the saddle with the Texans: day-by-day with Parsons's Cavalry Brigade, 1862-1865 / edited by Anne J. Bailey.
p. cm.
Includes bibliographical references and index.
ISBN 1-893114-48-1 (cloth)
1. Confederate States of America. Army. Texas Cavalry. Parsons's Brigade. 2. Texas--History--Civil War, 1861-1865--Regimental histories. 3. United States--History--Civil War, 1861-1865--Regimental histories. 4. Parsons, William Henry, 1826-1907. 5. Confederate States of America. Army. Texas Cavalry--Military life--Sources. 6. Texas--History--Civil War, 1861-1865--Cavalry operations--Sources. 7. Mississippi River Valley--History--Civil War, 1861-1865--Cavalry operations--Sources. 8. United States--History--Civil War, 1861-1865--Cavalry operations--Sources.
I. Bailey, Anne J.

E580.6.P37I5 2004
973.7'464--dc22

2004014587



McWhiney Foundation Press
McMurry University, Box 637
Abilene, Texas 79697
(325) 793-4682
www.mcwhiney.org

Printed in the United States of America

1-893114-48-1
10 9 8 7 6 5 4 3 2 1

Book Designed by Rosenbohm Graphic Design

Cover Illustration: "The Attack at Blair's Landing," *Harper's New Monthly Magazine*, April 1865.

# TABLE OF CONTENTS



# LIST OF ILLUSTRATIONS



(Maps 1 and 4 are from the *War of the Rebellion: A Compilation of the Union and Confederate Armies*. Maps 2 and 3 are from the *Official Records of the Union and Confederate Navies in the War of the Rebellion.)*

**For Samuel R. Hilburn**

# ACKNOWLEDGMENTS

Many people played a part in the development of this book. Steve Chapman, chair of the Trustees of the Nicholas P. Sims Library in Waxahachie, Texas, Susan Maxwell, head librarian, and all the staff at the library were generous in every way possible. Valuable support also came from the Summerlee Foundation, Order of the Southern Cross, Sons of Confederate Veterans, Order of the Confederate Rose, United Daughters of the Confederacy, and descendants of the men in Parsons's Brigade Association at Hill College, Hillsboro, Texas.

Yet this project would not have been possible if Sande Wilkinson of Waxahachie had not wanted to recognize her ancestor, Samuel R. Hilburn, who was a private in Company C, Nineteenth Texas Cavalry. She understood the historical significance of the Order Book of Parsons's Texas Cavalry Brigade, tucked away in the Special Collections at the Sims Library, and it was through her tireless efforts that it has been transcribed and published. She contacted me in 2000, asking me to take on the project. My graduate assistant, Carlyn E. Kahl, entered all the correspondence in a computer, spending many hours transcribing the often faded and hurried handwriting from the microfilm copy. Her assistance was invaluable, and allowed me the time to ponder the unreadable script. Carly and I passed many hours trying to decipher the words written more than one hundred forty years ago; it would have been a monumental task for one person to record the hundreds of orders in the collection. Finally, I must thank Gary D. Joiner, who helped me find the locations of obscure ferries and picket points in Louisiana, and graciously read the chapters on that state. Many other individuals, too many to name, helped me identify locations. I appreciate the help from all involved.

Anne J. Bailey

# A NOTE ON TRANSCRIPTION

The original spelling and punctuation has been retained, regardless of errors (i.e. Parson's for Parsons' or Parsons's) except in a few cases (calvary was changed to cavalry). The use of [*sic*] to indicate an incorrect spelling or other error is used only in cases where the original would appear as an obvious typographical error (although there are frequent phonetic spellings or just plain carelessness on the part of the writer where *sic* was not added). Because the adjutant oftentimes took dictation directly from the commander, he frequently composed the orders so rapidly that he did not worry about grammar or style. Since adjutants earned the position because of their friendship with the commander as well as their penmanship, one would hope their handwriting would be clear and concise. That was not always the case, and many of the orders indicate the lack of a polished vocabulary and evidence of poor grammar. Nonetheless, it could also be that adjutants may have employed a sort of shorthand for common words; for example, the use of "an" for "and" occasionally appears. A far more likely explanation is that the orders were hastily written with little care or attention to detail, for in many cases the handwriting was so sloppy that it was barely discernible and letters are obviously missing from simple words. Therefore, if the order is readable as written the editor has left any misspelled words or lack of punctuation marks without inserting further explanations. Nonetheless, the reader will note that the editor sometimes added letters to words in brackets to make the meaning precise, but in most cases the spelling was preserved as initially penned.

The editor has tried to be as faithful to the original as possible in transcribing these orders, but in some cases their fragile or deteriorated condition has made that very difficult. Often the writing is faded or complete sections of the orders are torn. The insertion of a question mark in parenthesis (?) means that the transcription was unclear or damaged and [torn] is inserted where part of the order is missing. Capitalization has been retained as written in the original.

Since many of the documents were not entered by date, it was necessary to place them in chronological order first, thus creating an accurate day-by-day portrait of the brigade. Both general and special orders are integrated together so that the story is told chronologically. While it was often difficult or impossible to read damaged and faded orders, only a handful had to be eliminated. Any errors in the text or dates are the fault of the editor, as transcribing the documents was by far the greatest challenge.

Chapters are divided by both date and the state where the men served at that time. The brigade fought in Arkansas in 1862, then moved to Louisiana in 1863, and alternated between Louisiana and Arkansas from 1863 until it returned to Texas in 1865. The chapter introductions are meant to help the reader understand the overall wartime situation while at the same time place the brigade in the context of military events as they unfolded in the Trans-Mississippi.

Individuals are identified by company and regiment (if possible), particularly Texas soldiers found in the "Compiled Service Records of Confederate Soldiers Who Served in Organization from the State of Texas" (Washington, D.C.: National Archives and Records Administration). Those men who served as officers—colonels, lieutenant colonels, majors, and company captains—have further information taken from the 1860 manuscript census records (Eighth Census of the United States, United States Bureau of the Census, National Archives, Washington, D.C.) the first time they are mentioned in the text. Those individuals, generally privates, who are not identified were not found in the Compiled Service Records (although they obviously joined the regiment at some point). Moreover, it was also often impossible to decipher some of the names of individuals making it possible to overlook a person simply because of bad handwriting or faded ink. Unfortunately, the records relating to soldiers in the Trans-Mississippi, particularly cavalrymen, are not always reliable, as individuals tended to change companies or regiments to join friends or relatives in other units. The muster rolls become less useful in the later years of the war, and this was frequently when men moved from unit to unit with ease. Since the goal of this work was to follow the wartime service of the Texans, only well-known Arkansas and Louisiana soldiers are identified.

Finally, there are going to some unavoidable errors in spelling, so a person looking for an ancestor should try various possibilities. The adjutants often wrote names phonetically and they were not always careful to insure the individual's given name or initials were correct. An underline indicates that a word or name could not be deciphered. If it appeared that an individual could be identified with some certainty, the full name or initials have been inserted in brackets. Unfortunately, it was not possible to determine the identity of every person mentioned in the documents.

# INTRODUCTION

The daily life of Confederate cavalrymen was not glamorous or exciting as many postwar writers have asked readers to believe. While flamboyant commanders such as J.E.B. Stuart and John Hunt Morgan certainly caught the attention of the southern press and became glorified southern cavaliers following the war, the typical rebel cavalryman served without any fanfare. Far more common were the hard-riding troopers who served under practical-minded commanders such as Nathan Bedford Forrest. Each day began before dawn and ended after dark. There was no father, mother, wife, or children to greet an individual when he rose in the morning or kiss him before he went to bed at night. His military company became his world. Instead of a bed, he slept on the ground. If he was wounded and died, he died without the comfort of his relatives. His messmates became his family; his home was wherever military commanders ordered his regiment.

In spite of never-ending hardships, those Texans who fought as cavalry in the Trans-Mississippi served throughout the war, for by doing so they protected their homes and families from invading armies. William Henry Parsons understood this dedication when he pointed out in 1878: "The Texas Regiments of Virginia may have for a time succeeded in keeping the Federal armies out of Richmond, but the army of the Trans-Mississippi . . . did keep formidable Federal armies out of Texas, and never permitted hostile foot to march over her soil." Writing thirteen years after the war ended, he lamented that Trans-Mississippi Confederates had received little recognition for their service, but noted that because of "the alertness and valor of this army whose praises and annals are yet unrecorded, and unrecognized," most of Texas escaped the destruction that had accompanied northern armies in other regions across the South.[1]

[1] W.H. Parsons to W.H. Getzendaner, June 24, 1878, *A Brief and Condensed History of Parsons' Texas Cavalry Brigade Composed of Twelfth, Nineteenth, Twenty-First, Morgan's Battalion, and Pratt's Battery of Artillery of the Confederate States: Together with Roster of the Several Commands as far as obtainable—Some Historical Sketches—General Orders and a Memoranda of Parson's Brigade Association* (Waxahachie, Texas: J.M. Flemister, printers, 1892), 19.

Parsons, an outspoken newspaper editor in Waco, raised a regiment of cavalry in North Central Texas just after the outbreak of the war and offered it for state service in the summer of 1861. Known originally as the Fourth Texas Dragoons, the official designation changed to the Twelfth Texas Cavalry after the unit mustered into the Confederate armed forces on October 28. The troopers first moved to camps of instruction near Houston, but by the spring of 1862 were anxious to head east. They hoped to join General Albert Sidney Johnston, a Texan who commanded the Confederate army in Kentucky. Instead the regiment received orders to report to Little Rock. In Arkansas, Parsons would eventually receive command of a brigade composed of the Twelfth, Nineteenth, and Twenty-first Texas cavalry regiments, Charles Morgan's battalion, and the Tenth Texas field battery. The troopers took part in the defense of Little Rock in 1862, and then reconnoitered in eastern Arkansas and northeastern Louisiana, generally scouting along the Mississippi River and its tributaries, from mid-1862 until the close of the war. Their participation in the Red River Campaign in 1864 was the highlight of their military service. Generally, however, the troopers spent little time in camp, as they were always in the saddle. While their duty as scouts was not exciting, it was essential.[2]

This is not a book about battles, instead it is a look at the real war—monotonous, harsh, and lonely. The soldiers who belonged to cavalry in the Trans-Mississippi fought in very few actual battles, and most of those are known only to the dedicated student of the war. Therefore, the value of this work is not found in well-known campaigns, but in the day-by-day story it tells of the men who served west of the Mississippi River.

Cavalrymen in the Trans-Mississippi were not the dashing cavaliers of folklore, instead they generally performed an often tedious but important service by keeping Union soldiers occupied west of the Mississippi River and unable to reinforce armies in other theaters. Moreover, they kept department commanders, first at Little Rock, and later at Shreveport, Louisiana, informed

[2] William Henry Parsons was born in New Jersey in 1826. His family moved to Montgomery, Alabama, when he was a small child and he attended Emory College at Oxford, Georgia, until leaving his studies to fight in the Mexican War. After the war he made Texas his home and he became a well-know newspaper editor. Shortly before the outbreak of the Civil War, Parsons founded a pro-southern newspaper in Waco, the *South West.* After Texas seceded, Parsons raised a regiment of cavalry. See also, George H. Hogan, "Parsons's Brigade of Texas Cavalry," *Confederate Veteran* 33 (January 1925): 17; *Condensed History of Parsons Texas Cavalry Brigade 1861-1865: Together with Inside History and Heretofore Unwritten Chapters of the Red River Campaign of 1864* (Corsicana, Texas, 1903); P.H. Goodloe, "Service in the Trans-Mississippi," *Confederate Veteran* 33 (January 1915): 31-32. For a complete history of the brigade, see Anne J. Bailey, *Between the Enemy and Texas: Parsons's Texas Cavalry in the Civil War* (Fort Worth: Texas Christian University Press, 1989).

of enemy movements. Parsons called his brigade the "sleepless eye, the good right arm" of the army, and noted that "whether in the incessant skirmish[es] on the enemy's out-post or lines, or in repeated attacks upon gun-boats on the White, the Mississippi, or the Red rivers," his men impressed the opposition "with a conception of number that had no existence in reality." During the Vicksburg campaign the cavalry watched Union activities on the Arkansas and Louisiana sides of the Mississippi.[3]

More than four thousand men served in the brigade during the war. Although Colonel Parsons never received a promotion to brigadier general, the members of the Twelfth and Nineteenth cavalry regiments displayed a strong devotion to their commander, even threatening to mutiny after his removal in 1863. Troopers in the Twenty-first Texas cavalry felt an equal loyalty to their colonel, George Washington Carter, and Parsons and Carter would vie for control of the brigade throughout the war. The dispute was not settled until Carter transferred his regiment to another brigade the end of the war.

These soldiers were typical Texans. Parsons's own regiment, the Twelfth Texas, was composed of young men who had joined at the beginning of the war and were anxious to fight for southern independence. The men of the Nineteenth and Twenty-first Texas delayed enlisting until the passage of the conscription act in 1862. Many of these recruits were married and had families at home, explaining their reluctance to leave Texas until the threat of being drafted into the infantry encouraged them to join the cavalry. Finally, the battalion commanded by Charles Morgan began as a squadron, grew to battalion strength, and by the end of the war attained regimental status. It was an assortment of unattached companies that often operated independently.

Nonetheless, whatever their background or allegiance to a commander, all these troopers had the same goal—to safeguard the Lone Star State from an invasion. They remained in the army throughout the war, only disbanding when the Confederacy dissolved. They protected their home state by keeping Federal soldiers confined to neighboring Arkansas and Louisiana. This order book offers a rare glimpse into the daily life of these mounted Texians.

This original correspondence was preserved by the Parsons's Texas Cavalry Brigade Association and eventually deposited in the Nicholas P. Sims Library at Waxahachie, Texas, near where the Twelfth Texas had organized in 1861. The association eventually published *A Brief and Condensed History of Parsons' Texas Cavalry Brigade*, a book that was privately printed in

[3] W.H. Parsons to W.H. Getzendaner, June 24, 1878.

Waxahachie in 1892. Yet the handwritten orders contained in the Order Book remained untouched until microfilmed in the late twentieth century. This work contains transcriptions of all the orders contained therein, and is intended as a research tool for those readers interested in the life of the typical Trans-Mississippi cavalryman. The reader will find that these daily orders are remarkably routine, often simply providing for such necessities as food and forage, but they indicate the true nature of war for a cavalryman serving in the Confederate Army on the west side of the Mississippi River.

CHAPTER 1

# ARKANSAS

## June 3–October 29, 1862

When the war began after the Confederate attack on Fort Sumter in Charleston harbor in April 1861, Texans rushed to join the military, fearful the fighting would end before they could enlist. Governor Edward Clark authorized prominent Texans to raise regiments for the new Confederate government, and by December 1861 the horsemen leaving the state outnumbered the infantry by twenty-four to one. British Colonel James Fremantle, who visited the southern states in 1863, noted that "it was found very difficult to raise infantry in Texas, as no Texans walks a yard if he can help it." Even Clark admitted that Texans were proud of the "peerless horsemanship" and were "unwilling, in many instances to engage in service of any other description unless required by actual necessity." Colonel William Henry Parsons had little trouble recruiting eager young men in the weeks following the events in South Carolina. His regiment, the Fourth Texas Dragoons, became the Twelfth Texas Cavalry Regiment when its men swore allegiance to the Confederacy in October at camps of instruction near Houston.[1]

Throughout the autumn and into the winter of 1862, Parsons taught the men what it meant to be a soldier. The news of the first major battle at Manassas Junction on Bull Run Creek in Virginia (August 1861) fueled the new recruits' desire to cross the Mississippi River as soon as possible. It was late February, however, before the colonel gave the men the welcomed news that they were headed for Kentucky or Missouri. Yet events conspired to

[1] Stephen B. Oates, *Confederate Cavalry West of the* River (Austin: University of Texas Press, 1961), 26-27; James A. L. Fremantle, *Three Months in the Southern States April-June 1863* (1863; reprint, Alexandria, Virginia: Time-Life Books, Inc.), 72. See also, *Governor's Message, November 1, 1861,* and Texas Adjutant General, *Report, November, 1861.*

keep this from happening, for their destiny lay not on the east side of the Mississippi, but in the states to the west.

In February 1862, following the Confederate loses at Forts Henry and Donelson in Tennessee, Secretary of War Judah P. Benjamin ordered Trans-Mississippi military commanders to send any available troops to Little Rock, Arkansas. There was concern for the safety of southern shipping along the Arkansas and Mississippi rivers, as well as a general apprehension about the welfare of the far-western Confederate states. By late winter the situation on the west side of the Mississippi had deteriorated. The Union Army of the Southwest under Brigadier General Samuel Ryan Curtis had moved from Missouri into northwest Arkansas, and Confederate Major General Earl Van Dorn had failed to halt Curtis's advance at the Battle at Pea Ridge in March 1862. Following the Confederate defeat, Van Dorn had transferred his army across the Mississippi River to join General Albert Sidney Johnston, leaving Arkansas virtually undefended. Although Van Dorn was too late to participate in the Battle of Shiloh on April 6 and 7, most of his soldiers never saw Arkansas again.[2]

With no Confederate army to protect the state, Arkansans feared Little Rock would fall without a fight. After Pea Ridge, Curtis occupied Batesville on the White River in north central Arkansas, less than forty miles from the state capital. Former Arkansas governor John Selden Roane threw together a hasty defense with any troops he could muster and, with the blessing of Confederate officials, detained Texas cavalrymen on their way to join Johnston. When Parsons's Twelfth Texas reached Memphis it was among those units rerouted. The Texans arrived in Little Rock in mid-May where they found a few Arkansas soldiers and various unattached companies of

[2] See Thomas A. DeBlack, *With Fire and Sword: Arkansas, 1861-1874* (Fayetteville: University of Arkansas Press, 2003); Anne J. Bailey and Daniel E. Sutherland, *Civil War Arkansas: Beyond Battles and Leaders* (Fayetteville: University of Arkansas Press, 2000); William L. Shea and Earl J. Hess, *Pea Ridge: Civil War Campaign in the West* (Chapel Hill: University of North Carolina Press, 1992); Mark K. Christ, ed., *Rugged and Sublime: The Civil War in Arkansas* (Fayetteville: University of Arkansas Press, 1994); David Y. Thomas, *Arkansas in War and Reconstruction, 1861-1874* (Little Rock: Central Printing Company, 1926); John L. Ferguson, ed., *Arkansas and the Civil War* (Little Rock: Pioneer Press, 1965); Michael B. Dougan, *Confederate Arkansas: The People and Policies of a Frontier State in Wartime* (Tuscaloosa: University of Alabama Press, 1976); Colonel Thomas L. Snead, "The Conquest of Arkansas," in *Battles and Leaders of the Civil War*, edited by Robert Underwood Johnson and Clarence Clough Buel, 4 vols. (New York: Thomas Yoseloff, 1956), 3:441-45; Judah P. Benjamin to Paul O. Hébert, February 24, 1862; Hébert to George W. Randolph, April 19, 1862; Robert E. Lee to Hébert, May 26, 1862; Hébert to Henry H. Sibley, August 8, 1862, U.S. War Department, *The War of the Rebellion: A Compilation of the Official Records of the Union and Confederate Armies*, 128 vols. (Washington, D.C., 1880-1901), 9:700, 707, 713, 729-30 (hereinafter cited as *OR*; unless otherwise indicated, all references are to Series I).

Texans, including the well-known Alf Johnson and his Texas Spy Company.[3] At the same time Arkansas state senator Robert W. Johnson met with General P.G.T. Beauregard, who had assumed command of the Confederate army at Corinth, Mississippi, after the death of General Johnston at Shiloh. In an effort to improve the situation near Little Rock, Beauregard ordered Brigadier General Thomas C. Hindman, a resident of Helena, Arkansas, to take charge in the state capital. Hindman arrived in late May and immediately took drastic measures to defend the state.[4]

During May mounted Texans and Arkansans skirmished daily with detachments from Curtis's army. The Federal supply line stretched all the way back to Missouri, and Curtis, running short on forage, needed to relocate to the fertile regions around Little Rock. To supplement his dwindling supplies, he ordered scouting parties to move through the countryside collecting foodstuff from local farmers. The Texans first chance for battle came when they attacked one of these foraging parties on May 19. After successfully routing the enemy, the rebels proclaimed victory near the little town of Searcy in what became known as the Battle of Whitney's Lane.[5]

Although no more than a skirmish, this Confederate triumph gave Arkansans hope. The *Arkansas True Democrat* reported that the Texans had accomplished "one of the most daring and brilliant feats of the war." Even Parsons proudly proclaimed that the handful of Texans had "so successfully impressed Curtis with the conviction that his further advance was opposed by a newly arrived army, that he precipitately fell back." Although Parsons

[3] Alf Johnson was probably the most renown of all the commanders whose Spy Company later joined Morgan's command. He was forty-five years old in 1860. A native of Alabama, he had enlisted in Collin County where he claimed his occupation as farming with $18,000 in real estate and $4,200 in personal estate. Johnson was already well-known in Arkansas by the time Colonel Parsons arrived; the Houston newspaper noted that "everybody in Texas knows Alf Johnson" for his exploits while serving with Ben McCulloch. He later received a commission to raise a "spy company" and his command was one of the only units of Texas horsemen in Arkansas in the spring of 1862. He was captured at Arkansas Post in January 1863 and died en route to prison. Bailey, *Between the Enemy and Texas*, 44-45.

[4] See Anne J. Bailey, "Henry McCulloch's Texans and the Defense of Arkansas in 1862," in Bailey and Sutherland, *Civil War Arkansas*, 21-30.

[5] See Scott H. Akridge and Emmett E. Powers, *A Severe and Bloody Fight: The Battle of Whitney's Lane and Military Occupation of White County, Arkansas, May and June 1862* (Searcy, Arkansas: White County Historical Museum, 1996); "The Battle of Whitney's Lane or The Battle of Searcy," *White County Heritage* 1 (1963): 7-10; Raymond Lee Muncy, *Searcy, Arkansas: A Frontier Town Grows Up With America* (Searcy, Arkansas: Harding Press, 1976), 46-48; Report of Eugene Kielmansegge, May 20, 1862, *OR* 13:73-75; Report of F.M. Chrisman, May 19, 1862, *Arkansas True Democrat* [Little Rock], May 22, 1862; E.W. Rogers to J.S. Roane, May 24?, 1862, *San Antonio Herald*, June 14, 1862; Report of Henry Neun, May 20, 1862, *OR* 13:78-79; Report of August Fischer, May 20, 1862, *OR* 13:73-75; Golliger, "The Fight near Searcy," May 24, 1862, *Houston Tri-Weekly Telegraph*, June 9, 1862; Report of Peter J. Osterhaus, May 19, 1862, *OR* 13:70-71; Report of John Kaegi, May 21, 1862, *OR* 13:77-78.

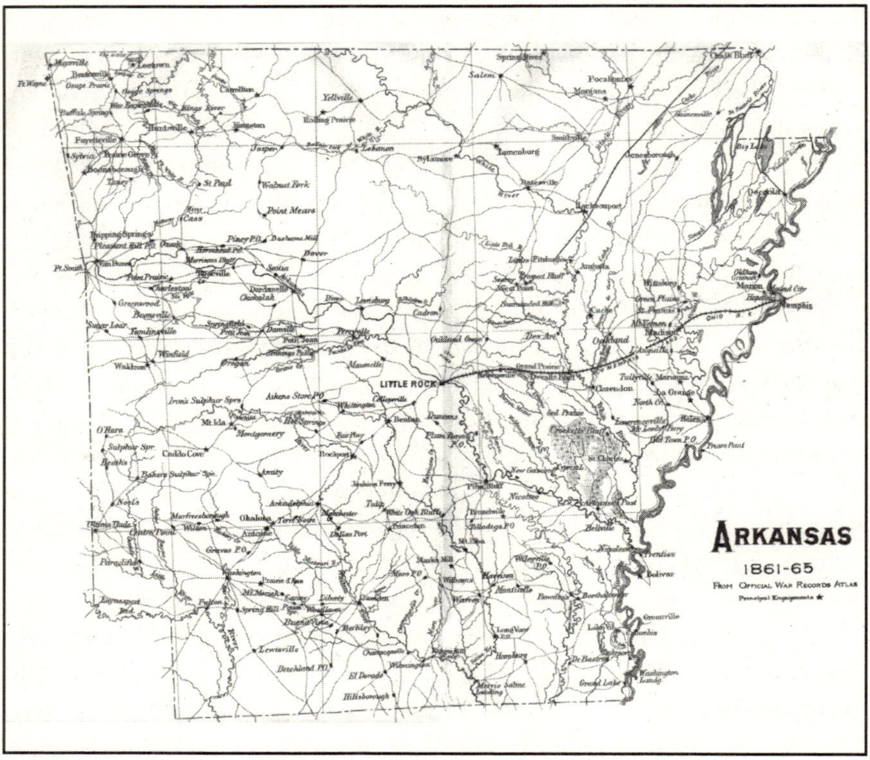


was proud of his men, the truth was that Curtis's advance stalled because of escalating supply problems.[6]

When the Twelfth Texas regiment reorganized a few days after the skirmish at Whitney's Lane, the men re-elected Parsons colonel by acclamation, and on May 28 he was given command of the Confederate troops north of the Arkansas River. To stop Curtis, Confederate officials established a line of defense west of Des Arc and used cavalry to harass any Federal units in the vicinity. Shortly thereafter, Brigadier General Albert Rust arrived in Little Rock and assumed overall command in the field. Rust was never popular with the Texas troops, partly because they objected to being led by an Arkansan, and preferred Colonel Parsons.[7]

The spring storms in late May and early June proved harsh for both Union and Confederate soldiers. When a rain of thirty-six hours further dis-

[6] *Arkansas True Democrat* [Little Rock], May 29, 1862; *Brief and Condensed History of Parsons' Brigade*, 19-20.

[7] Rust had represented the southern district of Arkansas in Congress at the time of secession. He raised a regiment and fought in Virginia before his assignment in Arkansas.

rupted Curtis's supply line, he observed: "The ox-train had brought me a supply of seven or eight days, and on this I hope to reach Little Rock. Now dry creeks are impassable and several days will transpire before I can cross streams, and during this time my bread supplies will probably run short. The country here and below cannot furnish flour, and I must depend mainly on the trains for bread."[8]

While Curtis pondered his logistical dilemma, Hindman, as commander in the Trans-Mississippi, organized a defense using whatever means necessary to achieve his goal. Some of his measures were not popular with the soldiers, both Texans and Arkansans. When locals complained about his conscript army, he had nine men shot without trials. Although the Texans disliked Hindman more than Rust, they had little time to complain. Not long after arriving in the state, they received orders to move into the mountainous country northwest of Little Rock. Parsons, as senior colonel, took command of the cavalry.[9]

Throughout June and July the Texans skirmished with scattered units of Federal troopers regularly. Texan Henry Orr claimed that the "enemy could not stand the Ranger's war-whoop," while another trooper added that the "Yankees are as afraid as death of the Texans and curse us for everything they can think of, for 'bushwhacking' them." A Union private noted that "fighting the Texans is like walking into a den of wildcats."[10]

Plagued by constant attacks from the rebel cavalrymen, the condition of Curtis's army continued to worsen. But after Memphis surrendered on June 6, the general knew that the odds were about to change. With the upper Mississippi River in friendly hands, he would soon receive aid. In mid-June, Union gunboats and transports moved into the White River carrying reinforcements and supplies to his hungry soldiers. Curtis quickly began marching his army in the direction of the small fleet, abandoning any thoughts of capturing Little Rock. The White River Expedition, as Curtis's

[8] Report of Samuel R. Curtis, May 24, 1862, *OR* 13:69-70.

[9] Diane Neal and Thomas W. Kremm, *The Lion of the South: General Thomas C. Hindman* (Macon, Georgia: Mercer University Press, 1993); "Saving the State," *Arkansas True Democrat* [Little Rock], October 1, 1862; John M. Harrell, "Arkansas," in Clement A. Evans, Ed., *Confederate Military History*, 12 vols. (Atlanta: Confederate Publishing Co., 1899), 10:98; Johnette Highsmith Ray, ed., "Civil War Letters From Parsons' Texas Cavalry Brigade," *Southwestern Historical Quarterly* 69 (October 1965): 212-13; Snead, "Conquest of Arkansas," 3:441-45.

[10] Letter of G.W. Sweet, June 11, 1862, *San Antonio Weekly Herald*, July 5, 1862, and Henry Orr to "Father and Mother," June 6, 1862, in John Q. Anderson, ed., *Campaigning with Parsons' Texas Cavalry Brigade, CSA: The War Journals and Letters of the Four Orr Brothers, 12th Texas Cavalry Regiment* (Hillsboro, Texas: Hill Junior College Press, 1967), 47-49; Jakie L. Pruett and Scott Black, eds., *Civil War Letters: 1861-1865; A Glimpse of the War Between the States* (Austin, Texas: Eakin Press, 1985), 34. See also, Daniel E. Sutherland, ed., *Guerrillas, Unionists, and Violence on the Confederate Home Front* (Fayetteville: University of Arkansas Press, 1999).

campaign became known, was the only real fighting the Texans saw in 1862. General Hindman opposed Curtis's movement south, but his command still only consisted of a few Arkansas troops and a handful of Texas regiments. Parsons's Twelfth Texas was one of the regiments in the fighting.[11]

The Federal army moved out of Batesville in late June, and Hindman sent General Rust with the Confederate cavalry to thwart the advance. Upon reaching Devall's Bluff one Texan observed: "No man is allowed to leave camp, and when we go out to graze our horses the whole command goes together with our arms and ammunition." Moreover, he added: "We have to sleep with our saddles under our heads and guns either in our arms or beside us," and the men "are nearly all wore out. During our force[d] march we only got two meals during the march, and six ears of corn for our beloved horses, but if we have the chance we will give them a good fight."[12]

As Curtis progressed south, the skirmishing intensified. The Houston newspaper reported that Alf Johnson's Spy Company "had been in the Valley for several days, and though it numbered less than one hundred men, it annoyed the enemy seriously, cutting off their foraging parties, killing their pickets, etc." Even Hindman noted that "Capt. Alf Johnson, commanding an unattached company of Texans, inflicted frequent defeats upon Federal scouting parties and won much distinction as a brave and skillful partisan. Upon one occasion he literally destroyed an entire Federal company."[13]

After Parsons's Twelfth Texas left Devall's Bluff, the regiment crossed the White River, turning east at Des Arc. Fording the Cache River late in the evening of July 6, the Texans neared Curtis's advance guard. The following day the two sides clashed in the Battle of Cotton Plant when several Texas regiments fought soldiers from the Thirty-third Illinois Infantry under Charles E. Hovey. Colonel Hovey also had several companies of the Eleventh Wisconsin Infantry and one gun from the First Indiana Cavalry. While the Federals received reinforcements, Rust mismanaged his side of the fighting and the Confederates retreated. Although both sides claimed success, it was a Confederate disaster.[14]

[11] See Snead, "The Conquest of Arkansas," 3:441-61.

[12] D.N. Shropshire to "My Beloved Sister," July 4, 1862, Shropshire Letters, Confederate Research Center, Hillsboro, Texas.

[13] Hindman's Report of Operations May 31-November 3, 1862, *OR* 13:36; "More Skirmishing in Arkansas," *Houston Tri-Weekly Telegraph*, June 27, 1862.

[14] For more see Edwin C. Bearss, "The White River Expedition June 10-July 15, 1862," *Arkansas Historical Quarterly* 21 (Winter 1962): 305-62.

Rust called the battle a "great victory," and praised Parsons and his men, but a soldier in the Seventeenth Texas Cavalry noted that the rebels had been "jenteely whipped." Union Brigadier General Frederick Steele reported that the "enemy was defeated and totally routed, with heavy loss on his part and comparatively small loss on ours." Another rebel soldier wrote, "Curtis out-generaled us on the 7th, and was soon out of danger, for I heard on the 10th that he was drinking champagne toasts with the other Generals on his return to Memphis." Most of the Texans believed that if Parsons, rather than Rust, had been in overall command that the outcome would have been different. In the debacle seventeen Texans from Parsons's regiment died and thirty-two were wounded, out of the four hundred men who saw action.[15]

After the fight at Cotton Plant, Curtis continued moving down river, and most of Arkansas was free from Union troops for the first time in several months. At Little Rock, Hindman took the opportunity to tighten his command structure. As a result of dwindling forage, he decided to dismount most of the cavalry. Since the Twelfth Texas had displayed disciplined fighting qualities, it was one of the few units allowed to retain its mounts. Also, when Parsons had visited Beauregard in May he had apparently received assurances that his men could keep their horses. But restrictions were tight as Hindman allowed each company only seventy-five men, and every horse had to pass inspection.

In spite of the limitations on cavalry, Parsons's numbers continued to increase. When the Twenty-first Texas Cavalry under Colonel George Washington Carter (commanded temporarily by Lieutenant Colonel DeWitt Clinton Giddings) arrived in Arkansas, the regiment immediately joined Parsons. Giddings attached the regiment to Parsons as soon as he realized that otherwise the men faced the prospect of losing their horses as a result of the general dismounting. Carter, who was absent in Richmond, was angry when he discovered what Giddings had done without his permission. Carter had brought a brigade of three mounted regiments to Arkansas, only to have two of them dismounted when they arrived, and he longed for an independent command. So Carter pointed out his commission came directly

[15] J.T.S., "Campaign in Arkansas: Battle of Cotton Plant," July 22, 1862, *Houston Tri-Weekly Telegraph*, August 4, 1862. James T. Scott was a captain and assistant adjutant general (A.A.G.) See also, Bryan Marsh to Araminta Marsh, July 29, 1862, "The Confederate Letters of Bryan Marsh," *Chronicles of Smith County, Texas* 14 (Winter 1975): 14-15; Report of Frederick Steele, July 20, 1862, *OR* 13:141-42; T.J.C., "Letter from Nelson's Regiment, September 16, 1862," in the *Houston Tri-Weekly Telegraph*, October 13, 1862; "Casualty Report of Parsons' Regiment, Texas Dragoons, in the Cotton Plant fight," July 22, *Houston Tri-Weekly Telegraph*, August 6, 1862.

from Richmond, ignoring the fact that Parsons had received his promotion first.[16]

Nonetheless, Carter lost the argument since the date of a commission determined rank, and overall command remained with Parsons. Fortunately this command dispute did not affect the performance of the troops. Throughout the summer, the Texans scouted near the Mississippi River and captured numerous prisoners, for at the beginning of the war Federal cavalrymen were not as skilled horsemen as their Confederate counterparts. One Union trooper judged that "Texas soldiers seem to know no fear," and a Texan proudly told his family that Union prisoners-of-war claimed that "they had long heard of our regiment and had wished that they might never come in contact with us."[17]

In late July, with an independent command of more than three hundred men of the Twelfth Texas and forty from Alf Johnson's Spy Company, Parsons decided to raid a Federal supply train headed for Helena. In fact, the commander, Lieutenant Colonel Oscar H. La Grange, had separated his wagons thinking there was no enemy cavalry in the area. Parsons targeted the detachment commanded by Major Henry S. Eggleston of the First Wisconsin Cavalry. Eggleston had twenty-seven wagons, about hundred horses and mules, and over one hundred sick soldiers. On August 3, when about a half-mile from the L'Anguille River in northeast Arkansas, mounted Texans hit his camp. The attack was such a surprise that the Union soldiers never stood a chance. One Texan recalled of the Federals: "They fought bravely for a few moments, thinking we were Missouri troops. But they couldn't stand Texas." The fighting ended in about half an hour.[18]

The Confederates captured several wagons, horses, mules, and burned what they could not carry back to Little Rock. (See the Appendix for captured correspondence.) The Federal loss was reported as almost a half a million dollars, with thirteen or fourteen men killed, around fifty captured, and some forty wounded. An estimated forty black refugees were killed and more than one hundred taken captive; Parsons lost two killed and ten

[16] Carter was born in 1826 in Virginia and had powerful family connections in the Confederate capital. He had been a professor of ethics at Soule University, located at Chappell Hill between Houston and Austin, in 1860. When the war came, he received permission directly from Richmond to raise a regiment of lancers, the Twenty-first Texas, and took three regiments: his own, the Twenty-fourth and Twenty-fifth to Arkansas in 1862. There he lost command of the latter two regiments, which eventually became dismounted cavalry. For more information on Carter, see Bailey, *Between the Enemy and Texas*. The order is found under Special Order, No. 25, August 4, 1862, in the Order Book of Parsons's Texas Cavalry Brigade.

[17] Henry Orr to [Mary & Sammie], July _, 1862, in Anderson, ed., *Campaigning with Parsons' Brigade*, 59-60.

[18] Henry Orr to "Parents," August 21, 1862, in ibid., 62-64.

wounded. A Wisconsin soldier claimed that after the fighting ended the rebel horsemen "took possession of the camp, and with the most fiendish barbarity murdered many negroes, both men and women, plundered and burned the train, and then with forty-seven prisoners besides negroes, returned, as rapidly as they came, toward Little Rock."[19]

As a result of this, and other successful engagements with the enemy, the Texans soon earned a reputation for their fierce fighting. A Texan noted that the Yankees "call us murderers, the 'Swamp Fox' Regiment." He considered the description accurate, as "we lie in the swamps in daylight and travel at night. We have done more to keep the enemy out of this country than all the balance of the troops combined." Moreover, a Houston newspaper reported that enemy soldiers in Arkansas "have a great deal more fear of Texas Rangers than they have of the devil."[20]

June and July had been trying months for the Texans under Parsons. "We have traveled a rough road since we've been in this state while all other soldiers have been lying at ease," wrote one soldier. The number of sick averaged more than one hundred, and without a hospital fund, the men had little medicine and no way to take care of the ill. Still, it was Parsons's troopers whom Hindman selected to watch the line near Helena and they continued to scout enemy movements. Parsons "is frequently down within a few miles of Helena," wrote an observer, "and is continually cutting off the enemy's foraging parties and driving in their picket." Throughout the late summer and into early autumn Parsons men scouted along the Mississippi River while the Federals worked to complete Fort Curtis at Helena, their main base in eastern Arkansas.[21]

Back in Little Rock, the Confederacy hierarchy changed when Theophilus H. Holmes succeeded Hindman as commander of the newly

[19] There are varying reports of killed and wounded. See Report of T.C. Hindman's Operations May 31-November 3, 1862, *OR* 13:37-38; Report of Henry S. Eggleston, August 9, 1862, ibid., 202-205; Report of O.H. La Grange, August 4, 1862, ibid., 202; *Arkansas True Democrat* [Little Rock], August 6, 1862; "The L'Anguille Battle," *Brief and Condensed History of Parsons' Brigade*, 29-33 (probably written by W.H. Getzendaner, who commanded the Fourth Squadron); "Battle of Anguille: A Wisconsin Regiments Experience in the Rebellion—Lost for Six Weeks in the Bayous of Arkansas," *Brief History of Parsons' Brigade*, 33-41 (the unnamed author of this account was a lieutenant in Company M, First Wisconsin Volunteer Cavalry and Getzendaner, who read this story in the *Milwaukee Sentinel*, July 31, 1881, reprinted it in the history of the brigade.) The author was probably Second Lieutenant John A. Owen, First Wisconsin Cavalry, whose story was taken from the *Chicago Republican*, January 2, 1866, and was printed in William DeLoss Love, *Wisconsin in the War of the Rebellion* (Chicago: Church & Goodman, and New York: Sheldon & Co., 1866).

[20] Henry Orr to W.T. Payne, August 12, 1862, in Anderson, ed., *Campaigning with Parsons' Brigade*, 61-62; "More Skirmishing in Arkansas," *Houston Tri-Weekly Telegraph*, June 27, 1862.

[21] Henry Orr to "Parents," August 21, 1862, in Anderson, ed., *Campaigning with Parsons' Brigade*, 62-64; A.J. Embree, senior surgeon of the Twelfth Texas Dragoons, sent a report of conditions to the Texas paper dated July 22, 1862, *Houston Tri-Weekly Telegraph*, August 6, 1862; letter to E.H. Cushing from Camp Hope, Arkansas, September 29, 1862, *Houston Tri-Weekly Telegraph*, October 22, 1862.

constituted Department of the Trans-Mississippi. In September Holmes reorganized the army. Colonel Parsons received command of a cavalry brigade consisting of the Twelfth and Twenty-first Texas as well as Francis M. Chrisman's Arkansas battalion. Joseph H. Pratt's battery from Jefferson, Texas, also joined the brigade.[22] Several unattached companies often operated with the brigade including Alf Johnson's Spy Company, and Charles Morgan's squadron, composed of Edward Vontress's and Frank Lemmon's companies. Occasionally Benjamin D. McKie's squadron of his own command and that of Milton M. Boggess[23] worked with Parsons. (These would eventually be consolidated into a battalion under Charles Morgan, but in 1862 they frequently operated independently.)[24]

Parsons also recruited Nathaniel M. Burford's Nineteenth Texas, giving the colonel three regiments besides the various unattached companies.[25] Although Burford's men were raw recruits just arrived from Texas, the merger worked well. Burford, a lawyer and judge from Dallas, had served with Ben McCulloch and was a former law partner of the postmaster general, John H. Reagan. Although popular, he had little to recommend him for such a position, and Lieutenant Colonel Benjamin Watson was in charge during Burford's frequent absences. Watson, as a soldier recalled, "displayed considerable genius in military affairs, and was always ready for service, gener-

[22] Pratt, a railroad builder from East Texas, raised his battery from Harrison, Marion, and Cass counties. A member of the command claimed that of the original seventy-two who joined in Jefferson, Texas, only seventeen surrendered in 1865. One hundred seventy-one names appear on the muster rolls, but Pratt lost so many men during the war that at one point he had to borrow from the cavalry. Pratt's tombstone in Oakwood Cemetery, Jefferson, Texas, indicates that he died of the effects of a wound received in the Missouri campaign on October 26, 1864. Bailey, *Between the Enemy and Texas*, 45, 311.

[23] Boggess was thirty years old in 1860. He was a native of Georgia who had enlisted from Rusk County. He gave his occupation as a clerk with no real or personal estate. He had raised an independent company that joined the First Texas Mounted Riflemen under Henry E. McCulloch in San Antonio and had remained in frontier service until the spring of 1862. Reorganized after the passage of the conscript act, the men eventually joined McKie's squadron, which became part of Morgan's command. Ibid., 228-31.

[24] Albert Castel, "Theophilus Holmes—Pallbearer of the Confederacy," *Civil War Times Illustrated* 16 (July 1977): 10-17. Chrisman's battalion subsequently became part of the First Arkansas Cavalry under Archibald S. Dobbin. Francis M. Chrisman became lieutenant colonel of the First Arkansas (he later resigned after being wounded). Chrisman's battalion consisted of Company A, "Corley's Spies," under Samuel Corley who died in combat September 10, 1863; Company B, "Anderson's Company Partisan Rangers," which was commanded by Rufus D. Anderson; Company C was an infantry company ordered mounted (previously Company I, Thirtieth Arkansas Infantry under James H. McGeehee); Company D was under George W. Rutherford from Batesville. Special Orders, No. 39, September 28, 1862, *OR* 13:883-85.

[25] A native of Tennessee, Burford had come to Texas at the close of the Mexican War. He arrived in Dallas in 1848 where he became a lawyer, forming a partnership with John H. Reagan. Both men prospered, and Burford became a district judge. When the war came he joined an artillery battery, but resigned in 1862 to organize a regiment of cavalry. He was ill-suited to be a commander, as he was more a politician than a soldier, and a fondness for drink added little to his military prowess.

ally commanding the regiment in trying moments." He often "distinguished himself by his coolness in action . . . and his gallant conduct."[26]

Holmes had also divided sixteen Texas infantry and dismounted cavalry regiments into two divisions, assigning eight to Brigadier General Henry McCulloch, and the rest to newly appointed Brigadier General Allison Nelson. Although Parsons had received command of a cavalry brigade, a promotion to brigadier general did not follow. Early in October Holmes ordered McCulloch's division, with Parsons's troopers as advance guard, to Devall's Bluff on the White River to discourage a possible offensive from Helena. Since cavalry companies often operated independently, the men from the Nineteenth Texas received an assignment to scout for two infantry regiments near Clarendon.[27]

A strange relationship developed between the Union troopers stationed near the Mississippi River and the Confederate cavalrymen watching their every movement; they occasionally came to know each other by name. Sometimes the two sides became friendly, trading goods across the lines, but at other times the fighting deteriorated into personal feuds. Although there were no major battles, the skirmishing never ended in the autumn of 1862. "Our men are having a fight, what might be called pretty heavy skirmishing every week, in the neighborhood of Helena—in all of which they get the better of the federals." Our soldiers "are cautious, but when they make a fight, they fight like devils. The Yankees, call them *Hell Yelpers*, from the fact that they allways raise the war whoop when they fight."[28]

The Texians' popularity with the civilian population became a proud topic of conversation for their families below the Red River, and their reputation grew accordingly. Moreover, they continued to distinguish themselves in the fighting in northeast Arkansas, and even earned the grudging respect of the enemy. The following orders detail the history of Parsons's command from June 3, soon after the Twelfth Texas arrived at Little Rock, through October 29, 1862, a day after the men in the Twelfth celebrated one year of service in the Confederate armed forces. Also included is an account

[26] *Ellis County History: The Basic 1892 book (With the Presidents Selection deleted) with Additional Biographies compiled by the Ellis County Historical Museum and Art Gallery, Inc. in Memory of the Courageous Pioneers and Builders of Ellis County* (Fort Worth and Arlington: Historical Publishers, 1972), 462-63, 698-99. For more on the creation of the brigade and information on all the commanders, see Bailey, *Between the Enemy and Texas*.

[27] Bailey, "Henry McCulloch's Texans and the Defense of Arkansas," 21-30.

[28] E.S.C. Robertston to Mary Robertson, November 14, 1862, Robertson Colony Collection, Special Collections, Central Library, University of Texas at Arlington. For the Union point of view, see William Forse Scott, *The Story of a Cavalry Regiment: The Career of the Fourth Iowa Veteran Volunteers from Kansas to Georgia 1861-1865* (New York: G.P. Putnam's Sons, 1893), 50-55.

of the Battle of Cotton Plant that appeared in the *Houston Tri-Weekly Telegraph.* Although the end of October signaled a year of service for the veterans of the Twelfth Texas, Parsons's Texas cavalry brigade, consisting of the Twelfth, Nineteenth, and Twenty-first Texas cavalries and a few unattached companies, had existed for only a few weeks.

D O C U M E N T S

# ARKANSAS

## June 3–October 29, 1862

Hd. Qrs. Advance of Army
of Trans Miss Dpt.
Stony Point, Arkansas,[29]
June 3d 1862

Special Order No 1[30]

(1) Westly Stamps private Capt. [Robert] Querry's Compy of Ark. Volunteers[31] detailed for special duty to go to the Critz neighborhood in White County, Ark. and direct all of the citizens to remove all of their bacon except what is necessary for the immediate use of their families to some point say, the Widow Bergers across Des Arc mountain and after moving the bacon to remove their corn and forrage to the same point. This is to be done, without delay. Compensation will be allowed for the same for Confederate use and the removal is imperative to prevent the supplies from falling into the hands of the invaders.

(2) Private Stamps is ordered to take charge of all the waggons needed to rendezvous at Stony Point along the Military Road and bring them up promptly to the point of rendezvous by 1/2 past 5 O'clock tomorrow morning.

By order of
Col. W.H. Parsons
Comdg Advance of Army of
Trans Miss Dpt.

J.T. Scott
Act. Adjt.

[29] When the Texans first arrived in Arkansas they operated on a line north/northeast of Little Rock, from near Searcy in White County to Des Arc and the White River to Cotton Plant, east of the Cache River.

[30] As the Federal supply problem increased, the Confederates looked for ways to make insure that hungry Union soldiers found as little food as possible.

[31] Co. B, Thirty-sixth Arkansas Infantry; however Stamps is listed in Co. H, Second Mounted Rifles.

* * * * * * * * * * * * *

Hd. Qrs. Advance of the Army
of Trans Miss Dist. Near
Bayou Des Arc, White Co, Ark.
June 3d 1862

Special Order No. 2

(1) Immediately upon the receipt of this order Major Headrick[32] will report to these hd. qrs. with his entire command leaving at Austin all surplus baggage.

(2) Major Headrick will bring with him his full train of waggons.

J.T. Scott
Act. Adjt.

By order of
Col. W.H. Parsons
Comdg.

* * * * * * * * * * * * *

Hd. Qrs., Advance of Army
of Trans Miss Dist.
June 3d 1862

Special Order No. 3

(1) Col. [A. Bell] Burleson[33] will communicate at once with Capt. [J.B.] Mosely[34] and state to him that he (Col. B) is sent to cover and protect his foraging parties

(2) Col. Burleson will aid Capt. Mosely in securing all the supplies in that section as more will be achieved thereby than by a victory in the field.

(3) Col. Burleson will avoid a fight unless sure of victory as the expedition is intended for foraging purposes & not to fight.

J.T. Scott
Act. Adjt.

By order of
Col. W.H. Parsons
Comdg.

[32] Headrick commanded Coleman's regiment of cavalry. (Probably W.O. Coleman's Forty-sixth Arkansas Infantry Regiment [Mounted].)

[33] Lieutenant Colonel of the Twelfth Texas Cavalry. Bell Burleson's uncle, Edward Burleson, had served as vice-president of the Republic of Texas, and Bell's father and uncles fought in the Texas Revolution. Despite his reputation for bravery, Burleson drank too much and by 1864 was in trouble with his superiors for insubordination and probably only escaped serious discipline because the war ended. Bailey, *Between the Enemy and Texas*, 210.

[34] Mosely was in Co. K, Thirty-second Arkansas Infantry.

* * * * * * * * * * * * *

Head Quarters Advance of
Army of Trans Miss Dist
June 3d 1862

Special Order No. 4

(1) Capt. [J.B.] Mosely will resume his foraging opperatives in the Dogwood section where he will secure all the corn & bacon possible—(2) Col. [A. Bell] Burleson & command are ordered to protect and support him while so engaged—(3) Capt. Mosely will report to Col. Burleson immediately.

J.T. Scott
Act. Adjt.

By order of
Col. W.H. Parsons
Comdg.

* * * * * * * * * * * * *

Hd. Qrs. Advance of Army
of Trans Miss. Dpt.

Special Order No 5

Col. [James R.] Taylor of the 17th Texas Cavalry & commanding detachment in Searcy Valley will at once take position to cover & protect the opperations of the citizens of the valley in removing their corn & bacon [to] South Des Arc Bayou.

Capt. [Francis M.] Chrisman recomends a position at Owens 2 mile west of Searcy—Showing your pickets eastward toward Gum Spring—this will be good fighting ground & a safe retreat if necessary. The enemy are demoralised and whilst in this position—The citizens west of that position can remove their supplies unmolested—depriving the enemy of their anticipated supplies will secure results worth a dozen fights—I am opperating in the same way in the west end of the district in the Dogwood Country press the people to act vigorously—Place your pickets from Smyrna through to Gum Springs nearly to West Point—Let your videttes report to you and lend daily expresses to me of any movement of the enemy. My men are opperating east of you, give orders to your pickets to permit all citizens with supplies to pass southward.

J.T. Scott
Act. Adjt.

By order of
Col. W.H. Parsons
Comdg.

* * * * * * * * * * * * * *

Hd. Qrs. Advance of Army
of Trans Miss Dist.
June 4th 1862

Special Order No. 6

(1) Capt. [P.H.] Wheat[35] will report with his company to these headquarters to take position for pickets duty on the crossings of Des Arc Bayou East of the Bayou.

(2) The pickets stationed on the road from West Point to Des Arc will destroy the ferry boat.

(3) Capt. Davy will establish pickets from Mr. Owen's west of Searcy to West Point along the Bayou by way of or near Gum Springs.

(4) Capts. Green & Corrall will make Des Arc Mountain their headquarters & establish pickets & patrol the roads going to Batesville & Searcy & all the crossings on the Bayou Des Arc—West to Nevills crossing—inclusive.

By order of
Col. W.H. Parsons
Comdg.

J.T. Scott
Act. Adjt.

* * * * * * * * * * * * * *

Hd. Qrs. Advance of Army of
Trans Miss Dist,
June 4th 1862

Special Order No. 7

Col. [James R.] Taylor[36] comdg detachment of the advance in Searcy Valley will promulgate this Official Order to wit—1st that all citizens above Des Arc Bayou are hereby required to haul with the aid of their own teams & negroes their supplies corn & bacon South of said Bayou to a post at the junction of the road 12 miles South of Quarles on the Searcy and Austin roads to prevent it from falling into the hands of the enemy.

(2) Col. Taylor will take pro[m]pt steps to enforce the order—by compulsion if necessary.

By order of
Col. W.H. Parsons
Comdg.

J.T. Scott
Act. Adjt.

[35] Wheat, in the First (Monroe's) Arkansas Cavalry, frequently operated with the Texans.

[36] Seventeenth Texas Cavalry Regiment.

* * * * * * * * * * * * *

Hd. Qrs. Advance of Army
of Trans Miss Dpt.
June 4th 1862

Special Order No. 8

Major Headrick Comdg Coleman's Regt. Cavalry C.S.A. will await instructions from Genl. [John S.] Roane & if not directed to join his regimental commander, or he will report promptly to these head quarters.

| | |
|---|---|
| | By order of |
| J.T. Scott | Col. W.H. Parsons |
| Act. Adjt. | Comdg. |

* * * * * * * * * * * * *

Hd. Qrs. Advance of Army
of Trans Miss Dist
June 4th 1862

Special Order No. 9

Col. [William] Fitzhugh comdg Regt Tex Cavalry[37] at Austin will move forward promptly with his command bringing with him every available man & all commissary stores in his possession he will report without delay to these head quarters.

| | |
|---|---|
| | By order of |
| J.T. Scott | Col. W.H. Parsons |
| Act. Adjt. | Comdg. |

* * * * * * * * * * * * *

Head Quarters Advance
of Army of Trans Miss
Dist, June 4th 1862

Special Order No. 10

The officer commanding detachment of Parsons' 12th Tex Dragoons at Austin will send forward every available man to this point without delay.

| | |
|---|---|
| | By order of |
| J.T. Scott | Col. W.H. Parsons |
| Act. Adjt. | Comdg. |

[37] Sixteenth Texas Cavalry Regiment.

* * * * * * * * * * * * *

Head Quarters Advance
of Army of Trans Miss Dst.
June 4th 1862

Special Order No. 11

Major [John] McClarty commanding detachment of [James R.] Taylor's 17th Tex. Cav. at Austin will bring every available man in his command & all commissary stores in his possession.

By order of
Col. W.H. Parsons
Comdg

J.T. Scott Actj. Adjt.

* * * * * * * * * * * * *

Head Quarters Advance
Army of Trans Miss Dist.
June 4th 1862

Special Order No. 12

Major [Lochlin J.] Farrar[38] commanding detachment of 12th Tex. Dragoons will upon the reception of this order bring forward all the men of his command who may be fit for duty.

(2) Major Farrar will also bring forward all waggons & teams with such supplies as he may have in charge

(3) Major Farrar will take charge of both men and trains report at these head quarters as soon as practicable.

By order of
Col. W.H. Parsons
Comdg.

J.T. Scott
Act. Adjt.

[38] Farrar raised a sixty-two man unit known as the "Limestone County Volunteers," but he failed to reach the necessary number to become a company. After reaching Parsons's camps of instruction near Houston, the unit disbanded and returned home. Farrar remained with Parsons and became major of the Twelfth Texas.

* * * * * * * * * * * * *

Head Quarters, Advance of
Army of Trans Miss. Dist.
June 4th 1862

Special Order No. 13

Major [Lochlin J.] Farrar will bring with forward him all ammunition belonging to the 12th Tex. Dragoons now stored in Peays warehouse in Little Rock. Major Farrar will also bring any other ammunition he may be enabled to obtain and remove it to Searcy.

By order of
Col. W.H. Parsons
Comdg.

J.T. Scott
Act. Adjt.

* * * * * * * * * * * * *

Head Quarters Advance of
Army of Trans Miss. Dist.
Searcy Ark, June 6th 1862[39]

Special Order No. 14

(1) All officers, non commissioned officers and soldiers belonging to the 12th Regiment Tex. Dragoons at Little Rock, Austin, on the road or else where, will immediately join their regiment and report for duty.

(2) No excuse will be received for disobedience of this order unless in case of sickness, certified by Surgeon in charge. (3) Officers commanding detachments of the regiment at Austin, Little Rock, & else where will forward comp[an]y and garrisons equipage to this place.

By order of
Col. W.H. Parsons Comdg.

J.T. Scott, Act. Adjt.

[39] Henry Orr wrote his parents on June 6: "We left Little Rock last Friday and arrived at Austin, thirty miles distant, Saturday evening; remained there till Monday morning when we resumed the march, taking with us one wagon to the squadron with a few cooking items, etc., and leaving the balance of the camp equipage with those not able for the scout and some to attend to them there. We came on within seven miles of this place [Camp Searcy] and stopped here to scout around." Henry Orr to "Father and Mother," June 6, 1862, in Anderson, ed., *Campaigning with Parsons' Brigade*, 48.

* * * * * * * * * * * * *

Head Quarters Advance of
Army of Trans Miss Dist.
Searcy June 7th 1862

Special Order No. 15

All officers commanding Arkansas State Troops will report in person to these head quarters.

By order of
Col. W.H. Parsons
Comdg.

J.T. Scott
Act. Adjt.

* * * * * * * * * * * * *

Head Quarters Camp Rust
Near Searcy June 13th 1862

Special Order No. 16

Regimental commanders will make immediate reports in compliance with the last Genl order issued by Genl. [Albert] Rust[40] relating to the amount of corn they have receipted for & the number of horse since the reduction of transportation & will then make requisitions as prescribed in said order upon Brigade Qr. Master.

By order of
Col. W.H. Parsons
Comdg. Post

J.T. Scott
Act. Adjt.

* * * * * * * * * * * * *

Head Quarters Camp Rust
Near Searcy June 13th 1862

Special Order No. 17

Regimental Adjutants are required to instruct all details ordered to report at Head Quarters to form in their respective camps under command of a Non Commissioned officer who will march them to head quarters & report there for duty

By order of
Col. W.H. Parsons
Comdg. Post

J.T. Scott
Act. Adjt.

[40] In late May, soon after the Twelfth Texas had reorganized, Parsons had taken command of all the Confederate troops north of the Arkansas River. Shortly after, Albert Rust arrived at Little Rock and replaced him. On June 11 the colonel of the Fifteenth Texas cavalry noted: "Brig. Gen. A. Rust commands us at this time, a clever gentleman and good officer; but the boys are quite clamorous for a Texas Brigadier and Major General to command them—a very natural feeling of State Pride, but I have no doubt they will do just as good fighting under any other man." Letter of G.W. Sweet, June 11, 1862, *San Antonio Weekly Herald*, July 5, 1862.

* * * * * * * * * * * * *

Hd. Qrs. 1st Brgd. 1st Div. of
the Army of the West, July 62[41]

Extract from Special Order No. 2[42]

Col. Parsons will take immediate steps & c (see Special Order on subject of dismounting).

1st In persuance to above order the now effective horses of Col. Parsons' Regt. will upon inspection & condemnation be sent in the manner prescribed to their homes. The men of said regiment who are dismounted, or whose horses are condemned as inefficient, will at once purchase from among the best horses of the brigade, get horses and remount themselves.

(II) The adjutant of Col. Parsons Regt. will report the number of effective men, belonging to the regiment and if there is a less number present than seven hundred & fifty men able to mount themselves as required under the special order in reference to dismounting the number will be completed by receiving well mounted armed men from the other four regts. composing the first brigade sufficient to make the five squaddrons full.

(III) The horses belonging to the men, composing the other four regts. of the 1st Brigade with the exception of those who may attach themselves to the Cavalry regt. or may be purchased for the use of the same will (in pursuance to Special Order above) be sent to their homes or such other place as the Genl. commanding may direct in the manner prescribed by said orders.

(IV) The organizations of the respective commands composing the 1st brigade will remain intact except so far as the arm of service, changed by the above special order.

(V) The men who are members of Col. Parsons Cavalry Regt. who cannot remount, where their horses are condemned as ineffective, will be privilleged to attach themselves to any other regiment in the brigade—and effectively mounted & armed men of the other regiments of the brigade are privilleged to exchange with numbers of Col. Parsons' Regt. who cannot remount or procure effective horses

(VI) In pursuance to special order from Comd of Division requiring the Cavalry regiment to be armed with the most effective cavalry weapons that can be selected from the entire brigade all members of the brigade having side arms such as six shooters will sell such numbers as may be neccessary to effectively arm the Cavalry regiment.

By order of
Col. W.H. Parsons
Comdg 1st brd. 1st Div
Army of the West

J.T. Scott
Act. Adjt.

[41] Parsons's regiment took part in the Battle of Cotton Plant on July 7. This order comes a few days after that cavalry fight.

[42] "We was dismounted on the13th & horses sent home," wrote Captain Bryan Marsh, Seventeenth Texas Cavalry, in July 1862. The men "unanimously objected," he noted, "but under the circumstances we could doo no better—our horses was starving for feed—scarcely half of them being fit for duty." Bryan Marsh to Araminta Marsh, July 29, 1862, "Confederate Letters of Bryan Marsh," 14-15. Although Parsons's cavalrymen remained mounted, all the horses were inspected and men whose steeds could not pass inspection were transferred to the infantry.

* * * * * * * * * * * * * *

Hd. Qrs. 1st Bridg, 1st Div.
Army of the West
July 12th 1862[43]

Special Order No 18

In pursuance to special order received by the commander of this Brigade a copy of which has been transmitted to each commander of Regts. composing the Brigade it is hereby ordered

(I) That the organization of the respective commands composing the 1st brigade will remain intact except so far as the arm of service changed by virtue of the special order relating to dismounting

(II) The basis of the Cav. Regt. of this brigade will be the 12th Tex Dragoons. All non effective horses will be condemned in said Regt. & the men and officers of the same Regt. to purchase good horses & remount

(III) The horses belonging to the men & all subaltern officers composing the other four Regts. of the first brigade, with the exception of those who may be purchased for the remounting of the Cavalry Regt. will be sent home, or such other place as the Genl. comdg may direct & in the manner prescribed by said order

(IV) All vacancies that may exist or be created in the Cavly. Regt. by the inability of any of the men to remount or where horses are declaired ineffective will be filled from the other regts. by men who are well mounted and armed & all men in the 12th Tex. Dragoons who cannot remount are privilleged to join any of the other Regiments

(V) In pursuance to Special order from this commander of division requiring the Cavalry Regt. to be armed with the most effective Cavalry weapons of the brigade. All the dismounted men of the brigade having side arms such as six shooters will sell such number as may be necessary to effectually arm the Cavalry regt.

By order of
Col. W.H. Parsons
Comdg 1st brdg.
1st Div. Army of the West

J.T. Scott
Act. Adjt.

[43] George W. Ingram wrote on July 13: "On tomorrow we are to take up the line of March for Little Rock. What this means I cannot say. The enemy have not crossed White River and report says that they have got on their gun boats & Transports and left the State." George W. Ingram to Martha F. Ingram, July 13, 1862, in Henry L. Ingram, comp., *Civil War Letters of George W. and Martha F. Ingram* (College Station: Texas A&M University Press, 1973), 29-30. Although the Union army was moving towards Helena, it had not yet left the region of the White River.

* * * * * * * * * * * * * 

Hd. Qrs. 1st Brig. 1st Div. Army
of the West. Camp near Brownsville
Arkansas July 19th 1862[44]

Special Order No. 19[45]

Sergeant I.D. [Thomas D.S.] Whittenburg of the 12th Tex Dragoons C.S.A. (Col. Parsons' Regt.) is hereby detailed with six privates from the same Regt. viz. J.M. Ince, W.L. Horn, J.F. Potterfield [Porterfield], G. Getton [Jetton], W.M. Fender & E.M. Gentry[46] to take charge of all the horses condemned in that Regt. and ordered to conduct them to Texas where he will distribute them to the counties in which they [were] obtained as rapidly as possible & return promptly to his regt. when this duty is accomplished with the men under his command Sergt. Whittenburgh [*sic*] will move by the most expeditious and convenient route & all persons on his road are requested to assist him in the execution of this order

By order of
J.T. Scott., Col. W.H. Parsons
Act. Adjt. Comdg 1st Brgd. & c.

* * * * * * * * * * * * * 

Hd. Qrs. 1st brgd. 1st div
Army of the West July 21/62

Special Order No 20

Lieut. [J.B.] Abbot[47] will go with one compy down White River as far as the "Cut Off" & observe closely—See what is going on—Do not depend upon neighborhood rumor—See every thing yourself or learn it from your scouts whom you know to be reliable. If any boats are in the river see what they are doing and whether they can navigate it without trouble. See if any troops are on board, and how many—communicate by courier with Col.

[44] On July 18 George Ingram told his wife: "All the Cavalry have been dismounted in this army except our Regiment and we are allowed only 75 men to the Company. Our surplus men have been transferred to the Infantry Regiments." George W. Ingram to Martha F. Ingram, July 18, 1862, ibid., 31. On July 15 Henry Orr was more concerned with telling his family about the recent battle and wrote from Brownsville: "Our movements have been very active since I last wrote to you. The command left Stoney Point the first of July on a forced march for Devalls Bluff and arrived there the third. Upon our arrival there, we learned there was no Federal force near, but that they were some thirty miles northeast on Cash [Cache] River. [Details of the Battle of Cotton Plant followed.] Henry Orr to "Father, Mother, Sister, and Brother," July 15, 1862, in Anderson, ed., *Campaigning with Parsons' Brigade*, 55-58.

[45] Unlike Union cavalry, Confederates furnished their own mounts. Horses were inspected by a board and a value assessed in case of loss. Those animals whose owners were dismounted in Arkansas were returned to their owner's families in Texas. Texan Henry Orr observed that few of Parsons's men had their horses rejected, and those who did quickly bought others. John W. Truss of Company D commented: "Most of the horses are dead on their feet," but the committee "announced my horse one of the best horses in the regiment." John W. Truss to Rebecca Truss, July 14, 1862, Ray, ed., "Civil War Letters from Parsons' Texas Cavalry Brigade," 214-15.

[46] Companies are as follows: Whittenburg-Co. I; Ince-Co. A; Horn-Co. B; Porterfield-Co. E; Jetton-Co. F; Fender-Co. G; Gentry-Co. K.

[47] Co. B.

[R.G.] Shaver[48] at Pine Bluff and with Genl. [Thomas C.] Hindman[49] by telegraph by way of Brownsville or Des Arc as you think best. Genl. Hindman is desirous that you should be active and vigilant report every thing of interest that occurs promptly that I (Col. Parsons) may be advised of it in time if it should be important to one as it may be—Major Johnson with a squaddron of Cavalry has been ordered from Pine Bluff across the country to cross White river at Clarendon, you may meet him—You will have to subsist yourself in the country, inflict no hardships & carefully prevent all depredations. Report to Gen. Hindman by courier at least once a day if possible. Dont strike the river lower down than Clarendon

By order of
J.T. Scott — Col. Parsons
Captain & A.A.G. — Comdg 1st brgd

The above order was compiled from Gen. Hindmans Telegraphic instructions to Col. Parsons

* * * * * * * * * * * * *

Hd. Qrs 1st brgd & c
July 20th 1862

Special Order No 21

Major [Lochlin J.] Farrar Comdg 12th Tex dragoons will furnish a detail of 50 men composed of five privates from each compy well mounted armed & rationed for five days. Two non Comd Officers will be furnished to the detail and the command is assigned to Lieut. [John I.] Richardson of compy F 12th Tex. Dragoons who will receive full instructions from Major Farrar

By order of
J.T. Scott — Col. W.H. Parsons
Captain & A.A.G. — Comdg 1st brgd & cav

* * * * * * * * * * * * *

Hd. Qrs. 1st Brg. 1st div.
July 20th 1862

Special Order No. 22

Every man reported for duty exclusive of those actually reported sick by the chief surgeon will at once hold himself in readiness for march at a moments notice

[48] Shaver commanded an Arkansas regiment at the beginning of the war and later various commands of Arkansas soldiers.

[49] Several weeks earlier George Ingram had told his wife: "Hindman say the Texans [are] a pack of d____d heathens and G_d d____d them, he intends to bring them under, that he intends to have some of [them] Shot the first chance that he has. Many of the boys in the different Texas Regiments have taken a vow to kill him the first opportunity." George W. Ingram to Martha F. Ingram, June 11, 1862, in Ingram, comp., *Civil War Letters*, 22-24.

The camp will be broken up and the waggons accompany the companies

J.T. Scott　　　　By order of
Capt. & A.A.G.　　　　Col. W.H. Parsons

* * * * * * * * * * * * *

Hd. Qrs. 1st Brg. & c.
July 21st 1862

Special Order No. 23

Major [Lochlin J.] Farrar comdg. 12th Tex dragoons will assume the line of march immediately.

By order of
J.T. Scott　　　　Col. W.H. Parsons
Capt. & A.A.G.　　　　Comdg & c

* * * * * * * * * * * * *

Campaign in Arkansas
Battle of Cotton Plant - Gallantry of Texians
Camp on Bayou Metoe Near Brownsville, Arkansas July 22, 1862[50]

Presuming that a brief history of our movements since leaving Texas, will be interesting to a large proportion of your readers, I avail myself of the opportunity afforded by the return of Dr. McNeil to Houston, and send you a synoptical sketch of our campaign up to the present moment.

You remember that the 12th Texas Dragoons, commanded by Col. W.H. Parsons, left Houston to rendezvous at Colbert's Ferry on Red River, en route to Fort Smith. While on the march however, Col. P. received orders from Gen. [Earl] Van Dorn, to change his route to Des Arc, by way of Little Rock. The Regiment consequently assembled at Clarksville in Red River county, Texas, whence they proceeded by squadron for the Capitol of Arkansas. But on reaching Red River their destination was again changed and they were ordered to push forward rapidly to Pine Bluff, whence they would be transported by water to Memphis. These orders were executed in the face of unparalleled difficulties. Many of the streams being swollen to such an extent that the ferrymen frequently declared their passage impracticable. In such cases the soldiers took possession of the boats and crossed themselves without a single accident in the entire command. Texians have surmounted the proverbial difficulties of being water bound in Arkansas.

From Pine Bluff, Col. P. traveled rapidly by steamer with his advance squadron to Memphis, where he heard for the first time, that Gen. [Samuel R.] Curtis with a large force was advancing upon Little Rock. Gen. P.G.T. Beauregard immediately countermanded the order for the transportation of the remaining companies to Memphis, and directed Col. P. to return with his advance to Little Rock. The Col. only remained long enough to obtain the funds necessary to pay off his regiment and supply the bounty of $50 per man, when he hurried back to Little Rock, paid his men, reorganized them under the conscript act, and

[50] From the *Houston Tri-Weekly Telegraph*, August 6, 1862.

was a second time elected by acclamation to command them.

Upon the return from Memphis we heard for the first time, of the splendid fight near Searcy, in which Major [Emory W.] Rogers, with a detachment of regiment, only 100 strong, after a forced march of over 50 miles engaged 400 of the enemy in ambush and in the short space of an hour killed 180 Federal soldiers, losing only Lieutenant [N. Brown] McDonald and 2 privates.

Our regiment no sooner reorganized, than on 28th of May, Col. Parsons was assigned the command of all Confederate troops North of Arkansas river and ordered forward with the regiment to select and establish a line of defense, he proceeded at once to occupy the Southern bank of bayou Des Arc, whence foraging and reconnoitering parties were thrown out in the face of the enemy, obstructing their advance and forming abattis for defence in case of attack.

These offensive demonstrations caused Generals Oysterhaus [Peter J. Osterhaus] and [E.A.] Carr, commanding the Federal advance, to relinquish their line of operations on Little Red River and retreat hastily to Batesville; thus it was the Federal army received their first check in advance upon Little Rock. Our commander immediately established his base of operations upon Little Red, established headquarters at Searcy, in White county, and commenced a concentration of forces at that point. In a few days Gen. [William M.] Rust arrived and assumed command, preserving the existing lines. The day succeeding his arrival, two of our videttes were captured by a body of the enemy, reported to be reconnoitering in force, three or four miles north of Searcy, when Col. Parsons was ordered in command of his own regiment, with [James R.] Taylor's and [William] Fitzhugh's regiments of Texas cavalry, to cross over and investigate their movements. He pressed rapidly forward, leaving a portion of Taylor's regiment at the ford, in reserve, and sending Fitzhugh to the right and east to intercept a flank movement; then with our regiment and an advance of 100 men, under Taylor, followed after the Federal. About 12 miles north of Searcy, Col. Taylor engaged them and reported to Col. P., who promptly formed line of battle and fell upon their flank. The enemy soon gave way and rushed, panic stricken, from the field.

We were then pressed forward in line of battle, and bivouacked on a deserted camp of the Federals, within 3 miles of their main body, where we remained until ordered to return. The audacity of this affair will be appreciated when I state that Col. Wood, of the Iowa cavalry, told Capt. Morgan (bearer of a truce flag) that at the moment of attack, he had, in position, 1,000 men, whose slight loss of 17 killed and 4 prisoners, arose solely from the rapidity with which they left the field. Parsons' force engaged was not 400, while he was 10 miles from any support, and the enemy near a large encampment of their forces, who stood upon their arms until 12 M. of the next day. In this skirmish several prisoners were taken. Among them a non-commissioned officer, by Capt. [F.H.] Ayres. Shortly after this engagement, we were moved up toward Batesville, to an encampment 30 miles north-west of Searcy, where we remained a few days and then sending the train with the sick and baggage to the rear, Parsons', [George W.] Sweet's, Taylor's, [Nicholas H.] Darnell's and Fitzhugh's regiments were ordered to advance upon the flank and rear of the enemy. They moved without forage and baggage, and with no rations save parched corn, by forced marches over a mountainous country, a distance of 150 miles, and only returned when needed to prevent a junction of the Federal army with their gunboats in White River.

Marching with great celerity they reached Duval's Bluff on that stream, then to Des Arc, where they crossed over and proceeded across the lake to attack the centre of Curtis' army with a force of few hundred men. The enemy in ambush fired on Parsons' advance, when the regiment was formed in line of battle by the Colonel, aided by Lt. Col. [A.B.] Burleson, Maj. [L.J.] Farrar and Capt. Ayres. The boys fell rapidly under a galling fire from a concealed foe, but encouraged by their officers stood like veterans and pressed on the enemy's position until they broke cover. Then the double barrels and six shooters of Texas well avenged the brave who had fallen. Parsons drove them from their position and held his ground more than three hours, until ordered by Gen. Rust to return, when he bought the entire command off in good order and perfect safety. I should here state that one company of Sweet's regiment and one of Fitzhugh's were the only ones of their respective commands brought into action. They suffered severely and did gallant service. For the part taken by our regiment in this fight, the Colonel received the warmest thanks of General Rust, who told him that he had covered himself, his regiment and his State all over with glory. That it was deserved and nobly earned the list of casualties fully proves; especially when considered that from sickness and details on detached service, scarcely more than 400 of the regiment stood the brunt of the fight.

The brigade was then placed in position on the lake to resist an attack, but much to our surprise Gen. Curtis declined the contest and proceeded by forced marched to Helena, on the Mississippi river, where he is now stationed.

We were consequently ordered to fall back on Bayou Metoe, where the entire cavalry was dismounted, save the old 12th, which, thanks to its fine drill and fighting reputation still preserves its mount.

Our Colonel has been appointed to command the 1st Brigade 1st Division Army of the West, composed of Texas troops, and at present is in the advance; the other regiments having been ordered to Little Rock for more thorough organization.

Col. Sweet has done good service and is wounded by the fall of the second horse killed under him during the campaign. Col. Fitzhugh also is badly wounded, but improving. Col. Taylor, too, has shown himself a fearless officer. In the Cotton Plant affair, he was ordered to move around the enemy by a very circuitous route, but owing to the stupidity of his guide, was placed in such position, that for the obstinate stand of Parsons' Regiment, he must have been cut off and sacrificed. Col. [Nicholas H.] Darnell, too, has shown himself a vigilant, effective officer. The enemy's loss in this engagement as reported by citizens, reached in killed and wounded, 300 or 400. We lost fully one eighth of all engaged. Even this dreadful mortality, worse than decimation, was light when the disparity of force, (ten to one) is taken in consideration.

The boldness of the attack evidently saved the entire army, for the enemy being thoroughly deceived by the daring move of our regiment, and thinking that it was certainly sustained by a large force, fell back before the mere handful opposed to them for nearly a mile. Thus you perceive our regiment has won an enviable reputation at the very opening of the campaign. They are proud of their country, their Colonel and themselves, and you may rest assured, that the honor of our well beloved State will never be tarnished while its flag is borne on the field by the 12th Texas Dragoons. I append a list of Doctors [A.J.] Embree, Reagan and [W.H.B.] Goodwin.

Before concluding this rambling account, I would say that in the Telegraph of the 19, just received, we observe a description of a fight reported, in which we are said to have taken a battery, but were unable to hold it after several unsuccessful charges. This account was sent you from Brenham on the 7th. It had no foundation of course, but singular as coincidence, our regiment was on that very day, the 7th, actually engaged in the battle near Cotton Plant, which your report describes very well save always the unsuccessful charges. Yours, &c, J.T.S.[51]

[51] J.T.S. was James T. Scott, captain and A.A.G. of the Twelfth Texas.

The following is a list of caualties in Parsons' Regiment, Texas Dragoons, in the Cotton Plant Fight, as reported by Dr. Embree J. Goodwin:[52]

Capt. Maddox' Company.—W.F. Luter, private, mortally wounded, (since dead); Lieut. B.F. Holder, wounded slightly; H.H. Harrison, private, wounded slightly.

Capt. Neal's Company.—A.W. King private, killed; A.R. Childers, private, killed; W.J. Neal, captain, wounded severely; J.V. Higgins, E. Ariola, privates, wounded severely, J.B. Eastham, private, slightly wounded; J.F. Barnes, private, missing (taken prisoner, but escaped and recently come in).

Captain Highsmith's Company.—N. Ponce, J.B. Standefer and W.L. Peveiser, privates, killed; T.J. Owen, private, mortally wounded, since dead; B.S. Reed, J.R. Robinson, J.M. Perry, J.R. Butler, J.H. Dancer, wounded severely; J. Goft and T. Standefer, wounded slightly; J.E. Pettie, missing, since found wounded.

Capt. J.C. Brown's company.—Lieut. T. Cureton, killed. Privates F.W. Webster, killed; F.M. Gregory, mortally wounded, (since dead); L.T. Folston and D.C. Nance,[53] wounded severely.

Capt. Hawkins' Company.—J.S. Burnett, corporal, killed; N.M. Massie, musician, killed; E.S. Forney, private, killed; J.W. Cornelius, sergeant, and privates O.S. Farron, J.M. Loyd, wounded severely; J.B. Pruet and H.M. Moor, wounded slightly

Capt. Morrow's Company.—A.R. Ragsdale, private, and C.N. Britt, corporal, killed; J. West, private, wounded severely; privates H.C. Wilberger, J.H. Poke, W.S. Sapp, and sergeant B.F. Knight, wounded slightly.

Capt. Veal's Company.—J.T. Pace, private, killed; T. Booth, sergeant, and private R.B. Rooken, wounded severely; privates J.O. French and R.S. Elkins, wounded slightly

Capt. Keyser's Company.—A. Rainer, private, killed; Lieut. J.M. Noble, wounded slightly.

Capt. Brown's Company.—W.R. Hammond, sergeant, wounded severely; private J.W. Meeks, wounded slightly.

Note.—Capt. Weir's Company does not appear, as they were at the time near Batesville on detached service under Col. Sweet, where they saw service, and behaved with bravery.

* * * * * * * * * * * * *

Hd. Qrs. 1st Brgd. 1st Div.
Army of the West,
Des Arc, Ark. July 27/62

Special Order No. 24

(I) Adjutant Scott will take command of the camps & train at Des Arc on the West side of White river & will exercise his own discretion in selecting a proper locality

[52] This probably refers to A.J. Embree and W.H.B. Goodwin. Periods added after initials in names to make the list readable.

[53] David C. Nance later wrote: "I don't know much . . . about the battle . . . for at the very first volley, a one-ounce ball hit my left cheek, coming out the back of my neck . . . another ball hit the right side of my neck." After pulling himself to a tree, out of the way of the charging horses, he was hit again, a ball passing through his right shoulder. Following his recovery from his wounds, he was assigned to a powder mill in Waxahachie and did not return to the regiment until the autumn of 1863. B.P. Gallaway, *The Ragged Rebel: A Common Soldier in W.H. Parsons' Texas Cavalry, 1861-1865* (Austin: University of Texas Press, 1988), 47-54.

(II) He is hereby empowered & authorised to purchase supplies of subsistence & forage for same & to give receipts for the amounts purchased which will be settled by officers of the proper departments.

By order of
Col. W.H. Parsons
Comdg

J.T. Scott Captain & A.A.G.

* * * * * * * * * * * * *

Little Rock, Ark. July 31/62

Extract
Special Order 2_

Col. Parsons will assume command of Lt. Col. [DeWitt Clinton] Giddings[54] battalion Major Johnson's battalion, Alf Johnson's spy Compy Capt. [Rufus D.] Anderson's Compy[55] and all other mounted men East of White River

By order of
Genl. [Thomas C.] Hindman
(Signed) R.C. Newton
[Assistant Adjutant General]

* * * * * * * * * * * * *

Hd. Qrs. 1st Brg. 1st Div.
of Army of the West
near Cotton Plant, Ark.
Aug. 4th 1862[56]

Special Order No. 25

Col. [DeWitt Clinton] Giddings[57] will move with his command at the earliest practi-

[54] Giddings was lieutenant colonel of the Twenty-first Texas Cavalry. As a Pennsylvanian by birth, he had initially opposed secession, but he carried a respected name in South Texas and was popular with the men. Thirty-four years old in 1862, he had enlisted in Washington County and was originally captain of Company F. He listed his occupation as a lawyer with $10,000 in real estate and $5,000 in personal estate. He was succeeded as captain by John C. Lusk, a native of Alabama. Lusk was thirty years old in 1862, and had enlisted from Washington County where he was a stable keeper with $4,000 in real estate and $1,700 in personal estate. Bailey, *Between the Enemy and Texas*, 220-21.

[55] Co. B, Chrisman's Arkansas Battalion.

[56] On August 3 Colonel Parsons had attacked the Union supply train at L'Anguille Ferry.

[57] Giddings commanded the Twenty-first Texas Cavalry in Carter's absence. After Giddings attached the regiment to Parsons's brigade without telling the colonel, Carter was understandably angry. As soon as Carter arrived in camp he argued that his commission, which came directly from the secretary of war, superceded any authority Parsons might have. But his complaints were in vain. Nonetheless, rather than having Carter around while he nursed his wounded pride, Parsons sent the newly arrived Texans to a camp on Bayou de View several miles from the Twelfth Texas with instructions to scout independently.

cable moment to West bank of Bayou De View near Cotton Plant & report to these hd. qrs. for futher orders.

| | |
|---|---|
| | By order of |
| J.T. Scott | Col. W.H. Parsons |
| Captain & A.A.G. | Comdg. |

* * * * * * * * * * * * *

Hd. Qrs. on Cache River, Ark.
Aug. 5th 1862

Special Order No. 26

Capt. Allen comdg. a portion of McNells[58] comd. will immediately report with his entire command to these head quarters enclosed Capt. Allen will find an Extract from Genl. [Thomas C.] Hindman's order assigning Col. Parsons to command all troops East of White river

| | |
|---|---|
| | By order of |
| J.T. Scott Captain & A.A.G. | Col. Parsons Comdg. |

* * * * * * * * * * * * *

Hd. Qrs. in the field
Aug. 7th 1862

Special Order 27

In accordance with orders received from Gen. Hindman—Major Horner is informed that his office is established at Jacksonport—to which place he will move at once & organize his dpt in Jackson Cty & to assist Major McCrery(?) in organizing in Independence County & Lawrence & Randolph Counties

| | |
|---|---|
| | By Order of |
| J.T. Scott | Col. W.H. Parsons |
| Capt. & A.A.G. | Comdg East of White River |

[58] Probably Archibald J. McNeill's Thirtieth Arkansas Infantry (also known as the Thirty-ninth Arkansas Infantry and the Fifth Trans-Mississippi Infantry Regiment).

* * * * * * * * * * * * *

Hd. Qrs. Cache River
Aug. 7th 1862[59]

Special Order 28

Lt. Col. [DeWitt Clinton] Giddings comdg detachment of Col. Carters Tex Cav. will send out small scouting parties of picked men in the direction of Clarendon, to watch any & all movements of the enemy & report the same promptly to these hd qrs

Lt. Col. Giddings will encamp his command at the point designated beyond Cotton Plant & furnish an alert & constant picket guard at the crossing on Bayou De View

By order of
Col. W.H. Parsons
Comdg

J.T. Scott
Capt & A.A.G.

* * * * * * * * * * * * *

Hd. Qrs. Tex. Cav. Brgd.
Aug. 13th 1862[60]

Special Order 29

Capt. Hicks post comdg at Hicks Station will furnish subsistence to the Hospital Steward at Brownsville for the sick belonging to Lt. Col. Giddings 1st Regt. of Carters Tex Brigade attached to this advance of Army of S.W.

By order of
Col. W.H. Parsons
Comdg
Adv. of Army S.W.

J.T. Scott
Capt. & A.A.G.

* * * * * * * * * * * * *

Hd. Qrs. Tex. Cav. Brg.
Aug. 20th 1862

Special Order No. 30

Lt. Col. Giddings & Lt. Col. [A. Bell] Burleson will require their respective Comds to march to water alternately twice every day in charge of a field officer.

By order of
Col. W.H. Parsons
Comdg & c

J.T. Scott,
Capt. & A.A.G.

[59] A.L. Orr reported his company camped fifteen miles above Little Rock on the Arkansas River on this date. On the twelfth, Henry Orr said he was fifteen miles below Clarendon and on the twenty-first gave his location as a camp on the Cache River. [A.L. Orr] to "Parrents," August 7, Henry Orr to "Lieut. Payne, Dear Friend," August 12, and Henry Orr to "Parents," August 21, 1862, in Anderson, ed., *Campaigning with Parsons' Brigade*, 60-64.

[60] On August 12 Henry Orr said that "Carter's Cavalry Regiment is now with us." [Henry] Orr to "Lieut. Payne, Dear Friend," August 12, 1862, ibid., 61-62.

* * * * * * * * * * * * *

Hd. Qrs. Tex. Cav. Brg.
Aug. 20th 1862

Special Order No. 31

(I) Lieut. Col. Giddings & Lieut. Col. Burleson will furnish from their respective regt daily details to form a Brigade guard for protection of citizens from depredations

(II) A Brigade officer of the day will be detailed from each regiment alternately whose duty will be to take general supervision of the guard & report daily upon the condition of the camps

(III) Each Regt. will hand in a roster of commissoned officers immediately

By order of
Col. W.H. Parsons
Comdg.

J.T. Scott
Capt. & A.A.G.

* * * * * * * * * * * * *

Hd. Qrs. Tex. Cav. Brgd.
Aug. 20th 1862[61]

Special Order No. 32

(I) In pursuance of Genl. order No. 32 of Maj. Genl. Hindsman, Surgeon Norris[62] of Lt. Col. Giddings Regt. Surgeon [W.H.B.] Goodwin[63] of Col. Parsons' Regt. & asst. surgeon [T. J.] Petty[64] to constitute the Medical Board of this Brigade

(II) All applicants for discharge will appear before these for examination at their regular sittings which will be arranged by the senior Medical Officer of the board

(III) They will duly notify the commanders of Regts & unattached compys of the time when such meetings will be held

By order of
Col. W.H. Parsons
Comdg

J.T. Scott,
Capt. & A.A.G.

[61] On August 21, J.C. Morriss of the Twenty-first Texas told his wife that his regiment was "some three or four miles from Cotton Plant," where they had camped "some weeks ago." He added that the men were "doing very well here—get plenty of forage for our horses and plenty to eat," however, there was "a good deal of fever in camp but a mild form." J.C. Morriss to Amanda Morriss, August 21, 1863, in Cecil E. Weller, Jr., ed., *My Dearest Amanda: The Civil War Letters of J.C. Morriss to his Wife* (Fayetteville: University of Arkansas Press, forthcoming). Since this work has not been typeset at the time this book went to press, there are no page numbers cited.

[62] Both J.T. Norris and Thomas Norris were surgeons in the Twenty-first Texas.

[63] Goodwin was a surgeon in the Twelfth Texas.

[64] Petty was a surgeon in the Twenty-first Texas.

* * * * * * * * * * * * *

Hd. Qrs. Tex. Cav. Brigade
Aug. 23d 1862

Special Order No 33

Capt. [Rufus D.] Anderson Comdg Co. of Ark. Vol.[65] attached to this brigade will remain on East side of White River closely watching the movements of the enemy—The knowledge of the Country possessed by his men renders them invaluable for such service & will enable Capt. Anderson to annoy the enemy constantly—Capt. Anderson will report by courier to Des Arc—Whence a line of courriers will be established to Col. Parsons hd. qrs. enabling him to communicate with Col. P. with celerity

By order of
Col. W.H. Parsons
Comdg

J.T. Scott
Capt. & A.A.G.

* * * * * * * * * * * * *

Hd. Qrs. Tex. Cav. Brigade
Camp Cache River Ark.
Aug. 23d 1862

Special Order No. 34

(I) Capt. [M.B.] Highsmith[66] in comd of Hospital Camps at Brownsville Ark, will turn over his comd to Capt. W.G. [William G.] Veal[67] of the 12th Tex Drags. C.S.A.

(II) Capt. Highsmith & Lieut. Armes [A.W. Arms][68] of the 12th Tex. Drags C.S.A. will report to Col. Parsons hd. qrs. without delay

(III) Capt. W.G. Veal will assume comd of the hospital camps at Brownsville & forward all convalescent soldiers who are fit for duty to their commands—He will also strenuously exert himself to ascertain the locality of all officers & soldiers belonging to the 12th Tex Dragoons C.S.A. who will be immediately ordered to form their regt irrespective of their condition provided they are able to ride

By order of
Col. W.H. Parsons
Comdg.

J.T. Scott
Capt. & A.A.G.

[65] Co. B, Chrisman's Arkansas battalion.

[66] Co. D ("Bastrop Cavalry Company"), Twelfth Texas. Malcijah B. (Kige) Highsmith, thirty-three years old when the war began, had been a farmer with $1,000 in real estate and $1,000 in personal estate. He was a native of Missouri, but enlisted from Bastrop County. As the son of the noted Texas Ranger Samuel Highsmith, Kige had experience fighting Indians on the Texas frontier. Bailey, *Between the Enemy and Texas*, 212-17.

[67] Co. F ("Texas Mounted Guards," "Texas Mounted Rangers," or simply the "Ellis Rangers"), Twelfth Texas. Veal was thirty-two when the war began. A native of Tennessee, he enlisted from Parker County. A prominent Methodist minister from near Weatherford, he was fairly wealthy with $8,000 in real estate and $1,500 in personal estate. He was known as the "Texas Bull" for his tenacity as a fighter and his men earned the name "Methodist Bulls." But his numerous liaisons with women over the years garnered for him the nickname the "Passionate Parson" and eventually forced him to leave the ministry. Nonetheless, he continued to be popular with the men, serving as president of the Parsons' Brigade Association for eleven years and master of ceremonies of the state Confederate convention in Dallas in 1892. Veal subsequently died at the hands of an angry husband. Ibid., 212-15.

[68] Co. D, Twelfth Texas.

* * * * * * * * * * * * *

Hd. Qrs. Tex. Cav. Brigade
Magberry's Aug 26st 1862

Special Order. No. 35

(I) Col. J.H. Winston[69] in command at Mitchel's will order Col. [William A.] Crawford[70] to detail sixty privates 6 non commissioned officers & 2 Commissioned Officers from his command for picket duty at the following points viz: Widow Harris, Peppers, Crockets, Mount Adams and St. Charles. Col. [William A.] Crawford will detail 1st Lieut J.W. Blanton & 2d Lt. Harden both of Capt. Ralston's compy[71] for the above service, and will select from his regt. without regard to comps men of known reliability

(II) Lt. Col. Burleson & Lt. Col. Giddings with their respective regiments with Lieut Falmen of the Tex. Artillery, Col. [William A.] Crawford & Major Johnson's commands will march to Fairdale 10 miles below Richland on the Arkansas river with as little delay as possible

(III) Col. J.H. Winston in command of Mo State Guard at Mitchel's will remain at that point with his infantry & artillery until further orders communicating with my hd. qrs. at Fairdale as often as a necessity may arise for so doing

By order of
Col. Parsons
Comdg

J.T. Scott,
Act. Adjt.

* * * * * * * * * * * * *

Aug. 26th 1862

Special Order 36

The waggons appropriated for transportation of com. stores for this brigade being inadequate in number & having been condemned as unfit for service—The comd is totally destitute of means to procure subsistence.

Therefore Mr. [J. Fred] Cox[72] A.A.C.T. is hereby ordered to proceed with the condemned wagons to Little Rock, where he will turn them over to the Q.M. Department & make requisition for the necessary transportation upon the Post Q.M.

By order of
Col. W.H. Parsons
Comdg.

J.T. Scott, Capt. & Adj.

[69] Winston commanded Missouri soldiers.

[70] Crawford led various Arkansas commands.

[71] Ralston commanded a unit known as Ralston's Guerrillas.

[72] Cox was one of the chaplains of the Twelfth Texas.

* * * * * * * * * * * * *

Hd. Qrs. Tex. Cav. Brgd.
Aug. 29th 1862

Special Order No. 37

This brigade having been detached from command of Gen. M. [Mosby M.] Parsons[73] & assigned to special service. Col. [William A.] Crawford comdg detached comp[any]s of Ark. Cav. will report to Genl. Parsons for duty & is not included in the Genl. orders issued from these hd. qrs. for the march

J.T. Scott
Capt. & A.A.G.

By ord. of Col. W.H. Parsons
Comdg.

* * * * * * * * * * * * *

Hd. Qrs. Tex. Cav. Brigade
Des Arc, Ark. Sept. 4th 1862

Special Order No. 38

Private A. Lopez of Co. F 12th Regt. Tex dragoons is permanently detailed for special duty on Col. W.H. Parsons Staff & will report to these hd. qrs. immediately

J.T. Scott
Capt. & A.A.G.

By order of Col. W.H. Parsons
Comdg

* * * * * * * * * * * * *

Hd. Qrs. Tex. Cav. Brdg.
Des Arc, Ark, Sept. 4th 1862

Special Order No. 39

Lt. Col. Giddings will select a competent & reliable officer from his regt. with 40 men & order him to proceed upon a scout in the direction of Helena. Lt. Col. Giddings will instruct the officer detailed for this service to use the greatest dispatch in obtaining & reporting to these hd. qrs. all the information that can possibly be obtained relative to the enemy their movements & plans & numbers.

J.T. Scott
Capt. & A.A.G.

By command of
Col. W.H. Parsons
Comdg

[73] Mosby Munroe Parsons, no relation to William H. Parsons, was a brigadier general from Missouri. He led a brigade at Wilson's Creek, Missouri, and Pea Ridge, Arkansas, and later in the Red River Campaign in 1864.

* * * * * * * * * * * * *

Hd. Qrs. Tex. Cav. Brigade
Des Arc, Ark, Sept. 6th 1862

Special Order 40

Officers comdg Regts. & Compys attached to this brigade will send in accurate reports of their respective commands to these hd. qrs. by 12 O'clock M. tomorrow.

| | By command of |
|---|---|
| J.T. Scott | Col. W.H. Parsons |
| Capt. & A.A.G. | Comdg. |

* * * * * * * * * * * * *

Hd. Qrs. Tex. Cav. Brigade
Des Arc Sept. 8th 1862

Special Order No. 41

Capt. [F.H.] Ayers will as fast as the commissary wagons are emptied send them back to Brownsville for supplies. The commissary fund is exhausted except $80.00 you will forward funds immediately.

| | By order of |
|---|---|
| J.T. Scott | Col. W.H. Parsons |
| Capt. & A.A.G. | Comdg |

Sent by Telegraph

* * * * * * * * * * * * *

Hd. Qrs. Tex. Cav. Brigade
Des Arc Sept. 8th 1862

Special Order No. 42

In consequence of the absence of all surgeons from the 12th Tex. Dragoons & the necessity for action in cases requiring discharge—Doctor Wm. [William] Bethel[74] Actg. Post Surgeon at Des Arc is hereby appointed to act in that capacity until the arrival of a regimental surgeon & he will examine all candidates for discharge in that regt. previous to their appearance before the brigade board

| | By command of |
|---|---|
| J.T. Scott | Col. W.H. Parsons |
| Capt. & A.A.G. | Comdg |

[74] Bethell was detailed as a surgeon in the Twelfth Texas.

* * * * * * * * * * * * *

Hd. Qrs. Tex. Cav. Brigade
Des Arc, Sept. 8th 1862

Special Order No. 43

(I) The comdg officer of the 12th Tex. Dragoons C.S.A. will move with his regt across White river tomorrow morning commencing the march at Day light

(II) He will also order Capt. [James C.S.] Morrow[75] & Lt. [Benjamin] Barnes[76] to regain their regt with their respective parties after sending spies across the river with orders to report with information at Camp on Cache river

By command of
Col. W.H. Parsons
Comdg.

J.T. Scott,
Capt. & A.A.G.

* * * * * * * * * * * * *

Hd. Qrs. Tex. Cav. Brgd.
Des Arc, Sept. 8th 1862

Special Order No. 44

Lt. Col. Giddings will station one compy East of the Battery in the encampment on Cache river & will picket all fords & points of approach as formerly

By order of
Col. W.H. Parsons
Comdg

J.T. Scott
Capt & A.A.G.

Lt. Col. Burleson's comdg will not cross White rivers until tomorrow

J.T. Scott,
Capt. & Adj.

[75] Co. I ("Williamson Bowies"), Twelfth Texas. Morrow was only twenty-two when the war began. He was a native of Kentucky who enlisted from Travis County. He was a dedicated Confederate in spite of the fact that his father was a Kentucky Unionist, and he missed only one of thirty-seven battles. He gave his occupation as a clerk in Austin with no real estate and only $100 in personal estate. (After the war he married a daughter of Sam Houston.) He had followed J.W. Mullen and Wiley Peace as captain of Company I. Mullen, who became lieutenant colonel, was fifty years old when the war began. A native of Delaware, he was one of two men who served as captain in the Twelfth Texas having been born in a non-slaveholding state. Mullen enlisted from Williamson County, where he was a farmer with $1,000 in real estate and $500 in personal estate. Peace, forty-three when the war began, also enlisted from Williamson County. He was a native of North Carolina, a stock raiser with $8,000 in real estate and $6,000 in personal estate. Bailey, *Between the Enemy and Texas*, 212-17.

[76] Barnes, twenty-eight years old when the war began, was a native of Georgia who enlisted from Johnson County. He was a stock raiser who had no real estate and $4,000 in personal property. He was also the third captain of Company C, following Neal and Haley. Ibid.

* * * * * * * * * * * * *

Hd. Qrs. Tex. Cav. Brigade
Des Arc, Sept 8th 1862

Special Order No. 45

(I) Orders having been received from Genl. Hd. Qrs. Tex. Requiring a change to be made in the disposition of troops—Lt. Col. Giddings with his command & Capt. Pratts Battery will move to the point in the "Surrounded Hill" recommended by Capt. [John R.S.] Alston[77]

(II) Lt. Col. Giddings will leave on Strong picket to sever the approaches to Des Arc & Cotton Plant at the main crossings on Bayou De View & Cache river

(III) He will also request Col Haralsen to bring all the meal that can be obtained in the vicinity of Cotton Plant near Camp referred to in order

By order of
Col. Parsons
Comdg

J.T. Scott,
Capt & A.A.G.

* * * * * * * * * * * * *

Hd. Qrs. Tex. Cav. Brigade
Des Arc, Sept. 10th 1862

Special Order No. 46

(I) Lt. Col. Giddings of the 21st Tex. Cav. will move with the whole brigade to the east bank of Cache river near Cotton Plant

(II) The baggage train will be brought out to the Cotton Plant & Des Arc road where it will be left for further instructions

(III) Only such wagons will be taken as are absolutely necessary to transport the requisite food & cooking utensils & these will be left on the Western bank of Cache River at the crossing.

(IV) Lt. Col. Giddings is requested to use great energy in execution of this order—it arises from an advance from Helena by the enemy & also from necessity for a speedy check to their advance

By order of
Col. W.H. Parsons
Comdg

J.T. Scott,
Capt. & A.A.G.

[77] Co. H, Twenty-first Texas. John Rutledge Smith Alston was twenty-seven years old when he enlisted in 1862 and led a company of men from Grimes County. Ibid., 220-23.

* * * * * * * * * * * * * *

Hd. Qrs. Tex. Cav. Brigade
Camp Haralson, Sept. 11th 1862

Special Order No. 47

(I) Capt. [James C.S.] Morrow & Lt. [Benjamin] Barnes[78] (of the 12th Tex. Dragoons) comdg scouts in West side of White river below Clarendon will at once place a picket opposite Clarendon in addition to the point already watched—guarded by them

(II) They will continue to watch & guard strictly all the crossings below Clarendon until relieved by Capt. Alf. Johnson's or some other company in an official manner when they will report with their respective commands to the hd. qrs. of their regt. where ever it may be

By command of
Col. W.H. Parsons
Comdg.

J.T. Scott,
Capt. & A.A.G.

Note—Capt. Morrow will please notify Lt. Barnes of this order by sending it to him after Capt. Morrow has taken a copy of it.

* * * * * * * * * * * * * *

Hd. Qrs. Tex. Cav. Brigade
Sept. 12th 1862[79]

Special Order No. 48

Lt. Col. Giddings having picketed the bridge on bayou De View—he will also station similar pickets at the crossings of Bayou De View 7 miles above the bridge and at Parley Hills—He will select for this purpose reliable, vigilant men & instruct them fully as to their duties

By order of
Col. W.H. Parsons
Comdg

J.T. Scott,
Capt. & A.A.G.

[78] Morrow-Co. I; Barnes-Co.C.

[79] A.L. Orr wrote on September 12: "There is eleven Texas regiments here and seven Arkansawers. If they keep coming, I don't know what we will do for something to eat, for provisions are getting tolerable scearce now. Our rations are three-fourth's of a pound of beefe pr day and one pound of bacon evry eight days, and one quart of meal a day. . . . Thire is about one third of our regiment barefooted and cant get shoos at no prise. I don't know what we will do this winter for shoos and blankets." A.L. Orr to "Father and Mother," September 12, 1862, in Anderson, ed., *Campaigning with Parsons' Cavalry Brigade*, 67-69.

* * * * * * * * * * * * * *

Hd. Qrs. Tex. Cav. Brdg
Camp Haralson Near Cotton Plant
Sept. 14th 1862

Special Order No. 49

(I) Immediately upon the reception of this order, Lt. [Thomas] James[80] Comdg Johnson's Tex. Spy Compy will relieve Capt. [James C.S.] Morrow & Lt. [Benjamin] Barnes[81] of the 12th Tex. dragoons of the duty which they are now performing in guarding the crossings on White river

(II) He will station pickets at Clarendon, Widow Harris, Peppers Ferry, Allen, St. Charles, Crocketts' Bluff & such other points as he may deem necessary.

(III) This duty has been assigned to the Tex Spy Co. at Col. Parsons special request & he confides it to them with full confidence that it will be performed with energy & vigillance

By command of
Col. W.H. Parsons
Comdg

J.T. Scott,
Capt. & A.A.G.

* * * * * * * * * * * * * *

Hd. Qrs. Tex. Cav. Brigade
Camp Haralson near Cotton Plant
Sept. 14th 1862

Special Order No. 50[82]

(I) The Col. Comdg is pained to hear that serious complaints have been made by the citizens of depredation committed upon their property by troops belonging to this brigade—He hopes never to hear of similar complaints in the future

(II) Comdg officers will immediately cause to be read in dress parade the order just received from Maj Genl. [Theophilus H.] Holmes.

By command of
Col. W.H. Parsons
Comdg

J.T. Scott,
Capt. & A.A.G.

[80] James would later command Company E, Johnson's Spy Company, in Morgan's battalion (later regiment). He was a native of Tennessee who had enlisted in Hopkins County. James was forty-four years old in 1860 and gave his occupation as a farmer. He claimed $1,000 in real estate and $2,300 in personal estate. Bailey, *Between the Enemy and Texas*, 228-29.

[81] Morrow-Co. I; Barnes-Co. C.

[82] Because of the drought of the preceding year, forage for men and horses was so scarce that troopers occasionally preyed on civilians. This would be a recurring problem during the war as resources in the Trans-Mississippi never met the needs of the army.

* * * * * * * * * * * * *

Hd. Qrs. Tex. Cav. Brgd.
Sept. 17th 1862

Special Order No. 51[83]

No furloughed men will be allowed to take with them their arms, which shall be retained for the use of the respective companies to which they belong in pursuance to a General order to that effect

By order of
J.T. Scott Capt & A.A.G. Col. W.H. Parsons Comdg

* * * * * * * * * * * * *

Hd. Qrs. Tex. Cav. Brigade[84]
Sept. 19th 1862

Special Order No. 52[85]

During the absence of Col. W.H. Parsons Snr. Col. commanding Texas Cavalry & Artillery Brigade—Col. Geo. W. Carter will assume command & be respected & obeyed accordingly.

By order of
J.T. Scott, Col. W.H. Parsons
Capt. & A.A.G. Comdg

* * * * * * * * * * * * *

Hd. Qrs. Tex, Cav. Brigade
Camp Haralson Sept. 25th 1862

Special Order No. 53

Capt. Terrel [R.A. Terrell][86] Q.M. of this Brigade will purchase ten horses for the artillery service & deliver them to Capt. [Joseph H.] Pratt comdg Pratt's Battery

By command of
J.T. Scott, Col. W.H. Parsons
Capt. & A.A.G. Comdg

[83] Confederate soldiers owned their weapons, but a shortage of guns made it necessary to keep them with the army whenever possible.

[84] On September 26, J.C. Morriss of Carter's regiment wrote that he was camped at Des Arc. J.C. Morriss to Amanda Morris, September 26, 1862, Weller, ed., *Civil War Letters*.

[85] Although Carter was frequently not with his regiment, he was available if he could command the entire brigade.

[86] R.A. Terrell served as quartermaster of the Twelfth Texas. Throughout the Order Book it is often difficult to distinguish between R.A. Terrell, quartermaster of the Twelfth Texas, and James E. Terrell, adjutant of the Nineteenth Texas. James E. Terrell died at Jackson, Mississippi, in November 1863 while on his way to Richmond. The editor has speculated in some instances when the right man is unclear.

* * * * * * * * * * * * *

Hd. Qrs. Tex. Cav. Brigade
Camp Haralson Sept. 26th 1862

Special Order No. 54

(I) Private J.H. Bonner of Compy B, 12th Tex. Drag's is hereby detached from his compy on special duty & ordered to report to Capt. F.H. Ayres[87] A.C.S. at Brownsville—who will give him further instructions & supply him with funds to subsist this command.

(II) Private Bonner will act as Asst Com of subsistence until the return of Capt Ayres from Texas

By command of
Col. W.H. Parsons
Comdg

J.T. Scott,
Capt. & A.A.G.

* * * * * * * * * * * * *

Hd. Qrs. Tex. Cav. Brigade
Sept. 26th 1862

Special Order No. 55

Lt. Col. Burleson will place Mr Cameron now under guard in charge of the waggon guard tomorrow morning with orders to conduct him to Des Arc & deliver him to the provost Marshal at that place—with the enclosed letter

By command of
Col. W.H. Parsons
Comdg

J.T. Scott,
Capt. & A.A.G.

* * * * * * * * * * * * *

Hd. Qrs. Tex. Cav. Brigade
Camp Haralson Ark, Sept 26/62

Special Order No. 56

(I) Capt. F.H. Ayres is hereby detached from this Brigade & will at once proceed to Texas to press forward the clothing intended for this command & also to recruit a sufficient number of soldiers to fill up the 12th Texas Dragoons & the 21st Tex. Cav. to the maximum standard authorized by Major Genl. [Theophilus H.] Holmes Comdg the Trans Miss Dpt.

(II) He will advertize that Majr Genl. Holmes authorizes Col. Parsons to recruit the companies in his brigade to 110 men each and that in consequence of this permission Col. Parsons Regt. (12th Tex Drags.) will receive 360 men & Col. Carter (21st Tex Cav) 315 men respectively

[87] Ayres was commissary of the Twelfth Texas.

(III) He will announce that Col. Parsons especially desires & invites such soldiers to enlist as may have previously served in his old regt. & that all who may volunteer must come provided with good horses & arms

(IV) Such recruits as may respond to this call will be directed to press forward with the utmost dispatch—either singly or in parties to this hd. qrs. of this Brg—whether in front of the enemy at Helena or St. Louis Mo.

(V) Capt. Ayres will execute this order with the utmost dispatch possible & return to his post for duty

By command of
Col. W.H. Parsons
Comdg

J.T. Scott
Capt. & A.A.G.

* * * * * * * * * * * * *

Hd. Qrs. Advance Brigade
Tex. Cav. Sept. 26th 1862

Special Order No. 57

(I) Two days rations of bread will be cooked & salt distributed to each man for 7 days rations

(II) The entire train belonging to the command will be sent tomorrow morning to Des Arc

(III) Arms will be inspected and ammunition distributed to day

(IV) The command will hold itself in readiness to move after to day at a moments notice

(V) Each man will carry from two to three blankets

(VI) The Q.M. & commissaries of the different commands belonging to the advance brigade will make the necessary arrangements to execute above orders relative to trains & subsistence

By order of
Col. W.H. Parsons
Comdg

J.T. Scott,
Capt. & A.A.G.

* * * * * * * * * * * * *

Hd. Qrs. Tex. Cav. Brgd.
Sept. 26th 1862

Special Order No. 58

Lt. Col. Giddings will as soon as his regt. is formed for the march report with his command upon the ground occupied viz his former encampment at the time designated in the above order

By command of
Col. W.H. Parsons
Comdg

J.T. Scott
Capt. & A.A.G.

* * * * * * * * * * * * * *

[Extract.]

Headquarters Trans Miss. Department,
Little Rock, Ark., Oct. 1, 1862

SPECIAL Order No. 43[88]

II. The present production of Salt in this Department is not sufficient for supplying the army and the people. The price demanded is extortionate, and great inconvenience has ensued, and much suffering will result from this cause. It is believed it can be remedied by carrying on the works on government account. Therefore all salt works within the State of Arkansas and the Indian Territory, which are not producing to their greatest capacity, will be taken possession of by an agent of the Confederate States, to be designated from these Headquarters, who will take steps at once to increase their production to the greatest extent possible. For this purpose he will be authorized to obtain by hire or purchase, or, if necessary, by impressment, the requisite labor and material. The Quartermaster and Commissary Departments will afford him every aid and assistance possible.

The agent will set apart monthly for Army use, such proportion of Salt manufactured by him as may be required by the Chief Commissary of the Department not to exceed one-half of the amount manufactured; the remainder he will sell to citizens at the price of one dollar and fifty cents ($1.50) per bushel, or less if the cost of manufacture is below that price, payable in Confederate money, or in corn, wheat, flour, pork, bacon, lard, and such other articles of subsistence as may be necessary, in due proportion of each, limiting the quantity of salt sold to each citizen to a reasonable supply for himself and family. The prices to be paid, in Salt, for subsistence, will be regulated by the Tariff: This applies when the articles are delivered at the place where produced, when delivered at government depots, the actual expense of transportation will be added.

It must be perfectly palpable to every one, that on the successful operation of this order will depend the ability of the people to provide provisions for another year. As soon as the emergency is passed, the order will be resinded. A fair compensation will be allowed the owners of the works seized.

Maj. C.P. King, S.C. is appointed agent for the government to carry out this order.

By command of
Maj. Gen. Holmes.
S.S. ANDERSON,
Lieut Col. and A.A. General.

[88] This is not a handwritten order but a copy published in an unidentified newspaper. It was probably an order of the commanding general of the department rather than a Special Order of Parsons's Brigade (thus explaining why the number is out of order). Salt was important to both the military and civilian population as it was the primary means of preserving meat. Therefore, the order concerning salt was distributed through the press. Salt was also used to pack cheese and eggs and preserve hides during processing. Antebellum Southerners had bought their salt from the North or from Europe, but the war made it necessary to find local supplies. There were three methods of making salt: extracting it from brine wells, extracting it from seawater or inland salt ponds, and mining deposits of rock salt. See Ella Lonn, *Salt as a Factor in the Confederacy* (Tuscaloosa: University of Alabama Press, 1965).

* * * * * * * * * * * * *

Hd. Qrs. Tex. Cav. Brigade
Cotton Plant Oct 2nd 1862

Special Order No. 59

(I) Lieut [A.H.] McDaniel[89] at Moro & Lieut [William M.] Walton[90] near Trenton will report to Col W.H. Parsons at Duvals Bluff[91] with their command as soon as practicable after being relieved by Mjr [Francis M.] Chrisman

(II) The above mentioned officer comdg scouts near Moro & Trenton will communicate this order to such men & officers as may be engaged upon scouts in their vicinity.

By command of
Col. W.H. Parsons
Comdg. Brigade

J.T. Scott
Capt. & A.A.G.

* * * * * * * * * * * * *

Hd. Qrs. Tex. Cav. Brgd.
Cotton Plant, Oct. 3d 1862.

Special Order No. 60

Lt. Col. Giddings & Major Farrar will take charge of the government horses at Col. Haralsen's & distribute them among the men of their respective commands who are most in need of them

By command of
Col. W.H. Parsons
Comdg

J.T. Scott,
Capt & A.A.G.

[89] Co. B, Twenty-first Texas.

[90] Late in September a detachment under Lieutenant William M. (Buck) Walton of Co. B, Twenty-first Texas captured nearly thirty men of the Fifth Kansas Cavalry. Walton and Major Samuel Walker of the Fifth Kansas met under a flag of truce a little over a week later, and the Federal officer vowed to "get even." Shortly after that some of Walton's men were captured while eating a hot meal in a private home. "The loss of the men were charged to me," lamented Walton, "and it somewhat cast a shadow on me for a time." William M. (Buck) Walton, *An Epitome of my Life: Civil War Reminiscences* (Austin: Waterloo Press, 1965), 32-33; *Official. Military History of Kansas Regiments During the War for the Suppression of the Great Rebellion* (Leavenworth: W.S. Burke, 1870), 108-11. Walton, who was thirty years old in 1862, was a native of Mississippi who had enlisted from Travis County. He gave his occupation as lawyer, with $12,000 in real estate and $6,250 in personal estate. He lived only a few doors from Sam Houston in Austin and owned two slaves. He had also served as Governor Francis Lubbock's private secretary before the war and claimed to have given the first secession speech on the capitol grounds. His book is a treasure of information about the wartime experiences of the Texans in the Twenty-first cavalry regiment. Bailey, *Between the Enemy and Texas*, 220-21.

[91] The Du Valls family settled on the bluffs along the White River sometime after 1838, and the town became Du Valls Bluff. There are various spellings, including De Valls or Devall's Bluff. It is located on the White River between Clarendon and Des Arc. The spelling has been left as it was written on the order.

* * * * * * * * * * * * *

Hd. Qrs. Tex. Cav. Brigade
Cotton Plant Oct. 3d 1862

Special Order No. 61

Lieut. Hinson [H.C. Hynson] of Pratts Battery[92] commanding detachment will immediately join his compy & report with his detachment to Capt. [Joseph] Pratt for duty

| | |
|---|---|
| | By command of |
| J.T. Scott, | Col. W.H. Parsons |
| Capt. & A.A.G. | Comdg |

* * * * * * * * * * * * *

Hd. Qrs. Tex. Cav. Brgd
Oct. 3rd 1862

Special Order No. 62

(I) Major [Francis M.] Chrisman will order Capt. [Rufus D.] Anderson's compy[93] to move down toward Helena in order to watch & report all movements of the enemy.

(II) If Capt. Anderson's compy can supply Maj. Chrisman with caps he will remove the remainder of his command in the same direction on the same duty—If not however Maj. Chrisman will remain on that side of White river until the deficiency in his ammunition is supplied.

| | |
|---|---|
| | By command of |
| J.T. Scott | Col. W.H. Parsons |
| Capt. & A.A.G | Comdg. |

* * * * * * * * * * * * *

Hd. Qrs. Tex. Cav. Brgd
Oct. 3d 1862

Special Order No. 63

Lieut [Lafayett] Kinkle[94] comdg Capt [Rufus D.] Anderson's compy of Ark. Cav. will instantly take steps to secure the arrest of "Jack Watson" of Philips County Ark who is

[92] Tenth Texas Field Battery.

[93] Apparently Anderson had already left on the scout, as J.C. Morriss wrote on October 1: "Capt. Andersons spy company went down to Helena a few days ago and had a fight with Fed. Anderson had about 80 men and the Feds sent out about 1500 to cut him off and capture him; and Anderson retreated followed in full tilt by the Feds, and he whip[p]ed out in the bushes and as they came by he opened fire on them and killed about 20 and captured 20 odd horses & mules and got off without loosing a man." J.C. Morriss to Amanda Morris, October 1, 1862, Pruett and Black, eds., *Civil War Letters*, 35-38.

[94] First lieutenant, Co. B, Dobbin's Arkansas Cavalry.

now en route for that place. Lieut Kinkle will send parties on all the roads leading to Helena & use every exertion to intercept him & send him to these hd. qrs.

By command of
Col. W.H. Parsons
Comdg

J.T. Scott,
Capt. & A.A.G.

* * * * * * * * * * * * *

Hd. Qrs. Tex. Cav. Brgd.
Cotton Plant Oct. 3d 1862

Special Order No. 64

Lt. [W.N.] Kenner[95] comdg train at Des Arc will cause the prisoner John Bugle (alias Wm. Johnson) to be carried before the Provost Marshal at Des Arc who will hear the charges prefered against him & dispose of his case.

By command of
Col. W.H. Parsons Comdg

J.T. Scott, Capt & A.A.G.

* * * * * * * * * * * * *

Hd. Qrs. Tex. Cav. Brgd
Camp near Duvals Bluff
Oct. 6th 1862[96]

Special Order No. 65

(I) Mjr. [Francis M.] Chrisman's Comdg Batt of Ark Cav. will immediately distribute to Capt. [George W.] Rutherford's compy the caps sent per courier & then take the field without delay

(II) He will carry out the instructions previously given him to cover the post watch & report all movements of the enemy. He will establish a line of couriers (as he descends the country) connecting with Switzer's & report the stands to these hd. qrs.

(III) Major Chrisman will obtain by impressment if necessary a sufficient no. of negroes to repair the bridge over Bayou de View. He will place the negroes in charge of some reliable citizens or soldier with orders to perform the repairs without delay.

By order of
Col. W.H. Parsons
Comdg

J.T. Scott
Capt. & A.A.G

[95] Co. E, Twelfth Texas.

[96] On October 6 Henry Orr wrote from De Valls Bluff that "Buford's Regiment has at last got here; it is at Clarendon. . . . Carter's Regiment still with us. Buford's will also be in our brigade." He added at the end of the letter: "Col. Buford is under arrest at the Rock for getting drunk and stopping his command out of the rain while on a forced march, on order signed by Gen. Holmes." Henry Orr to "Father and Mother," October 6, 1862, in Anderson, ed., *Campaigning with Parsons' Brigade*, 72-74.

Note—Major Chrisman is expected only to cover the approaches from the mouth of Spring Creek Eastward—Especially the St. Francis & Spring Creek roads—Col. Giddings[97] guards the approaches from Trenton west towards Clarendon

J.T. Scott, Capt. & A.A.G.

* * * * * * * * * * * * *

Hd. Qrs. Tex. Cav. Brgd 1st Div.
Army of S.W. Oct. 8th 1862

Special Order No. 66

Circular

Comdg Officers of Regts, Comps & detachments will forward to these hd. qrs. without delay monthly returns of their respective commands for September

By command of
Col. W.H. Parsons
Comdg

J.T. Scott,
Capt. & A.A.G.

* * * * * * * * * * * * *

Hd. Qrs. Tex. Cav. Brigade
In camp near Duvals Bluff
Oct 8th 1862

Special Order No. 67

Capt. [James C.S.] Morrow[98] of the 12th Tex. Dragoons is detailed with his company to remain at or near Duvals Bluff in order to picket the river at that point & the vicinity in

[97] On October 11 Lieutenant Colonel Giddings rode upon a party of the Fourth Iowa Cavalry heading for Helena. After successfully attacking a detachment, killing three, wounding two (one later died), and capturing fifteen, he continued on his scout. But Giddings and eleven of his men were captured. In retaliation for helping the rebels, soldiers in the Fifth Kansas burned at least two homes. This also began a vendetta between Major Samuel Walker and Giddings's seventeen-year-old nephew, Edmund Giddings, that ended with the boy being killed by Federal troops. Colonel Giddings was sent to prison in St. Louis and exchanged two months later. Scott, *The Story of a Cavalry Regiment,* 50-55; "Fight Near Helena, Arkansas," from our Special Correspondent, Helena, October 12, 1862, D.C. Giddings's Papers, Eugene C. Barker Texas History Collection, The Center for American History, Austin, Texas. The official history of the Fifth Kansas stated: "From the time of arrival at Helena until mid winter, the regiment was engaged weekly, and almost daily, in skirmishing with the rebel cavalry hovering around that post, and with invariable success. Major [Samuel] Walker became a terror to all guerilla bands, capturing from time to time many men and horses." *Official. Military History of Kansas Regiments,* 108-11. But J.C. Morriss proudly told his wife: "Those prisoners that we took in the fight when Col. Giddings was taken, all said that we were the best clothed & the best armed men that they had ever seen in the Confederate service. They gave us the praise of treating our prisoners better than any other troops that had ever taken any of them prisoners and that if they were ever taken prisoners they wished to be taken by the Texas Rangers. They treated Col. Giddings very kindly in Helena." J.C. Morriss to Amanda Morriss, November 27, 1862, Weller, ed., *Civil War Letters.*

[98] Co. I, Twelth Texas.

accordance with the instructions already given him. He will remain upon this only until releived [*sic*].

By Command of
Col. W.H. Parsons, Comdg Brig
J.T. Scott, Capt & A.A.G.

* * * * * * * * * * * * *

Hd. Qrs. Tex. Cav. Brg
Des Arc, Ark. Oct. 8th 1862

Special Order No. 68

(I) Major [Emory W.] Rogers[99] of Waxahachie, Ellis County Texas is authorized & requested to receive & muster into service all recruits volunteering for regiments or compys attached to Col. Parsons' Tex. Cav. Brg. Army of the South-West.

(II) Col. Parsons Regt. will receive 360 men and Col. Carter's 21st regt. will receive 315 men respectively.

(III) The brigade consists of

| | |
|---|---|
| The 12th regt. of Tex. Drags. | (Col. Parsons) |
| " 21st " " " Cav. | ( " Carter) |
| " [19th] " " " " | ( " Burford) |
| " Batt. Ark. " | (Maj. Chrisman) |
| Tex. Compy of Artillery | (Capt. Pratt) |

(IV) The deficiencies existing in other regts. Batts. & compys than Col. Parsons & Col. Carter's will be communicated to Majr Rogers as soon as accurate reports can be obtained—he will then recruit to the full extent of the deficiencies in all commands attached to this brigade & forward recruits in compys—squads or singly as they may volunteer to the hd. qrs of the Brgd. where ever it may be

(V) Capt. F.H. Ayres is at present in Texas on similar duty to that assigned Major Rogers in this order—a copy of the orders given Capt. Ayres is forwarded here with—nothing in them conflicting with this order.

By command of
Col. W.H. Parsons
Comdg Brg.

J.T. Scott,
Capt. & A.A.G.

[99] Rogers, a proprietor of a hotel in Waxahachie, had come to Texas around 1847, and donated the land for the original town site. Bailey, *Between the Enemy and Texas*, 10.

* * * * * * * * * * * * * *

Hd. Qrs. Tex. Cav. Brigade
Des Arc Ark. Oct 9th 1862

Special order No. 69

The officer comdg Col. [Nathaniel M.] Burfords Regiment of Texas Cavalry will report with his command at the head quarters of this Brigade at the earliest practicable moment.

By command of
Col. W.H. Parsons Com of Tex.
Cav. Brigade

J.T. Scott
Capt. & A.A.G.

* * * * * * * * * * * * * *

Hd. Qrs. Tex. Cav. Brigade
Des Arc, Ark. Oct. 9th 1862

Special Order No. 70

(I) Lieut. [John B.] Ashford of the 21st Tex Cav comdg Post at Des Arc—will at once forward all men who are fit for duty to their respective commands—except such as are indespensably needed for service in the hospital at this place—

(II) Lt. Ashford will also arrest & send to their respective commands any soldiers or officers remaining in Des Arc or vicinity—without a surgeons' certificate—a leave of absence from competent authority or not on duty—He will exert himself to the utmost to prevent all straggling on the part of soldiers or officers fit for duty

By command of
Col. W.H. Parsons
Comdg Brg.

J.T. Scott,
Capt. & A.A.G.

* * * * * * * * * * * * * *

Hd. Qrs. Tex. Cav. Brg.
Des Arc, Ark, Oct 9th 1862

Special Order No. 71

(I) Comdg officers of this Brigade will require all officers & soldiers who are absent from their respective commands without leave of absence certificates from army surgeons—or not on duty to join their regts & compys without delay

(II) Compy commanders will make details of one or two men from each compy to go through the compy & enforce this order

By command of
Col. W.H. Parsons Comdg Bgd

J.T. Scott
Capt & A.A.G.

* * * * * * * * * * * * *

Hd. Qrs. Tex. Cav. Brgd.
Des Arc, Ark, Oct 9th 1862

Special Order No. 72

(I) Capt. [William G.] Veal[100] comdg Post at Brownsville will send to these respective regiments & comps all men in Brownsville or vicinity who are fit for duty—None will be excused unless in possession of surgeon's certificate, a leave of absence from proper authority or an order assigning them to duty & justifying absence

(II) All the sick who can be moved to Des Arc will be at once transported to the Hospital at this place—All who are unable to be moved to this point will be sent per rail road to Little Rock & placed in the hospital.

(III) Surgeon [Thomas. D.] Lorence will join his regt. & report for duty & Capt. Veal is relieved from the command of the post at Brownsville & if his health will permit will report to his regt. commander for duty—if unfit for duty he will forward a surgeon's certificate of the fact & apply for furlough

(IV) The hospital & post at Brownsville are hereby discontinued & all officer & soldiers attached to either one or the other on duty will join their respective commands immediately

J.T. Scott
Capt & A.A.G.

By command of
Col. W.H. Parsons
Comdg Brgd

Sent by Telegraph

* * * * * * * * * * * * *

Hd qrs 12th Texs Dragoons
Cotton Plant October 12th 1862

Order No

The commanding offi[cer] of companies composing the 12th Texas Drag[oons] in obedience to the order of Genl [Theophilus H.] Holmes [marked out] reference to clothing, will proceed at once to make an estimate of the amount of clothing necessary for their respective companies and hand in their estimates to the adjutant by 4 O'clock P.M.

By order of
L.J. [Farrar]
Comdg 12th Texas Dragoons

[100] Co. F, Twelfth Texas.

* * * * * * * * * * * * *

Hd qurs 12th [Texas] Dragoons
Cotton Plant October 12th 1862

Genl Order No[101]

In [hole] the order of Genl [Henry E.] McCulloch upon the [hole] of firing guns. Officers will be held respons[ible and] under arrest for a violation of that ord[er and] the men will be put on ten days [hole] for firing their guns without per[mission] of the Brigade commander.

By order of
Farrar Major
Comdg 12th Texas Dragoons

L.L. Wren
actg adj

* * * * * * * * * * * * *

Hd. Qrs. Tex. Cav. Brgd.
Cotton Plant, Oct. 13th 1862

Special Order No. 73

I Commanding officers, will require their adjutants to furnish to <u>these</u> hd. qrs. an accurate morning report of their respective commands by 7 O'clock A.M. to morrow

II Regimental commissarys will immediately furnish to Mjr [A.J.] Byrd[102] A.C.S. Regimental requisition for seven days rations.

By order of
Col. W.H. Parsons
Comdg

J.T. Scott,
Capt. & A.A.G.

* * * * * * * * * * * * *

Hd. Qrs. Tex. Cav. Brigade
Cotton Plant, Oct. 15th 1862

Special Order No. 74

I Capt. Terrel [R.A. Terrell] A.Q.M. 12th Tex dragoons will at once place the wagons & teams in condition for mounting at a moments notice

II He will see that arrangements are made to turn over the exhausted mules & occupy their places with others fit for service

By order of
Col. W.H. Parsons
Comdg Brgd.

J.T. Scott,
Capt & A.A.G.

[101] Shortages in the Trans-Mississippi resulted in prohibitions on the unauthorized use of ammunition.

[102] Byrd later wrote *A History and Description of Johnson County, and its Principal Towns* (Marshall, Texas: Jennings Brothers, 1879), and has a brief description of his wartime experience. He was also Parsons's brother-in-law and a member of the colonel's staff.

* * * * * * * * * * * * *

Hd. Qrs. Tex. Cav. Brigade
Cotton Plant, Oct. 15th 1862

Special Order No. 75

Col. Carter's Regt & the 12th Tex. Dragoons will prepare immediately for the march & hold them selves in readiness to move promptly when the signal is given

| | |
|---|---|
| | By order of |
| J.T. Scott, | Col. W.H. Parsons |
| Capt & A.A.G. | Comdg |

* * * * * * * * * * * * *

Hd. Qrs. Tex. Cav. Brigade
Oct. 15th 1862

Special Order No. 76

Col. Carter will detail Lt. [Augustus Daniel] Edwards of Compy H, 21st Texas Cav with 12 men to reinforce Capt [John R.S.] Alston on out post duty

| | |
|---|---|
| | By order of |
| J.T. Scott | Col. W.H. Parsons |
| Capt. & A.A.G. | Comdg & C |

* * * * * * * * * * * * *

Hd. Qrs. Texas Cav. Brigd
Camp near Bayou Deview
Oct. 16th 1862

Special Order No. 77

I Col. Carter will station a picket at the mouth of the lane leading into the Cotton Plant road—It will consist of 1 non comd officer & six men & will be relieved & continued by Col Carter until further orders—[103]

II He will also relieve Lieut. Bradly [Daniel Bradley][104] & place the pickets & scouts on the outposts & on the roads from Spring Creek road to Trenton under command of Lieut. Walton

[103] Part of Carter's regiment had been scouting in the region around Clarendon and De Valls Bluff. J.C. Morriss noted that the civilians were extremely helpful. "There is nothing the people have down here that is to [*sic*] good for a Texas Ranger. They give us the best they have and charge nothing for it." Daily encounters with Union horsemen were typical, but the cold, rainy autumn weather made the men miserable. J.C. Morriss to Amanda Morriss, October 16, 1862, Weller, ed., *Civil War Letters.*

[104] Co. E, Twenty-first.

III No officer or soldier will be permitted to pass the inner line of pickets without a permit signed by his Regimental Commander

By order of
J.T. Scott, Col. W.H. Parsons
Capt & A.A.G. Comdg.

* * * * * * * * * * * * *

Hd. Qrs. Tex. Cav. Brgd
Camp near Bayou Deview
Oct 16th 1862

Order No. 78

I Col. [Nathaniel M.] Burford will continue to picket the bridge over Bayou De view until further orders

II He will also detail 1 non comd officer & 42 privates well mounted, armed & rationed for picket service to report promptly at these hd. qrs. tomorrow morning at 7 O'clock under command of his Regimental Adjutant

III No officer or soldier will be permitted to pass the inner pickets without a permit from his Regtal comdr

By order of
J.T. Scott, Col. W.H. Parsons
Capt & A.A.G Comdg

* * * * * * * * * * * * *

Hd. Qrs. Tex. Cav. Brigade
Camp near Bayou De view
Oct. 16th 1862

Special Order No. 79

I Major [Lochlin J.] Farrar[105] will relieve Lt. McDaniel comdg picket at Moro by stationing a picket consisting of a sergeant & six men at that place

II Major Farrar will station & releive [*sic*] da[i]ly a picket of 1 non comd & 6 men 2 mile above hd. qrs. via the lane

III No soldiers or officers will be allowed to pass the inner pickets without a permit from his regimental commander unless on duty—

By order of
J.T. Scott, Col. W.H. Parsons
Capt & A.A.G Comdg

[105] Twelfth Texas.

* * * * * * * * * * * * *

Hd. Qrs. Tex. Cav. Brgd.
Camp near Bayou Deview
Oct 16th 1862

Sp. Order No. 80

I Capt. [James C.S.] Morrow[106] comdg picket comp[an]y near Duvalls Bluff is relieved from duty at that point & will report with his comp[an]y to Lt. Col. [A. Bell] Burleson at Des Arc with the greatest possible dispatch

II Capt. Morrow's comp[an]y will if it arrives at Des Arc in time to do so constitute the military escort at the funeral of the late Capt. [William Jeff] Neal[107] of the 12th Tex. Dragoons.

III Immediately after the funeral of Capt Neal—Capt. Morrow with his comp[an]y will rejoin his Regt without delay—

By order of
J.T. Scott Col. W.H. Parsons
Capt. & A.A.G. Comdg

* * * * * * * * * * * * *

Hd. Qrs. Tex Cav. Brigade
Camp on Bayou De View
Oct 16th 1862

Special Order No. 81

I Col. Carter will order Capt. [William M.] Rust[108] with his company to accompany Mr. I.C. Davisson to the vicinity of the country in which Lt. [William M.] Walton is operating.

II Capt. Rust will report at these head quarters immediately for special instructions

By order of
Col. W.H. Parsons Comdg.
J.T.Scott Capt & A.A.G.

[106] Co. I, Twelfth Texas.

[107] Neal was captain of Co. C ("Johnson County Slashers"), Twelfth Texas. He was twenty-six years old when the war began. Born in Tennessee, he had enlisted from Johnson County. He was a lawyer with $40 in real estate and no personal estate, probably indicating he owned no slaves. He died as a result of wounds from the Battle of Cotton Plant. His body was returned to Texas where he was buried at Buchanan, the seat of Johnson County in 1862. Nothing remains of the town near Cleburne except the cemetery. Bailey, *Between the Enemy and Texas*, 212-16.

[108] Co. B, Twenty-first Texas. Rust was thirty-seven years old in 1862. A native of Virginia, he had enlisted from Burnet County. He was a farmer with $4,000 in real estate and $6,000 in personal estate. His recruits called themselves the "Austin City Light Infantry," and came from the frontier west of the capital. In 1864 Rust resigned to build a powder mill near his home and invested $25,000 of his own money in the venture. Ibid., 219-21.

* * * * * * * * * * * * *

Hd. Qrs Tex Cav. Brigade
Camp on Bayou De View
Oct 16th 1862

Special Order No. 82

Col Burford will order his men to prepare rations of bread for two days & hold himself in readiness to move with 400 men at sunrise tomorrow morning

By command of
Col. W.H. Parsons Comdg.
Cav. Brig.
J.T. Scott, Capt & A.A.G.

* * * * * * * * * * * * *

Hd. Qrs. Tex. Cav. Brigade
Camp on Bayou De view

Special Order No. 83

Doctor [E.W.] Herndon[109] Act. Asst. Surgeon in charge of Hospital at Cotton Plant will sign all requisitions & receipts for supplies obtained for Hospital use at that place—They will be approved by his Regimental commander

J.T. Scott,
Capt & A.A.G

By order of
Col. W.H. Parsons
Comdg Brgde

* * * * * * * * * * * * *

Hd. Qrs. Tex. Cav. Brigade
In camp on Bayou De View
Oct 16th 1862

Special Order No. 84

I Special order No 82, assigning Col Burford to hold himself in readiness for the march to-morrow morning is hereby revoked.

II Col. Burford will require a daily drill of one hour, beginning at 8 o'clock A.M. for his regimental officers.

III He will also require a regimental drill of 2 hours daily beginning at 2 o'clock P.M.

IV These drills will be continued while in stationary camp until further orders.

By order of
Col. W.H. Parsons. Comdg Brig.
J.T. Scott Capt & A.A.G.

[109] Herndon was a senior surgeon of the Fourth Brigade, Sterling Price's division, in late 1863. He was in charge of a hospital in Arkansas.

* * * * * * * * * * * * *

Hd. Qrs. Tex Cav. Brigade
In Camp on Bayou De View
Oct 16th 1862

Special Order No. 85

I Capt. [William M.] Rust[110] will move with his command to the position occupied by Lt. Walton on the road from Helena to Clarendon, and will direct scouting parties belonging to the 21st Tex. Cav. & the 12th Tex. Drags—now in the field near that point, to report to him in order to secure concert of actions.

II He will take command of all individual or private scouts belonging to the 12th Tex Drags.

III He will cooperate with Capt. [Samuel] Corley[111] and the other companies of the Ark. Cav Battalion. and will establish a line of couriers from his positions to these head quarters.

IV He will cooperate with the companies composing the Ark. Cav Battalions for concert of actions.

V He will keep his videttes close to the enemies lines, closely observing their movements, reporting the same promptly to these head quarters by couriers.

VI Capt Rust will direct Lieut Bradly [Daniel Bradley] to report to his company at these hd. qrs.

By command of
Col. W.H. Parsons Comdg Brg.
J.T. Scott, Capt. & A.A.G.

Copied from Col Parsons notes
J.T.S. A.A.G

* * * * * * * * * * * * *

Hd. Qrs. Tex Cav Brig.
Camp on Bayou De View
Oct. 17th 1862

Special Order No. 86

I Col. Carter will detail Capt [George R.] Freeman[112] with all the available men of his company & order him to proceed without delay—to occupy the roads & country now held by the Scouts before Helena & en route to that vicinity.

[110] Co. B, Twenty-first Texas.

[111] Co. A, Chrisman's Arkansas Battalion.

[112] Co. D, Twenty-first Texas. Freeman lived in Austin, although he had raised a company primarily from Bell County. Born in Kentucky, he had enlisted in Travis County. He was a wealthy lawyer, counting his real estate at $20,000 and his personal estate at $5,000. Bailey, *Between the Enemy and Texas*, 220-23.

II Capt. Freeman will cooperate with Capt [William M.] Rust & other officers on similar duty near the positions to which he is ordered.

By command of
Col. W.H. Parsons, Comdg. Brig.
J.T. Scott, Capt. & A.A.G.

* * * * * * * * * * * * *

Hd. Quarters, Tex. Cav. Brigade
In camps. Oct. 17th 1862

Special Order No. 87

I Capt. [George R.] Freeman comdg compy on scouting duty will place a courier at six miles south of Mr. Switzer's & inform the officer with whom he comes in contact of the fact: to facilitate the transmission of reports to these Hd. qrs.

By order of
Col. W.H. Parsons
Comdg Brg.

J.T. Scott,
Capt & A.A.G.

* * * * * * * * * * * * *

Hd. Qrs. Tex. Cav. Brgd.
Oct. 20th 1862

Special Order No. 88

I No soldier will ride out of a trot before either the color or brigade line

II Regimental officers will instruct their guards to arrest any person riding faster than a trot in the ground indicated.

III All Officers of the Brigade are instructed to enforce this order rigidly.

By order of
Col. W.H. Parsons Cmdg
J.T. Scott, Capt & A.A.G.

* * * * * * * * * * * * *

Hd. Qrs. Tex. Cav. Brgd.
Oct. 21st 1862

Special Order No. 89

Capt. Kuyser [H.W. Kyser][113] of the 12th Tex. Dragoons will take command of the Post & move his camps according to instructions already given

By command of
Col. W.H. Parsons Comdg
J.T. Scott, Capt & A.A.G

* * * * * * * * * * * * *

Hd. Qrs. Tex. Cav. Brig-
Camp on Cache River-
Oct 24th 1862

Special order No 90

I Capt McGhee [James H. McGeehee][114] comdg. co of Ark. Cav. Chrismans Batt. will immediately move with his command to Madison where he will take position to cover all the approaches to the St. Francis River & scout the county towards Memphis.

II He will watch the enemy & report their movements promptly to these Hd. Qrs

III He will also secure the cooperation of Capt. Harris Co. & Mjr. Barton Squadron

____ to be communicated
to Capt. [Samuel] Corley comdg
Chrismans Batt, J.T.S.

By command of
Col. W.H. Parsons,
comdg Brig
J.T. Scott, Capt. & A.A.G.

[113] Co. G ("Kaufman Guards"), Twelfth Texas. Kyser was thirty-eight when the war began. A native of Tennessee, he had enlisted from Kaufman County. He had been the county surveyor with $800 in real estate and $200 in personal estate. Bailey, *Between the Enemy and Texas*, 212-18.

[114] Co. C, Chrisman's Battalion.

* * * * * * * * * * * * *

Hd. Qrs. Tex. Cav. Brig.
Oct 24th 1862

Special order No 91

I Col. Burford 19th Tex. Cav. Mjr [Lochlin J.] Farrar 12th Tex Dragoons & Capt. [Joseph] Weir[115] 12th Tex Drags. are hereby detailed to constitute a court of inquiry to investigate charges performed against Lt. [Samuel M.] Snead[116] & other officers of Col Burford Regt by Brig Gen. [Henry E.] McCulloch—Col Burford will act as president of the court.

II The court will convene at Col Burfords Hd. Qrs. immediately; transact the business referred to them & report the results as early as possible to these hd. qrs.

By command of
Col W.H. Parsons Comdg Brig
J.T. Scott, Capt & A.A.G.

* * * * * * * * * * * * *

Hd. Qrs. Tex. Cav. Brig-
Camp on Cache River, Oct 24th 1862

Sp. Order No. 92

I Lt. Col. Burleson, Col. Burford & Col Carter will each furnish from their respective Regiments a detail of 1 Lt. 1 sergt & 20 men mounted rationed and armed for a scout of three days.

II The officers & men will be selected with care for scout service & will report at these hd. qrs. promptly at 1 o'clock P.M. to day.

By command of
Col. W.H. Parsons Comdg
Cav. Brig.
J.T. Scott, Capt & A.A.G.

[115] Co. A ("Hill County Volunteers"), Twelfth Texas. Wier (also seen Weir) was thirty years old in 1861, and a resident of Hill County. He had been born in Virginia and was an attorney when the war began. His real estate was valued at $4,000 and his personal estate at $4,000. He had represented Hill and Navarro counties in the secession controversy although he owned only two slaves. Wier often operated as the regiment's senior captain and was fatally wounded in the Red River Campaign in May 1864. Bailey, *Between the Enemy and Texas*, 211-13.

[116] Co. C, Nineteenth Texas.

* * * * * * * * * * * * * *

Hd. Qrs. Tex Cav Brigade
Camp Burford. Oct 26th 1862

Special order No. 93

Private J.M. [James M.] Scales of Co. I. 19th Regt Tex Cavalry is detailed on special duty in the commissary department until further orders & will report to Major [A.J.] Byrd for instructions.

By command of
Col. W.H. Parsons Comdg Brig.
J.T. Scott Capt & A.A.G.

* * * * * * * * * * * * * *

Hd. Qrs. Tex. Cav. Brigade
Camp Burford, Oct 27th 1862

Special order No. 94

Capt. W.G. [William G.] Veal[117] of the 12th Tex. Dragoons is hereby detailed to visit Little Rock in order to obtain tents & other supplies for his Regt.

By command of
Col. W.H. Parsons
Comdg Cav Brig
J.T. Scott Capt & A.A.G.

* * * * * * * * * * * * * *

Hd. Qrs. Tex. Cav. Brigade
Camp Burford, Oct. 27th 1862

Special Order No 95

I In accordance with genl. order No 5 of Majr Genl. [Thomas C.] Hindman—Lt. Col. [Benjamin] Watson[118] of the 19th Tex Cav. Capt. J.P. [Joseph P.] Wier[119] 12th Tex Dragoons

[117] Co. F, Twelfth Texas.

[118] Watson, a native of Virginia, was thirty-two years old when he enlisted in Ellis County in 1862. He claimed $7,000 in real estate and $26,000 in personal estate. He was a farmer who rose to lieutenant colonel of the Nineteenth Texas. He "displayed considerable genius in military affairs, and was always read for service, generally commanding the regiment in trying moments." Popular with the men, he "distinguished himself by his coolness in action . . . and his gallant conduct." Bailey, *Between the Enemy and Texas*, 40, 224-25.

[119] Co. A, Twelfth Texas.

& Capt. J. Alston[120] 21st Tex Cav. are hereby detailed as a board of examiners before whom all officers entitled to promotion by seniority of rank or election who are attached to this brigade will appear for examination as prescribed in the above mentioned order of Gen Hindman

II Lt. Col. [Benjamin] Watson[121] will act as president of the board

III The board will meet at some convenient place in camps or its vicinity which they will designate to Regimental Comdrs—as also their hours of meeting

IV Comdrs of Regts & Compys will require all officers of their respective commands designated by Gen. Hindman's orders to appear before the board promptly & will also require a certificate of proficiency from the board in every instance before any further continuance on duty of any officer subject to examination

V The board will report to the brigade cmd. the names of all parties who pass or fail to pass an examination

By order of
Col. W.H. Parson Comd
J.T. Scott, Capt. A.A.G

* * * * * * * * * * * * *

Hd. Qrs. Tex. Cav. Brigade
Oct. 27th 1862

Special order No 96

Private J.H. Bonner Actg. Commissary, will turn over to Lieut [J.B.] Abbot[122] A.A.C.S. all funds, supplies, transportation & property belonging to the commissary departments, that may remain in his hands at this time.

By command of
Col. W.H. Parsons, Comdg
J.T. Scott, Capt & A.A.G.

[120] Co. H, Twenty-first Texas.

[121] Nineteenth Texas.

[122] Co. B, Twelfth Texas.

* * * * * * * * * * * * *

Hd. Qrs. Tex. Cav Brigade
Oct 28th 1862

Spl. Order No. 97

I Capt. Hanner [J.H. Hannah][123] of the 21st Tex. Cav. is detailed to supply the vacancy in the brigade board for the examination of officer occassioned by the absence of Capt [John R.S.] Alston[124] of the 21st Tex. Cav

II Capt Hanner will report to Lt. Col. [Benjamin] Watson president of the board

By order of
Col. Parsons Comdg
J.T. Scott, Capt & A.A.G

* * * * * * * * * * * * *

Hd. Qrs. Tex. Cav. Brigade
Camp Burford Oct 28th 1862

Special Order No. 98

Hereafter comdg officer of Regiments & companies composing this Brigade will send to these hd. qrs. daily at 10 o'clock A.M. accurate morning reports of their respective commands

By order of Col W.H. Parsons,
Comdg.
J.T. Scott. Capt & A.A.G.

* * * * * * * * * * * * *

Hd. Qrs. Tex. Cav. Brigade
Camp. Burford. Oct 28th 1862

Special order No. 99

I Commanding officers of this Brigade will require their Regimental Quarter Masters to furnish full and accurate statements of the forage received & issued by them from the 7th of Oct 1862 to the 31st Oct. 1862 inclusive to Major [Thomas] Johns Brigade Q.M.

II These statements must be furnished without delay—

By command of
Col. W.H. Parsons, Comdg
J.T. Scott, Capt. & A.A.G.

[123] Co. G, Twenty-first Texas. Hannah was thirty-eight years old in 1862. He was born in the District of Columbia and had enlisted from Orange County. He gave his occupation as merchant with no real estate and $3,000 in personal estate. Bailey, *Between the Enemy and Texas*, 220-21.

[124] Co. H, Twenty-first Texas.

* * * * * * * * * * * * *

Hd. Qrs. Tex. Cav. Brigade
Camp Burford. Oct 29th 1862

Special order No. 100

Capt. Corly [Samuel Corley][125] comdg Battalion & Ark. Cav. will dispatch a courier to Capt McGhee [James H. McGeehee][126] at Madison, with orders for Capt McGhee to rejoin Capt Corleys Battalion with his company—unless movements of the enemy render it imprudent for him to evacuate his position.

By order of
Col. W.H. Parsons, Comdg.
J.T. Scott, Capt & A.A.G.

* * * * * * * * * * * * *

Hd. Qrs. Tex Cav. Brig.
Camp Burford. Oct 29th 1862

Special order No. 101

I Col. Burford comdg 19th Tex Cav will furnish a detail of 1 Lieutenant 1 N.C. officer & 34 men. to report to Capt [J. T.] Scott A.A.G. at these hd. qrs to morrow morning at 7 o'clock, mounted & armed with rations for 2 days.

II Capt [Anthony M.] Branch[127] comdg 21st Tex. Cav. will furnish a detail of 1 Lieutenant, 1 N.C. officer & 31 men to report to Capt Scott A.A.G. at the same time & place provided & armed with rations for 2 days

III Mjr [Lochlin J.] Farrar comdg 12th Tex Drags will furnish a detail of 30 men under Capt J.P. [James P.] Brown[128] to report to Capt J.T. Scott A.A.G. at the same time & place. Mounted & armed with rations for 2 days.

[125] Co. A, Chrisman's Arkansas Battalion.

[126] Co. C, Chrisman's Arkansas Battalion.

[127] Co. A, Twenty-first Texas. Branch was thirty-eight years old when he enlisted in 1862. He was a native of Virginia and a resident of Walker County. Listing his occupation as a lawyer, he owned $5,960 in real estate and $5,350 in personal estate (including four slaves). He was elected to the Confederate Congress in 1863. He was succeeded in office by George Washington Farris, a native of Tennessee who also enlisted from Walker County. Known as "Black Wash" for his dark complexion and black hair, he had fought in the Mexican War. He generally commanded the company when Branch was absent. Bailey, *Between the Enemy and Texas*, 220-21, 320.

[128] Brown was thirty-two years old when the war began. He was born in Georgia, but enlisted from Limestone County. He gave his occupation as a farmer with $1,500 in real estate and $7,500 in personal estate. He was the second captain of Company K ("Eutaw Blues"), Twelfth Texas. The first captain had been Anson F. Moss, who had been forty-six when the war began. A native of North Carolina, Moss also enlisted from Limestone County. He was the wealthiest man to serve as captain in this regiment with $27,000 in real estate and $14,000 in personal estate. He owned nine slaves and three different farms where he tried to raise tobacco. Because of his age, he resigned from the army. Bailey, *Between the Enemy and Texas*, 212-17.

IV Mjr. [Thomas] Johns Brigade Q.M. will furnish a detail of 9 wagons with driver for each, to report promptly at these hd. qrs. to Capt J.P. Brown, 12th Texas Dragoon at 7 o'clock A.M. tomorrow.

V As soon as the above details assemble at the hour indicated, Capt. Brown will join them into a detachment of which he will assume the command and proceed to carry out verbal instructions that will be given him by the Comdg col.

By command of
Col. W.H. Parsons comdg Brig
J.T. Scott Capt. & A.A.G

## CHAPTER 2

# ARKANSAS

## November 2-December 31, 1862

By late 1862 the Texans under Colonel Parsons had so successfully harassed Union scouting parties operating along the Mississippi River that the *Houston Telegraph* could report the Federals were "fulminating all kinds of threats as to what they will do with him *when they catch him*." A captain in the Seventeenth Texas Infantry observed that "Parsons is a trump." The Federals "never make a play but he catches them. They hate him as the devil."[1]

Although Confederate cavalry attacked Federal supply trains and foraged in the vicinity of the Union base at Helena, it was difficult to find enough food for man and beast. The region west of the White River offered little sustenance, as the armies marching through the area the previous spring had stripped it clear. Although corn was brought by boat from southern Arkansas, when the river dropped it was impossible to navigate. The troopers had to move to camps east of the White and Cache rivers where they could find supplies. Discontent spread as cold weather arrived and food grew scarce.

As winter approached, Confederate authorities in Richmond debated ways to safeguard the vital waterway of the Mississippi while at the same time protect the Arkansas state capital. General Holmes received instructions to forward seven regiments to Virginia, a request he ignored, replying instead that he needed the Arkansas soldiers east of the river returned to

[1] Letter to E.H Cushing, from Camp Hope, Arkansas, September 29, 1862, *Houston Tri-Weekly Telegraph*, October 22, 1862; E.P. Petty to Ella Petty, October 26, 1862, in Norman Brown, ed., *Journey to Pleasant Hill: The Civil War Letters of Captain Elijah P. Petty, Walker's Texas Division, C.S.A.* (San Antonio: Institute of Texan Cultures, 1982), 96-97.

him. While President Jefferson Davis and Secretary of War George Randolph squabbled over who should make decisions regarding the Trans-Mississippi, Holmes continued to defy Richmond. For Holmes, the state of Arkansas took priority. When Adjutant and Inspector General Samuel Cooper told him to forward ten thousand reinforcements to Vicksburg, Holmes answered that he had no men to spare. He was worried about an attack on his own position, particularly the Post of Arkansas on the lower Arkansas River. The loss of the Post would open the way to Little Rock, and he told the authorities that to deprive his command of troops was the "equivalent to abandoning Arkansas."[2]

Control of the Mississippi was vital for both sides, and Vicksburg was the most important port remaining open for Southerners. New Orleans on the southern end of the river had fallen in April 1862 and Memphis to the north had surrendered in June. Vicksburg had clearly become the Federal objective. The city, situated on the steep bluffs of a sharp horseshoe bend in the river, connected the Trans-Mississippi with the rest of the Confederacy. A railroad ran from the Mississippi state capital at Jackson to Vicksburg, while a ferry connected the city with the recently completed Vicksburg, Shreveport and Texas Railroad that continued on to Monroe, Louisiana.

As the Union campaign to take Vicksburg took shape, Memphis became a base of operations. Since the Federal depot at Helena continued to concern authorities in Little Rock, Parsons's men remained scouting in northeast Arkansas watching enemy movements. Their goal was to prevent supplies from reaching Helena by land, supplies that could be used in the river war. The first significant action against Vicksburg came in December 1862 when Grant pushed overland along the Mississippi Central Railroad while William T. Sherman led an expedition against Chickasaw Bluffs, just a few miles to the north of the city. But Confederates under Earl Van Dorn attacked Grant's supply depot at Holly Springs while Nathan Bedford Forrest's cavalry destroyed the railroad. When Sherman's river campaign also failed, Grant temporarily abandoned his plans.

Yet actions along the Mississippi River were not the only concerns for the people in Arkansas. In the northwest, Brigadier General James G. Blunt's

[2] Samuel Cooper to T.H. Holmes, October 15, 1862, *OR* 13:888; T.H. Holmes to Samuel Cooper, November 2, 1862, ibid.; Samuel Cooper to T.H. Holmes, November 19, 1862, ibid., 921; T.H. Holmes to Samuel Cooper, November 22, 1862, ibid., 926; T.H. Holmes to Samuel Cooper, November 25, 1862, ibid., 926-27; T.H. Holmes to Samuel Cooper, December 5, 1862, ibid., 17: pt. 2, 783-84; Samuel Cooper to T.H. Holmes, December 6, 1862, ibid., 17: pt 2, 786; T.H. Holmes to Samuel Cooper, December 8, 1862, ibid., 17: pt. 2, 787-88; Anne J. Bailey, "The Abandoned Western Theatre: Confederate National Policy toward the Trans-Mississippi Region" in *Journal of Confederate History* V: 35-54.

division of John Schofield's Army of the Frontier threatened the region around Fayetteville. In early December General Hindman attacked the Federals at Prairie Grove. After a confusing battle, the Confederates withdrew, retreating down the Arkansas River toward Little Rock. General Holmes faced a predicament. He needed both to reinforce Hindman to the west of the state capital while at the same time prevent a Union movement up the Arkansas River from the southeast. To add to his dilemma, he continued to receive requests to send reinforcements to Vicksburg.

While Holmes argued with Richmond over the availability of troops to reinforce the river port, he made changes that directly affected the Texas cavalry: he replaced Parsons with James M. Hawes, a brigadier general who had arrived in Arkansas in late September. Hawes, born in 1824, had enjoyed an early life among the prominent families in Lexington, Kentucky. He had graduated from West Point in 1845, twenty-ninth in a class of forty-one. Upon graduation he had promptly been sent to Texas, where he had fought in the Mexican War. Following the war he taught infantry and cavalry tactics as well as mathematics at West Point and traveled to Europe to observe French military tactics. In the 1850s he was briefly posted in Texas, then took part in the Mormon expedition in Utah, and finally went to Kansas. He resigned from the army when the secession crisis came and offered his services to the Confederacy. Accepting a captain's commission, he rose quickly through the ranks. He was a favorite with his old friend, Albert Sidney Johnston, and although the general recommended him for promotion to brigadier general, that did not happen until the spring of 1862. General Braxton Bragg, who assumed command of the army following Johnston's death at Shiloh and Beauregard's decision to leave the army, did not think Hawes showed potential. Bragg indicated a dislike for Hawes, complaining that he was "unsuited for [his] responsible position." Although it is unclear why Bragg felt this way, shortly thereafter Hawes was transferred to Little Rock.[3]

Although most of the Texans thought that Hawes was an effective leader, he was also a strict disciplinarian and that was not popular among the democratically-minded Texians. Private Henry Orr complained that "some of the

[3] Hawes would remain in the Trans-Mississippi for the rest of his career. Although he took command of the cavalry, he would soon move to command infantry, never retaining a position for long and often offending the authorities, both civilian and military. Mark M. Boatner III, *The Civil War Dictionary* (New York: David McKay Company, Inc., 1959), 386; Ezra J. Warner, *Generals in Gray: Lives of the Confederate Commanders* (Baton Rouge: Louisiana State University Press, 1959), 128-29; William C. Davis, "James Morrison Hawes," *The Confederate General* (Harrisburg, Penn.: National Historical Society, 1991), 74-75.

boys are put under arrest most every day . . . but the offences are trifling—no one has been punished yet . . . some of the command dislike him—I have found no fault with him yet." And Lieutenant George Ingram decided that he was "a good disciplinarian and an unasuming gentleman. . . . He is a Kentuckian but claims to be a Texan."[4]

In December, as a result of the spreading discontent (partially because Hawes enforced regulations), some men from the Nineteenth Texas serenaded the general in a "disrespectful manner" that "created a sensation." Hawes immediately issued a special order in which he said he was "much gratified" that the men from the Twelfth and Twenty-first Texas regiments and Pratt's battery, were not "engaged in the disgraceful & mutinous scene of last evening."[5]

Parsons was not in camp to see this exhibition of frustration on the part of the troops, as he had left for Texas. He planned to visit the state's military commander and see if he could obtain permission to detach his brigade from Hawes and return it to duty in Texas. At the same time, various regimental officers attempted to transfer their companies to Shreveport, out from under Hawes's command. Neither endeavor proved successful. In the midst of controversy, the brigade received orders to report to Fort Hindman at Arkansas Post to prevent a Federal advance up the Arkansas River toward Little Rock.[6]

The following orders cover the last two months of 1862 before the brigade moved from northern Arkansas to the southeast part of the state. Many of the men in the brigade would never see northeastern Arkansas again.

[4] Henry Orr to Mary Orr, November 24, 1862, and Henry Orr to "Father," December 17, 1862, in Anderson, ed., *Campaigning with Parsons' Brigade*, 84-86; George W. Ingram to Martha F. Ingram, November 30, 1862, in Ingram, comp., *Civil War Letters*, 39-40.

[5] Henry Orr to "Father," December 17, 1862, in Anderson, ed., *Campaigning with Parsons' Brigade*, 85-86; General Order No. 17, December 9, 1862, Special Order Book of Parsons's Brigade.

[6] John W. Truss to Rebecca Truss, November 5, 1862, Ray, ed., "Civil War Letters From Parsons' Texas Cavalry Brigade," 217-19; George W. Ingram to Martha F. Ingram, December 22, 1862, in Ingram, comp., *Civil War Letters*, 42-43.

DOCUMENTS

# ARKANSAS

## November 2-December 31, 1862

Hd Qrs White River District
Near Cotton Plant Nov 2nd 1862

Gen Order No 5

I Commanders of outposts and pickets will in future retain at the outposts all prisoners captured from the Enemy. When the number of prisoners becomes sufficient to incommode the outposts or pickets in the discharge of their duty—they will be sent under guard to the rear far enough to secure them from escaping or recapture

II In every case a statement of the circumstances attending the capture with full name & rank, Regt, Compy & citizenship of each individual known will be sent to these Hd Qrs promptly where parols will be prepared & forwarded to the ouposts & pickets from which all prisoners will hereafter be paroled.

By order of
Brig Genl [James M.] Hawes[7]
J.[T.] Scott A.A.Genl

[7] James Morrison Hawes (1823-1889) replaced Parsons as commander of the cavalry brigade, and Parsons promptly left for Texas where he worked for authorization to detach his regiment and have it reassigned to him south of the Red River. On November 4 Henry Orr wrote "Gen. Hawes, a Kentuckian—took command a few days since. Don't know how we will like him yet. He looks to be about forty-five years of age. So Col. Parsons comes to his regiment [retirement?]. I judge he *does not feel so elevated as he has been feeling.*" Henry Orr to "Mother and Father, November 4, 1862, Anderson, ed., *Campaigning with Parsons' Brigade*, 75-78. On November 30 George Ingram, wrote: "Col. Parsons has gone home on a visit. We are highly pleased with Gen. Haw[e]s. He is a good disciplinarian and an unasuming gentleman." George W. Ingram to Mat Ingram, November 30, 1862, in Ingram, comp., *Civil War Letters*, 39-40.

* * * * * * * * * * * * *

Head Qrs White River District
Camp near Cotton Plant
Nov 5th 1862

Extract
Gen Order No 6

The following named officers having been declared proficient by the Brig Board of Examiners are announce[d] and will at once enter upon the discharge of these duties.

| | |
|---|---|
| Thomas Haly [Haley][8] Capt | Co K.[C] 12th Texas Dragoons |
| Geo. W. Ingram[9] 1st Lieut | " A " " " |
| W.N. Kinner [Kenner] 1st Lieut | " D [E] " " " |
| W.H. Getzendanner [Getzendaner] 2nd Lieut Snr | Co D [E] Tx Dr |
| James M. Jackson " " Jr | Co A " " |
| John Haly [Haley] " " Jr | Co K [C] " " |
| H.B. Smith " " Sr. | Co A " " |

By order of
Brig Genl [James M.] Hawes
J.T. Scott Capt & AAG.

* * * * * * * * * * * * *

Hd Qrs Trans Miss Dept
Little Rock Ark Nov 5th 1862

Spl Orders No 36

I Col M J White corps of Artillery Provisional Army being the Senior Artillery officer in this Department announced as chief of artillery of the Same

II Maj G.H. Hill P.A.C.S. is announced acting Inspector Genl of the Trans Miss Dept

By command of
Major Gel [Theophilus H.] Holmes
S.S. Anderson A A Genl

A true Copy
J L Robertson A A Genl

[8]Thomas F. Haley became captain of Company C upon the death of Captain Neal after the Battle at Cotton Plant. He was forty-four years old in 1861, and had enlisted from Johnson County. Born in Alabama, he was a farmer with $3,150 in real estate and $15,205 in personal estate. He was seriously wounded in the Red River Campaign in 1864 and returned home where he died of complications in February 1865. Bailey, *Between the Enemy and Texas*, 212-16.

[9] Ingram was thirty-one years old when the war began. Born in North Carolina, he had enlisted from Hill County. He was a stock raiser with real estate valued at $1,000 and a personal estate valued at $2,000. Bailey, *Between the Enemy and Texas*, 212-13.

* * * * * * * * * * * * *

Head Quarters Trans Miss Dept
Little Rock Nov 12 1862.

Colonel

I am instructed by the Major General commanding the Department to say to you he has received with great satisfaction and pride the vindication of yourself and command from the charges of pillage and plunder as shown in the resolutions passed by the Citizens of Des Arc, which now seem were made in malevolence and that he received the high opinion of the gallantry and good conduct of his officers and men as expressed in those resolutions as the sure exponent of their future

The General directs me further to say he wishes you to furnish Brigadier General [James M.] Hawes with a copy of those resolutions

I am Colonel very respectfully
You[r] most obnt Servt
S.S. Anderson
Asst Adjt General

Col W.H. Parsons
(True Copy)

* * * * * * * * * * * * *

Hd Qrs Dist Wh River
Cotton Plant Nov 15th 1863

Sp order No 25

The following details will be made daily from each Regiment and in accordance with the following Regulation

Every evening at 4 Oclock each Regt commander will detail 2 commissioned officers and thirty men to have on hand cooked rations for 24 hours to be s[up]plied Inlying pickets[10]

This detail will be required to remain within the Regimental lines holding themselves in readiness to be called out any moment for any duty ordered at these Hd Qrs. for picket or any other duties

By order of
Brig Genl [James M.] Hawes
J.L. Robertson Ast. Adj

[10] Scouting towards Helena was a daily occurrence. "We are the advance gard [*sic*] of the army," wrote J.C. Morriss of Carter's regiment, "and consequently, will have to be on the alert all of the time." J.C. Morriss to Amanda Morriss, November 8, 1862, Weller, ed., *Civil War Letters*.

* * * * * * * * * * * * *

Hd Qrs Dist Wh River
Near Cotton Plant Nov 16th 1863[11]

All applications for furlough, leave of absence and communications of any kind, should be folded and endorsed on back [hole]

Br[ig.] Genl [James M.] Hawes
[J.] L. Robertson A.A.G.

Application for leave of absence for

______________
___ Co ____ Rgt
for ______ days

Approved & forwarded
Capt Comdg
Compy _______

[hole]

______ Regt

* * * * * * * * * * * * *

Hd. Qrs Dist Wh River
[hole, Nov.?] 23rd Des Arc

Genl Order No 12

The attention [of] commanders of Regiments & c is called to paragraph [hole] Order No ____ Application for discharges, furloughs & [leave] of absence will be forwarded by & through the adjts of [hole] & companies in detached service will forward [hole] application through the regular couriers & in [hole] will the applicant himself be allowed leave to [hole] the same

Comdrs are held responsible for the enforcement of this order

[By] order Brig Genl [James M.] Hawes
J L Robertson A.A.G

[11] George Ingram wrote from Des Arc on November 18: “Our command is now crossing the [White] River and will remain here for a while. . . . We are quartered in good houses with good fire places and would be glad to stay here this winter. . . . *I* am so fat that I can not button the top button on my new Pants. My beard is very long. I have not shaved since May last. . . . The Feds are at Helena and also about the northern boundery of the State. We will not be troubled with them here unless White River gets up and the Gun Boats come. If so we will have to get away from here.” George W. Ingram to Mat Ingram, November 18, 1862, in Ingram, comp., *Civil War Letters*, 37-39.

* * * * * * * * * * * * *

Hd Qrs Dist Wh River
Des Arc Ark Nov 27 1862

Genl order No 14

I In accordance with paragraph [_______] Genl orders No 72 Adjt & Insp Gen Office Richmond Va The following regulations will be observed

II A medical Board of Examiners for the examination of applicants for discharge by reason of disability and applicants for furlough on account of sickness or wound is hereby appointed.

Detail for the board

| | | |
|---|---|---|
| Surgeon | [William H.] Pyle[12] | 19th Texas Cavalry |
| " | Dashiel [William Bond Dashiell][13] | " " " |
| " | [W.H.B.] Goodwin | 12th " " |

III All applicants of the nature stated above will be forwarded properly approved to surgeon Pyle together with the applicant for the action of the Medical Board and when action shall have been by the board properly approved the application will be forwarded to Capt [Joseph P.] Weir comdg the Post who will take final action in the report of the Medical Board

IV No [fur]lough Will be granted to applicants in camp, [hole] the Hospital and only in cases where [the] Medical board of Examiners deem it practicable [hole] furloughs for the speedy recovery of the applicant [hole]

V Paragraph [hole] Genl order No 7 from these Head Qrs is hereby revoked [hole]

By [order] Brig Genl [James M.] Hawes
J [L. Robertson] A.A.G.

* * * * * * * * * * * * *

Head Qrs 12th Tex Drag
Des Arc Nov 28th 1862

Genl Order No

The companies constituting this command will resume the letters they need after the Reorganization of the Regiment on the 25th May last, and all the officers belonging to this command will be careful to make use of their original letters in all communications and all returns and reports of whatever description to prevent any confusion in the future

For the better infomation of the command it is announced that the Alphabetical arrangement of the companies will stand thus; without being affected by any future ~~reorganization~~ promotion. ~~made at any future time~~.

[12] Pyle was a surgeon in the Nineteenth Texas.

[13] Dashiell was assistant surgeon in the Nineteenth Texas.

| Capt | | |
|---|---|---|
| [Joseph P.] | Weir will be Company | A |
| [Appleton M.] | Maddux[14] | B |
| [Thomas F.] | Haley | C |
| [M.B.] | Highsmith | D |
| | Jno. C. Brown[15] | E |
| [William G.] | Veal | F |
| [H.W.] | Kyser | G |
| [J. Em.] | Hawkins[16] | H |
| [James C.S.] | Morrow | I |
| | Jas. P. Brown | K |

This order [hole] does not affect the present position of [com]panies & Squadrons in the formation of line of battle or in camp

By order of

J.W. [John W.] Walden — Maj L.J. [Lochlin J.] Farrar
Act Adjt — Comdg 12th Tex Drag

* * * * * * * * * * * * *

Hd Qrs 12th Texas Dragoons
Des Arc Nov 28 1862

Sp order No

In fu[tu]re when any details are made for <u>any</u> purpose to report at Genl Head Qrs the orderly Sergt will instruct the men so detailed to report first to the adjutant of the Regt and the details will in no case go to Genl Hd Qrs without instructions and orders from these Hd Qrs.

By order of

J W [John W.] Walden — Maj L.J. [Lochlin J.] Farrar
Lt & Act Adjt — Comdg 12th Tex Drag

[14] Maddux was twenty-eight years old when the war began. Born in Alabama, he had enlisted from Freestone County. He was a farmer with $2,600 in real estate and $15,709 in personal estate. He was the captain of the "Freestone Boys," later Company B, a unit he financed with his own money. Bailey, *Between the Enemy and Texas*, 212-16.

[15] Brown was thirty-two years old when the war began. Born in Tennessee, he had enlisted from Ellis County. He was a farmer with no real estate and $1,450 in personal property. His father, however, was worth almost $20,000 and owned seven slaves. Ibid., 212-14.

[16] Hawkins was thirty-one years old when the war began. He was a native of Indiana, one of only two men from non-slaveholding states to serve as a captain in the Twelfth Texas (he owned thirteen slaves). When the war began he was a lawyer in Ellis County with $4,575 in real estate and $7,000 in personal estate. He lived in the Waxahachie Hotel with his Cherokee wife and was remembered as someone who had "infinite good humor" and "never lost an opportunity to perpetrate an innocent joke." Hawkins led the company until he was wounded at Lake Providence in 1863 and resigned the following year. He had succeeded W.J. Stokes, who at thirty-six, did not remain in the service long. Stokes, a native of Tennessee who had enlisted from Ellis County, had been a stock raiser with $725 in real estate and $5,300 in personal estate. He served as the first captain of Company H, also known as the "Ellis Blues" or "Hell Roaring Blues." Ibid., 212-14.

* * * * * * * * * * * * *

Head [hole] 12th Tex Dragoons
Des Arc [hole] Nov 28th 1862

Regt Sp Order No

[Daniel] Price[17] of Capt J.C.S. [James C.S.] Morrows Company is hereby [hole] appointed ordnance sergeant of this Regiment [hole] and will immediately enter upon his duties in the [hole] Department

By order [of] Maj L J [Lochlin J.] Farrar
[John W.] Walden Act Adjt

* * * * * * * * * * * * *

Hd Qrs Dist Wh River
Des Arc November 28th 1862

Special Order No 45

The command will be prepared to move at day light to morrow morning. The order of march will be announced verbally when the command is ordered to [hole] The Regimental trains will move in rear [hole] in order of their Regt Each Regimental train [will] be under control of Regimental Q Master [hole] Wagon Master and the whole under super[vision of] Major Headington

Those of the sick [hole] unable to march in ranks will march [hole] the train, of their respective regiments and [in no] case will straggling be allowed—

[By order of] Brig Genl [James M.] Hawes
[J.L.] Robertson A.A.G.

* * * * * * * * * * * * *

Hd Qrs Dist Wh River
Des Arc Ark Nov 29th 1862

Genl Orders No 15

I Paragraph [hole] Genl order No 14 from these head Qrs is modified [as] follows—Surgeon [W.H.B.] Goodwin is relieved from duty [on] the Medical Board and Asst Surg [R.P.] Sweatt appointed [in] his stead

II Capt [Joseph P.] Weir[18] is left in command of the Post and will make his report to the Brig Genl Comdg

[17] Company I, Twelfth Texas.

[18] Company A, Twelfth Texas.

III Surgeon [William H.] Pyle will remain in charge of the hospital at this point—Asst Surgons DeShiel [William Bond Dashiell], [R.P.] Sweatt & [D.C.] Hewson[19] will report to Surgeons Pyle for duty—all other Surgeons and asst surgeons will join their commands at once

IV Col [George W.] Carter will remain with his command at this point & carry out instructions given him by the Brig Genl Commanding

By order of Brig Genl [James M.] Hawes
J L Robertson A.A.G.

* * * * * * * * * * * * *

Hd Qrs [hole] River District
Des Arc [hole] 29th 1862

Sp Order No 46

Order for preparation for to morrow morning is revoked, but the command should be prepared to move at short notice

[By order of] Brig Gen [James M.] Hawes
[J.L.] Robertson A.A.G.

* * * * * * * * * * * * *

Hd Qrs Dist Wh River
Des Arc Nov 29th 1862

Special Order No 48

The 12th and 19th Texas Cavalry and Pratts Battery will be prepared to move in accordance with special No 45 at Sun Rise tomorrow morning

By command of Brig Genl [James M.] Hawes
J.L. Robertson A.A.G.

* * * * * * * * * * * * *

Hd Qrs Dist White River
Des Arc Nov 29th 1862

Special order No 50

I Owing to the assignment of Major [Joel T.] Daves[20] of the 19th Texas Cavalry to Lt [W.H.] Getzendaner of the 12th Tex Cavalry to other duty, Capt W G [William G.] Veal and Lt J.B. Abbott of the 12th Texas Cavalry are detailed to their stead to act on the Brigade

[19] Hewson was assistant surgeon in the Twenty-first Texas.

[20] Daves was a major in the Nineteenth Texas. Before the war he had been a Methodist minister and in 1863 he resigned and returned to his congregation. Major General John G. Walker wrote: "The reasons offered for this resignation are insufficient, but as it seems to be a case of conscience I recommend its acceptance." Bailey, *Between the Enemy and Texas*, 41.

Board for the Examination of officers

II Capt W G Veal will act as President of the board & convene at such time and place as may be necessary and [send] proceedings to these Head Quarters

III The board [hole] consists of the following officers

| | | |
|---|---|---|
| Capt | Veal[21] | President |
| Lieut | Abbott[22] | 12 Tex Cav |
| " | Hunt[23] | 19th " |

[By] command of
Brig Genl [James M.] Hawes
[J.L.] Robertson A.A.G.

* * * * * * * * * * * * *

Hd. Qrs Wh River District
Lake Bluff[24] Dec 1st 1862

Sp Order No 54

I Hereafter these details are made with orders to report at these Hd Qrs. the order for the detail will be copied at Regt Hd Qrs and the original order sent with the comder of detail in order to show what the detail was made for

II The attention of [co]mpany commanders is called to the necessity of [hole] Capt [Joseph P.] Weir[25] comdg Post at Des Arc with a [hole] list of & account of each man sick in hospital [hole] will be furnished at once

III All sick [in] camp or that may hereafter be too sick to remain in camp while at this point will be sent to hospital [at] Des Arc.

By [order] of
Brig Genl [James M.] Hawes
J L Robertson A.A.G

[21] Company A, Twelfth Texas.

[22] Company B, Twelfth Texas.

[23] Company K, Nineteenth Texas.

[24] Lake Bluff is about twelve miles from Des Arc. On December 24 J.C. Morriss complained: [W]e had not been here but a few days before we had the most intolerable rain that I ever saw fall; it rained one entire night and raised White River until it is now out of its banks and is still rising. It looks impossible for us to stay here, it is so wet and boggy, and it looks like it would be impossible for us to get away from our trains." J.C. Morriss to Amanda Morriss, December 24, 1862, Weller, ed., *Civil War Letters.*

[25] Company A, Twelfth Texas.

* * * * * * * * * * * * *

Hd Qrs. Dist Wh River Ark
Lake Bluff Dec 1/62

Sp order No

Maj [Lochlin J.] Farrar will detail 1 NCO & 9 men for Brig guard and will report to Capt [J.T.] Scott at these Hd Qrs at 9 A M to morrow.

By command of Brig Genl [James M.] Hawes
J L Robertson A.A.G.

* * * * * * * * * * * * *

Head. Qrs. Trans. Miss. Dist.
Little Rock, Ark Dec 1 1862

Genl Order No 42

I Major Rhetts [Thomas G. Rhett] corps of artillery C.S. Army having reported at these Hd Qrs in obediance to special order No 24 current series from the department of war will relieve Major C.I. (?) Alexander in the duties of Chf. of Ordnance for the Trans Miss Dept

II Major Alexander is assigned to the command of the post at Arkadelphia and the superintendancy of the ordnance at that point and will also have charge of the manufacturing and purchasing for that portion of the Army in Arkansas.

Signed S.S. Anderson
A.A.G.

By Comdg of
Major Genl [Theophilus H.] Holmes

* * * * * * * * * * * * *

Hd Qrs Dist Wh River
Lake Bluff Dec 1st 1862

Maj J.L. Robertson A.A.G.[26]

We have before us charges and specifications against Jno. Stein Co. K.—Jessie Craft Co. C.—W.M. Falkner Co. C.—Jo Buress Co. G.—W.H. Bradley Co. D.—J.W. Uptol Co K.—J. Cook Co F.—G.W. Jones Co. B.—G.M. Sullivan Co D.—Alvis Lockhardt Co H.—J R Brook C[o.] G.—P.H. Woods Co. G.—J.D. Jones Co B.—J R Pope Co. F.—G.W. Parker Co. B.—R.A. Fenler Co. G.—P.S. Smith Co. G.—W.S. Lawrence Co. E.—T.H. Clare Co. G. All of the 12th

[26] It is possible that these arrests stemmed from the same violation of Special Order 45 (see November 28, 1862), as noted in the following order.

Texas Dragoons—None of the above parties have been arrested, The first named Jno Stein is off on scout with Tom Keenan and Jessie Craft is reported here as our orderly In the case of Henry ____ four of the Witnesses are absent—Witnesses in many of the cases are detailed or absent

A.M. [Anthony M.] Branch
Judge Advocate

Endorsement

Maj [Lochlin J.] Farrar will have the within named men arrested i[mmed]iately and placed under guard

By order [of] Genl [James M.] Hawes
J [L.] Robertson A.A. Genl.

* * * * * * * * * * * * *

Hd Qrs Dist Wh River
Dec 2nd Lake Bluff

Special Order No 56[27]

1st Lt Wm M. [William M.] Campbell[28] Co "H" 12th Regt Tex Dragoons—charged with violation of Special order No 45 from these Hd Qrs [while] on the march from Des Arc to this point is [here]by placed in arrest & confined to his quarters

[By] command of
Brig Genl. [James M.] Hawes
J L Robertson A.A.G.

* * * * * * * * * * * * *

Hd Qrs Dis Wh River
Decr 2nd 1862

Sp order No

Major [Lochlin J.] Farrar will detail Capt [William G.] Veal and 20 men to report (unmounted) to Major Headington Brigade Qr M immediately.

By order of
Brig Gen [James M.] Hawes
[J.T.] Scott A.A.G.

[27] Incidents like this one, the enforcement of military regulations, only served to fuel discontent and a rising dislike of General Hawes. Henry Orr wrote on November 24: "Military discipline is now enforced to the letter. . . . A soldier—or officer—caught one mile from town without a properly approved [torn] is arrested and court martialed [torn] are several under arrest now." Henry Orr to "Mollie [Mary]," November 24, 1862, in Anderson, ed., *Campaigning with Parsons' Brigade*, 84-85.

[28] Campbell was twenty-one years old when the war began. He was a native of Tennessee who had enlisted in Ellis County. He gave his occupation as a clerk with no real estate nor personal estate. Bailey, *Between the Enemy and Texas*, 212-13.

* * * * * * * * * * * * *

Decr 2nd 62

Sp order No

Maj [Lochlin J.] Farrar will detail 1 com off 1 NCO & 10 privates to report to Capt [J.T.] Scott at 9 A M tomorrow

By order of Brig Genl [James M.] Hawes
J.L. Robertson AAG

* * * * * * * * * * * * *

[Hea]d Qrs Dist Wh River
Decr 3rd 1862

Sp Order No

Comdg officer 12th Tex Dragoons will detail 2 men as teamsters to report to Maj [A.J.] Byrd at his Qrs at once

By command of
Brig Genl [James M.] Hawes
J L Robertson A.A.G.

* * * * * * * * * * * * *

Hd Qrs Dist White River
Lake Bluff Decbr 3 1862

Sp Order No

Comdg 12th Tex Dragoons will detail one man as courier to go to Cotton Plant with orders to report here at once, will detail one who knows the <u>trailway</u> to Cotton Plant

By order of Brig Genl [James M.] Hawes
J.L. Robertson AAG

* * * * * * * * * * * * *

Head Qrs Dist Wh River
Lake Bluff Decr 3-1862

Special Order No

Maj [Lochlin J.] Farrar will detail 2 N.C.O. & 9 men for Brig Guard to report to Capt [J.T.] Scott at 9 oclock A.M. tomorrow

By command of
Brig Genl [James M.] Hawes
J.L. Robertson A.A.Genl.

* * * * * * * * * * * * *

Head Quarters Dist. White River
Lake Bluff Decr 3rd 1862

Special Order No

Major [Lochlin J.] Farrar will relieve private Clements and four men that where [were] with him from duty for four days

By order of
Brig Genl [James M.] Hawes
J.L. Robertson A.A.G.

Pevehouse, Logan & Brown Co K
Richardson Co D

* * * * * * * * * * * * *

Hd Qrs Dist W.R. Decr 4th 1862

Special Order No

Major [Lochlin J.] Farrar will detail 1 Corp & 4 men for fatigue duty to report at these Hd Qrs at once

By order of
Brig Genl [James M.] Hawes
J.L. Robertson A.A.G.

* * * * * * * * * * * * *

Head Quarters Dt White River
Lake Bluff Decr 4th 1862

Special Order No

Major [Lochlin J.] Farrar will detail 1 Lieut 1 N.C.O. & 9 privates for Brig guard to report to Capt [J.T.] Scott tomorrow at 9 o'Clock A.M.

By command of
Brig. Genl. [James M.] Hawes
J L Robertson A A Genl

* * * * * * * * * * * * *

Head Qrs White River Dist.
Lake Bluff Ark Decr 4th 1862

Special Order No 58
Extract

Comdr of 12th Texas Dragoons will keep in camp until after ~~the~~ examined as witnesses before the Genl Court Martial now in session the following named officers & men

| | | | | |
|---|---|---|---|---|
| Lt J.L. [Levi] Smith | Co H | Private | B I Bigmore | Co B |
| " Burgess | " D | " | W Hays | " F |
| Capt [Joseph P.] Weir | " A | " | Jas Reagan | " I |
| Lt. [H.B.] Smith | " " | " | Jno Williams | " " |
| | | " | Geo Tanner | " " |
| | | " | W.T. Gray | " C |
| | | " | W Hogan | " H |
| | | " | W Richards | " B |
| | | " | J.H. Jeffers (?) | " D |
| | | " | S Hays | " F |
| | | " | Rigsby | " B |
| | | Sergt | T F Sitton | " E |
| | | | J Woods | " D |
| | | | J H Clay | |
| | | | C. Cadwell | |

By order of
Brig. Genl [James M.] Hawes
J.L. Robertson A A. Genl
Head Quarters Dt. W.R.

* * * * * * * * * * * * *

Head Quarters Dt W. R.
Lake Bluff Decr 4, 1862

Special Order No[29]

Major [Lochlin J.] Farrar will detail 2 men as couriers and will report at these Hd Qrs at 8 oClock A M tomorrow.

By command of
Brig Gen [James M.] Hawes
J.L. Robertson A.A.G.

[29] This order appears twice with slight variations in each.

* * * * * * * * * * * * * *

Head Quarters Dist White River
Lake Bluff Decr 4th 1862

Special order No

Captain [Thomas F.] Haley[30] is detailed as field officer of the day and will report at these Hd Qrs at 9 o'Ck A.M. tomorrow.

By command of
Brig. Gen'l [James M.] Hawes
J L Robertson A A Genl

* * * * * * * * * * * * * *

Hd Qrs White River Dist
Decr 5th 1862

Special Order No

Major [Lochlin J.] Farrar will detail 1 com off & 10 men to report at once to these hd qrs for fatigue duty.

By order of
Brig Gen [James M.] Hawes
J L Robertson A.A.G.

* * * * * * * * * * * * * *

Head Qrs Dist White River
Dec 5th 1862

Special order No

Major [Lochlin J.] Farrar will furnish a detail of 1 Non com off. & 4 men with axes to report at once to Mr. Saddler at the Blacksmiths shop.

By order of
Brig. Genl [James M.] Hawes
J.L. Robertson A.A.G.

[30] Company C, Twelfth Texas.

* * * * * * * * * * * * *

Hd. Qrs. White River Dist
Decr 5th 1862

Special Order No

Major [Lochlin J.] Farrar will detail the four men that were with Mr. [Benjamin W.] Watson yesterday [and they] will report here at once

By order of
Brig Genl [James M.] Hawes
J L Robertson

* * * * * * * * * * * * *

Hd Qrs White River Dist
Decr 6th 1862

[torn] order

Comand'g officer of 12th Texas will detail [torn] Woody as a permanent Teamster to report to [Wagon] Master Saddler at Blacksmiths shop immediately

By order of
Brig Gen'l [James M.] Hawes
J.L. Robertson A.A.G.

* * * * * * * * * * * * *

Hd Qrs White River Dist
Decr 6th 1862

[torn] order

Commd'g officer 12th Texas will furnish a detail [torn] (seven) men to report at once to Wagon Master Saddler at [torn] Blacksmiths shop—Also one—6 mule team & driver to haul [torn] for coal to report at the same place

By order of
Brig Genl [James M.] Hawes
J.L. Robertson A.A.G.

* * * * * * * * * * * * *

[order marked out and not completed]

H'd Qrs White River Dist
Decr 6th 1862.

[torn] Order

Commdg officer of 12th Texas will detail Chas Fox of Compy B as permanent Teamster for the

* * * * * * * * * * * * *

Hd Qrs White River Dist
Decr 6th 1862

[Spec]ial Order No

Commd'g officer of 12th Texas will detail 4 men [to] report at the ferry to J M Scales for fatigue duty at 11 oclock

By order of
Brig Genl [James M.] Hawes
J.L. Robertson A. A. G

* * * * * * * * * * * * *

Head Quarters Dist White River
Lake Bluff Decr 6th 1862

[Spe]cial Order No -

Major [Lochlin J.] Farrar will detail 1 Lieut, 1 N.C.O. & 10 men for Brig. Guard and will report to Capt [J.T.] Scott at 9 ock AM Tomorrow

By order of
Brig Genl [James M.] Hawes
J.L. Robertson A.A.G.

* * * * * * * * * * * * *

Head Qrs Dist White [torn]
Lake Bluff Dec [torn]

Special Order No

Major [Lochlin J.] Farrar will detail one [torn] guard duty to report at these Hd Qrs at on[ce] [torn]

By Command [of]
Brig Genl [James M. Hawes]
J.L. Rober[tson]

* *. * * * * * * * * * * *

Head Quarters Dist [torn]
Lake Bluff [torn]

Special Order No

Major [Lochlin J.] Farrar will detail 2 [torn] 9 men for Brig Guard to report to Capt [J.T.] Scott at [torn] tomorrow

By order of
Brig. Genl [James M.] Hawes
J L Robertson A[AG]

* * * * * * * * * * * * *

Head Qrs White River
Decr 6 1862

Special Order No

The commandg officer of 12th Texas will de[tail] _____ men to report at once to J.R. Grover[31] at the flat boat for duty

By order of
Brig. Genl [James M.] Hawes
J L Robertson

* * * * * * * * * * * * *

Head Qrs White River Dist
Decr 6th [torn]

Special Order No

Commd'g officer of 12th Texas will detail [Charles] Fox of Co. B. as permanent teamster for the Com'y train to [covered up] the Blacksmith's shop to Mr Saddler at once, also Saml Sad_____ of Company 'I' for the same purpose—& to report at the same

By order of
Brig Genl [James M.] Hawes
J.L. Robertson A.A.G.

[31] Grover was quartermaster of the Twelfth Texas.

* * * * * * * * * * * * *

Head Quarters Dis White River
Lake Bluff Ark
Dec 8th 1862

Genl Or No 16

I The Brig Genl comdg the District has heard with mortification that the troops of his comdg have so far divided from rules of discipline and solderly conduct as to bring down upon them the comdemnation of officers, soldiers & citizens who respect and revere the true and disciplined soldiers, and for the better discipline of the troops of the comdg & in order that officers and citizens may be treated with that respect due the soldier and gentleman—the following will be observed by all concerned.

II The practice of soldiers challenging the paserby with such ludeness and foolish, and ungentleman[l]y expressions as "Get out of that _____" & c. shows a like [lack] of discipline and is not seen in an Army that is properly governed by its officers and in order that it may be remedied Should any soldier or citizen be accosted in such manner, and any com officer of this command known to be within hearing of such soldier challenging and does not arrest the soldier for disobedience of this order, the coms officer shall be arrested and tried before Genl Court Martial [for] neglect of duty and disobedence of orders of superior officers. All officers com and non com who respect discipline and order are called upon to assist in in [*sic*] the enforcement of this order.

* * * * * * * * * * * * *

Head Qrs White River
Lake Bluff Ark. Dec 8th 1862

Special Order No

Major [Lochlin J.] Farrar will detail a Brigade Guard unmounted of 2 N.C.O. & 10 privates to report at the usual hour

By comd of Brig. Genl. [James M.] Hawes
J.L. Robertson A.A.G.

* * * * * * * * * * * * *

Hd Qr White River Dis
Dec 8th 1862

Sp Ord

Major [Lochlin J.] Farrar will detail 24 men and 2 non com officers for Brig Guard to report to Capt [J.T.] Scott unmounted and will move immediately.

By Order of
Brig Genl [James M.] Hawes
J.T. Scott Capt A A.G

* * * * * * * * * * * * *

Head Qrs White River
Dis. Dec 9th 1862

Spl Ord No

Major [Lochlin J.] Farrar will detail 1 NCO and ~~ten~~ 14 men to report to [J.R.] Grover at these Hd Qr at once mounted and unarmed

By Comdg of
Brig Genl [James M.] Hawes
J L Robertson A.A.G.

* * * * * * * * * * * * *

Head Quarter White
Rive[r] Dis. Dec 9th 1862

In addition to the guard detailed already for Brig guard Major [Lochlin J.] Farrar will detail 1 Liet 3 NCO and 21 men to report at the same time

By order of
Brig Genl [James M.] Hawes
J L Robertson

* * * * * * * * * * * * *

Head Qr White River
Dis. Dec 9th 1862

Spe Order No

Major [Lochlin J.] Farrar will detail 1 man to go to Little Rock, to report at these Hd Qr at once.

By order of Brig Genl [James M.] Hawes
J.L. Robertson A.A.G.

* * * * * * * * * * * * *

Hed Quarters White River
Lake Bluff Dec 9th 1862

Special order No

Major [Lochlin J.] Farrar will detail 6 to drive Beavs to Report to Maj [A.J.] Byrd at once

By Command of
Brig Genl [James M.] Hawes
J L Robertson A A Gen

* * * * * * * * * * * * *

Head Qr White River
Dis. Dec 9th 1862

Spl Or No -

Major [Lochlin J.] Farrar will detail 1 com off and 10 men to report at these Head Quarters at 10 O'ck for provost guard.

By Order of
Brig Genl. [James M.] Hawes
J.L. Robertson A.A.G

* * * * * * * * * * * * *

Hed Quarters Dt White River
Lake Bluff Dec 9th 1862

Special order No

Major [Lochlin J.] Farrar will detail one non com officer & 11 men mounted for Brg Guard to Report at the usual hour

By Command of
Brig Gen [James M.] Hawes
J L Robertson A A Gen

* * * * * * * * * * * * *

Hed Quarters
Camp Lake Bluff

Special order No

The following named persons who were detailed on Brigade guard last night having been ordered by the general commanding to Be releaved of one Houer of guard duty for the prompt execution of their duty as soldiers and sentinals and here By excused from one Houer of guard sentence and the Capt will See that the persons named Below are not put upon guard duty at their next regular Term viz

| | |
|---|---|
| W A Wuller | Corp guard |
| Mc [McCoy] Redding | Co I |
| S Monsun [Swan Mondon] | " " |
| John Shropshir [Shropshire] | Co C |
| T.J. Scott | " H |
| E.M. Chisolm [Chisum] | " K |
| R Hamair (?) | " " |
| Joseph Berry | " D |

L.J. [Lochlin J.] Farrar
Major Comdg

* * * * * * * * * * * * *

Head Qrs White River Dist
Camp Lake Bluff Ark
Dec 9th 1862

Gen order No. 17[32]

The Genl Comdg is much gratified to know that the 12th & 21st Texas Regt & Pratts Battery were not engaged in the disgracful & mutinous scene of last evening.

The conduct of these commands shows a high state of discipline & that the officers & men can be relied on in the enforcement of discipline in the hour of danger & on the day of battle.

It is with a real pride & with feelings of gratituion that the Genl comdg makes this order

[32] On December 17 Henry Orr wrote: "Gen. Hawes is a strict disciplinarian—and some of the boys are put under arrest most every day—the Brigade Court Martial sits most all the time—but the offences are trifling—no one has been punished yet—some of Burford's Regiment serenaded him in a disrespectful manner some time ago, which created a sensation—some of the command dislike him—I have found no fault with him yet." Henry Orr to "Father," December 17, 1862, in Anderson, ed., *Campaigning with Parsons' Brigade*, 85-86. One soldier noted that although he was "a Kentuckian" he claimed to be "a Texan." He apparently felt this was a personal insult to Texas. George W. Ingram to Martha F. Ingram, November 30, 1862, in Ingram, comp., *Civil War Letters*, 39-40.

He is proud to have such troops in service & gratified that the State of Texas & the country have such loyal soldiers

Special dress Parade is ordered at 4 ock this morning at which this order will be read,

By condg of Brig Genl [James M.] Hawes
J.L. Robertson A.A.G.

* * * * * * * * * * * * *

Hd Qrs White River
Lake Bluff Ark Dec 9th 1862

General order No 18

For the prompt & spirited Execution of his duty as a sentinal in firing upon an insubordinate soldier Private F. Ainsworth of Co C 19 Regt Texas Cav is released from six hours of guard duty

By order of
Brig Genl [James M.] Hawes
J [T] Scott A.A.G.

To be read any dress parade

* * * * * * * * * * * * *

Hd Quarters Ds White River
Lake Bluff Dec 10th 1862

Spl Order No

Maj [Lochlin J.] Farrar will detail a man to go to Des Arc to Report to these head Quarters.

By command of
Brig Gen [James M.] Hawes
J L Robertson A.A.G.

* * * * * * * * * * * * *

Head Qrs White River Dist
Dec.- 10th 1862

General Order No 63

Extract

The following named officer having been declared proficient by the Brig. Board of Examiners are announced & will enter at once upon the discharge of their duties—

| | |
|---|---|
| Jrn. 2nd Lt—Wm J. Montgomery | Co. I 12th Tex. Dragoons |
| " " " W.A. Nichols | " D " " " |

By order of
Brig Genl [James M.] Hawes
J.L. Robertson A.A.G-

* * * * * * * * * * * * *

Head Qrs White River Dist-
Lake Bluff Dec. 10th 1862

Special order No

Major [Lochlin J.] Farrar will detail 1 Lieut 1 N.C.O. & 10 men for Brig. Guard to report at the usual hour

By comdg of Brig Genl [James M.] Hawes
J.L. Robertson A.A.G.

* * * * * * * * * * * * *

Hd Qurs White River Dst
Dec 10th 1862

Spl Ord

Major [Lochlin J.] Farrar will detail 1 non com officer 10 men mounted & un armed to report to J R Grover At once at the river for fatigue duty

By order of
Brig Genl [James M.] Hawes
J L Robertson A.A G

* * * * * * * * * * * * *

Head Qrs White River Dist
Dec 11th 1862

Special Order No

Major [Lochlin J.] Farrar will detail 4 men for fatigue duty to report to Brig. Wagon Master at the Black S.[mith] shop—

By order of Brig. Genl [James M.] Hawes-
J.L. Robertson A.A.G.

* * * * * * * * * * * * *

Hed Qrs Dt White River
Lake Bluff Ark Dec11th, 62

Major

The Genl directs that Dr [E.W.] Herndon be discharged from Service dating from 1st Dec. He has been ordered from Des Arc to this point

I am Major
Your Obt Svt
J L Robertson

Major [Lochlin J.] Farrar
Comdg 12th Texas

* * * * * * * * * * * * *

Hd Qrs Dist White River
Lake Bluff Dec 12th/62

Spl order No

Major [Lochlin J.] Farrar will furnish 10 men for fatigue duty to report at once to Capt Harris of Steam Boat Tom _____.

By order of Genl [James M.] Hawes
J L Robertson A A G

* * * * * * * * * * * * *

Dec 12th 63
Hd Qrs Dist White River

Spl Ordrs

Major [Lochlin J.] Farrar will detail 1 com off 1 non com offr & 40 men (forty) to report at the steam boat landing to J R Grover mounted & unarmed immediately

By order
Brig Genl [James M.] Hawes
J L Robertson A.A.Gen

Dec 12th/62

* * * * * * * * * * * * *

Head Qrs White River
Lake Bluff Ark Dec 12th/62

Genl Orders - No 19-

I B[ei]ng little attention has been paid to orders issued from these Head Qrs that have reference to sending and bringing up communications and that orders may be enforced the following will be observed

II All Genl Orders and Special orders in which company may be interested will be copied and each company commander furnished with a copy

By Order of
Brig Genl [James M.] Hawes
J L Robertson A A Genl

* * * * * * * * * * * * *

Head Qrs White River Dist
Lake Bluff Dec 12th/62

Special Ordr No.

Major [Lochlin J.] Farrar [will] detail 1 NCO & 10 men for Brig guard to report at the Head qur

By comd of
Brig Genl [James M.] Hawes
J L Robertson A A G

* * * * * * * * * * * * *

Hed Qrs Lake Bluff
Dec 12th/62

Special Order No

Major [Lochlin J.] Farrar will detail 1 Lieut 1 NCO & 11 men for Brggade [Brigade] guard to report at the usual hour

By Command of
Brg Genl [James M.] Hawes
J L Robertson A A Genl

* * * * * * * * * * * * *

Head Qurs White River Dist
Dec 12th/62

Special Order No

Major [Lochlin J.] Farrar will furnish a detail of 1 non com oficer [*sic*] & 3 men to take charge & guard the corn boat at the steam boat landing Also a detail of 6 men for fatigue duty to report at these head qurs to Mr. Dennison (?) emediatly [*sic*]

By comand of
Brg Genl [James M.] Hawes
J L Robertson A A Genl

* * * * * * * * * * * * *

Head Quarters Dist White
River Lake Bluff Dec 12th 1862

Special Order No

Capt [Thomas F.] Haley[33] is detailed as field officer of the day and will report at these Head Quarters at 9 O clk AM tomorrow.

By command of
Brig Genl [James M.] Hawes
J L Robertson A A Genl

[33] Company C, Twelfth Texas.

* * * * * * * * * * * * *

Head Qurs Lake Buff [*sic*]
Dec 12th 1862

Special order No

Major [Lochlin J.] Farrar will detail 2 men for couriers to report at these hd quarters at 8 O clk A M tomorrow

By Order of
Brig Genl [James M.] Hawes
J L Robertson A A Genl

* * * * * * * * * * * * *

Head Qurs White River
Dec 13th 1862

Special Order No

Major [Lochlin J.] Farrar will detail 1 N O offi[cer] & 3 men unmounted to guard corn boat at the steam boat landing

By order of
Brig Genl [James M.] Hawes

* * * * * * * * * * * * *

Head Quar Dist White River
Lake Buff [*sic*] Dec 13th 1862

Special Order No

Major [Lochlin J.] Farrar will furnish 1 NCO & 6 men to gard [*sic*] ordinance stores at Devalls Bluff to report at these Hd Quarters immediately

By command of
Brig Genl [James M.] Hawes
J L Robertson A A Genl

* * * * * * * * * * * * *

Head Quarters Dist
White River Lake Bluff
Dec 13th 1862

Special Order No -

Major [Lochlin J.] Farrar will furnish a detail 1 com officer 1 non com officer & 7 men & the officer & non com officer & 4 men to start early to morrow morning with a flat Boat to St Charles to carry ordinance stores, the other three to lead their horses by land to St Charles to start at the same time, all provisions for three days. The com officer will report at these Head Quarters this evening without delay for instructions

By command of
Brig Genl [James M.] Hawes
J L Robertson A.A.G.

* * * * * * * * * * * * *

Head Quarters Dis White River
Lake Bluff
Dec 13th 1862

Special Order No -

Major [Lochlin J.] Farrar will detail 1 non com off & 10 men for fatigue duty mounted and unarmed to report to [J.R.] Grover at 7 Ocl A.M. to morrow at Mjor Headington's office.

By Order of
Brig Genl [James M.] Hawes
J L Robertson A A. Genl

* * * * * * * * * * * * *

Head Quarters
Lake Buff [*sic*] Dec 13th 62

Special Order No

Maj [Lochlin J.] Farrar will detail 1 Lieut 2 NCO & 11 men for Brg gard [*sic*] to report at the usual hour

By commd of
Brg Genl [James M.] Hawes
J L Robertson AAG

* * * * * * * * * * * * *

Head Qurs Dist White River
Extract

Special Order No 63

The following named officers having been declared proficient by the Brg Bord of examiners are announced & will enter at once upon the discharge of their duties

| | |
|---|---|
| G.W. Moore from 2nd Lieut | Co D 12 Texas Dragoons |
| B.F. [Benjamin F.] Knight | " I " " " |

By Order of
Brig Genl [James M.] Hawes
J L Robertson A A Genl

* * * * * * * * * * * * *

Head Quarters White River Dist.
Lake Bluff Dec 14th 1862

Special Order No 65

On statement of facts made by Capt [William G.] Veal[34] 12th Texas Cavalry The genl comdg is please to release Lt. [John W.] Wright[35] of the same Regt from arrest Lt. Wright will resume his sword and return to duty

By Order of
Brig Genl [James M.] Hawes
Clinton McClarty A A Genl

* * * * * * * * * * * * *

Head Qurters Dist White Ri[ver]
Lake Bluff Dec 14th 1862

Genl Order No 27

With the consent of the parties concerned, the following change in the Staff of the General commanding Dist, is announced for the information of all concerned Clinton McClarty ordnance officer to be A A Genl Capt J.L. Robertson, A.A. Genl to be ordnance officer.

Official
Clinton McClarty A.A.G.

By Command of
Brig Genl [James M.] Hawes

[34] Company F.

[35] Company F.

* * * * * * * * * * * * *

Head Quarters Dist White River
Lake Bluff Dec 14th 1862

Spl. Order No -

Capt [H.W.] Kyser[36] is detailed as field officer of the day [and] will report at these Head Quarters at 9 Ock A.M. to morrow.

By command of
Brig Genl [James M.] Hawes
Clinton McClarty A A Genl

* * * * * * * * * * * * *

Head Quarters Dist
White River Lake Bluff
Dec 14th 1862

Special ord. No -

Major [Lochlin J.] Farrar will detail 1 Lieut 1 Non com officer & 10 men for Brig guard to report at [the] usual hour.

By Command of Brig Genl
[James M.] Hawes
Clinton McClarty A.A.G.

* * * * * * * * * * * * *

Head Quarters Dist White River
Lake Bluff Dec 14th 1862

Special Or No -

Major [Lochlin J.] Farrar will detail 3 men to ferry the river and will report at once,

By Command of
Brig Genl [James M.] Hawes
Clinton McClarty A. A. Genl

[36] Company G, Twelfth Texas.

* * * * * * * * * * * * *

Head Quarters Dist White River
Lake Bluff Dec 15th 1862

Special Or No -

The commanding officer of the 12th Texas Regiment of Cavalry will detail fifteen men to report forthwith to these Hd. Qr. for fatigue duty.

By Order Brig Genl [James M.] Hawes
Clinton McClarty A.A. Genl

* * * * * * * * * * * * *

Head Quarters Dist White River
Lake Bluff Dec 15th 1862

Sp- Or- N-

M.F. [Major Lochlin J. Farrar] will detail 1 N.C.O. & 6 men for Fatigue to report immediately—

By order Brig. Genl [James M.] Hawes
C.- McClarty AAG

* * * * * * * * * * * * *

Lake Bluff

Special Ord No 64

The Regimental Quarter Master of this Brigade are directed to turn over forthwith to Capt A. Harwood A Q M acting Brigade Quarter Master all pay Master funds in their hands[37]

By ord of Brig Genl
[James M.] Hawes
C McClarty- AAG

[37] Money was always an issue. On November 8, J.C. Morriss of Carter's regiment had written: "Our Quartermaster has gone to Little Rock after our pay, and they say that the money is there ready for us. I think that it is time that we were paid off, as we have been now in the service eight months and have never received a dollar, and I have spent about seventy five dollars of my own money since I left home." J.C. Morriss to Amanda Morriss, November 8, 1862, Weller, ed., *Civil War Letters*. Although Harwood was the quartermaster of the Nineteenth Texas, this does indicate that some funds were on hand by December for the men in the Twenty-first Texas.

* * * * * * * * * * * * *

Hed Qrs WRr Dist Lake Bluff
Dec 15th 1862

Special Order No

M [Lochlin J.] Farrar will detail on[e] Sergeant to report [to] Lt [J. Fred] Cox at the Brg gar [brigade guard] House

By ord Brg Genl [James M.] Hawes
C McC[l]arty

* * * * * * * * * * * * *

Head Qrs Whit[e] River Dis
Lake Buff [*sic*] Dec 15th

Special Ord

The comdg officer of the 12 Texas Cavalry [will] detail one discrete man for duty as special courier to report at these head qarters imed[iately]

By order of Brig Genl [James M.] Hawes
C McClarty A A Gen

* * * * * * * * * * * * *

Hed Qrs Whit[e] River Dist Lake Buff [*sic*] Dec 15th 1862

Special Order No

Maj F [Lochlin J. Farrar] will detail 1 NC off & 15 men to report at these Head Qrs early Breakfast on 16th for fatigue [duty]

By order Brig Genl [James M.] Hawes
C McClarty A A Gen

* * * * * * * * * * * * *

Hed Qrs Wh River
December 15th 1862

Special Order No

Cap [J. Em.] Hawkins[38] is detailed as field officer of the day to report at 9 ock AM at these Hed Qrs.

By order of
Brig Genl [James M.] Hawes
C McClarty A A Gen

[38] Company H, Twelfth Texas.

* * * * * * * * * * * * *

Head Qrs Dec 15th 1862

Special order No

Major F [Lochlin J. Farrar] will detail 2 NCO offi[cers] & 11 men for briggade guard to report the usual Hour

By ord of Brig. Genl [James M.] Hawes
C McClarty A A Gen

* * * * * * * * * * * * *

Head Qrs Dec 15th 1862

Special Order No

Major F [Lochlin J. Farrar] will detail 1 NOC [*sic*] & 5 men for fatigue at the ferry at early brekfast [*sic*]

By order of
Brig Genl [James M.] Hawes
C McClarty A A Gen

* * * * * * * * * * * * *

Circular

Hed Qrs Trans Miss Department
Little Rock Dec 17th 1862

Sir-

In obedience to instructions from Secretary of War Major Genl [Theophilus H.] Holmes comdg Trans Miss department directs that without delay you cause to be made out and forwarded to this office a list of all officers belonging to your command who are disabled by wounds or Sickness from active service in the field the full name rank regiment the present address of the officer as far as known on the nature of his disability

I am Sir very respectfully
your obdt Servent
(Signed) S.S. Anderson
Asst Adjt Genl

Official
C McClarty
A.A. Genl

* * * * * * * * * * * * *

Regimental Orders

A.P. Martin of Co. H. is hereby detailed in the Commissary Dept. from this date.

Dec. 19th 1862
Lake Bluff, Ark
W.M. Daviess[39] Adjt

By order of L.J. [Lochlin J.] Farrar
Major com 12 Tex Drg

* * * * * * * * * * * * *

Genl Orders from Hd Qrs at Little Rock or Brigade-
Hed Qrs White River Dist
Lake Buff [*sic*] Dec 19th 1862

General Order No 22

I Accounts for mileage commutation of rations for detached servs pickets & c and travling [*sic*] expenses of all parties on detached service will only be paid by the Brigade Commissary & Quarter Master and all such accounts must be approved by the Brigade Commander

II Regimental Commissaries & Quarter Master will make no disbursements of money except in the payment of their employes or when their regiment is detached from the Brigade

III Requisitions for funds on the Brigade Qarter Master & commissaryes for the payment of employes requir the approval of the Brigade Commander

By order of Brig Genl [James M.] Hawes
C McClarty AA Genl

* * * * * * * * * * * * *

Hed Qrs Dist White Riv
Lake Buff [*sic*] Dec 20th/62

Special order No

Capt M.B. Highsmith is detailed as field officer of the day an[d] will report at these Hed Qrs at 9 Ock A M tomorrow

By order of Brig Genl [James M.] Hawes
C McClarty A A Genl

[39] William M. Daviess was adjutant in the Twelfth Texas.

* * * * * * * * * * * * *

Office Adjut Genl White River Dist
Lake Buff [*sic*] Dec 20th 1862

The Adjutant of 12th Texas Cavalry will without delay make out and transmit to this office the list required on the above circular of Said Regiment [dated December 17th].

Clinton McClarty
A A Genl

* * * * * * * * * * * * *

Hed Qrs 12th Tex Cavalry
Dec 20th 1862

Special Order NO

Hereafter all letters to be mailed & wished to to be sent thro the adjt office will be sent in each morning by the 1st Serg & immediately Sent up thro He Qrs to Little Rock & no letters will be received through us at every hour of the day

By order of L.J. [Lochlin J.] Farrar
Major comd 12 Tex Wm Daviess

* * * * * * * * * * * * *

Hed Qrs Dist White River
Lake Buff [*sic*] Dec 21st 1862

[Sp]ecial order No

Major Fr [Lochlin J. Farrar] will make the following detail for gard [*sic*] duty viz One commission officer, One Sergant and one corporal 7 men to report at these head Qrs for Brigade Gard [*sic*] at 9 Ock

By order of
Brig Genl [James M.] Hawes
C McClarty A A Genl

* * * * * * * * * * * * *

Hed Qrs Dist W. R
Lake Buff [*sic*] Dec 22/63

Special order NO

Major [Lochlin J.] Farrar will detail one Lieutenant and 1 N.C.O and 9 men for Brig guard to report at the usual hour

By Command Brig Genl [James M.] Hawes
Clinton McClarty A A Gn

* * * * * * * * * * * * *

Head Qrs Lake Buff [*sic*] Dec 22

Special order NO

Commanding officer of the 12th Texas will furnish a detail of 1 NC Officer an[d] Six men mounted an[d] armed to report as as [*sic*] soon a[s] they can get their Breakfast

By order of Brig Genl [James M.] Hawes
Clinton McClarty A A Genl

* * * * * * * * * * * * *

Head Qurs White River Dist
Lake Bluff Dec 22nd 1862

General order No. 23-

Capt R W Graham[40] AQM is relieved from duty with the Regiment and will forthwith assume the duties of Brigade Quarter Master Capt Harwood acting Brigade QM will turn over to Capt [Robert] Graham all funds and the papers pertaining to the Briade [*sic*] Quarter Master Department in his posession

By order of
Brig Genl [James M.] Hawes
Clinton McClarty A A Genl

[40] Graham was a quartermaster in the Twenty-first Texas.

* * * * * * * * * * * * *

Hed Qrs Lake Buff [*sic*] Dec 23rd/62

Special order No

Capt J P Brown[41] is detailed as field officer of the day and will report at these Hed Qrs at 9 Ock A M tomorrow

By order of Brig Genl [James M.] Hawes
C McClarty

* * * * * * * * * * * * *

Hed Qrs Lake Buff [*sic*] Dec 23rd/62

[Spe]cial order [N]o

Commanding officer will make the [fo]llowing detail for gard [*sic*] duty viz One Sergeant two Corporals 9 men to report to the usual hour

By command of
Col G W [George W.] Carter
C McClarty A A G

* * * * * * * * * * * * *

Hed Qrs Lake Buff [*sic*] Dec 23

[Spe]cial order [N]O

Major [Lochlin J.] Farrar will detail 1 NCO [an]d 10 men to Bucher [*sic*] hogs to report immediately after [brea]kfast to morrow morning at the company hed Qrs

By order of Brig Genl [James M.] Hawes
C McClarty A A Genl

* * * * * * * * * * * * *

Head Qrs White River Lake Bluff
Dec 24/1862[42]

Spl Order No.

Commanding Officer 12th Texas Drags will make the following detail for Q.M. One commissioned and ten soldiers to report at these Hd Qrs immediately

By Order of Brig Gen. [James M.] Hawes
Clinton McClarty A.A.G.

[41] Company K, Twelfth Texas.

[42] On December 24, J.C. Morriss of Carter's regiment wrote from Lake Bluff: "It is understood in camp that we are going to leave here tomorrow. To what point we are going it is impossible to say. Some think that we are going to Napoleon, some to Fort Smith, and some to some point on the Arkansas River and some go as far as to say that we are going to Shreveport." J.C. Morriss to Amanda Morriss, December 24, 1862, Weller, ed., *Civil War Letters*.

* * * * * * * * * * * * *

Head Qrs Dist White River
Lake Bluff Dec 24/62

Spl Order No

Commanding officer will make the following detail for fatigue duty viz one wagon and team and four soldiers to report at the steamboat landing to J R. Grover immediately.

By order of Brig. Gen. [James M.] Hawes
Clinton McClarty A.A.G.

* * * * * * * * * * * * *

Hd. Qrs Dist. White River
Lake Bluff Dec 24 1862

Spl order No.

Comdg officer 12th Regt. will make the following detail for fatigue duty viz 1 Non commissioned officer and 12 men to report at the steamboat landing immediately to J.R. Grover

By Command of
Brig Gen [James M.] Hawes
Clinton McClarty A.A.G.

* * * * * * * * * * * * *

Head Qrs Dist White River
Lake Buff [*sic*] Dec 24th 1862

Special Order NO

Comdg officer 12th Texas Cavalry will make the following detail for guard duty viz 1 Lieutenant one Sergt 2 Corporals 9 men to report at the Brig Guard House at 9 Ock tomorrow

By order of
G W [George W.] Carter Col Comd
C McClarty A A G

* * * * * * * * * * * * *

Hed Qrs Lake Buff [*sic*] Dec 24

Special order NO -

Comdg officer will detail 2 men as Special courier to report at 7 Ock tomorrow

* * * * * * * * * * * * *

Head Qrs Lake Buff [*sic*] Dec 25

Spl order NO

Commanding officer of 12th Texas Cavalry will detail 1 com officer & 30 men to report at these Head Qrs to Capton [*sic*] [Robert] Graham Q M

By order of G W [George W.] Carter
C McClarty A A Genl

* * * * * * * * * * * * *

Head Qrs Lake Bluff Dec 25

Special order NO

Commanding officer of the 12th Texas will make the following detail for guard viz
One Sergeant
Two Corporals & 9 men to report at the brig Guard House at 9 Ock
AM tomorrow.

By order of Col G W [George W.] Carter
comdg Clinton McClarty A A Genl

* * * * * * * * * * * * *

Head Qrs Lake Bluff Dec 26

Special order NO

Comdg officer 12th Texas make the following detail for guard duty 1 NC Officer 3 men to report at these Head Qrs immediately

By order of
Col [George W.] Carter
C McClarty A A Genl

* * * * * * * * * * * * *

Head Qrs Dist W River
Lake Bluff Dec 26th 1862

Special Order NO

Commanding officer 12th Regiment will make the following detail for guard duty viz
One Lieutenant
One Sergeant
One Corporal
Nine men to report at the Brig Guard House at 9 Oclock A M tomorrow

By order of G W [George W.] Carter
Col comdg Brigade
Clinton McClarty

* * * * * * * * * * * * *

Head Qrs Lake Bluff Dec 26th 1862

Special order NO

Commanding officer of the 12th Regiment will make the following detail for guard duty

One Sergeant and Six Soldiers to report at the Brig Guard House at 9 Oclock tomorrow

By order of G W [George W.] Carter Col
Comand C McClarty A A G

* * * * * * * * * * * * *

Head Qrs Lake Bluff Dec 26

Special order NO

Commanding officer of the 12th Reg will make the following detail for a tour of five days guard duty dismounted one non commissioned officer and Six Soldiers they will take their Rations and report at these Hed Qrs at 7 oclock A M tomorrow

By order of
Col G W [George W.] Carter
Commdg Brig C McClarty A A Genl

* * * * * * * * * * * * *

Head Qrs Lake Bluff
Dec 26th 1862-

Special order NO

Commding officer 12th Regiment will make the following detail for fatigue duty for too days an[d] will carry rations an[d] axes with them One commissioned officer and eight Soldiers to report at these Hed Qrs at 7 oclock A M tomorrow

Also will detail eight Soldiers for five days fatigue duty and will take rations the [w]hole to be dismounted and report at these Head Qrs at 7 oclock A M tomorrow

By order of Col G W [George W.] Carter
Comdg Reg
Clinton McClarty A A Genl

* * * * * * * * * * * * *

Head Qrs Lake Buf [*sic*]
Dec 26th 1862

Special order NO

Commandg officer of 12th Texas will detail one N[C]O officer an[d] 20 men to report to Cap [Robert] Graham at this Hed Qrs immediatly for fatig[e] duty mounted & unarmed

By order of
Col [George W.] Carter Comdg
C McClarty AAG

* * * * * * * * * * * * *

Head Qrs Lake Buff [*sic*] De 26

Special order NO

Commandg officer of 12th Texas Cav will detail 1 discrete and rel[i]able [man] as courier to go to Little Rock an[d] back

By order of
Col [George W.] Carter comdg
C McClarty A A Genl

* * * * * * * * * * * * *

Head Qrs Dist White River
Lake Bluff Dec 28th 1862

Special order No -

Commanding officer 12th Regiment will make the following detail for immediate guard duty viz Two Soldiers to report to the officer of guard at Brigade guard house immediately

By order of
Col G W [George W.] Carter Comdg
Clinton McClarty A.A.G.

* * * * * * * * * * * * *

Hd Qrs Lake Bluff Ark Dec 28 1862

Sp order No

Com Off 12 Tex will make the follow detail for guard duty viz one corp—six soldiers to report at the Brig G. House at 9 A.M. tomorrow

By order of Col. G.W. [George W.] Carter
Com. C. McClarty A.A.G.

* * * * * * * * * * * * *

Hd Qrs Dec 29 1862 Lake Bluff

Spl Order

Com off 12 Tex will detail 1 N.C.O. & 10 men to report mounted & unarmed to Capt [Robert] Graham immediately at these Hd Qrs

By order of Col. G. W. [George W.] Carter
Com C. McC A A G

* * * * * * * * * * * * *

Hd Qrs Lake Bluff Ark Dec. 29 1862

Sp order

Com Off. 12—Tex will detail for guard duty 1 Lt 2 Corps & nine soldiers to report at Brigade G. House tomorrow at 9 oclk

Also for Patrol duty 1 Com Off & 4 soldiers to report at Brig G. House at 9 o'clk tomorrow

By order of Col G.W. [George W.] Carter
Com Brig C. McC AAG
Sp. Order

Capt A.M. Maddux[43] detailed as field off of day to report at 9 o'clk

By order & Col [George W.] Carter & c

* * * * * * * * * * * * *

Hd Qrs Lake Bluff
30 Dec. 1862

Sp order

Com. Off. 12 Texas will detail 1 N.C.O. & 6 men to report forthwith mounted, unarmed & with knives at Maj. Pyles [William H. Pyle] Hd Qrs to [butcher hogs]

By order Col. [George W.] Carter & c & c

* * * * * * * * * * * * *

Hd Qrs Lake Bluff Dec 30 1862

Sp. Order

Com. Off. 12 Tex will detail for guard duty 1 Sergt 1 corp—& 9 soldiers to report at the Brig. G. House at 9 o'clk to mor[row]

By order of Col. [George W.] Carter
Comdg Brig. C. McC A.A.G.

[43] Company B, Twelfth Texas.

* * * * * * * * * * * * *

Hd Qrs Lake Bluff Dec 30

Sp. Order

Com. Off. 12 Tex. will detail for couriers for two days—Two soldiers to report at Head Qrs at 7 ockl tomorrow

By Order Col [George W.] Carter & c & c

* * * * * * * * * * * * *

Hd Qrs Lake Bl Dec 30

Sp. Order

Com. Off. 12 Tex. will detail private [W.M.] Couch Co E to drive the Brig. Ammunition wagon until further orders & will report at these Head Quarters at once.

By Order of Col. [George W.] Carter
Comdg C. McClarty AAG

* * * * * * * * * * * * *

Hd Qrs Lake Bluff Dec 30

Sp. Order

Com. Off. 12 Reg. will make a detail of 2 men to assist in guarding corn to report to Mr. Seales at the steam mill forthwith

By order of Col [George W.] Carter
Com Brig. C. McClarty A.A.G.

* * * * * * * * * * * * *

Hd Qrs Lake Bluff Dec 31

Sp order

Com. Off 12 Texas will detail 1 NCO & 12 men to report to Capt [Robert] Graham dismounted immediately for fatigue duty

* * * * * * * * * * * * *

Hd Qrs 12 Texas Drag- Dec-31 1862

Spe. Order No -

Com off. Comp B & H must see that their details report more promptly—as they will be held responsible for tardiness of duties or neglect of non com officers

By order L J [Lochlin J.] Farrar
Major 12th Texas

W M Daviess
Adjutant

CHAPTER 3

# ARKANSAS

## January 1-June 17, 1863

The new year opened with confusion for the soldiers as well as the commander in Little Rock. General Holmes initially ordered the Texas cavalry brigade to move in the direction of Hindman's beleaguered Confederates, who were retreating after the defeat at Prairie Grove in northwest Arkansas on December 7. But he changed these orders before the men even broke camp. His indecision stemmed from his fear of a Federal offensive from the southeast where he anticipated an enemy advance up the lower Arkansas River. "Yesterday was a busy time in camps," wrote George Ingram on January 2. "Night before last we received orders to take up the line of march for Hindman's army. Yesterday was spent in making preparations for the trip but last night the order was countermanded."[1]

Holmes's concern turned toward the lower Arkansas River. Grant and Sherman had failed miserably in their attempts to take Vicksburg from the north, and Union authorities had to rethink their strategy. But before another operation could take place, some commanders felt it was important to remove the Confederate defenders at Arkansas Post. The post, situated on the Arkansas River, was about forty miles from the mouth of the Mississippi. The Confederates had constructed Fort Hindman to protect the state capital from an attack upstream, but it could also be used as a base of operations for rebel activities in the region. Union soldiers had built a supply depot at Milliken's Bend, just a few miles above Vicksburg on the Louisiana shore, and the Federals did not want an enemy citadel in their rear.

[1] George W. Ingram to Martha F. Ingram, January 2, 1863, in Ingram, ed., *Civil War Letters*, 46-47.

Over the previous few weeks, Holmes had steadily increased the number of soldiers at the fort. By the beginning of the year, there were almost five thousand men, all under the command of Brigadier General Thomas J. Churchill. Many of these were Texas cavalrymen who had been dismounted earlier in the summer. Colonel Carter had lost two regiments from his brigade of lancers—Franklin C. Wilkes's Twenty-fourth Texas and Clayton C. Gillespie's Twenty-fifth Texas—and these soldiers now manned the trenches in the Arkansas swamps. Holmes also ordered the Fifteenth, Seventeenth, and Eighteenth Texas, men who had fought at Cotton Plant and who were now dismounted, to the post. A mounted company under Samuel J. Richardson[2] had arrived from Marshall in early December to join the Louisiana horsemen under L.M. Nutt and W.B. Denson on picket duty outside the fort.

The plan to attack Arkansas Post was the idea of Major General John A. McClernand, a political general with little to recommend him for his rank except a friendship with Abraham Lincoln. Grant, of course, was not happy to discover that McClernand had gone directly to his friend in the White House, but was also annoyed to find that the Illinois politician wanted to use soldiers from his department. When Grant diverted the units McClernand had personally raised in the Midwest, the politician-turned-general complained to Secretary of War Edwin M. Stanton: "Either through the intention of the General-in-chief or a strange occurrence of accidents, the authority of the President and yourself, as evidenced by your acts, has been set at naught, and I have been deprived of the command that has been committed to me."[3]

McClernand knew he had the support of the president, and he headed for Milliken's Bend to claim his army. He had intentions to lead a combined army and navy operation, with Admiral David D. Porter providing the vessels. It was a hastily planned operation, but by the second week of January the navy was within three miles of the fort unloading thousands of men. A surprised

[2] Certainly the most colorful of the company captains, Samuel Richardson was a native of Virginia who enlisted in Harrison County. He was thirty-five years old in 1860. He raised the "W.P. Lane Rangers" in Marshall, a unit named after a leading citizen. The Rangers joined the Second Texas Cavalry under Colonel John S. Ford, and served on the Texas frontier the first year of the war. After the reorganization in 1862, Richardson took his company to Arkansas where it was among those captured at Arkansas Post in 1863. After his parole he rejoined his company and was sent to guard Federal prisoners at Camp Ford in East Texas. In 1864 the company officially joined Morgan's regiment. Bailey, *Between the Enemy and Texas*, 228-31. Richardson, dressed in leopard skin pants, is seen in a photograph in W.W. Heartsill, *Fourteen Hundred and 91 Days in the Confederate Army* (1876; rpt., Jackson, Tenn.: McCowat-Mercer Press, 1954).

[3] J.A. McClernand to Edwin Stanton, January 3, 1863, *OR* 17, 2:528-30. See also, Edwin C. Bearss, "The Battle of the Post of Arkansas," *Arkansas Historical Quarterly* 18 (Autumn 1959): 237-79; David D. Porter, *The Naval History of the Civil War* (New York: Sherman Publishing Co., 1886); and Robert S. Huffstot, "The Battle of Arkansas Post," a souvenir booklet from the editors of *Civil War Times Illustrated* (Harrisburg, Penn.: Historical Times, Inc., 1969).

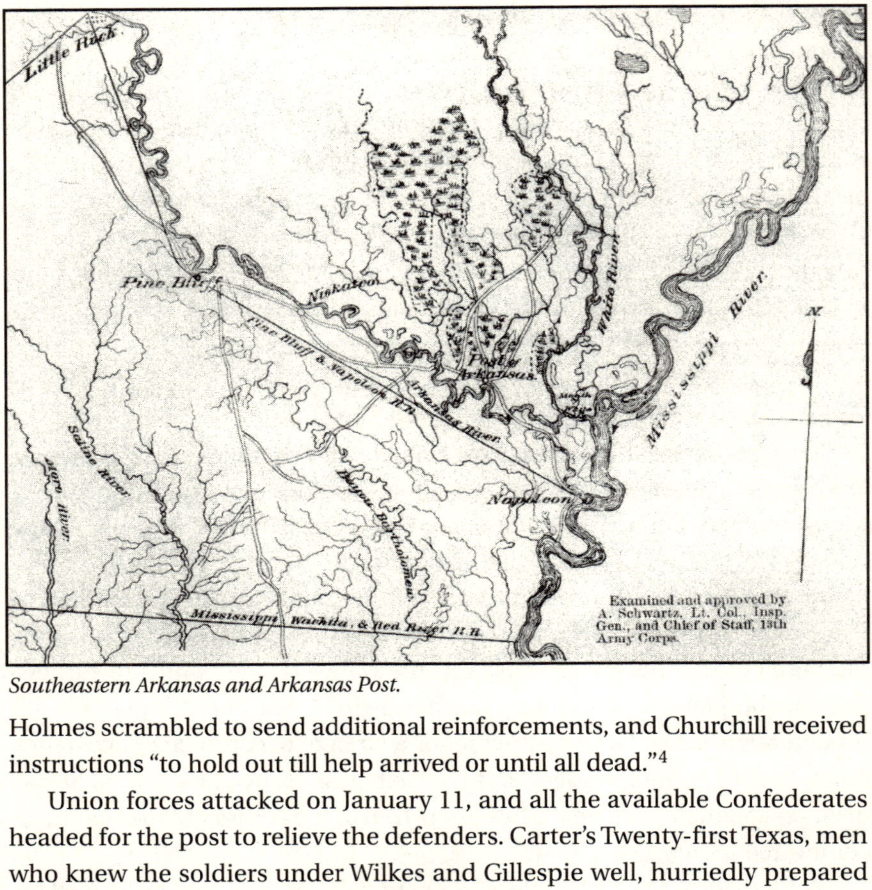


*Southeastern Arkansas and Arkansas Post.*

Holmes scrambled to send additional reinforcements, and Churchill received instructions "to hold out till help arrived or until all dead."[4]

Union forces attacked on January 11, and all the available Confederates headed for the post to relieve the defenders. Carter's Twenty-first Texas, men who knew the soldiers under Wilkes and Gillespie well, hurriedly prepared to ride south, while the Twelfth Texas was soon on the road. An infectious enthusiasm spread through the ranks, as the Texans felt they were on an important mission to save friends and relatives. "A song would be started at the head of the column," noted Captain Martin M. Kenney[5] of the Twenty-first Texas, "generally some old camp meeting hymn which would be taken up all along the line to the rear."[6]

But reinforcements failed to arrive in time. The steady assault coming from Porter's gunboats and the overwhelming number of infantrymen who stormed the fort quickly proved too much for the greatly outnumbered Confederates,

[4] Report of T.J. Churchill, May 6, 1863, *OR* 17, 1:780-82.

[5] Kenney was thirty years old in 1862. He was a native of Illinois and lived in Goliad. He was a lawyer with no real estate and $300 in personal estate. Bailey, *Between the Enemy and Texas,* 220-21.

[6] "Letter from Arkansas," M.M. Kenney to "Sister," January 27, 1863, *Bellville* [Texas] *Countryman*, March 21, 1863; Log of events, January 10, 1863, in Anderson, ed., *Campaigning with Parsons' Brigade*, 89.

and a white flag appeared in the lines late in the afternoon. Everyone blamed someone else, but Churchill later noted, "I was forced to the humiliating necessity of surrendering the balance of the command." When the Texas cavalry reached the Arkansas River on Tuesday, the horsemen learned the fort had surrendered Sunday evening. Henry Orr, who had two brothers captured, declared that everyone he saw censured "Holmes for not getting [John G.] Walker's Division at the Post before Churchill was compelled to surrender" and Texan John Truss added: "If we could have got there we could have held the post in spite of all their efforts. Our forces was too much scattered." Another horseman recalled, "[t]here were no more songs in our camp after these dismal tidings reached us, the sky was overcast with dark and threatening clouds, and the men prowled gloomily about the glaring camp fires."[7]

The next few days were miserable for man and beast. The weather deteriorated as the temperature dropped. The horsemen camped on a nearby plantation where the troopers took shelter in barns and vacant slave cabins. Captain Kenney, with forty men, allowed ten inside at one time but, he noted, "the thirty outside froze faster than the ten inside could thaw and so we passed a miserable night; after dark it turned to a snow and snowed all night and all next day, being near a foot deep." It was worse for the infantry and artillery with General Walker; the soldiers suffered through "mud knee deep." Building fortifications of snow and ice, the infantrymen dubbed their new home "Camp Freeze Out." One man recalled: "There we lay for six or seven days without tents and with but little food." The snow was eight inches deep and "with but one blanket apiece, [we were] shivering around our campfires."[8]

[7] Churchill later reported: "My great hope was to keep them in check until night, and then, if re-enforcements did not reach me, cut my way out." Report of T.J. Churchill. *OR* 17, 1:780-82. Secretary of War James A. Seddon wrote to Jefferson Davis: "The strange circumstances causing the capture of the Arkansas Post demand investigation. I recommend a court of inquiry, and that meanwhile Colonels Garland and Wilkes, and I inclined to think General Churchill likewise, should be relieved from their present commands over the men surrendered." J.A. Seddon to Jefferson Davis, May 9, 1863, ibid., 782. Churchill, unable to live down the embarrassment of surrendering the post, was later replaced by James Deshler. See also for the quotes, Henry Orr to "Father," January 21, 1863, in Anderson, ed., *Campaigning with Parsons' Brigade*, 90, and John W. Truss to Rebecca Truss, January 3, 1863, Ray, ed., "Letters from Parsons' Brigade," 219-20. (Since Truss is telling his wife about the surrender of Arkansas Post, the letter would have to be after January 11, probably January 13 or 23), and Kenney, "Letter from Arkansas." McClernand reported his casualties as 134 killed, 898 wounded and 29 missing for a total of 1,061. Churchill's incomplete return listed the dead as not exceeding 60, with 75 or 80 wounded. Confederate prisoners numbered 4,791. See also, *OR* 17, 1:708, 716-19, 782.

[8] Kenney, "Letter from Arkansas;" Entry for January 13, 1863, J.P. Blessington, *The Campaigns of Walker's Division by a Private Soldier* (New York: Lange, Little & Co., 1875), 70; John Simmons to Nancy Simmons, February 5, 1863, in Jon Harrison, ed., "Civil War Letters of John Simmons," *Chronicles of Smith County, Texas* 14 (Summer 1975): 31.

Although Parsons's troopers did not take part in the battle, Charles Morgan[9] gained three companies for his battalion as a result of the surrender. Those men from Johnson's Spy Company and Richardson's Rifles not captured at the post joined Morgan as Company E (Captains Alf Johnson, Thomas James,[10] and R.B. Carr[11]) and Company I (Captain Samuel Richardson). Also, Company H of the Eighteenth Texas Dismounted Cavalry, not at the fort when the battle began, became Company D in Morgan's battalion under Captains Franklin L. Farrar[12] and later William Ivy Coggins.[13]

After Fort Hindman fell, the troopers remained in southern Arkansas scouting in the region east of Pine Bluff along the lower Arkansas and White rivers. The Twenty-first Texas occupied a plantation belonging to a man named Jordan, and Colonel Carter and his staff lived on the upper floor of a two-story frame mansion. As the weather improved, his soldiers made fairly comfortable quarters in the slave cabins. Henry Orr of the Twelfth Texas wrote from Judge Thomas H. Fletcher's plantation on the Arkansas River in February: "Our command 'infests' this River for many miles." Conditions for his regiment were not comfortable as those of Carter's Twenty-first, and he confided to his sister, "I tell you, I would give a dollar for as many good biscuits as I could devour. I have not seen one in a coon's age."[14]

Nevertheless, there was some good news for the men of the Twelfth Texas when the announcement of Hawes's resignation reached the regiment. Although he had led the troops for less than two months, he had never gained the confidence of the Texans. (He would soon command an

[9] Charles L. Morgan could claim the distinction of being a native Texan. He enlisted in the Eighth Texas Cavalry (Terry's Texas Rangers) when the war began and was elected first lieutenant of Company D when he was twenty-one years old. Although he went to Kentucky, he returned to Texas in December 1861 (citing a disability) and joined the Eighteenth Texas Cavalry, a regiment in which his brother Hiram commanded a company. He was soon elected major. By September 1862 he headed a squadron of about one hundred fifty men operating near Little Rock. After his brother was captured with the regiment at Arkansas Post, Charles continued to lead independent companies. The evolution of his regiment is hard to follow because they seldom fought together. They were not known by the typical letter designations; rather the companies were known by their commander's name. Bailey, *Between the Enemy and Texas*, 44, 227-34.

[10] Thomas James, a native of Tennessee, was forty-four years old in 1860, and gave his occupation as a farmer in Hopkins County with $1,000 in real estate and $2,300 in personal estate. Ibid.

[11] R.B. Carr was a native of Tennessee who had enlisted in Collin County and served in Alf Johnson's Spy Company. He was twenty-eight years old in 1860 and gave his occupation as a farmer with $11,160 in real estate and $6,000 in personal estate. Ibid.

[12] Franklin L. Farrar was thirty-eight years old in 1860. He was a native of South Carolina and had enlisted in Ellis County. A farmer, he claimed no real estate and $9,500 in personal estate (the agricultural census indicated he farmed twenty acres and owned three slaves). He had fought in the Regulator and Moderator War in East Texas. His company had belonged to the Eighteenth Texas Cavalry but was not with the regiment when it was captured at Arkansas Post in January 1863. He died at Austin, Arkansas, from a wound he suffered in 1862 and, according to family tradition, from a lack of food. Ibid., 228-32.

[13] William Ivy Coggins was twenty-six years old in 1860. He was a bricklayer in Ellis County, but it is possible that this occupation was postwar. Ibid.

[14] Henry Orr to "Sister," February 22, 1863, in Anderson, ed., *Campaigning with Parsons' Brigade*, 92-93.

infantry brigade under General Walker.) Since Colonel Parsons was still in Texas, Colonel Carter assumed command of the brigade. This arrangement did not last long, however, as Parsons arrived in the camps and reclaimed his troopers. Holmes, recognizing the dispute over seniority that plagued the brigade, decided to send the Virginian on a special assignment. Carter, with the Nineteenth and Twenty-first regiments and a section of Pratt's battery, would take part in John S. Marmaduke invasion of Missouri in April-May 1863. While these Texans would participate in several battles in Missouri, the men of the Twelfth Texas, remaining in southeastern Arkansas, continued to watch Union movements along the Mississippi River.

As winter turned to spring, the Texans monitored enemy activities between Helena and Milliken's Bend. Before joining Marmaduke, the Tenth Texas battery under Joseph Pratt had made occasional assaults upon passing vessels steaming up and down the Mississippi. Henry Orr observed in February that two gunboats and four transports had landed men in an attempt to capture Pratt as he was "playing along the river." Both Grant and Sherman considered the enemy firing on Union shipping as a serious crime. Sherman even authorized the destruction of houses in the vicinity of the incidents. Pratt, however, evaded capture throughout the war.[15]

By June 1863, General Holmes, now relegated to the command of only Arkansas, had received instruction from General Edmund Kirby Smith, the new commander of the Department of the Trans-Mississippi, to send a force of at least brigade strength to the bayou country around Lake Providence, just below the Arkansas-Louisiana border above Milliken's Bend. As the hot summer months approached, the Texans would leave Arkansas and head for the uninviting swampland of northeast Louisiana.

The following orders cover the activities of the Texans as they operated in southeast Arkansas. They spent their time scouting in the directions of Federal strongholds and watching shipping on the Mississippi River, counting transports and supply vessels. There are no documents preserved in the Order Book regarding the Missouri raid, so the daily activities of men in the Nineteenth and Twenty-first Texas and Pratt's Battery went unrecorded for posterity. When the Parsons's Brigade Association formed following the war, it was primarily through the initiatives of veterans from the Twelfth Texas Cavalry, explaining why more documents were preserved relating to that regiment. The Brigade Association organized at Waxahachie, the site of the muster-in of the Fourth Texas Dragoons (Twelfth Texas) in July 1861.

[15] Henry Orr to "Father and Mother," February 18, 1863, and Henry Orr to "Father," February 13, 1863, ibid., 90-92.

CHAPTER 3

# DOCUMENTS

## Arkansas: January 1-June 17, 1863

Special Orders from Head Quarters- Brigade-

Hed Qrs White River Dist.
Lake Buff [*sic*] Jan 1st 1863

Spe Orders No -

The Commanders of the 19th Texas Cavalry and of the 12th Texas Dragoons are directed to proceed with these commands to Des Arc on the morning of the 3rd Jan at as early an hour as practicably. The extra baggage of Said commands will be left under sufficient [men to] guard them respectfully & shipped by them to Des Arc.

By Order of Brig Gen [James M.] Hawes
Clint McClarty A.A.G.

* * * * * * * * * * * * *

Head Quarters Dis White River
Jan the 1st/63

Spe Order No -

Adjutant Davis [W.M. Daviess] will report at these Head Qrs at 4 ock PM to day to mount Brig Guard.

By Order of Brig
Gen [James M.] Hawes
Clint McClarty A. A. Genl

* * * * * * * * * * * * *

Hd Qrs Jan. 1 1863

Sp. Order

Com. Off. of 12 Reg. Tex. Drag. will detail 1 N.C.O. & 10 men to report immediately to Maj [A.J.] Byrd Hd Qrs mounted tomorrow & with knives to butcher hogs—

By order & c & c

* * * * * * * * * * * * *

Hed Qrs Lake Bluff Jan 1st

Special order NO

Comdg officer of 12th Tex will detail 2 men as Special courier mounted

By order of
Brig Genl [James M.] Hawes
Clinton McClarty A A G

* * * * * * * * * * * * *

Hd Qrs Lake Bluff Jan. 1 1863

Sp. Order

Com. Off 12 Reg. will make the following detail viz one wagon & team & 2 soldiers to report to Capt [Robert] Graham immediately to haul corn from East side White River with 5 days rations.

By com- Brig Gen [James M.] Hawes
C. McC[larty] A.A.G.

* * * * * * * * * * * * *

Hd Qrs Lake Bluff Jan. 1 1863

Sp. Order

Com. Officer 12 Reg will make the following detail to assist in guarding corn viz—2 soldiers to report to the miller at the steam mill forthwith

By com of Brig. Genl. [James M.] Hawes
C. McC[larty] A.A.G.

* * * * * * * * * * * * *

Hd Qrs Lake Bluff Jan, 1 1863

Sp. order

Com Off 12 Regt will make the following detail for guard duty 1 Sergt, nine soldiers—to report at the Brig. G. House at 4 o'clk P.M. today.

Com- of Brig. Genl [James M.] Hawes
C McC[larty] A.A.G

* * * * * * * * * * * * *

Head Qrs Lake Bluff Jan 1 1863

Special order NO

Comdg officer of the 12th Texas Regiment will make detail of 5 men to report at the Brg wagon Master at these Head Qrs forthwith

By order of
Brig Genl [James M.] Hawes
Clinton McClarty

* * * * * * * * * * * * *

Lake Bluff Hd Qrs 12th Texas Jan 2- 1863

Sp. Order

Capt J P Brown, Lieut [W.H.] Getzendaner & Lt. [John W.] Wright are appointed as a "board of survey" to examine into the loss of Property of Q.M. Department—viz the wagon belonging to Co. K 12 Texas—and are ordered immediately to investigate the matter & report theron—

By order of L.J. [Lochlin J.] Farrar Major
Com 12- Texas Dragoons

W.M. Daviess Adjutant

* * * * * * * * * * * * *

Head Qrs Lake Bluff Jan. 2

Sp. Order

Com. Off. 12 Reg. will make the following detail viz one wagon & team: Two soldiers to report to Capt [Robert] Graham at this office at 7 o'cl'k tomorrow

By order & c C McC[larty]

* * * * * * * * * * * * *

Hd Qrs Jan 2

Sp. Order

Com. off. 12 Reg. will make the following detail to guard corn 1 N.C.O. & 3 men to report to these Hd Qrs forthwith—

By order & c C McC[larty]

* * * * * * * * * * * * *

Hd Qrs Jan 2- 1863

Sp. orders

Com. off 12 Tex will detail 1 NCO & 6 men to report [forthwith] at the mill to haul corn

Sp order

Also will detail 15 men to shell corn at the mill forthwith

Sp order

2 men to help them

By order & c

* * * * * * * * * * * * *

Hd Qrs Lake Bluff Jan 2-1863

Sp order

Com. Off. 12 Tex will detail 4 men to drive hogs to report immediately to Maj [A.J.] Byrd's Hd Qrs

By order & c C McC[larty]

* * * * * * * * * * * * *

Hd Qrs Jan 2- 1862[3][16]

Sp. Order

Com. off. 12 Texas will detail 1 N.C.O & 3 men to report to Capt [Robert] Graham A.Q.M. at his quarters in the above mill

By order c
C McC[larty]

* * * * * * * * * * * * *

Hd Qrs Jan 3- 1863

Special order NO

Commanding officer of the 12 Texas Cavalry will make the following detail for fatigue duty. One non commission officer & Twenty men to report to Capt [Robert] Graham at these Hd Qrs at 7 oclock

By order of Brig Genl [James M.] Hawes
Clint McClarty A A Genl

* * * * * * * * * * * * *

Hdd Qrs Jan 3rd 1863

Special Order NO

Commanding officer of the 12 Texas Cavalry will detail 5 men for fatigue duty to report to morrow at 7 oclock A M with knives for Major [A.J.] Byrd

By order of Brig Genl [James M.] Hawes
Clint McClarty A A Genl

[16] J.C. Morriss of Carter's regiment observed on January 2 that his unit was on the move, for "we received the order night before last to be ready to start the next morning on a forced march for Fort Smith, so yesterday morning we struck our tents loaded our waggons and started for Fort Smith, but before the rear of the collumn [*sic*] got out of camp the order was countermanded and we were orderd [*sic*] back into camp—The enemy had fled beyond the Mo. line." J.C. Morriss to Amanda Morriss, January 2, 1863, Weller, ed., *Civil War Letters.*

* * * * * * * * * * * * *

Hed Qrs White River Dist
Lake Bluff Jan 3rd 1863-

Genl order NO 3

The General Commanding the District has the Satisfaction of announcing that on the 29th day of Decm last Lieut Col [DeWitt Clinton] Giddings[17] of the 21st Texas Cavalry with a detachment of twelve (12) men entered the inner line of the enemy pickets—and captured one Lieut 4 Sergents & 21 privates and succeeded in bringing them off without the loss of a man—

The boldness and brilliancy of this expedition whiltes it reflects the highest credit upon the gallant officers and men who executed it and has merited and received the unqualified commendation of the Genl commdg [should] stimulate their fellow Soldiers to an emulation of deeds of like daring and valour

By order of
Brig. Genl [James M.] Hawes
Clinton McClarty A A Genl

* * * * * * * * * * * * *

Hed Qrs Dist White River
Des Arc Jan 4th 1863

Genl orders NO 1

The Regimental Quarter Master an[d] Commissaries of this command and their employes and subordinates are forbidden to have quarters within the town and are expressly ordered to keep their quarters at all times in the incampments of their respective Regiments or commands

II Capt [Joseph P.] Wier[18] commander of the post of Des Arc is charged with the executions of this order

By order of Brig Genl [James M.] Hawes
Clint McClarty A A Gen

[17] In a previous expedition Giddings had not been so lucky when he had been captured. His captors described him as "a tall, fine-looking man, over six feet high," and "a brave officer." But he was "thoroughly devoted to the cause of the Rebellion, believing firmly in its ultimate success." "Fight Near Helena, Arkansas," D.C. Giddings Papers.

[18] Company A, Twelfth Texas.

* * * * * * * * * * * * *

Hed Qrs Dist of White River
Des Arc Jan 4th 1862[3]

Genl orders NO 2

Col. G.W. [George W.] Carter 21st Regiment Texas Cavalry will exercise command over the camp of the Cavalry Brigade issue orders for discipline police and drill and see them executed, give leves [*sic*] of absence an[d] passes for the day and in necessary cases for the night establish guards & patrols to carry out all prisoner[s], orders and regulate regimental camps hospitals and moving off sick to the Post of Des Arc

* * * * * * * * * * * * *

Morning Reports of Regimts [*sic*] leaves of absence for over one day furloughs & c will heare to fore be sent to Hed Qrs of the District All orders not in conflict with this will still be in force Orderly hours at District Hed Qrs will be from 10 to 11 Oclock A M

* * * * * * * * * * * * *

Hd Qrs White River Dist
Bayou Des Arc-
Jan. 5 1862[3]

Sp. Order

Com. off. 12 Tex will detail 1 N.C.O & 10 men to report to Wagon Master Saddler with axes at the old Quarters of gen in town

By order Gen. [James M.] Hawes
C. McC[larty] - A A G

* * * * * * * * * * * * *

Hed Qrs Des Arc Jan 6 1863

Genl orders NO 9

Upon application of the parties and the consent of their respective captons [*sic*] and Regimental commanders Private J F [Joseph F.] Bond of Com A 12th Texas Cavalry is transfered to Co D 19th Texas Cavalry and private Campbell Ince of Co D 19th Regiment of Texas Cavlry is transfered to Co A 12th Regiment of Texas Cavalry They will report respectly according to this transfer

By order of
Brig Genl [James M.] Hawes
Clint McClarty A A Genl

* * * * * * * * * * * * *

Hed Qrs White River Dist
Jan 7th 1862[3]

General order NO 4

Major R H Dyer AQM CSA is announced Chief Quarter Master of this District Capt [Robert] Graham Chief Quarter Master is Relieved and will turn over to Major Dyer all money property & papers belonging to Said Department

By Order of
Brig Genl [James M.] Hawes
Clint McClarty

Duplicate.

* * * * * * * * * * * * *

Brigade Hd. Qrs. Jan 9, 1863

Spl. Order No

The Commanding officer 12th Regt. will detail 10 men for Fatigue duty to repair the Road and report to Lt. White at these Hd Qrs immediately the men will bring axes and spades

By Order of Col G W
[George W.] Carter Com'g, Brigade
P. W. Connell[19] A.A.A.G.

* * * * * * * * * * * * *

Hed Qrs 12th Texas Dragoons
Camp Des Arc Jan 9th 1862[3]

Special Order NO -

I No horse will be allowed on the Parade ground beyond the Horse line

II No horse will be alowed [*sic*] losse [*sic*]

III No one will be alowed [*sic*] to ride in the water but must use buckets for watering horses

IV Every compy com is ordered immediatly to provide sinks for their company

V Each commanding officer of the diferent [*sic*] companys is required to drill in Infantry from the hours of 9 oclock [to] 10 1/2 AM

Upon any violation of the above orders it is made the duty of the officer of the Guard to arrest all such parties for disobedience of this order

W M Daviess
Adjut

By order of
L.J. [Lochlin J.] Farrar
Major Commanding 12th Tex

[19] Connell was quartermaster of the Twenty-first Texas.

* * * * * * * * * * * * *

Hd Qrs Defenses Lower Ark
Pine Bluff Jan 29th 1863[20]

Genl Order No -

In their application for Leaves of Absence Commissioned Officers will state the number of officers present within their Companies—

By order
Major Genl [John G.] Walker[21]
R.P. McClay
Maj & A A Gen

Official
Clinton McClarty

* * * * * * * * * * * * *

Head Qrs 12th Texas Cav

Special Orders No

Roll call will bee as heartofore [*sic*] three times a day Accurate Morning Reports will be prepaired [*sic*] each Morning by 7 Oclck & countersigned by the captons [*sic*] before brought in

By order M B Highsmith Capt Comdg

[20] The cavalry had left the region around Des Arc as soon as it was apparent that Union forces intended to attack Arkansas Post. Since the brigade was on the move in early January, there were no orders issued. By the end of January the headquarters for the Confederate command in the region was Pine Bluff. Henry Orr kept a brief log and the entry for January 10 stated, "news of the fighting at the Arkansas Post; ordered to have two days' rations cooked and to march for the Post by sunset . . . travelled thirty-seven miles. . . . Tuesday, January 13th: Rose three hours before day, started at daylight. . . . Evening: learned the result of the fight at the Post which commenced on Friday evening and continued till four o'clock Sunday evening, when our forces were compelled to surrender to a Federal forced estimated at 50,000." His brothers James and Lafayette were among the Confederates captured. Anderson, ed., *Campaigning with Parsons' Brigade*, 89.

[21] As a major general, Walker commanded all the infantry and cavalry in the vicinity. Walker's Texas Infantry Division, to which Parsons was attached, became one of the best known units in the Trans-Mississippi and Walker became one of the most respected commanders. He was a native of Virginia, had fought in the Mexican War, and was appointed brigadier general in January 1862. He fought at Antietam before his promotion to major general in November 1862. Walker led infantry in the Trans-Mississippi for the remainder of the war. See Richard G. Lowe, *Walker's Texas Division, C.S.A.: Greyhounds of the Trans-Mississippi* (Baton Rouge: Louisiana State University Press, 2004).

* * * * * * * * * * * * *

Head Qrt 12th Texas Cavalry

Special Order No

Capt Thomas Haley[22] Lieut John [W.] Wright[23] & Lt John [W.] Walden[24] are appointed as a Bord [*sic*] to examin into the removal of St_____ Box & report assess damag done

By order of M B Highsmith
Capton [*sic*] comdg 12th Texas

* * * * * * * * * * * * *

[no date]

Wee the bord [*sic*] above appointed agreeably to order that we have examined the Box & find that the place has been used by W J Mercer John [T.] Lott of Co B & W A Heaster [J.A. Hester] of Co H to keep their horses and assess the damage at eight dollars

Thomas Haley
Capt comd Co C
John W Wright-
1st Lt compy F 12 Texas
John W Walden
2nd Lt. Compy H 12th Cav

* * * * * * * * * * * * *

Head Qrs 12th Texas Cavalry
Febr 1st 1862

Special order No

Comdg officer of Co B & H will collect from cash of the above men in their respective camp the sum of $2.66 to be paid now & in case of refusial to pay for doubled this to be placed as Stopage on them

M B Highsmith[25] Capt Comdg.
12th Texas Cavalry

[22] Company C, Twelfth Texas.

[23] Company F, Twelfth Texas.

[24] Company H, Twelfth Texas.

[25] Company D, Twelfth Texas.

* * * * * * * * * * * * *

Transportation to Texas troops on Furloughs & Discharges-

Hd Quarters Lower Arkansas
Pine Bluff Febry 8th 1863

Genl order No. 3

According to the regulations of the War Department Soldiers receiving furloughs on account of ill health and discharges for disability are allowed actual transportation to their homes and in the former case transportation back to their regiment This regulation is beneficial only to such soldiers as are serving in those portions of the confederacy convenient to Railroads and failes to be of any benefit to Texas troops serving in Arkansas—to whose homes their are neither Railroad Steamboats nor Stages as it is supposed that no portion of the soldiers in the service of the country are intended to be excluded from the benefits of this regulation referred to—It is ordered that the Quarter Master of this command will in the case of discharged soldiers, on certificates of disability commute the transportation to their homes at the rate of ten cents per mile and in the case of furloughs granted upon the recommendation of Medical Bord [*sic*] for ill health the soldier so furloughed shall be entitled to his mileage from the place where the return of the Soldier to his Regiment at the expiration of his furlough he shall receive mileage at the same rate

Official
Clint McClarty

By order of Maj Genl [John G.] Walker
W A Smith Capt & A A Genl

* * * * * * * * * * * * *

Hd Qrs Defenses Lower Ark
Pine Bluff Feb. 9/63

Special orders No. 32

To enable the soldiers who escaped from the Ark. Post in the late attack to draw their pay it is hearby ordered that pay rolls to include 31st Dec. 1862 be made out by the commands of the companies to which the men are temporarily assigned; an affidavit being made by each man to[o] as to the duty place of his enlistment, & a period of last payment—The Rolls will be needed—Master & Pay Rolls of a detachment of soldiers refugees from Post of Ark. temporarily attached to ______ Compy ______ Regt___ A certificate of the fact of affidavit being made as prescribed above will be endorsed upon the Rolls signed by the Compy Commanders—Approved by the Regt commanders & Brigade & forwarded to these Hd Qrs for final action

Official
Clinton McClarty AAG
(true copy W.M. Daviess Adjt.)

By order of
Maj Genl [John G.] Walker
R.P. Mcclay Maj & A A G

* * * * * * * * * * * * *

Head Quarters Defenses Lower
Pine Bluff Febry 10/6_

Special Order No. 33-

I In consequence of the number of forged & unauthorized furloughs and discharges in possession of deserters from the army in Ark it is hereby ordered that in future all discharges and furloughs granted Soldiers of this comd will in addition to the Signature of the comp & Regimental commanders—be countersigned by the Brigade Commanders

By order of
Major Genl [John G.] Walker
(Signed) R P McClay Maj A A Genl

Official
Clint McClarty
Extract

* * * * * * * * * * * * *

Hd Quarters Defenses Lower Ark
Pine Bluff Febry 13th 1863

Special Order No 35

All public property pertaining to the command lately stationed at the Post of Arkansas and now accounted for by or in the possession of every officer or soldier of this command will at once be turned over to the proper officer. The Q Master Stores to Maj Stone Division Q Master and the ordnance & ordnance stores to Capt Galt ordnance officer

By command of
Maj Gen Hawes
(Signed) R P Maclay
Maj & AA. Genl

Official
Clint McClarty A A Genl

* * * * * * * * * * * * *

Hd Quarters Dept Lower Ark.
Pine Bluff Febry 17 1863[26]

Special Order No. 41

G.L. Massier having reported for duty is assigned temporarily to these Hd Qrt as Medical Director

By Order of
(Signed) Maj Genl [John G.] Walker
R T Mcclay A A G

* * * * * * * * * * * * *

Hd Quarter Defenses Lower Arkansas
Pine Bluff, Feb. 19th 1863[27]

Circular

Brigade commander will require the Senior Medical Officer of each Brigade to report to these Head Quarters the name rank & date of appointment of each Medical Officer in Brigade

By order of Maj Genl [John G.] Walker
(Signed) R.P. Maclay A A A Genl

* * * * * * * * * * * * *

Hed Quarters Walker Division
Pine Bluff Febry 19th 1863

Genl Order No 3

Those Soldiers over 40 years of age whose term of service will not extend thru month after the first of March 1863 by authority of Special Order No 3 from Hd Quarters Department dated Jan 3rd 1863 will be discharged—but subject to the operation of the conscript

[26] On February 18 Henry Orr wrote of Pratt's battery from Parsons's brigade: "There are one or two gunboats in the cutoff fifteen or twenty miles below here; Pratt with two guns is playing along the [Arkansas] River between them and Napoleon and below on the Mississippi River, fires into a transport occasionally. Report says he sunk one and crippled another which the gunboats towed off. We hear firing down there almost every day. The cannonading was quite brisk on Sunday evening, which was the gunboats shelling the bottom." Henry Orr to "Father and Mother," February 18, 1863, Anderson, ed., *Campaigning with Parsons' Brigade*, 91.

[27] On February 18 Henry Orr wrote: "Colonel Parsons arrived the 12th and started the next day on a lookout of defensive position down the River. When he returns, he will take command of the brigade. . . . Col. Carter has been commanding the brigade for some time, Gen. Hawes having got sick and gone to Hot Springs." Henry Orr to "Father and Mother," ibid.

Law in their respective districts. Such Soldiers will be [torn] to full pay from the date of enlistment to date of discharge and transportation from place of discharge to their home

By command of
(Signed) Maj Genl [John G.] Walker
R P Maclay A A [Genl]

Official
Clint McClarty A A Genl

* * * * * * * * * * * * *

Hd Qrs. Defe[n]ce Low. Ark
Pine Bluff Feb. 19- 1863

(Circular)

Colonel,

Also in case of any desertion or absence without leave from your command, you will immediately notify each of these officers, at the same time furnishing them with a descriptive list & such other information as may lead to the arrest of the soldier.

Capt J.C. Means[28] 28th Texas Cav. [Horace] Randals Brigade counties of Henderson Anderson Cherokee Nachodoches Shelby Sabine Angelina San Augustine Houston Houston & vicinity—address Palestine Texas—1—C.F. Mallet [George] Flournoys Regt [Henry] McCullochs Brigade counties of Lamar Bowie Titus Harrison Upshur Rusk Smith Wood Hopkins Panola & Van Zandt address Marshall Texas—

Capt Jno F. [John N.] Wilson [Overton] Youngs Brigade counties of Freestone Navarro Ellis Kaufman Dallas Hunt Collin Fannin Grayson Tarrant Denton & Wise address Dallas Texas, 1 Lt. S.S. Brooke 10 Tex Inf

Counties of Walker Polk Tyler Jasper Newton Orange Jefferson Liberty Harris Montgomery Grimes Madison & Brazos—Address Houston Texas.

I am Colonel very respy
Yr. obt. Servant
W.A. Smith A A Genl-

Col. Parsons
Comd. Brigade

[28] Company H. See M. Jane Johansson, *Peculiar Honor: A History of the 28th Texas Cavalry, 1862-1865* (Fayetteville: University of Arkansas Press, 1998), 88.

* * * * * * * * * * * * *

Head Quarters Trans Miss Departmt
Little Rock February 20, 1863

Extract
Special Order NO 50,

VII Private A.H. Lamb of Co A Parsons Regiment Texas Cavalry is detailed on extra duty in the ordnance Department and will report without delay to Major T P Rhett [Thomas G. Rhett] Chief of Ordnance QM Depart at Little Rock

By Command of
Lieut Genl [Theophilus H.] Holmes
S S Anderson A A genl

Pvt. Lamb
Thru Gen Walker

* * * * * * * * * * * * *

Mrs. Smith near the post of Ar[k]
Capt. [M.B.] Highsmith commanding 12 Texas
[no date]

Special ord NO

Capt

Have two captains, four Lieutenants, & one hundred privates, mounted, armed, equipped & with two days rations, in readiness to move under Command of Lt Col [DeWitt Clinton] Giddings to this point at 10 oclock AM tomorrow—These men are designed for special service and this order must be promptly executed[29]

Very Respectfully
Your Obt Servt
Geo W [George W.] Carter
Col Comdg Cav Out Post

[29] On February 19 J.C. Morriss wrote: "Col. Carter is going to start in a few days to the other side of the Mississippi for the pupose of establishing a line of couriers between here [near Arkansas Post] and the army on the other side of the river. . . . Col. [William H.] Parsons is now in command of our Brigade." J.C. Morriss to Amanda Morriss, February 19, 1863, Weller, ed., *Civil War Letters.*

* * * * * * * * * * * * *

Hed Qrs Texas Cav Brigade
Silver Lake [Arkansas] Febry 20th 1863

Genl Order

I Commanders of companies are directed at once to the execution of Special Order No 32 from Head Qrs Defenses Lower Arkansas in reference to the payment of Soldiers who escaped from the Post of Arkansas and which is on file in the respective Regimental Adjutants office [See February 9th].

By order of Col W H Parsons
Comdg Clinton McClarty A A Genl

* * * * * * * * * * * * *

Hed Qrs. Texas Cav Brigade
Silver Lake Febry 22th 1863[30]

Genl Order NO

In consequence of the absence of the members [of] companies [on] the examing Bord [*sic*] of Physicians & the exigencies of our Military Position on the Out Post it is found imposable to execute to the letter Genl Order Num 14 dated 27th November 1862 Said order is therefore modified in this. The Surgeons of the respective Regiments and Batt[er]y of this command are hereby authorized and empowered to examine & grant certificates of disability for discharg furloughs & leaves of absence & so much of Genl Order No 14 as make up requirements under this subject is hereby revised as provided. W.H.P.

* * * * * * * * * * * * *

Adjt & Inspector Genl
Richmond- Va-

Extract
Special Orders No -

V The following acting Medical officers, having been rejected by the Army Medical Board will have their names dropped from the Rolls & cease to be officers in C.S. Army

Dr. Wm H.B. Goodwin

By order
Secretary of War

Rec & Delivered-
Feb- 25 1863-

Asst Adjt Genl

[30] Henry Orr stated on February 22 that "our command 'infests' this River [Arkansas] for many miles." Henry Orr to "Sister," February 22, 1863, Orr, *Campaigning with Parsons' Brigade*, 92.

* * * * * * * * * * * * *

Head Qrs. Tex. Cav. Brigade
Silver Lake Feb. 28 1863

Genl order No -

I The Commissary Officers of Regt. Detachment & the Battery of this Brigade are especialy called upon to notice Paragraph II of Genl Order No. 104 from Adjt & Inspection Genl office Richmond forbidding mounted men in camps to ride their horses except on duty—And to enforce due execution of the same, the practice becoming too prevalent in this command of racing horses is in direct violation of the order alluded to & will be attended with result dangerous to the efficiency of the troops whilst on duty This and all other practices in violation of the Paragraph aforesaid will at once be discontinued.

II A post patrol will be detailed each day in charge of a com officer with orders to arrest any soldier riding 2 mile beyond his post unless with pass or on duty.

By order
Col. W.H. Parsons
Comd Brigade
C. McClarty A.A.G.

* * * * * * * * * * * * *

Hd Qrs. Defenses Lower Ark.
Pine Bluff- March 1 1863

Special orders No 47

I On the mutual application of the men approved by their respective commanders, the following transfers are ordered to take effect 1 inst, viz—

Pvt John S. Perry of [James C.S.] Morrow's comp I 12 Texas Cav. to [Edward H.] Vontress's[31] compy Morgans Squadron

Pvt Geo. Meredith of Vontress's Compy—[Charles] Morgans Squadron to Morrows comp I 12 Texas Cavalry &

Pvt. G.H. Long of Morrow's comp I 12th Texas Cavalry to Maltby's Co. G. Allens[32] 20 Tex—Inf ___ X X X X

For
Com off 12- Tex-
____ Col. Parsons-

By order Maj. Genl [John G.] Walker
R.P. Maclay
A A A Genl

[31] Vontress was a native of Kentucky who enlisted from Williamson County. He was thirty-three years old in 1860. A judge in the Seventeenth District and a legislator, he claimed real estate valued at $22,150 and personal estate valued at $2,400. He had raised an independent company after the state senate granted him a three-month leave of absence (he was still in the field two years later). He was struck and killed by lightning after the Red River Campaign in 1864. Bailey, *Between the Enemy and Texas*, 228-32.

[32] Robert T.P. Allen commanded the Seventeenth Texas Infantry in Walker's division, so the regimental number is probably a mistake.

* * * * * * * * * * * * *

Head Qrs- Walkers Division
Pine Bluff March 2 1863

Private J.H. Calloway comp. of Sappers & Miners is at his own request transfered temporarily to Capt [William G.] Veals[33] Co. 12th Regt Tex. Drag & will report to Col. Parsons Com Cavalry Brigade—

By order Maj. Genl [John G.] Walker
W.A. Smith A.A. Genl

* * * * * * * * * * * * *

Hd Qrs 12- Texas
March 2- 1863-

Special Orders NO -

Capt [William G.] Veal Lieut [B.F.] Holder[34] & Lieut Smith[35] are appointed a committee of Investigations to examine into outrages committed—in breaking open School House, & Masonic Hall & to report immediately in writing the result of investigations—

By order of M.B. Highsmith[36]
Capt com- 12th Texas

* * * * * * * * * * * * *

Investigation

The Result of the foregoing committees was implication of John Lauderdale Comp C 12th Tex against whom the following charges here brought by Capt [M.B.] Highsmith Com 12—Texas

"Charges preferred by Capt [M.B.] Highsmith com 12 Texas against John Lauderdale private comp C. 12—Texas

Charge 1st Violation of 54 Art. of War—

Spec, 1st In this that he the said John Lauderdale private in Comp C, 12—Texas did on or about [_____] day of Feb, 1863. break open the doors of Masonic Hall in Silver Lake Ark. Co. Ark—

Spec, 2nd In this that he the said Lauderdale on or about the [_____] day of Feb. 1863 did break open or otherwise unlawfully enter the desk of Masonic Lodge at Silver Lake

Spec, 3rd In this that he the said Lauderdale did on or about the [_____] day of Feb. 1863 injure or destroy the records of said Lodge

[33] Company F, Twelfth Texas.

[34] Company B, Twelfth Texas.

[35] Not positively identified.

[36] Company D, Twelfth Texas.

Charge 2nd Theft

Spec. 1st In this that he the said Lauderdale did on or about the [_____] day of Feb. 1863 carry off the records of said Lodge—

* * * * * * * * * * * * * 

Hd Qrs- Tex. Cav. Brigade
Silver Lake Mch. 5- 1863

Genl order No -

The com officers of Regt are directed to send some reliable & trustworthy non com officer with written authority to arrest & bring to their Reg's all soldiers absent from there respective regts & especially those soldiers East of White River, as complaints have been made to Hd Qrs Trans. Miss. Dept that soldiers of the three Reg of this Brigade are depredating upon citizens of Phillips County

By order Col. W. H. Parsons
Com Brigade

* * * * * * * * * * * * * 

H Qrs. Trans Miss. Dept
Med. Directors Off.
Little Rock Ark
March 6- 1863

Sir,

You will proceed without delay to the Lower Ark & report to Col. Parsons comd 12 Tex. Cav. in the field for Duty with his Regiment.

By order of
Lt Genl T.H. Holmes
John M. Haden
Med. Director

Surg. Thom M. Mathews
Little Rock
Ark

* * * * * * * * * * * * * 

Head Qurs Defenses Lower Ark
Pine Bluff Mch' 7th 1863

General Order NO 6

It has come to the knowledge of the Major General commanding that the officers of at least one Regt of this command have failed to comply with the regulation requiring the articles of War to be read to their commands at Stated times It is therefore hereby ordered that on the first evening parade ensuing after the reception of this order in the company of any Regt Batt Squadron or Detached Company of this command the Article of War will be read to the command by a commissioned officer & that in future they will be read on dress parade to each & every separate Regt Batt Squadron or detached company by a commissioned officer on the last day of each month

Official                                        By order of Major Genl [John G.] Walker
Clint McClarty AA Genl                          Signed R P Maclay A A A Genl

* * * * * * * * * * * * *

Hd Qrs. Tex. Cav. Brigade
March 10 1863

Special order No -

The following details are confirmed from date Jan. 30—Robt. Johns—Co. E. 12 Tex Dragoons—

By order Col W.H Parsons
com Tex

* * * * * * * * * * * * *

Hd Qrs.- Tex. Cav. Brigade
March 10, 1863

Special order N -

Upon the application of the parties with the approval of officers concerned the following transfers are made

| | | |
|---|---|---|
| | Geo. C. Leonard | Co. E. 12 Tex to Co. C. 19 Tex |
| | Peyton Sevier | Co. C. 19 " Cav. to Co. E. 12 Tex Dragoons |

By order Col. W.H Parsons - comd

* * * * * * * * * * * * *

Hd- Quars 12th Texas
March 11th 1863

Special Order No -

Sergt major [Henry A.?] Highsmith will report at once to these Hd Qur for duty

By order of
W M Daviess                                     Capt W G [William G.] Veal
Adjt                                            Comdg 12th Texas

* * * * * * * * * * * * *

Head Quarters Texas Cavalry
Silver Lake March 11th 1863

Special Order

Lieut Davis [W.M. Daviess] of 12th Texas Dragoons is temporarily assigned to duty to these Hd Qur as asst-adjutant Genl of this Brigade

By Order of
W H Parsons Col
Commanding Brig

* * * * * * * * * * * * *

Hd Qrs Tex Cav. Brigade
Silver Lake Mch 13- 1863

Genl orders

All absentees of this comd who have been absent without leave & have come into camps will be arrested & charges preferred against them for a genl C. Martial

W.H. Parsons
Col. Comd. Brigade

* * * * * * * * * * * * *

Hd Qrs 12- Texas Drag
March 14 1863

Special order

E. [Elisha] Terry of Co. B 12 Texas Drag is appointed Chaplain of the Regt & will enter upon his duties at once—

By order
L.J. [Lochlin J.] Farrar
Maj. Com 12 Tex

W M Daviess
Adjt

* * * * * * * * * * * * *

H Qrs T.C.B. Sil. Lake Mch 15 1863

Special order

The genl order recently issued directing the arrests of all who have been absent without leave must apply to all who have come in & who may come in unless the officer of the Co. & Reg. are satisfied upon sufficient evidence that the absentee was unavoidably detained beyond his time by sickness or otherwise.

By order Col. Parsons
Comd Brigade

* * * * * * * * * * * * *

Hd Qrs T. Cav. Brig
Silver Lake Mch 15/63

Special order

In compliance with Genl. Order of num 12 from Division Hd Qrs you will have made out a <u>Roster</u> of all the comd officers of your Regt showing the Name Rank, Regiment, Company & date of commission & appointment & forwarded immediately.

S.G. Ward[37] AAAG

By order
Col. W.H. Parsons com

* * * * * * * * * * * * *

Hd Qrs, Tex, Cav Brigade
Silver Lake Mch 15
1863

Surg. Thomas M. Mathews will report immediately to the comdg officer 12 Tex Cav. for duty

S.G. Ward A.A.A.G.
Chaplain

By order Col. W.H. Parsons
Comdg Brigade

[37] Ward was an adjutant in the Twenty-first Texas.

* * * * * * * * * * * * *

Hd Qr 12th Texas Dragoons
Silver Lake
Mar 20th/63

Received of Lieut Col. A B [A. Bell] Burleson Seven hundred and thirty $730.00 Dollars as a Hospital Fund placed in his hands by the citizens of Texas.

W.H. Parsons
Col. Com Brg

* * * * * * * * * * * * *

Transfer

Hd Qrs Defenses Lower Ark Pine Bluff
March 20- 1863

Col,

Pvt David Wilson of Comp I [Roger Q.] Mills Regt is temporarily attached to your Regt for duty—

By order Maj Genl [John G.] Walker
R.P. Maclay AAAGenl

* * * * * * * * * * * * *

Hd Qurs Defenses Lower Arkansas
Pine Bluff Mch 24th 1863

Circular

The attention of Quarter Master is called to the pay accounts approved for payment of refugees from the Post of Arkansas

The approval extends to giving authority for the payment but does not extend to authorizing any pay or allowance more than is given by law to enlisted men

The monthly pay allowances & all calculations must be verified by the Q Master before making the payment[38]

By order of
Maj. Genl. [John G.] Walker
(Signed) R.P. Maclay
A.A.A.G.

Official
W M Daviess
Adjt

[38] J.C. Morriss of Carter's regiment noted on March 3: "We have drawn pay again but only drew 48$ two months pay." J.C. Morriss to Amanda Morriss, March 3, 1863, Weller, ed., *Civil War Letters.*

* * * * * * * * * * * * *

Hd Qurs Department Lower Ark
Pine Bluff March 25, 1863

General Order NO 5-

In accordance with Par 1 Genl Order 107 dated Richmond Dec 17th 1862 Surg Certificate disability upon which to forward application for leaves of absence for officers or furloughs for soldier will in future be only given when in the opinion of Medical Officer the health of the applicant requires his removal or change of climate which oppinion will be stated in the certificate

| | |
|---|---|
| | By Order of |
| Official | Maj Genl [John G.] Walker |
| W M Daviess | W H Smith |
| Adjt | A A Genl |

* * * * * * * * * * * * *

Hd Qrs. Defenses Lower Ark. Pine Bluff
Mch 26, 1863-[39]

Special Orders No 63-

VIII Upon the mutual application of the parties properly approved this following transfers will take effect from 1 Apr

Corp Jas. A. [J.H.] Willison Comp K [Richard] Waterhouse Regt Co. F 12 Tex Drags & Pvt Jas M. Belacey of Co F, 12 Tex to Comp K, Waterhouse Regt.

By order Maj Genl [John G.] Walker
(Signed) R.P. Maclay A A A G

* * * * * * * * * * * * *

Hd Qurs Texas Cavalry Out Post
Silver Lake, Mch 31 1863

General Order No -

Commanders of Regt. detached and all out Post of the Lower Arkansas of this command are hereby required to enforce the regulations in regard to sentinel duty and every officer & non com officer shall give the necessary instructions to be followed on Post. No

[39] A letter from Henry Orr on March 29 stated his detachment was at Bledsoe's Station, having left Silver Lake. He occasionally went down to the Mississippi River where "we silently lay behind the levee, having received orders not to let ourselves be seen or to fire at them [steamers]." Henry Orr to "Brother Sammie," March 29, 1863, in Anderson, ed., *Campaigning with Parsons' Brigade*, 94. Apparently the Arkansas River was not a concern, as J.C. Morriss noted that the "Ark. River is too low now for the Fed Gun Boats to come up, and unless there is another rise this spring we are safe from an invasion up the Ark. River for this season." J.C. Morriss to Amanda Morriss, March 27, 1863, Weller, ed., *Civil War Letters.*

such conduct as a sentinel playing cards, laying aside his gun, failing to walk his post—to hail or salute in proper manner will be allowed—Any violation of the duty the officer comdg guard will be held to a strict accountability

By order of
W.H. Parsons Col Comdg & c
Wm M. Daviess Adjt

* * * * * * * * * * * * *

Hd. Qurs Texas Cavalry Out Post
Silver Lake April 5th 1863[40]

Special Order No -[41]

Capt R A Terrell will immediately turn over to Capt Kuyser [H.W. Kyser[42]] funds for the payment of Capt [Joseph P.] Wier's Compay A 12th Texas Dragoons upon the estimate made by Capt Wier taking receipts of Capt Kuyser for the same

By order of Col. W.H. Parsons
W.M. Davies Adjt-

* * * * * * * * * * * * *

Hd Qurs Texas Cavalry Out Post
Silver Lake April 10th 1863

Special order

A Regimental Court Martial is hereby appointed to meet at Goodlow's Plantation on the 11th day of April or as soon thereafter as practicable for the trial of M. Dejarnett [William T. DeJarnette] of Co. C 12th Texas Dragoons & work other prisoners as may be brought before

Detail for the Court
Capt. M.B. Highsmith Co. D. 12th Tex. Dragoons
J.C. [James C.S.] Morrow
Lt. B. [Benjamin] Barnes Co C
Lieut J.B. Abbott Judge Advocate

By order of
A.B. [A. Bell] Burleson
Lieut Col. Comdg
Wm M. Davies Adjt.

[40] On April 4, Henry Orr observed: "About ten boats per day on an average pass our station on the River [Bledsoe's Station], mostly transports. . . . There is talk of our whole company coming down here to stay at this stand. We have a good stand on the Mississippi River. I have no doubt but that the Feds are aware of our being down here, but I think they will not attempt to take us so long as we do not disturb them. We could easily shoot into their transports, but are forbid doing so." Henry Orr to "Father," April 4, 1863, ibid., 95. By this time Union commanders had warned that if the Confederates fired on their shipping, they would retaliate by burning homes of civilians in the vicinity of the incident.

[41] This order appears twice with slight variations in each.

[42] Company G, Twelfth Texas.

* * * * * * * * * * * * *

Hd Qrs T.C. Out Post
Silver Lake April 14-

Special Order No -

Capt. F.H. Ayers [Ayres] A.C.S. 12 Texas Dragoons charged with conduct unbecoming an officer & a gentleman is hereby placed in arrest & confined to his quarters

By order Lt. Col. A.B. [A. Bell] Burleson
W.M. Daviess Adjt.

* * * * * * * * * * * * *

Hd. Qurs. Texas Cav Out Post
Silver Lake April 14th 1863

Special Order

Lieut [J.E.] Bonner of Co B is temporarily assigned to the duties of A.C.S. Capt Ayer [F.H. Ayres] A.C.S. being in arrest

By order of
Lieut Col A.B. [A. Bell] Burleson
Wm M. Davies Adjt-

* * * * * * * * * * * * *

Regt. Order

Hd Qrs Tex. Cav. Out Post
April 21 1863

Special Order No -

Lt [J.E.] Bonner[43] Act. A.C.S. will turn over to Lt [W.N.] Kenner[44] commutation of rations for Six men for two days—ordered off on special duty—

[43] Company B, Twelfth Texas.

[44] Company E, Twelfth Texas.

* * * * * * * * * * * * * *

Endorsement on Discharge & Furloughs

Hd Qrs. Defenses Lower Ark
Pine Bluff April 21

The within papers for discharges & furloughs with one exception are informal not being signed by the Asst. Surg of the Reg If the Senr Off. is sick or on Leave the signature of the Asst Surg _____ show him to be in charge of Regt.

E.J. Beall
Resp Refd Chf. Surg. Divis-

* * * * * * * * * * * * * *

Adjutant & Inspector Generals office
Richmond April 23d 1863

General Order No. 49

The following regulation is made and will hereafter be observed in the army relative to the clothing of diseased Soldiers up on the death of any soldier the Surgeon in charge of the Hospital at which it occcurs, will cause an inventory to be made of al his military clothing an[d] will make a fair appraisement of each arcital [article] there of. It will then be turned over to the nearest quartermaster for reissue The original apprasiment shal be fowared to the second auditor to send its value to the personal representative of the deseased Soldier, and a copy their of be furnished to the receving quartermaster who will issue the clothing at the appraised price, and not those set forth in General Ord No 100 last series

By order of
S. [Samuel] Cooper Adj & I- Genl

Official J M Brandon AAG

* * * * * * * * * * * * * *

Hospital Steward

Hd Qrs May 1 1863. Tex Cav. Out Post

Special order No -

Pulaski Terrill [Tyrrell] of Comp. E. is hereby appointed Hospital Steward for 12 Regt Texas Dragoons—

Thos. M. Mathews
Surg 12- Texas Drag-

Approved
W.H. Parsons
Col. Comdg

By order Col W H Parsons
W.M. Daviess
Adjt

* * * * * * * * * * * * *

Hd Qurs Texas Cavalry Out Post
Silver Lake May 3 1863

General Order No 6

I All communications & dispatches intended for these Hd. Qurs. during the absence of Col. Parsons will be directed to Lieut Col. A.B. [A. Bell] Burleson comdg 12th Texas Dragoons

II Couriers and other having business with the comdg officer will find him most of the time at Red Fork Station

By order of
Lieut. Col. A.B. [A. Bell] Burleson
Comdg & c
Wm. M. Daviess Adjt

* * * * * * * * * * * * *

Hd Qurs Tex Cav Out Post
Silver Lake May 8, 63

Genl Order NO - 7

In obedience to orders from Brig Gnl [Daniel M.] Frost[45] Commanding Defenses lower Ark no more furloughs will be issued to the troops of this command for a longer time than three days

By order
Lieut Col. [A. Bell] Burleson
Comdg. 12th Tex Drags
Wm M Daviess Adjt.

* * * * * * * * * * * * *

Head Quarters Tex Cav Out Post
Silver Lake May 8th 1863

Orders No -

I Lieut John Healey [Haley] of Company "C" 12th Texas Dragoons will take command of Eighteen privates and two non-commissioned Officers to be furnished by Capt [Thomas F.] Haley of Co 'C' 12th Texas Dragoons

II He will go in the direction of Helena and remain in the vicinity of Helena a few days using every effort to kill or capture as many of the enemy as possible—

[45] Frost, an 1844 graduate of West Point, had lived in St. Louis before the war and led Missouri soldiers in the Confederate army. He fought with Hindman at Prairie Grove in December 1862 and held various positions within Arkansas in 1863.

III He will keep strict order and not allow any man to leave his command and is especially enjoined not to allow any depredations committed by the men under his command—

IV He will procure forage and rations for his men in the country where he may be, giving receipts for the same and retaining duplicates taking three days rations from Camps

V He will call on the ordnance Srgt for ammunition

VI He will take charge of all the men in the vicinity of Helena belonging to the 12th Texas Dragoons and will bring them to camps on his return

By Order of Lt Col. [A. Bell] Burleson
Wm Daviess Adjt

* * * * * * * * * * * * *

Head Quarters Texas Cav Out Post
Silver Lake May 8- 1863

Special Order No -

Capt [R.A.] Terrell A.Q.M. 12th Texas Dragoons will furnish Lieut. John Haley[46] money to buy forage for Twenty (20) Horses Twenty Days taking his receipt for the same

By order
Lieut Col [A. Bell] Burleson
Comdg 12th Tex Drags
Wm M Daviess Adjt-

* * * * * * * * * * * * *

Head Quars Tex Cav. Out Post
Silver Lake May 8- 1863

Special Order NO -

Lieut [J.E.] Bonner A.A.C.S. will furnish Lieut. [John] Haley[47] with money to buy rations for Twenty men Seventeen days—

By order
A B [A. Bell] Burleson
Lt Col Comdg
W M Daviess Adjt

46 Company C, Twelfth Texas.

47 Company C, Twelfth Texas.

* * * * * * * * * * * * *

Head Quarters Texas Cav Out Post
Silver Lake May 9- 1863

Genl. Order NO -

Owing to the increased value of Horses & c Since the valuation of those belonging to this command; commanders of companies will select three disinterested citizens and have all horses, Equipments and private arms, revalued as soon as practicable and send report to these Head Quarters—

By order of
A B [A. Bell] Burleson
Lt. Col Commanding
Wm M Daviess Adjt.

* * * * * * * * * * * * *

Hd Qrs defenses Lower Ark.
Pine Bluff. May 9 1863.

Gen Orders No - 4

I Surgeon A.S. Small, P.A.C.S. having reported for duty at these Hd Qrs in obedience to Special Orders No 4 Adjt & Insp Genl office Richmond is hereby assigned to duty as Chf. Surgeon of this comand—

By order of Brig Genl [Daniel M.] Frost
(Signed) T.T. Taylor
A.A. Genl

* * * * * * * * * * * * *

Great and good men are seldom found W G. [William G.] Veal[48]

* * * * * * * * * * * * *

Hd Qrs Tex. Cav. Out Post
May 10 1863

Genl order No - 9

(I) 120 Sabres will be distributed to each squadron. Requisitions will be made for additional sabres, if there are soldiers without any after distribution.

(II) Comp. Commanders will see that each private will as soon as practicable sharpen his sabre 18 in. fr. point to hilt & that each sabre shall be habitually worn the Mexican

[48] Company F, Twelfth Texas.

Style attached to the left by the saddle & examined with the other arms at the regular semi weekly inspection for each squadron 11 A.M. Wednesday & Saturday

(III) Comp. Commanders will take memorandum of the men's names to whom sabres are distributed & for each sabre lost or sold by any private the sum $45 wil be charged & deducted upon pay roll.

John Flenn
W W. Evans

By order Col. W.H. Parsons Comdg.
W.M. Daviess Adjt

* * * * * * * * * * * * *

Hd. Qurs. Texas Cavalry Out Post
May 11th 1863

Special Order No -

(I) P.H. [P. Harper] Goodlow[49] of 12th Texas Dragoons is hereby appointed Sword Master of the Regt. & will hold a drill of one hour every other day in each squadron on the line of detachments

(II) The officers & men of each squadron will without exception turn out the whole strength of their companies for sword drill—The officer will render every assistance in giving the men as rapid proficiency as possible

By order of
Col. W.H. Parsons
Wm M. Daviess Adjt-

* * * * * * * * * * * * *

Hd. Qurs. Texas Cavalry Out Post
Silver Lake May 13th 1863

Special Order No -

Comdg Officer of Squadron at Goodlow's will arrest J.H. Calloway of Compy G., Bell's Regt who is now attached to compy F. 12th Texas Dragoons: as a deserter and send him under charge of two men to report to Brig Genl. [Daniel M.] Frost, Pine Bluff, Ark. without delay

By order of
W.H. Parsons Col Comdg
Wm M. Daviess Adjt

[49] Goodlow, from Ellis County, became Parsons's aide-de-camp. He later wrote "Service in the Trans-Mississippi," which appeared in the *Confederate Veteran* 33 (January 1915): 31-32.

* * * * * * * * * * * * *

Hd. Qurs. Texas Comdg Out Post
Silver Lake, May 13/63

Special Order No -

(I) Capt. F. Ayers [F.H. Ayres] A.C.S. will whilst under arrest no longer perform any functions of his office as it is a breach of arrest—

(II) Lieut [Robert C.H.] Good will perform the duties of the office by special order—Lieut [J.E.] Bonner having been relieved

Capt Ayers must know the military impropriety of ~~executing~~ exercising any function whilst in arrest complaint has been made & the above order must be ~~exeuted~~ observed

W.H. Parsons Col. Comdg

* * * * * * * * * * * * *

Hd. Qurs. Lower Defenses
Ark. May 13th 63

Special order

(I) Lieut J.E. Bonner is relieved from duty as A.C.S. of the 12th Texas Dragoons

(II) Lieut [Robert C.H.] Good (Co. K) is ordered to duty as A.C.S. of 12th Texas Dragoons & will report at once to these Hd. Qurs.

W.H. Parsons Col. Comdg

* * * * * * * * * * * * *

Head Quarters Tex Cav Out Post
Silver Lake May 13/63

Special Order No -

Sergt. A.B. Denison of company "I" is hereby detailed on courier line, and will report to Lieut Ben Knight for duty at once—

By order of
Col. W.H. Parsons
Comdg
W.M. Daviess Adjt

* * * * * * * * * * * * *

Head Quarters Texas Cav Out Post
Silver Lake May 13- 1863

Special Order NO -

Capt F.H. Ayers [Ayres] asst commissary of Subsistence will turn over to Lieut. R C H [Robert C.H.] Good all Commissary Stores now in his possession taking Lieut Good's receipt for the same.

By Order of
W H Parsons
Col Comdg
W.M. Daviess Adjt.

* * * * * * * * * * * * *

charges vs. Capt. [F.H.] Ayers

Hd Qrs T.C. Out Post May 13 1863

Special order No

Surg [Thomas M.] Matthews[50] & Capt. Ayers [F.H. Ayres] will proceed immediately to Pine Bluff & report to Genl [Daniel M.] Frost to procure the settlement of charges made vs. Capt. Ayers.

By order Col. W.H. Parsons
W.M. Daviess Adjt

* * * * * * * * * * * * *

Hd Qrs T.C. Out Post May 14 1863

Special order No -

Alonzo [L.] DeSpain of Comp. C. is hereby detailed to take care of team at these Hd Qrs in absence of driver

By order of W.H. Parsons
W.M. Daviess Adjt

[50] Matthews was a surgeon in the Twelfth Texas.

* * * * * * * * * * * * *

Head Quarters Texas Cav Out Post
Silver Lake May 14th 1863

General Order

Comdg Officer comdg at Goodloe's will retain the man Childers under guard as a deserter

By order of
Col. W.H. Parsons Comg
Wm M. Daviess Adjt.

* * * * * * * * * * * * *

Hd. Qurs. Texas Cavalry Out Post
Silver Lake May 14th 1863

Special Order

Comdg Officer at Goodloe's will have the sentence in the case of Pvt. L.L. Hardeman[51] executed forthwith

By order of
Col. W.H. Parsons Comdg & c
Wm M Daviess Adjt

* * * * * * * * * * * * *

Head Quars Tex Cav. Out Post
Silver Lake May 14 1863

Special Order No -

All Piquettes and detachments will be on the look out for a man "Houston" a spy Traveling under pass port given to Capt Moore—Any man showing a passport to pass [as] Capt Moore will be arrested & sent to these Hd Qurs

By order of
W H Parsons
Col Comdg
W M Daviess Adjt

[51] Company E, Twelfth Texas.

* * * * * * * * * * * * *

A & I Genl Office
Richmond Va May 16 1863

Genl Order No 62-

I In accordance with an act entitled an act to better provide for the Sick and Wounded of the Army in hospitals approved May 1st 1863 The following modifications in Genl Order No 95 last series from this office are Published

The Commuted value of rations for sick & disabled soldiers in hospitals (Field & Hospitals) will until further orders be one dolar and Twenty five cents

II Hospital laundresses will be paid Twenty five dolars per month and allowed rations and quarters

| | |
|---|---|
| Official | By Order of |
| J M Brandon | S[amuel] Cooper |
| Astjdt Genl | A & I. Genl |

* * * * * * * * * * * * *

Head Quarters Texas Cav Out Post
Silver Lake May 17th 1863

General Orders No 10-

The Col. Comdg being in apprehension of an attack on some part of our line is pained to notice that men of this command wander far off in the country from their respective quarters therefore with a view of our own safety & utility in case of an attack it is ordered

(I) That there shall be three [blacked out] Reville, Meridian and Retreat

(II) There shall be a daily Dress Parade of each squadron at Retreat

(III) No man or officer not on duty shall be allowed to leave this camp—save to graze horses & then the whole compy shall go at one time under charge of a coms. officer

(IV) No man or officer will be allowed to be absent from roll call or dress parade

The Genl. Comdg this Dept. having specially enjoined on this command great vigilance & the strictest discipline consequent on our isolated position constantly invites, attack & occupying the most important ~~important~~ entrance to the State

The officers of this command will therefore be held strictly accountable for any violation of this order which will be read this evening at Dress Parade

By order of Col. W.H. Parsons Comdg
Wm M. Daviess Adjt-

* * * * * * * * * * * * *

Hd. Qurs. Texas Cavalry Out Post
Silver Lake May 17th 1863

Special order No

Capt [M.B.] Highsmith[52] will send a detail of men & officers or non-coms. off. to Coots Ferry & move the ferry boat from that point to Red Fork at it is deemed unsafe for a boat so low down & on the opposite side of the river

By order of
Col. W.H. Parsons
Comdg & c
Wm M. Daviess Adjt

* * * * * * * * * * * * *

Adjutant & Insp Generals Off
Richmond May 18th 1863

General Order No 60

I The exigencies of the Service requiring a larg number of artillry horses all public horses Sutable for that purpose employed in transportation or other wise with armies in the field will be turned over to the chif Quartermasters of Said armies and will Supply their places when necessary with mules; The chief Quarter Master of Armies are changed with the prompt execution of this Order under the direction of the Commanding General

II At Post or depots other than those immediately belonging to armies in the field, all publick horses Suted for Artillery will Be Collected under the Orders of Maj A G Cole Inspector General of Fiel[d] Transportation for the purpose named above and [torn] Substituted where necessary

By Order of
S [Samuel] Cooper
Adj & Insp Genl

Hd Qurt Comd Nov 18th 1863
Official
Wyatt C. Thomas
AA genl
Official J M Brandon A A Genl

[52] Company D, Twelfth Texas.

* * * * * * * * * * * * *

Morning Reports

Hd. Qurs Tex. Cav. Out Post
Silver Lake May 18th 1863.

General Order No 11

The Captains of Companies of 12th Texas Dragoons will early to morrow morning May 19th 1863 send to these Hd. Qurs. their orderly Sergeant with a full morning Report properly signed—upon the failure of any orderly sergeants to report here the Capt Comdg will be held strictly accountable

By order of
Col W.H. Parsons Comdg
Wm M. Daviess Adjt

* * * * * * * * * * * * *

Hd. Qurs. Texas Cavalry Out Post
Silver Lake May 19th 1863

Special order No -

Capt. F.H. Ayers [Ayres][53] A.C.S. of 12th Texas Dragoons will take immediate steps to feed Capt. [Appleton M.] Maddox's Squadron

By order of
Lieut Col. A.B. [A. Bell] Burleson
Comdg
W.M. Daviess Adjt.

* * * * * * * * * * * * *

Hd. Qurs. Texas Cavalry Out Post
Silver Lake May 20th 1863

Special Order

Capt F.H. Ayers [Ayres] A.C.S. 12th Texas Dragoons is hereby authorized to impress any bacon that he may find providing that the owner has the same for sale is not willing to take the Government price 30 cts per lb by he Capt Ayers paying the money for the same

[By order of] A.B. [A. Bell] Burleson
Lt. Col. Comdg & c

[53] Whatever charges were brought against Ayres (see the May 13 orders) do not seem to have prevented him from returning to duty within days.

* * * * * * * * * * * * *

Hd. Qurs. Texas Cavalry Out Post
Silver Lake, May 20th 1863

Special Order No 49

Comdg Office at Goodlow's will send under a strong guard with non com. officer the prisoners,

Gree & Emerson

They will ride government mules which the guard will bring back

By order of
Lt. Col. A.B. [A. Bell] Burleson comdg
W.M. Daviess Adjt-

* * * * * * * * * * * * *

Hd. Qurs. Texas Cavalry Out Post
Silver Lake, May 21st 1863

Special Order 50

Capt. [Appleton M.] Maddox[54] comdg at "Cut Off" is hereby ordered to stop all soldiers going into Napoleon unless with authority from their Hd. Qurs.

By order of
Lieut. Col. [A. Bell] Burleson comdg
Wm M. Daviess Adjt-

* * * * * * * * * * * * *

Arms of Regiments

Hd Qrs T.C. Out Post
May 21 1863

Genl Order No 12

(I) The first or advanced squadron will at once be armed with Sharp Shooting guns.

(II) The four other Squadrons will be armed with double barrelled guns

(III) The Col comg has made every exertion to procure a sufficiency of good guns for those who are destitute & there are no more to be obtained & as by requiring the 1st Squadron to lay aside their double barrels there is no excuse for any soldier destitute to be without a gun. They are hereby ordered to purchase guns within five days, for the use of which the govt allows full compensation

[54] Company B, Twelfth Texas.

IV. No soldier will be excused hereafter from going into action for the want of guns & every one will be required to keep _____ & keep it in good order—

V All _____ orders will be read on evening Dress Parade in each Squadron.

By order of W.H. Parsons
W.M. Daviess Adjt.

* * * * * * * * * * * * *

Head Quarters Tex Cav. Out Post
Silver Lake May 22- 1863

Special Order No - 51

Commanders of Companies will report at once to these Head Quarters whether there is a Negro by named "Jim" in their commands who ran away from the Steam Boat "Bracelett"

By Order of
W H Parsons
Col Commdg
W.M. Davies Adjt.

* * * * * * * * * * * * *

<u>Capt Terrell & Grover</u>

Head Quarters Texas Cavalry Out Post
Silver Lake May 26th 1863

Special order No - 52-

Capt R.A. Terrell is hereby relieved from duty as A.Q.M. 12 Texas & will turn over all property belonging to Q.M. Department to Capt [J.R.] Grover who will at once enter upon the duties of A.Q.M. 12 Texas

By ordr Col. W.H. Parsons
W.M. Daviess Adjt.

* * * * * * * * * * * * *

Hd Qrs. Tex Cav. Out Post
May 26- 1863-

Special Order No 53

Capt J.R. Grover A.Q.M. 12 Texas will furnish Sergt A.B. Dennison [Arthur B. Denison][55] with a mule if any for courier duty

By order Col. W.H. Parsons
W.M. Daviess Adjt.

* * * * * * * * * * * * *

clothing washed

Hd Qrs. Tex. Cav. Out Post
May 26, 1863

Genl Order No - 13

Comdg officers of Squadrons will allow one man to the mess to go out & get clothes washed for the mess & to be gone only sufficiently long for the purpose

By order Col. W.H. Parsons
W.M. Daviess Adjt

* * * * * * * * * * * * *

Head Quarters Texas Cavalry Out
Post May 26 1863

Special Order No. 54-

Lieut [Benjamin F.] Knight[56] & Sergt [A.B.] Dennison will report immediately at these Head Qrs.

By order Col. W.H. Parsons
W.M. Daviess Adj

[55] Company I, Twelfth Texas.

[56] Company I, Twelfth Texas.

* * * * * * * * * * * * *

Hd. Qrs. Texas Cav. Out Post
Silver Lake May 26- 1863

Special order No <u>55</u>

Lieut B F Knight will take the detached men from Burfords Txs. Cav. Regt. and use them on his line of Couriers

By Order of
W H Parsons
Col Comdg
W M Daviess Adjt,

* * * * * * * * * * * * *

Head quarters Tx Cav. Out Post
Silver Lake May 26- 1863

Special order No - 56

The A.C.S of 12th Texs Dragoons will pay to Lieut B F Knight Command'g Courier line One Hundred ~~and there~~ dollars ~~& fifty cents~~ as commutation of rations for three men one courier one month—

By order of
W H Parsons
Col Commdg
W.M. Daviess Adjt.

* * * * * * * * * * * * *

Head Qrs Cav. Out Post
May 26- 1863

Special Order NO - 57

(I) In re establishing his courier line Lieut B F Knight will call on Capts Commdg sqdron & c for men sufficient to make communication expeditions

(II) Commanding of sqdrons & cos will furnish the details required without further orders—

By order Col Parsons
W M Daviess Adjt,

* * * * * * * * * * * * *

Hd Qrs. Tex. Cav. Out Post
May 31 1863-

Special order No. 58-

Special order No 52 from these Hd Qrs is hereby revoked & Capt R.A. Terrell will continue in the exercise of his duties as A.Q.M. 12 Texas until further orders

By order Col. W.H. Parsons
W M Daviess Adj.

* * * * * * * * * * * * *

Hd. Qurs. Texas Cavalry Out Post
Silver Lake May 31st 1863

Special Order

Capt R.A. Terrell A.Q.M. of 12th Texas Dragoons is directed to go to Pine Bluff on official business

By order of
Col. W.H. Parsons Comdg &
W.M. Daviess Adjt-

* * * * * * * * * * * * *

Hd. Qurs. Texas Cavalry Out Post
Silver Lake, May 31st 1863

Special Order

Capt. W.G. [William G.] Veal[57] of 12th Texas Dragoons is detailed to accompany the A.Q.M. of this comd—to Pine Bluff

By order of
Col. W.H. Parsons Com'dg
W.M. Daviess Adjt-

[57] Company F, Twelfth Texas.

* * * * * * * * * * * * *

Hd, Qurs. Texas Cavalry Out Post
Silver Lake, June 7th 1863[58]

Special Order

(I) Lieut [B.F.] Knight comdg detachment of couriers is hereby releived from duty on courier line by Lieut [H.B.] Smith[59] of Co. A.

(II) Lieut Knight will turn over to Lieut Smith all property that may belong to the courier line and will furnish him with all necessary instructions

(III) Lieut Smith will report to these Hd. Qurs for ___ _____ _____ detail for couriers

By order of
Col. W.H. Parsons Comdg & c
W.M. Daviess Adjt.

* * * * * * * * * * * * *

Hd. Qurs. Texas Cavalry Out Post
Silver Lake June 8th 1863

Special Order No

Capt [R.A.] Terrell A.Q.M. will furnish Lieut [H.B.] Smith compy A Comdg couriers with one quire paper for couriers use

By order of
Col. W.H. Parsons Comdg & c
Wm. M. Daviess Adjt-

* * * * * * * * * * * * *

Head Qurs. Texas Cavalry Out Post
June 9, 1863

Special Order

Captain Ayers A.C.S. will furnish J.A.C. [Joseph A.C.] Scales[60] Serg. in 19th Texa. Cav commutation for 15 men for five days

By order of
Col. W.H. Parsons Comg.
W.M. Daviess Adjt-

[58] The battle at Milliken's Bend was on June 7.

[59] Company A, Twelfth Texas.

[60] Company G, Nineteenth Texas.

* * * * * * * * * * * * *

Hd. Qurs. Texas Cavalry Out Post
June 9th 1863

Special Order

Comdg officer at Goodlow's will detail seven men to supply the place of Burford's men at Clay & Jordan's

They will be relieved to morrow

By order of
Col. W.H. Parsons Comdg
W.M. Davies Adjt

* * * * * * * * * * * * *

Hd Qurs Texas Cavalry Out Post
June 9th 1863

Special Order

Lieut [H.B.] Smith comdg couriers will detail one man each from compys A.C.E.F.G. & K. to supply places at Clay & Jordan's of Burford's men also one man each from compys D & I to report at Bledsoe's for courier

By
Col. W.H. Parsons comd. & c
W.M. Daviess Adjt.

* * * * * * * * * * * * *

Hd. Qurs. Texas Cavalry Out Post
June 9th 1863

Special order

Capt. [R.A.] Terrell A.Q.M. will furnish J.A.C. [Joseph A.C.] Scales[61] Serg. 19th Texas Cavalry with funds to forage 15 horses for five days—also funds for forage

By order of
Col. W.H. Parsons Comd
W.M. Daviess Adjt

[61] Company G, Nineteenth Texas.

* * * * * * * * * * * * *

Hd Qrs. Tex Cav Out Post
Silver Lake June 17th 1863[62]

Special Order NO

Capt. J.R. Grover AQ.M 12th Tex will provide transportation for the 12th Texas Dgns to La

By order of Col. W.H. Parsons.
M. Daviess Adjt.

[62] George Ingram told his wife on June 17 that there was a lot of activity around his camp, as two regiments of infantry and two batteries of artillery had passed through. Although he was unsure where they were going, he added a postscript that read: "Since writing the foregoing we have received orders to march. We leave our present encampment and take up the line of march across White River at 5 o'clock just two hours from this time." George W. Ingram to Martha F. Ingram, June 17, 1863, in Ingram, comp., *Civil War Letters*, 52-53. He was headed for northeast Louisiana.

## CHAPTER 4

# LOUISIANA

## June 18-November 10, 1863

The Union plan to control the vital waterways in the nation's heartland had begun with Grant's capture of Forts Henry on the Tennessee River and Fort Donelson on the Cumberland River in early 1862, and continued through the Shiloh campaign in the spring of that year. By late 1862 he had made little progress down the Mississippi, but the capture of Arkansas Post in January 1863 had sent fear through residents along the western bank. In April, General Kirby Smith told Holmes, who now commanded the District of Arkansas, that Federal General Nathaniel P. Banks had left Baton Rouge with an army, and appeared ready to invade western Louisiana. There were reports of another force under John McClernand at Richmond below Milliken's Bend. "Order General Walker without delay with his division to Camden, with instructions to move to Monroe [Louisiana] should the movements of McClernand render it necessary," instructed Smith. By April 19 Smith added: "Please hasten Walker's movements."[1]

Early in the year Grant had tried many different schemes to take Vicksburg, for it remained the only important river port not under Union control. He even considered diverting the flow of the Mississippi River in an effort to bypass the Confederate stronghold. Since the river constantly changed course and cut new channels at will, engineers thought this a real possibility. At that time Vicksburg sat on the eastern bank of a sharp horseshoe bend in the river. De Soto Point, at the open end of the horseshoe, was the perfect place to dig a canal and thus render Vicksburg worthless, a fortified city on an unused waterway. But efforts in 1862 had failed, and even though Grant

[1] E. Kirby Smith to Theophilus H. Holmes, April 14, 1863, *OR* 15:1,041; Smith to Holmes, April 15, 1863, ibid., 1,042-43; Smith to Holmes, April 19, 1863, ibid., 828.

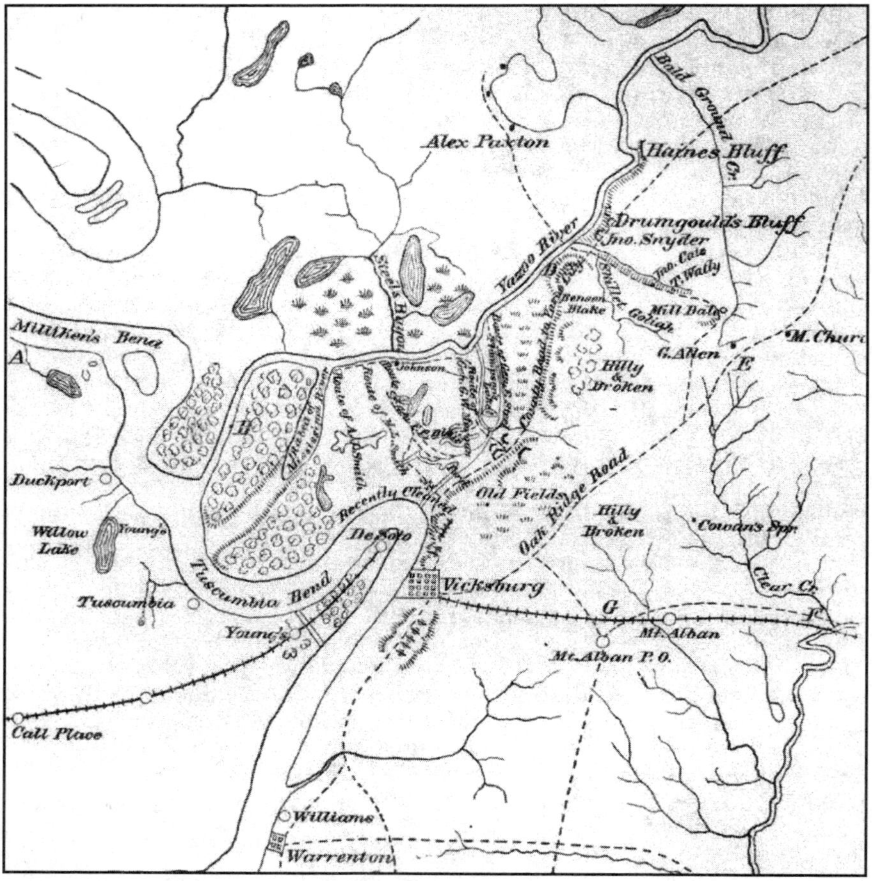

Vicksburg and vicinity.

revived the idea in 1863, the project again failed. The second failure was not because of the low water that had destined the first attempt to miscarry, but insufficient equipment and often too much water, inundating the channel dug by former slaves now employed by the Federal government. With constant harassment from Confederate cavalry, Grant finally abandoned the work in March. He also suspended another venture to cut a canal through the Louisiana bayous and enter the Mississippi below Vicksburg.[2]

[2] Although Grant was embarrassed by his failure to divert the Mississippi River, when he was president in 1876 the river cut across De Soto Point and formed a new channel very near the wartime effort, leaving Vicksburg an inland town on a lake (the former horseshoe bend in the river). It was not until 1903 that the U.S. Army Corps of Engineers diverted the lower end of the Yazoo River into the oxbow lake and opened the river at Vicksburg again. Even though Union efforts were not able to change the course of the river in time to be useful for military operations in 1863, the river later proved it could be done. David F. Bastian, *Grant's Canal: The Union's Attempt to Bypass Vicksburg* (Shippensburg, Penn.: Burd Street Press, 1995), 53-55.

By April 1863 none of Grant's various schemes had worked and he decided to move his army directly through the Louisiana bayous to a point below the port where Porter's fleet, after steaming past the Vicksburg batteries, could ferry the men to the eastern shore. The night of April 16 Porter moved his vessels safely by Confederate gunners on the bluff, and joined Grant's men at Hard Times. Union forces landed on the Mississippi bank on April 30, and Confederates in the Trans-Mississippi began serious preparations to help the Vicksburg defenders. As May opened, Grant launched the final saga of his Vicksburg campaign.

Soon after Kirby Smith took command of the Trans-Mississippi he had devised plans to reinforce Major General Richard Taylor in Louisiana. Holmes had sent Walker's infantry division to help defend Alexandria, but soon realized that Alexandria was not the Federal objective. Union troops under Banks moved outside of Port Hudson while Grant marched on Jackson, the Mississippi state capital. In an attempt to aid the Vicksburg defenders, Confederates struck Milliken's Bend and Young's Point, both Federal supply depots, early in June. Their instructions were to raid plantations run by the Federal government, destroy crops, and capture any African Americans who had been liberated by Union forces.[3]

On June 7, infantry under Henry McCulloch attacked Milliken's Bend in one of the most significant operations that Trans-Mississippi Confederates launched to relieve the situation at Vicksburg. If Milliken's Bend and Young's Point, eleven miles below, could be taken then the Confederates might disrupt operations on the Louisiana shore. The Confederates also wanted to "throw supplies into Vicksburg from the west bank of the river." The camp at Milliken's Bend consisted of white soldiers and a brigade of African American for a total of more than one thousand men. Most of the ex-slaves had only been in the army since late May. The garrison also served as protection for former slaves working on the cotton plantations, thus releasing white troops from that duty and allowing more white soldiers at the front. Milliken's Bend proved to be more controversial as a battle involving black soldiers than as a battle with any military significance. After the garrison surrendered, the question of black prisoners-of-war came to the forefront.[4]

As the fighting along the river opposite Vicksburg increased, Holmes ordered Parsons's brigade to Louisiana. The Twelfth and Nineteenth were in

[3] Report of Richard Taylor, June 11, 1863, *OR* 24, pt. 2, 461-62; Report of J.G. Walker, July 10, 1863, ibid., 466.

[4] E. Kirby Smith to John C. Pemberton, May 30, 1863, ibid., 24, 3:935-36.

southeast Arkansas; the Nineteenth having recently returned from Missouri. Carter's Twenty-first had remained near Helena after the Missouri raid. The troopers were scouting between the lower White River and the St. Francis and Mississippi rivers when orders came to move south. J.C. Morriss reported one typical incident along the Mississippi when he told his wife: "We fired into two boats; the first we fired twelve shots through it, and it was reported that she afterwards sunk, but I doubt the truth of the report. The second one that we fired into was a hospital boat, and we aimed to fire in front of her, but by some mistake the ball hit her and passed through her just at the wheel house."[5]

Parsons's brigade was not in Louisiana when McCulloch attacked Milliken's Bend; the first military engagement for the mounted Texans came a couple of weeks later. In late June, the horsemen captured a Union supply depot and then raided along the levee toward Lake Providence burning houses, cotton, cotton gins, and capturing blacks who worked on Federally-run plantations. The Union commander who followed in the tracks of the Texans claimed they plundered the homes of Union sympathizers. When the horsemen reached the little town of Lake Providence there was a brief fight and although the battle was short, it was fierce. "I don't know whether I was scared or not," wrote one soldier, "but I do know that I was not too *badly* scared to observe him [Parsons] closely. I *know* that *he* was not scared. He watched every movement and gave his orders as deliberately as though he was in no danger . . . and though the balls rattled all around him, he gave his orders and directions as coolly as if he was on drill."[6]

The Texans fought "Indian or Texas fashion," noted one soldier, and it was a "pretty hot fight." Captain J. Em Hawkins, at the head of his men, was seriously wounded. In a charge of the Nineteenth Texas a participant recalled to "have heard the real Texan yell they sent forth and seen those brave deter-

[5] Special Orders, No. 71, June 2, 1863, ibid., 22, pt. 2, 851; J.C. Morriss to Amanda Morriss, July 14, 1863, Weller, ed., *Civil War Letters.*

[6] J.E.T., "Letter from Burford's Regiment, July 18, 1863, *Dallas Herald,* August 5, 1863. J.E.T. was probably James E. Terrell, adjutant of the Nineteenth Texas. See also, Alfred W. Ellet to D.D. Porter, July 3, 1863, U.S. Naval War Records Office, *Official Records of the Union and Confederate Navies in the War of the Rebellion,* 30 vols. (Washington, D.C., 1894-1922), series 1, 25:215-16 (hereinafter cited as *ORN*; unless otherwise indicated all references are to series 1).

mined men, as they dashed off, urging on their jaded horses, you would have cried with me, the 'Lone Star' is in hands of which she may well be proud."[7]

The behaviors of the rebels in the operations from Milliken's Bend to Lake Providence resulted in a sharp exchange between Grant and the Confederate commanders in Louisiana. General Walker admitted that it was "an unfortunate circumstance that any armed negroes were captured," while Grant issued a warning to Richard Taylor after rumors spread that blacks had been murdered in northeast Louisiana. "It may be you propose a different line of policy toward black troops and officers commanding them, to that practiced toward white troops," wrote Grant. "If so, I can assure you that these colored troops are regularly mustered into the service of the United States." To Confederates, any African Americans in Union blue became legitimate targets. Not only had they enlisted to aid the enemy, but an armed black was illegal in the South. Moreover, their presence on the west bank of the Mississippi proved another complication in Confederate designs to aid the Vicksburg defenders.[8]

In reality, the soldiers on the Louisiana side of the river could do little to help the beleaguered port. General Walker lamented on July 3: "If there was the slightest hope that my small command could relieve Vicksburg, the mere probability of its capture or destruction ought not, and should not, as far as I am concerned, weigh a feather against making the attempt, but I consider it absolutely certain, unless the enemy are blind and stupid, that no part of my command would escape capture or destruction if such an attempt should be made."[9]

Although Trans-Mississippi Confederates could not offer much assistance to the Vicksburg defenders from the Louisiana side of the river, Confederates in Arkansas did attack the Federal stronghold at Helena on

[7] Soldat, "Col. Parsons' Cavalry Raid in the valley of the Mississippi, nearly opposite Vicksburg," *Houston Tri-Weekly Telegraph*, August 4, 1863; J.E.T., "Letter from Burford's Regiment;" George W. Ingram to Martha F. Ingram, July 18, 1863, in Ingram, comp., *Civil War Letters*, 55-56; Henry Orr to "Sister," July 2, 1863, in Anderson, ed., *Campaigning with Parsons' Brigade*, 111-13. For a detailed description of the raid, see Anne J. Bailey, "A Texas Cavalry Raid: Reaction to Black Soldiers and Contrabands," in *Black Flag Over Dixie: Racial Atrocities and Reprisals in the Civil War*, edited by Gregory J.W. Irwin (Carbondale: Southern Illinois University Press, 2004), 1-33.

[8] Report of J.G. Walker, July 10, 1863, *OR* 24, 2:466; U.S. Grant to Richard Taylor, June 22, 1863, ibid., 3:425-26; Richard Taylor to U.S. Grant, June 27, 1863, ibid., 443-44; U.S. Grant to Richard Taylor, July 4, 1863, ibid., 469. While there are a number of books that discuss the black troops at Milliken's Bend, one of the most recent is Noah Andre Trudeau, *Like Men of War: Black Troops in the Civil War, 1862-1865* (Boston: Little, Brown & Co., 1998), 46-59. Some classics are Benjamin Quarles, *The Negro in the Civil War* (Boston: Little Brown & Co., 1953); Dudley Taylor Cornish, *The Sable Arm: Black Troops in the Union Army, 1861-1865* (Lawrence: University Press of Kansas, 1956); and James M. McPherson, *The Negro's Civil War* (1965). See also, Brown, *Journey to Pleasant Hill*, 234-36, and Bailey, *Between the Enemy and Texas*, 138-41.

9. J.G. Walker to E. Kirby Smith, July 3, 1863, *OR* 22, pt. 2, 915-16.

July 4. The diversion failed, and to make a bad situation worse, Vicksburg surrendered that same day. J.C. Morriss of Carter's regiment wrote his wife ten days later from near Monticello, "some think that the news of the fall of Vicksburg is true . . . others think that the news of the surrender is false, and that we are going to make another advance into Mo. Gen. Holmes and Gen. Price were repulsed at Helena on the 4th the same day that it is reported that Vicksburg fell. We hear so many different reports that I do not know whether to believe it or no; I will try to disbelieve it untill [*sic*] I find out for certain whether it is true or false." He added, however, "we have reports that Gen. Lee has captured Harrisburg the capitol of Penns. And burned the capitol and is threatening Philadelphia." Trans-Mississippi Confederates soon learned of Lee's defeat in the Battle of Gettysburg. To further dishearten the southern soldiers, they found out that the rumors of Vicksburg's surrender were true.[10]

The fall of Vicksburg ended a Union campaign that had begun in 1862. With the river in enemy hands, the cavalry took on a more important role, scouting in the direction of Lake Providence and Milliken's Bend. The men particularly disliked the humid bayous and boggy deltas of northeastern Louisiana. "We would," wrote Captain George Ingram, "like to get out of this swamp." He blamed the unhealthy climate for a variety of woes, and noted that illness plagued the command. "You never saw a worse looking set in your life. Two thirds of them have not courage enough to fight an army of old women. We have not more than 25 men in our company that I could depend upon in a close place in their present condition. This swamp fever seems to make them indifferent to everything but eating and they have not life enough to cook that," he observed. Although there was a brief Union invasion into northeast Louisiana in August, with Federal soldiers making it as far west as Monroe, nothing else happened to alleviate the boredom. As a result, discipline suffered. Forced to live off the land, local citizens complained to authorities about the men's behavior.[11]

The inactivity that bred the troublesome discontent ended when the Federal troops moved on Little Rock in the autumn of 1863. The state capital surrendered on September 10, and Pine Bluff fell a few weeks later. In early November, the troopers in Louisiana headed back to Arkansas. When

[10] J.C. Morriss to Amanda Morriss, July 14, 1863, Weller, ed., *Civil War Letters.*

[11] George W. Ingram to Martha F. Ingram, July 18, 1863, in Ingram, comp., *Civil War Letters*, 55-56.

it appeared that Union commanders had no intention of advancing further south than Pine Bluff, the Texans returned to the monotonous activity of watching enemy movements and harassing shipping along the Mississippi River.

The following orders cover the months spent in northeast Louisiana. Since this was the most activity the men had seen since the surrender of Arkansas Post in January, the early summer was a particularly exciting time. After Vicksburg fell, however, the Texans returned to routine scouting, and with too much free time on their hands their unruly actions often exasperated local residents. Included with the following documents are two newspaper accounts of the cavalry raid into northeast Louisiana. The first, written by an officer in the Twelfth Texas, appeared in the *Houston Tri-Weekly Telegraph*. The second, written by an officer in the Nineteenth Texas, was published in the *Dallas Herald*.

CHAPTER 4

# DOCUMENTS

## June 18-November 10, 1863

Office of Provost Marshal
Shreveport June 18th 1863[12]

Charles L. Taylor & G.G. [George] Pinson have this day been sworn into the Confederate States Service into Capt. Maddox's [Appleton M. Maddux][13] Compy [B] Col. Parson's Regt. and I have this day granted them a leave of absence for eight days to join their command at the expiration of which time they will report to their command or be considered deserters

D.M. Stovall Capt & Pro. Marsh

The above men have been ordered to duty in Capt. Maddox's Co. [B] 12th Texas Dragoons

By order of Lt. Col. A.B. [A. Bell] Burleson
Comdg & c
Chas. J. Miller Act [Adjt]

[12] Henry Orr told his parents that the Twelfth Texas received orders to march to Louisiana on June 19. On the twenty-first he said he met Carter's regiment, Pratt's battery, and Morgan's squadron, and noted that Burford's regiment would join them at Monticello. Henry Orr to "Pa and Ma," June 19, 1863, in Anderson, ed., *Campaigning with Parsons' Brigade*, 109.

[13] Company B, Twelfth Texas.

* * * * * * * * * * * * *

Hd. Qurs. 12th Texas Dragoons
June 27th 1863[14]

Special Order No -

Capt F.H. Ayers [Ayres] A.C.S. 12th Texas Dragoons is hereby relieved from duty with this command and will turn over to T.J. [Thomas J.] Payne,[15] all names, property and effects belonging to C.S.

By order of
Lieut Col. A.B. [A. Bell] Burleson
Comdg & c
Chas. J. Miller Act Adjt.

* * * * * * * * * * * * *

Hd Qurs 12th Texas Dragoons
June 27th 1863

Special order No -

T.J. [Thomas J.] Payne of Co. C. 12th Texas Dragoons is hereby appointed Commissary of 12th Texas Dragoons with the rank & pay of Capt. in C.S.A. and will receive & receipt Capt Ayers [F.H. Ayres] for all monies, property & effects turned over by him

By order of
Lieut Col. A.B. [A. Bell] Burleson
Comdg & c
Charles J. Miller Actg Adjt

* * * * * * * * * * * * *

Hd Qrs 12th Tex Dragoons
June 27th 1863

Received of Lieut Col. A.B. [A. Bell] Burleson Two Hundred and Sixty Dollars. Hospital fund.[16]

Thos. M. [Thomas M.] Matthews
Surgeon 12th Tex Drag.

[14] On June 28 Henry Orr told his father that "The scout started just after sunrise; all in the highest spirits. I have been told today (as coming from an officer) that a general attack at Lake Providence is at once contemplated; think it will commence in the morning." Henry Orr to "Father," in Anderson, ed., *Campaigning with Parsons' Brigade*, 111. The raid on the Federal supply depot and Lake Providence was one of the major operations for the Texans in northeast Louisiana.

[15] Company C, Twelfth Texas.

[16] One of the main complaints of the troopers after they arrived in northeast Louisiana would be the prevalence of sickness associated with the unhealthy mosquito-infested bayous. The brigade hospital was often filled with men suffering from a variety of maladies.

* * * * * * * * * * * * *

Hd. Qrs. Texas Cav Brigade
Camp Lyon July 2d '63[17]

Special Order No -

The following officers are appointed a board of survey to examine and condemn Government horses:—

Captain W.G. [William G.] Veal[18] of 12th Tex. Drag
Captain [Nicholas T.] Sneed[19] of 19th Tex. Cav.
Lt. I.A. [Isaac A.] Clare[20] of Pratts Battery

By orders of
Col. W.H. Parsons
Comdg. & c
W.M. [William M.] Daviess A.A.A.G.

* * * * * * * * * * * * *

Hd. Qrs. Texas Cav. Brigade
Camp Lyon July 3rd 1863[21]

Special Orders No -

Major Thomas Johns Brigade Q.M. will proceed to sell at public auction to the highest bidders the 22 Hd of Gov. Horses condemned by board of Survey on the 2d inst.

By orders of
Col. W.H. Parsons
Comdg. & c
W.M. Daviess A.A.A.G.
Head Qrs. Texas Cav. Brigade

[17] On July 2 Henry Orr wrote that "the command stormed a Negro fort on last Monday, and after a short fight they surrendered their fort [which] was an Indian mound fifty or sixty feet high with steps or pegs on one side to descend. In it were 150 commanded by four Federal officers. The others, some 800 in number—big, little, old, and young—were around the quarters; all that tried to escape were killed. They were sent to Monroe." Henry Orr to "Sister," July 2, 1863, in Anderson, ed., *Campaigning with Parsons' Brigade*, 111-12.

[18] Company F.

[19] Company I. Sneed was thirty-six years old when he had enlisted in Navarro County in 1862. He was a native of Tennessee who gave his occupation as farmer and his worth as $1,200 in real estate and $4,000 in personal estate. Bailey, *Between the Enemy and Texas*, 224-25.

[20] Clare, who was twenty-six years old when he had enlisted, had been appointed on April 4, 1861, to survey the boundary between Marion and Cass counties. Ibid., 256.

[21] On July 7 Henry Orr wrote: "Our train moved Friday evening to go up to Poplar Bluff, Arkansas, and then down Bayou Bartholomew to the Louisiana line. We thought this would be our permanent train encampment, but on yesterday we received orders to go to Floyd, a village some forty miles distant and rather below Lake Providence. . . . Our command is down about Delhi [Louisiana]. They have taken upwards of 1,300 Negroes in the employment of the Feds on plantations around Lake Providence and a good deal of property and burnt every dwelling, gin, barn, crib, etc. in that country. The boys from the command report fighting at or around Vicksburg every day." Henry Orr to "Father," July 7, 1863, in Anderson, ed., *Campaigning with Parsons' Brigade*, 113.

* * * * * * * * * * * * * * *

Col. Parson's Cavalry Raid in the Valley of the Mississippi, nearly opposite Vicksburg
Floyd, Carroll Parish, La. July 7, 1863[22]

Editor *Telegraph*: As you see by the caption of this, the 12th Texas Dragoons have taken another rapid and sudden flight from Silver Lake in the valley of the Arkansas, where it had so long guarded the key to the South West, unexpected appearing, about sunrise one bright morning, near "DeSoto Mound" in the Valley of the Mississippi, to the infinite surprise and consternation of sundry Federals and numerous "U.S. volunteer soldiers of African descent." But I must not anticipate lest I spoil the narrative, and the whole be misunderstood.

Some time during the day of the 17th of June, Madam Rumor, ever busy, as you know, came bustling into our usually quiet camp, rousing the most listless, and producing a wonderful stir among the "boys" by telling that the "gallant Twelfth" had marching orders! From every lip came, of course, "When?" "Where?" "For what?" But alas for the curious, there was no one found who could answer, though all guessed. Yet, fortunately all remained in blissful ignorance and "*mirabile dictu*" continued so, till, to us, the memorable morning of the 29th, about eight o'clock, when the mighty secret was unfolded and became plain.

It is unnecessary to speak of the long and rapid march we made over hills and through swamps full of bogs and marshes. Such a narration will present nothing new or of interest either to yourself or readers. Suffice it to say, that on the evening of Friday, the 26th, the command, having the day before been joined by the 19th Texas Cavalry, (Col. Burford's Regiment), Lieut. Col. [B.W.] Watson commanding, with one section of Pratt's Battery, halted for the night on the east bank of the Boeuf River, in Morehouse Parish. Here we rested the next day, when we were joined by Col. W.H. Parsons, our brigade commander. He had preceeded us, and, Jackson like, been scouting single-handed and alone, on his own hook, thro' the swamps, keeping his own counsel and learning the whereabouts of the Federals, and finding the best point for striking a telling blow; which self-imposed task, as the sequel proved, he accomplished most successfully, verifying the old addage, "If you wish anything done, send someone else, but if you wish it *well* done, do it yourself."

On Saturday night the two regiments, without his knowledge, marched up in fine order, and surrounding the little deserted negro cabin in which Col. Parsons was quartered, took him completely by surprise, with the cry of "Col Parsons" "Col. Parsons." He came forth promptly at the call, and, though tired and worn, addressed his troops in a stirring, eloquent speech of some half an hour's length, and, as it forcibly struck me, much as a father would talk to his boys, of whom he was proud. He told them of the brave garrison at Vicksburg—of their struggles and their heroism—that he could not take them there, but that he would take them where they would hear the sullen boom of Vicksburg cannon—that they should and would have work to do, and that while they listened to the bass of the big guns, they might make the tenor with their double barrels.

But I cannot give even a synopsis of the address. Suffice it to say, the men quietly returned to their bivouacs, delighted with having heard the cheering words of their

[22] This article appeared in the *Houston Tri-Weekly Telegraph* on August 4, 1863.

favorite and beloved leader, and, full of the heroism which swelled his bosom, eager for the fray, resolved to follow where he would lead, and nobly do or die for Vicksburg.

At this point, leaving our train and the few sick, early on the 28th we took up the line of march, and in the afternoon, reaching Bayou Macon [Maçon], and halting just long enough to feed our horses and take a snack ourselves, we again set out at dark, crossing the Macon on a pontoon bridge hastily constructed. We halted at three o'clock in the morning at the camp of Gen. [John G.] Walker, near Tensas Bayou, and about ten miles distant from the Mississippi River. Here we rested an hour, when the bugle again sounded "to horse," and we set out for the open plantations immediately on the river. Just before emerging from the dense forest and thick underbrush through which we passed, we overtook Gen. [James C.] Tappan's and Col. Randall's [Horace Randal] brigades of infantry, and Col. [Isaac F.] Harrison's regiments of Louisiana cavalry.[23] The latter for the time, was placed under the command of Col. Parsons, together with two batteries—one of Mississippi, the other of Louisiana. The cavalry and artillery then dashed forward. Col. Harrison's cavalry, with the Louisiana battery, taking the right towards Goodrich's Landing; the 12th Dragons and 19th Texas cavalry, with the Mississippi battery, filing to the left to attack the fortified position, "Desoto Mound," while the Infantry followed to render any assistance needed. As we filed out of the timber into the open plantations, this stupendous work of the aborigines burst suddenly upon the sight, and here let me pause awhile in my narrative.

The mound stands about the centre of one of the finest plantations several thousand acres in the heart of the most magnificent valley the world contains. It rises in a constant form to the height of about one hundred feet, and at the top is about forty feet square. On this Mound was newly constructed fort, while around its base were the _____ and tents of the garrison's colony of negroes; or, in Federal parlance, "U.S. citizens of African descent." The fort, as I said, was not yet finished up on this high mound. There were two others near the base of the large one, but they were comparatively insignificant. There was dug a rifle pit some two and a half or three feet deep, with the dirt thrown up on the outside so as to form a light breastwork. In this ditch the garrison stood armed with the Enfield rifle, and provided with heavy timbers to roll down on their assailants should they be rash enough to attempt to scale the precipitous sides. This, however, was useless, since a single glance was sufficient to convince any one that such a thing as climbing that mound, except up the narrow pathway on the south side, was simply impossible. Besides, for a distance of fifteen or twenty feet from the top downward the earth was dug up loosely, so that one attempting to climb, even did he get so far, must there inevitably lose his footing. There were as yet no cannon there, though there was a very formidable looking log of wood about the size of an eight-pounder, with a vicous looking hole, some three inches in diameter, bored in one end of it. This was in position, and looked formidable at a distance. So much for the fortress, and now to return to the troops whom we left about a mile off, emerging from the wood, but who, of course, did not remain there.

Immediately forming the line of battle as they came out, they dashed up to the Mound; the 19th on the left, the 12th on the right, with the artillery in the centre. At a distance of about eight hundred yards they halted, whilst the battery opened on the fort, and a body of sharpshooters was sent to occupy one of the smaller mounds. These had a few rounds with the garrison, when Col. Parsons sent up the flag demanding the uncon-

[23] Harrison's cavalry brigade eventually included his Third Louisiana, the Fourth Louisiana under A.J. McNeill, the Fifth Louisiana under Richard L. Capers, and the Sixth Louisiana under William Harrison.

ditional surrender of the fort; and at that instant this demand was made, by his order the Infantry deployed from the wood and formed line of battle ready to do his bidding. The Federal commander seeing this, and seeing himself completely in our power, surrendered on the terms that the *white officers* should be treated as prisoners of war. For the negro soldiers no reservation was made. These terms Col. P., having consulted with Gen. Tappan, accepted, to prevent the effusion of blood, for, said he, "I would not give one of my brave men for the whole of them." The garrison then marched down, grounded their arms, and were turned over to the Infantry.

There were two companies of negroes, officered each by three white men—a captain and two lieutenants. These negroes were *well drilled*, and used their guns with a precision equal with any troops, and here were killed three of the four men we lost. The fourth was wounded by a negro, and has since died.

The buildings, & c., were fired, the colony [of] negroes, or Yankee peons, were sent to the rear with the Infantry, and the Cavalry and Artillery dashed on up the valley towards Lake Providence, to capture more negroes, burn the cabins and gins, and houses too, where occupied by negroes.

And here let me say, Mr. Editor, lest we too be called house-burners and thieves, that the owners of all these estates, or their authorized representatives, were themselves present, and not only assented to, but applied oftentimes the consuming torches with their own hands, nobly asserting that they preferred a pile of ashes for themselves, rather than the most stately mansion, when used by their enemy as his palace. Noble Louisianians, posterity claims herself to reward your lofty, disinterested patriotism. Yourselves, your wives and your children, are homeless and houseless by your own hands and those of your friends; but a righteous God accepts the sacrifice, and history will right your names upon her brightest page.

But two of the fine mansions from Goodrich's to Providence were left, while not a negro cabin or a gin or outhouse of any kind remains beside. These houses sheltered ladies who had not left their homes. The mansion house was left standing at each place, while all else was burned.

At one of the places, the order was given to burn. The lady, on hearing it, took her rocking chair and, moving out, took her seat upon the levee. Just at this moment Col. P. rode up, and, seeing her there, ordered the troops to spare the house; when, in an instant, there burst from the lips of the men a huzza for Col. Parsons that made the welkin ring again.

But I have wandered from the thread of my story, and, in doing so, have anticipated. As we dashed up the valley at a rapid trot march—the day being one of the hottest I ever felt, and the horses of the 19th Regiment being not yet recovered from their hard Missouri trip—the Louisiana Cavalry, as stated, having gone below and not yet come up, the 12th Dragoons got considerably in advance, and, in passing through a skirt of timber which made out into the plantations, fell into an ambuscade.

The Regiment, save the 5th Squadron, here at once fell into line, and, finding the enemy concealed, were ordered to dismount to fight, and went to work Indian or Texas fashion, driving the enemy about three hundred yards.

Col. Parsons here ordered up the Battery, preceded by the 5th Squadron, which came dashing up; in which charge Capt. J.E.M. Hawkins and 2d Jr Lt. Levi Smith both of Company H, were wounded, the former very dangerously. A few shells from the Battery drove the enemy from his lair, leaving about forty killed, and several wounded.

Col. P., being now informed that the "Feds"—1st Kansas, 16th Wisconsin, and a regiment recently sent up from Vickburg to reinforce Providence—in all 1500 strong were in full retreat, ordered Col Watson, with his (the 19th) Regiment, to charge them. Could you, Mr. Editor, have heard the real Texan yell they sent forth and seen those brave determined men, as they dashed off, urging on their jaded horses, you would have cried with me, the "Lone Star" is in hands of which she may well be proud, and thus the exciting race continued for five miles, and within a mile of the town of Providence. But the Federal horses, being fresh, outran our horses and the jaded condition of both man and beast, with the falling shades of evening, admonished our cool, but brave and gallant leader, twas time to return else Providence, too, would have been left with but a heap of ashes to mark the spot where it stood.

As it was, we learned that, thinking we were coming, the troops there had all embarked on board their boats, and the authorities stood ready to surrender the town. But night was coming shutting in the rays of the most fiery sun I ever felt. The column turned, with twelve long miles to go before its men and horses worn out—we had been out of the saddle but eight hours in sixty and had eaten but one meal a day for some four of five—yet not a murmur was heard.

A gunboat having come up the river, and also a transport mounting two guns on the hurricane deck, began to play upon our column, and the long cavalcade of captured negroes we were bearing along in our leisurely march down the levee, near the river bank. But their shells burst harmlessly above and around us, doing no other damage than killing three negroes.

Mr. Editor, the sight was the grandest I ever witnessed, and, were I to live threescore years and ten more, perhaps will never see again. Words are impotent well nigh, for 'twas almost beyond description. As that long and tortuous line of cavalry slowly wound its way through what was once the garden spot of the great Mississippi Valley, now reduced almost to a wilderness—as it marched leisurely along through the Yankee peon cotton farms, with the lurid shells from the gunboats bursting—but, guided by the hand of Deity, bursting harmlessly around and about us—while in every direction might be seen the thick tall columns of black smoke of the burning houses rising to the blue arch of heaven, and ever and anon the red flame darting forth, casting its sickly light over the land—the sullen boom of the distant signal guns, as they bore the news to Vicksburg, telling its heroic defenders that a blow had been struck *for*, and the besiegers, that a blow had been struck *against* them—the nearer roar of the bursting shells, the heavy dull tramp of the parting horses—the rattle of the sabres of the galiant and dashing 12th, never yet defeated—the hushed hum of the busy voices of the men—the deep sobs of the female and childish portion of the negro captives—the time, twilight—the occasion, the destruction of the Yankee cotton farming experiment—all conspired to render the scene "grand, gloomy and peculiar."

Thus we moved on till, some time after night-fall, we reached the positions of Col. Randall and Gen. Tappan who, with their Infantry falling in our rear, marched with us to the camp of Gen. Walker, which we reached a little after midnight.

Thus ended the first successful, and the most important cavalry raid ever made on the west bank of the Mississippi. We captured 1500 negroes, including negro uniformed soldiers, or as the negro-loving Yankee delights to call the, "U.S. citizens of African descent," about 10 prisoners, and 450 head of horses and mules, ten or twelve tents, a goodly quantity of camp equipage of every kind, and some 200 stand of arms.

Our loss in killed, was two dead on the spot—two have since died of their wounds, and seven wounded, as follows, viz.:

Of 12th Texas Dragoons, Lt. Col. A.B. Burleson, commanding—killed, none. Wounded, Capt. J.E.M. Hawkins, commanding Co. H, left arm at the elbow joint slightly, also in the left side dangerously; Private J.J. Russell, right leg above the knee, severely; Jr. 2nd Lt. J.L. Smith, Co. H, right hand, slight seemingly, has since proved severe; Private Jas. K. Moody, Co. E, head, two scalp wounds slight, right arm and hand severe; J.P. Thomason, Co. K, right hand (accidental) slight.

Of the 19th Texas Cavalry, Lt. Col. W.B. [B.W.] Watson commanding—Killed, A. Poteet. Co. F; R. Veal, Co. D, and John Humble, Co. A. Wounded; Capt. A. Beard, Co. B, right arm slight; Private Jas, Mayouse (Mexican) Co. D, right arm severe; Private J.J. Hagan, leg slight at first, since mortified and dead.

Our wounded were moved in ambulances to Delhi, and thence by rail to Monroe, where, when last heard from, they were doing well. The next morning the Federals, being greatly exasperated, came out as far as the Tensas, within two miles of our camp—Gen. Walker's whole command had left at daybreak, leaving us only two companies of sharp-shooters—threw a few shells about us, but, being afraid to come out into an open space and give us a fair fight, they left; and we, having skirmished with them some two hours, made our exit in the direction of Delhi, in obediance to Gen. Walker's orders to fall back, covering his rear. We are here now, but where we will be ten hours hence no one knows.

SOLDAT[24]

* * * * * * * * * * * * * *

Letter from Burford's Regiment[25]
Camp of Parson's Brigade near Delhi, La.
July 18, 1863

Editor of the *Dallas Herald* I don't know that you have a correspondent in this "lay out." A few items may not be uninteresting.

After the return from the raid into Missouri in the spring, Col. Burford's Regiment lay encamped on Coley's [Crowley's] Ridge (that most beautiful and abundant portion of Arkansas, save perhaps Washington and Benton counties, N.W. corner) recruiting men and horses. Allow me to say par parenthesis; that the 19th Regt was far from receiving justices in the reports of the raid. I cast blame on no one, but such is the fact. It is a fact established beyond controversy that the 19th Regt. bore the brunt of the entire raid, ever in front driving the enemy before them on the upward march, and like Marshal Ney a devoted band hovering around the rear of Napoleon's hosts, on the retreat from Moscow, they were there found at all times between the foe and our retreating columns. Impartial judgment has accorded it the name of a Regiment of most gallant fighting men and officers.

[24] Soldat, sometimes seen as Solidat, was a member of the Twelfth Texas, probably someone on the colonel's staff, who wrote numerous articles for the Houston Paper.

[25] This article appeared in the *Dallas Herald* on August 5, 1863. It was written by James E. Terrell, adjutant of the Nineteenth Texas.

But to resume. About the 10th of June we very suddenly received marching orders for Pine Bluff. Reaching that point we were ordered to report to Col. W.H. Parsons, and joined his command about 80 miles below Pine Bluff on Bayou Bartholomew.

The object of the expedition proved to be to break up a nest of federals who were cultivating cotton and corn in the valley of Bayou Macon [Maçon] and on the Mississippi on the "free labor" system that is to say with hired negroes.

Under the leadership of our deservedly popular and able commander (for he's nothing less) we proceeded so cautiously and securely (which was necessary for the success of the enterprise that we were actually charging upon the enemy's strong hold before they were at all aware of our approach.) This strong hold was a mound about 80 feet in height and perhaps 30 paces in diameter, at the top which was level and was situated in the midst of an extensive open field. Secure trenches had been formed around the entire mound in which the enemy took refuge. The official report has doubtless reached you ere this, I shall therefore not give you the details of the fight; suffice it that after a very sharp engagement in which we lost three men killed and several wounded, Col. Parsons demanded an unconditional surrender which was acceded to. Col. P. having given the 19th the post of honor it was the only Regt. actually, sustained by a Louisiana battery.

Col. P. then led off with his own Regiment in advance in the direction of Lake Providence (this mound being ten miles below Lake P. and 1 1/2 from the river.) The 19th was left in the rear to support the battery. While passing through a dense wood covered with heavy undergrowth the head of the column was suddenly fired upon. Forming his men promptly and coolly, Col. P. threw forward his sharp shooters and a fierce engagement ensued. Col P. was everywhere in the midst of it, and though the balls rattled all around him, he gave his orders and directions as coolly as if he was on drill. Capt. [J. Em] Hawkins was here severely wounded. Col. Parsons Regiment fought like veterans. They not only maintained their ground heroically against a greatly superior force, but constantly and devotedly advanced. The battery and the 19th coming up, the battery opened on them the 19th was ordered to charge and completed the route already begun, driving them square into Lake Providence under cover of their gun boats.

The next morning Col. Parsons was himself again under heavy fire, both of artillery and small arms. Our pickets supported by three companies of sharp shooters, engaged a force of the enemy across Tensas Bayou for near two hours. Col. P. was on the ground directing every movement in person. We lost several men killed and wounded.

I was by the side of Col. Parsons throughout these several engagements. I don't know whether I was scared or not, but I do know that I was not too *badly* scared to observe him closely. I *know* that *he* was not scared. He watched every moment and gave his orders as deliberately as though he was in no danger. The raid was a complete success. It resulted in thorough breaking up of the nest of Yankees, the capture of some fifteen hundred negroes, four hundred head of mules and horses, two hundred stand of arms, & c, & c.

The condition in which we found their crops proves the folly of their system. Though one of the most fertile and productive regions of the South, and having at their command all the necessaries and some of the luxuries of life, their crops were outgrown and chocked [choked] by weeds and grass. They looked yellow and unhealthy, and very small portions, if any, would have come to any sort of maturity, and this too when they (the negroes) had task masters over them, though nominally free.

It is not for me to particularize our officers. I candidly believe that every one of them was really "eager for the fray." The 19th was under command of that man of tired courage and coolness, Lt. Col. B.W. Watson. We had left Col. Burford in Pine Bluff, to the very great regret of his Regt. for every man in it loves and esteems him as no other col. ever was esteemed.

[Signed] J.E.T.

You will find below a list of killed and wounded of the 19 Reg't. Texas Cavalry in the charge upon the "Nigger Mound" early in the morning of the 29th June last and the charge upon the town of Lake Providence in the afternoon of the same day

Killed—John Humble Co, A, shot in the neck; Dickson Veal, Co. D, shot in the head; Ananias Patull, Co. F. shot in the abdomen and died the night of 29th

Wounded—John Heger Co I, shot in the calf of leg died three days after from mortification; James Mayors Co. D, shot in the arm; Capt Allen Beard Co. B, shot in the arm.

Capt. Beard and James Mayors are both doing well.

Respectfully,
W. Bond Dasheill
Surgeon 19th Reg't. Texas Cavalry

* * * * * * * * * * * * *

Hd Qrs. forces in front
July 20th 1863[26]

Special Order No

Maj. Thomas Johns Brigade A.Q.M. will proceed at once to Shreveport at once to get pay funds for the troops of this Brigade—[27]

By order of
W.H. Parsons
Col Comdg
W.M. Daviess A A A Gnl

[26] Henry Orr reported on July 20 that the command was still in the vicinity of Delhi. Henry Orr to "Sister," July 20, 1863, ibid., 114-15. George Ingram also wrote his wife from Delhi saying: "We left Arkansas Post one month ago to day. We came down Bayou Bartholemew opposite to Lake Providence and then moved in the direction of that place. When we arrived within fifteen miles of that town we found Gen. Walkers Division. This was on the 29th of June. We had marched all the day and night previous." After describing the attack on the fort he added: "Our Cavalry artillery moved off towards Lake Providence burning all the Negro Quarters and capturing all the Negros we could find." There was some skirmishing with Union soldiers before the Texans withdrew and Ingram concluded by saying: "We would like to get out of this Swamp." George W. Ingram to Martha F. Ingram, July 18, 1863, in Ingram, comp., *Civil War Letters*, 55-56.

[27] Because cavalrymen were often away on scouts or serving as pickets along the rivers and bayous, pay could be very irregular and a source of frequent discontent.

* * * * * * * * * * * * *

Hd Qrs Tex Cav Brig
July 21st 1863

Special order No - [12th & 19th]

For the convenience of the command and to avoid inconvenience at these Hd Qrs all persons wishing to send letters off will bring them up early on Mondays Wednesdays and Fridays

By Order Col W H Parsons
Comdg Brig
W M Daviess Adjt

* * * * * * * * * * * * *

Hd. Qrs.Tex Cav Brig
Camp Taylor July 21st 1863

Special Order No -

Owing to complaints being made of cavalry letting down the fences of Plantations adjoining this camp & letting out of beef cattle it is ordered that no horses of this command will in any case be turned in the said adjoining field[28]

By order Col W H Parsons
Comg Brig
W M Daviess Adjt.

* * * * * * * * * * * * *

Hd Qrs Tex Cav Brig
Camp Taylor July 21st 1863

Special order No -

J.R. [J. Fred] Cox acting Brig commissary will issue out days Rations of Bacon for Sixty men.

By orders
Col W. H Parsons Comg Brig
W M Daviess Ajt

[28] Obviously civilians were not happy when cavalry camped in the vicinity of their farms and plantations, as the troopers tended to use facilities at will forcing the authorities to issue orders prohibiting this practice. At this time, most of the brigade was near Delhi and camped in Carroll Parish near the Mississippi River.

* * * * * * * * * * * * *

Hd. Qurs. 12th Texas Dragoons
July 22nd 1863.

Special Order No -

Capt. J.R. Grover A.Q.M. 12th Texas Dragoons is hereby relieved from duty with the command and will turn over to Capt. [M.B.] Highsmith all monies, property and effects belonging to C.S

By order of
Lieut Col. A.B. [A. Bell] Burleson
Comdg 12th Texas
Char. J. Miller Actg Adjt

* * * * * * * * * * * * *

Hd. Qurs. 12th Texas Dragoons
July 22nd 1863

Special Order No

Capt M.B. Highsmith of Co. D. 12th Texas Dragoons is hereby appointed A.Q.M. of 12th Texas Dragoons and will receive & receipt Capt. [J.R.] Grover for all monies, property and effects turned over by him

By order of
Lieut Col. A.B. [A. Bell] Burleson
Comdg & c
Chas. J. Miller Actg Adjt-

* * * * * * * * * * * * *

Hd Qrs. Tex Cav Brigd
July 27th 1863

Special Order No -

(I) Comdg. Off 12th Texas will detail 1 Lt. & Ten (10) men to report the morning for Picket duty immediately

By order of Col W.H. Parsons
W.M. Daviess Adjt.

(II) Also will detail 1 Off of the Day & Six men to report at 9 oclock for Brig Guard

By order of Col W.H. Parsons
W.M. Daviess
Adjt

* * * * * * * * * * * * *

Hd Qr Tex Cav Brig
Waco May 15th 1863 July 27th 1863

To the commanding Off Parsons Regt

Sir-

Enclosed please find $260.00 for the use of the Hospital of your Regt from the ladies of McClennan [County].[29]

* * * * * * * * * * * * *

Head Quarters Texas Cav Brig
Camp Taylor July 27th/63

Special orders No -

Commanding Off 19th Tex will detail 1 Lt. Off. of the Guard. 1 Non com. Off. 4 Privates—to report at 9 oclk for Brig Guard.

By orders of Col.
W.H. Parsons
Comdg
W.M. Daviess Adjt.

* * * * * * * * * * * * *

Hd. Qrs. Tex. Cav. Brig.
Camp Taylor July 27th 63

Special Order No - [19th Texas]

Comdg officer 19th Texas will until change of orders detail each day to report at 9 o'clk A.M. for Brig Guard 7 Non com off & 5 Privates & will alternate each day with an off of the day detailing tomorrow an offr of the Guard

By order Col W H Parsons Comg Brig
W M Daviess Adjt

[29] While several of the companies in the brigade came from McLennan County, it was also where Colonel Parsons had been living at the outbreak of the war.

Special Order No. - [12th Texas]

Comdg offr 12th Tex will untill change of orders detail each day to report at 9 o'clk A.M. for Brig Guard 7 non com off 5 Privates & will alternate each day with an off. of the day & offr. of the Guard detailing tomorrow an off. of the day.

By order Col W H Parsons Comg Brig
W.M. Daviess Adjt-

* * * * * * * * * * * * *

Hd Qrs. Tex. Cav. Brig.
Camp Taylor - July 28th 1863

Special Order No. - [12th Texas]

Comdg Off. 12th Texas will detail 1 Off. of the Guard 1 Non Com. Off & 6 Privates at 9 o'clk for Brig. Guard.

By order Col. W.H. Parsons Comdg Br.
W.M. Daviess Adjt.

Special Order No. - [19th Texas]

Comdg Off. 19th Tex. will detail 1 N.C.O. & 5 Privates 1 Off. of the Day—at 9 o'clk for Br. Guard.

By order Col. W.H. Parsons Comdg Br.
W.M. Daviess Adjt.

* * * * * * * * * * * * *

Hd Qrs Tx. Cav. Br
July 28th 1863

Comg. - Off 12 & 19 Texas,

I am instructed by Col. Parsons to notify you that a volunteer scout of thirty men will start tomorrow morning, to scout on Bay[ou] Tensas & Miss- [River]

I am Respy
W.M. Daviess Adjt

* * * * * * * * * * * * *

Head Quarters 12 Tex Dragoons
Camp Taylor July 29 1863

Special order No -

Capt W.G. [William G.] Veal[30] is hereby authorized to arrest and place in hands of Enrolling Officer or Provost Marshall Miles J. Skinner of Co D 12 Tex Dragoons who is absent without leave or any other member of the 12 Tex Drags who are absent without leave

By Order
Lieut Col A.B. [A. Bell] Burleson
Comdg 12 Tex Dragons
C.J. Miller Act Sergt Maj

* * * * * * * * * * * * *

Hd Qrs Tex Cav Brig
Camp Taylor July 29th/63

Special Order No -

Comg Offs of 12th & 19th Texas will report to these Hd Qrs all articles needed in the Ord Dept.

By orders Col W.H. Parsons
W.M. Daviess Adjt.
W.J. Mercer Act Ord Off

* * * * * * * * * * * * *

Hd Qrs Tex Cav. Brig
Camp Taylor July 30th 1863

Special Order No -

Mjr [Richard L.] Capers[31] Capt McNeil [A.J. McNeill][32] or any officer comd company on Bayou Mason [Maçon] will furnish Lt. [William A.] Nichols[33] or Lt Terrill [James E. Terrell][34] each commanding scouting companys with guides familiar with the county in which they will respectively scout

By order Col W H Parsons Comg Brg.
W M Daviess Adjt

[30] Company F, Twelfth Texas.

[31] Capers commanded the Thirteenth Battalion Louisiana cavalry (Partisan Rangers), also known as the Fifth Louisiana, that was part of Isaac F. Harrison's cavalry command.

[32] McNeill commanded the Fourth Louisiana in Isaac F. Harrison's cavalry command.

[33] Company D, Twelfth Texas.

[34] This could be James E. Terrell, who served as adjutant of the Nineteenth Texas.

* * * * * * * * * * * * *

Hd Qrs Tex Cav Brig
Camp Taylor July 30th 1863

Special Order No -

Lt. [William A.][35] Nichols will repair to Floyd & obtain guides from Capt. McNeil or Johnson & move due East & scout as near enemies lines as practicable beyond Bayou Tensas. He will move south make a circuit so as to return by Delhi He will direct Capt McNeil or Johnson & Mjr [Richard L.] Capers to inform the Pickets and out Post of the presence of a Confederate Scout beyond their lines He will discover enemies number position & if possible movements.[36]

By order Col W H Parsons Comg Brig
W M Daviess Ajt.

* * * * * * * * * * * * *

Hd Qrs Tex Cav Brig
Camp Taylor July 30th 1863

Special Order No

Lt. Terrill [James E. Terrell] will proceed with his scout to Floyd—obtain guides of Capt McNeil or Johnson & scout as near enemies lines as practicable beyond Bayou Tensas for purposes of discovering enemies position numbers & possible movements— He will scout from a line due East of Floyd—North to the state [line] He will direct Capt McNeil or Johnson to inform their pickets & scouts above of the presence of a Confederate scout beyond their lines.

By order
Col. W H Parsons Comg Brig.
W.M. Daviess Ajt.

[35] Company D, Twelfth Texas.

[36] Federal forces continued to hold a number of positions along the Mississippi River, many of which were garrisoned by African American soldiers. The Federal government had also confiscated plantation lands along the west side of the river where the cotton was cultivated by former slaves before being sent to New England mills. The land, fertile from the overflow of the Mississippi, had attracted many planters in the antebellum years. The abundance of bayous allowed steamboats easy access to the cotton. In Madison Parish, by 1859, there had been nine slaves for every white person. Federal authorities had forbidden local residents to flee, although many left after Sherman arrived at Milliken's Bend in late 1862. For an excellent account of the people living in Madison and Carroll parishes, see John Q. Anderson, ed., *Brokenburn: The Journal of Kate Stone, 1861-1868* (1955; rpt., Baton Rouge: Louisiana State University Press, 1995). Brokenburn, a large cotton plantation, was about thirty miles west of Vicksburg in what is now Madison Parish. Kate's mother owned 1,260 acres and about 150 slaves. The family fled in April 1863, before the Texans arrived in the region.

* * * * * * * * * * * * *

H Qrs. Tex. Cav. Br.
July 30th 1863

Special order No. -

Major [Richard L.] Capers will order a scout of 30 men to go beyond Tensas as near the enemies lines as practible to move out from Delhi[37] & return after making the circuit beyond Tensas by the way of Warsaw & report the result of the reconnassance. Similar scouts will be made simultaneous along the whole lines above by troops from the rear Major Capers will notify his pickets outposts and scouts that a confederate scout is beyond their line going East from Floyd making a circuit and returning by Delhi he will report the exact location of his picket and posts from Poverty Point[38] to Warsaw & the district in which his scouts are operating beyond Mason [Maçon].

By order
Col W H Parsons

* * * * * * * * * * * * *

Hd Qrs Tex Cav Brig
July 30 1863

Special Order
19th 12th & Battery

Comdg 12th Tex will send in to these Hd Qrs three times a week Mondays Wednesdays and Fridays a morning Report of the entire strenth Present & Absent

By order Col W H Parsons
W M Daviess Ajt.

[37] Delhi is about halfway between Monroe, Louisiana, and Vicksburg.

[38] Poverty Point is below Lake Providence on Bayou Maçon.

* * * * * * * * * * * * *

Hd Qrs Tex Cav Brig
Camp Taylor July 30th 1863

Gen. Order No.
19th 12th & Pratts Bat

Upon the statement of the Surgeon of the Regts that the sickness in this command is in a great measure owing to bathing in the River. It is therefore ordered that no bathing will be allowed between the hours of 7 A.M. & 6 P.M. and it is suggested by the Physicians that no one remain in the water beyond one half hour.[39]

By order Col W H Parsons Comg Br.
W.M. Daviess Ajt.

* * * * * * * * * * * * *

Hd. Qrs. Texas Cavalry Brigade
Camp Taylor August 1st 1863

Special Order No.

Capt. M.B. Highsmith[40] A.Q.M. of 12th Texas will furnish Mr. [J. Fred] Cox one wagon & team immediately. To report to the Depot.

By order of
Major L.J. [Lochlin J.] Farrar
Comdg
W.M. Daviess Adjt.

* * * * * * * * * * * * *

Head Qrs 12th Tex Dragoons
August 1st 1863.

Special Order No

Capt. M.B. Highsmith AQM 12th Texas Dragoons will assume the duties of comd in compliance with Genl Orders No 70 from Richmond & will receipt T.J. [Thomas J.] Payne agent for Capt. F.H. Ayers [Ayres] A.C.S. for 12th Texas Dragoons, for all monies, property Comisary Stores, and effects belonging to his Department,

By order of
Lieut Col. A.B. [A. Bell] Burleson
Comdg

Chas L Miller
Act. Adjt.

[39] Orders such as this indicate the lack of understanding of the causes of the various maladies.

[40] Captain, Company D.

* * * * * * * * * * * * *

Head Quarters 12 Tex Dragoons

Special Order No

Jacob Hesse (?) is announced as Commissary Sergeant for this Regt & his appointment will take effect from the first of this month

L.J. [Lochlin J.] Farrar Maj
Comdg 12 Tex Drags
C.J. Miller Actg Adjt

* * * * * * * * * * * * *

Head Qrs. Texas Cav. Brigade
Camp Taylor La: August 1st 1863

Special Order

W.J. Mercer, acting ordnance officer, Texas Cav. Brigade, will proceed to Shreveport La to procure ordnance for the Brigade.

By order of
W.H. Parsons
Col Comdg
W.M. Daviess AAA Grnl.

* * * * * * * * * * * * *

<u>Maj. [Richard L.] Capers Pickets.</u>

Poverty Point, Jacksons Ferry, Lester's Ferry, Harrold Ferry, Millers Ferry, R.R. Bridge Burford Couches—Maybins—Butlers—Owens Ferry—McLanes Ford—Warsaw—at the ferry below Warsaw—many others—[41]

[41] Poverty Point, Lester's and Jackson's ferries all crossed Bayou Maçon in Carroll Parish. Owen's Ferry crossed Beouf River in Carroll Parish. Warsaw Landing was on Bayou Maçon just northeast of Crowville and almost due east of Baskinton in Franklin Parish.

* * * * * * * * * * * * *

Hd. Qurs. 12th Texas Dragoons
August 1st 1863

Special Order No -

Capt. T.J. [Thomas J.] Payne of 12th Texas Dragoons is hereby relieved from duty as comy [commissary] of this comd and will turn over to Capt. [M.B.] Highsmith A.Q.M. all monies, property and effects belonging to C.S.

By order of
Lieut Col. A.B. [A. Bell] Burleson
Comdg & c
Chas. J. Miller Actg Adjt.

* * * * * * * * * * * * *

Hd. Qurs. 12th Texas Dragoons
August 1st 1863

Special Order No -

Capt. M.B. Highsmith A.Q.M. of 12th Texas Dragoons will assume the duties of comsy [commissary] in compliance with Genl Orders from Richmond and will receipt Capt [Thomas J.] Payne for all monies, property & effects belonging to C.S.

By order of
Lieut Col. A.B. [A. Bell] Burleson
Comdg & c
Charles J. Miller Actg Adjt-

* * * * * * * * * * * * *

Hd. Qurs. Texas Cavalry Brigade
Camp Taylor August 1st 1863

Special Order No

Mr. [J. Fred] Cox Actg Brigade Commissary will have a man detailed to act in his place at the hospital to purchase supplies for the 12th and 19th Regts. of Cavalry

By order of
Maj L.J. [Lochlin J.] Farrar
Comdg & c
W.M. Daviess Adjt.

* * * * * * * * * * * * *

Hd Qrs. Tex. Cav. Brigade
Camp Taylor August 2d 1863.

Special Order No.

The commanders of Regiments will order company commanders to employ Black Smiths and have their horses shod

By order of
W H. Parsons
Col comdg
W.M. Daviess A.A.A.G.

* * * * * * * * * * * * *

Head Quarters Texas Cavalry Brigade
Camp Taylor August 3rd 1863

Special Order No

Leave of absence is hereby granted 2nd Lieut B.F. [Ben F.] Knight Company I 12th Texas Dragoons for sixty days at the expiration of which time he will rejoin his command

By order of
Lieut Col. A.B. [A. Bell] Burleson
Comdg Brgd
W.M. Daviess Adjt.

* * * * * * * * * * * * *

Head Quarters Texas Cavalry Brigade
Camp Taylor, August 3rd 1863

Special Order No

Commanding Officer of 19th Texas Cavalry will have 3 coms officers detailed to act as a Board of Survey to report immediately at Capt [Jefferson J.] Mallard's Quarters

By order of
Lieut Col. A.B. [A. Bell] Burleson
Comdg Brigade
W.M. Daviess Adjt-

* * * * * * * * * * * * *

Head Quarters Texas Cavalry Brigade
Camp Taylor, August 3rd 1863

Special Order No

One man from Co. D. 12th Texas Dragoons is hereby detailed to go with Lieut [William A.] Nichols of the same Co. & Regt. to Monroe

By order of
Lieut Col. A.B. [A. Bell] Burleson
Comdg Brigade
W.M. Daviess Adjt.

* * * * * * * * * * * * *

Head Quarters Tex Cav Brigade
Aug 3d 1863

Genl Order No

Comdg Officer of each Company of this Brigade will detail immediately one suitable man from his company to send home for clothing & send papers to these Head Quarters for approval

By Order Lieut Col A.B. [A. Bell] Burleson
Comdg Brigade
W.M. Daviess Adjt

* * * * * * * * * * * * *

Head Qurs Texas Cavalry Brigade
[no date]

General Order NO -

No sick of this Brigade will be sent to the Hospital without written orders from the regimental Surgeon to report to Capt Brown Comdg Post

By Order of Col W. H. Parsons
Comdg Brigade
W.M. Daviess A.A.A.G

* * * * * * * * * * * * *

Hd Qurs Dist North La.
Monroe Aug 4th 186[3]

Special Order No. 48

In compliance with Special orders No 101 Hd Qrs Trans Miss Dept Shreveport La Aug 1st 1863 Brig Gen J.C. Tappan is relieved of the command of the forces in front in the field upon the withdrawl of Brig General Tappans Brigade Col. W.H. Parsons will assume the immediate command of the forces in front

Official
W.M. Daviess
Adjt.

By Orders
Brig Gen P.O. Hebert [Paul O. Hébert][42]
(Signed) Isaac N. Dennis A.A. & A G Genl

* * * * * * * * * * * * *

Head Quarters Texas Cavalry Brigade
Camp Taylor Aug. 4th 1863

Special Order No

The attention of Mr. [J. Fred] Cox Actg. Brigade Comsy. of 12th Texas Cavalry Brigade is called to Genl. Order No. 70 from Richmond requiring Brigade Comsys to sell provisions to officers

By order of
Lieut Col. A.B. [A. Bell] Burleson
Comdg Brgd
W.M. Daviess Adjt-

* * * * * * * * * * * * *

Head Qrs. Sub. Dist. No La.
Monroe La. Aug 5th 1863.

Col. W.H. Parsons
Comg. & c.
Girard Station

Col.

I send some blanks returns which you will please have distributed & send one as <u>soon</u> <u>as</u> <u>possible</u> the monthly Returns of all the troops now under your command—including Col. [Isaac F.] Harrison,[43] Maj. [Richard L.] Capers & c.—for the month of July.

[42] Paul Octave Hébert, an 1840 graduate of West Point, commanded the Sub-District of Northern Louisiana.

[43] Col. Isaac F. Harrison's Louisiana cavalry operated with Parsons's command, along with a battery from Mississippi and another from Louisiana. Soldat, "Parsons' Cavalry Raid."

Please have this attended to at once as the returns are required at Dist. Hd. Qrs.
I have the honor to be very respty your obt. servt.

Official (Signed) Isaac N. Dennis
W.M. Daviess A.A.A. A.A. & A.I. Genl.

Sir—In compliance with above instructions you will please forward as "soon as possible" the July "monthly returns"

I am sir Respty. & c.
W.M. Daviess A.A.A.G.

Sent to Col. Harrison & Maj. Capers

* * * * * * * * * * * * *

Head Qur Tex Cav Brigade
Aug 5 1863

Special order No -

Comdg Officer of the 12th Tex Dragoons will send a courier to report to the Telegraph operator at Girard station to bring dispatches to Brigade Hd Qurs on Lake Lafouch [Lafourche] at Jones Ferry the courier will make the best arrangements [blacked out] for forage & subsistence

J.B. Daves
Maj Comdg

* * * * * * * * * * * * *

Camp Bartholomew Ark Aug 6 1863

W F Kenner

Will proceed to Col W H Parsons Regiment & report to him for duty being transfered to John Browns Co. of Said Reg

A True Copy B D McKie[44]
W G Evans Capt Comdg Squadron
W M Daviess Texas Rangers
Adjt

[44] Benjamin D. McKie was major of Morgan's regiment. He was a thirty-four-year-old native of Tennessee who had been wounded twice in the Mexican War. In 1861 he had organized the "Navarro Spies," which became the "Independent Mounted Rangers" in August 1863 (Company F, Morgan's regiment). By 1863 he was commanding his own squadron under Morgan. Before the war he had been a doctor who claimed $8,000 in real estate and $7,000 in personal estate. Wounded at least three times during the Civil War, he eventually found it physically impossible to continue fighting. Bailey, *Between the Enemy and Texas*, 44, 228-29.

* * * * * * * * * * * * *

Hd Qrs. Texas Cav Brigade
Aug 6th 1863

Special orders No -

Maj. Thos. [Thomas] Johns Brigade Q.M. will furnish Captain J.P. [Joseph P.] Weir[45] funds to forage One Hundred Hd Govmt Horses for seven days.

By order of
Col W.H. Parsons
Comdg Brigade
W.M. Daviess AAAG

* * * * * * * * * * * * *

Head Quarters Texas Cavalry Brigade
Camp Dennis, August 6th 1863

Special Order No

Major Thos. [Thomas] Johns A.Q.M. Texas Cavalry Brigade will furnish Capt. [Jefferson J.] Mallard Brigade Commissary with transportation

If he cannot obtain upon requisition or pu[r]chase he will hire

By order of
Col. W.H. Parsons
Comdg Brigade
W.M. Daviess A.A.A.G.

* * * * * * * * * * * * *

Hd. Qrs. Forces in Front
August 8th 1863.

Special Order No.

In compliance with Part IV & V Special orders 48 Hd. Qrs. Sub. Dist. N. La. Aug. 4th 1863, relieving Infy. Force at Rail R. Bridges—& c. & c. enclosed—Col. [Isaac F.] Harrison will have such guard placed at the Bridges as in his judgment may be deemed necessary.

By order Col W.H. Parsons
Commanding Forces in Front
W.M. Daviess A.A.A.G.

[45] Company A, Twelfth Texas.

* * * * * * * * * * * * *

Hd Qur Forces in Front
Aug 8/63 Camps on Lake LaFourche

Comdg Officer
12 Tex Dragoons

Sir you will Detail one Lt & ten men to report at these Hd Qurs immediately for Picket duty.

By Order Col. W.H. Parsons
Comdg Forces in Front
W.M. Daviess A.A.A.G.

* * * * * * * * * * * * *

Hd. Qrs. Forces in Front
Aug. 8th 1863

Special Order No.

Col. [Isaac F.] Harrison comg. & c. will immediately forward to these Hd. Qrs. a complete Roster of commissioned off. in his command—name, Rank, Regiment and date of appointment.

By order Col. W.H. Parsons
Commanding Forces in Front
W.M. Daviess A.A.A.G.

* * * * * * * * * * * * *

Head Quarters Forces in Front
Camp Dennis Aug. 9th 1863.

Special order No -

Captain M.B. Highsmith[46] A.Q.M. 12th Texas Dragoons will turn over to W.J. Mercer Brigade ordinance officer the wagon and harness & 6 mules for his department which was originally designed and used as such.

By order of
(Signed) W.H. Parsons
Col. Comdg. & c.

[46] Captain, Company D.

* * * * * * * * * * * * *

Hd. Qrs. Forces in Front-'63
Camp Dennis Aug 10th

Special order No. -

The A.Q.M. at Girard will turn over to Pvt. [Albert] Chalmers[47] of the 19th Tex. Cav. all the ordinance & medical stores for the Brigade shipped from Monroe by Captain [William] Oliver A.Q.M.

By order
W.H. Parsons
Col. Comdg. Forces in Front
Lt. R.C.H. [Robert C. H.] Good A.A.A.G.

* * * * * * * * * * * * *

Hd. Qrs. Forces in Front
Aug. 10th 1863.

Special Order No. -

The commanding officer of 12th Texas Dragoons will have a man detailed for Regimental Tailor.

By order
Col. W.H. Parsons
R.C.H. [Robert C.H.] Good
Lt. & A.A.A.G.

* * * * * * * * * * * * *

Hd. Qrs. Forces in Front
Aug 13th 1863

Special order No -[48]

Comdg. Officers of 12th Texas Dragoons will send Company B to report to I.N. Dennis A.A & A Ins. Gl. at Monroe to-morrow morning—they will take baggage and equipage—

By order
Col. W.H. Parsons
Comdg. & c.
Robt. C.H. Good Lt. & A.A.A.G.

[47] Company H.

[48] This order appears twice with slight variations in each.

* * * * * * * * * * * * *

Hd Qrs. Forces in Front
Camp Dennis Aug 13,'63

Special Order No -

Col. [Isaac F.] Harrison
Comdg. Regt

Col.

(I) You will relieve the infantry guard at Beoff River Bridge with 9 men, also place same number at Crew lake bridge. The infantry guard at Beoff River Bridge will be directed when relieved to join their command at Monroe.

(II) Col. [Isaac F.] Harrison will also have a monthly return of his command forwarded to these Hd Qrs. as soon as possible, in compliance with previous orders for the month of July—

By order of
Col. W.H. Parsons
Comdg. Forces in front
Robt. C.H. Good Lt & A.A.A.G.

* * * * * * * * * * * * *

Hd. Qrs. Forces in Front
Aug. 13th 1863

Special Orders No -

Maj. Thos. [Thomas] Johns Brigade Q.M. will permit private James [P.] McMahon of Co H. 12th Texas Dragoons to exchange his horse for a Government mule—his horse having been disabled in battle.[49]

By order of
W.H. Parsons
Col. comdg Forces in Front
J.M. Brandon A.A.G.

[49] Although riding a government mule was certainly not what any trooper wanted, it was preferable to transfer to the infantry.

* * * * * * * * * * * * *

Hd. Qrs. Forces in Front
Aug. 13th 1863

Special Order No -

Lt. Col. B.W. [Benjamin W.] Watson Commanding 19th Texas Cav will turn over the command of his Regiment to Maj. J.T. [Joel T.] Daves and assume Command at once of the Texas Cav. Brigade.

By order of
W.H. Parsons
Col. Commandg.
R.C.H. [Robert C. H.] Good A.A.A.G.

* * * * * * * * * * * * *

Head Quarters Dept Trans Miss
Shreveport La
Aug 14th 1863

General Order No 36

All clients and employees in the military service, liable to conscription in the Trans Miss Dept will be immiadiately enrolled, and within 20 days thereafter sent to camps of instruction in their respective Districts; All able bodied men, except officers, Mechanics, who are now serving in the several staff [positions] will be relieved and ordered to join their proper Companies and Reg unless especially detailed by the district commander upon proof of neccessity of service—Their place will be supplied by those who are not capable of active service in the field whether of age, sex or physical ability—

By command of
Lt Gen E Kirby Smith
S.S. Anderson
Asst Adjt Gen

By order
P.O. Hebert [Paul O. Hébert] Brig Gen
Isaac N Dennis A.A & A Ins Gen

* * * * * * * * * * * * *

Hd Qrs. Forces in Front
Aug 15th 1863.

Special Order No -

In obedience to order "No. 58" from E.S. McCall of Co. A. [Isaac F.] Harrisons Regiment, Partisan Rangers will report as soon as possible with his company for duty to Lt. Col. G.W. Logan at Harrisonburg[50] La. until further orders.

By order of
W.H. Parsons
Col. Commanding
R.C.H. [Robert C.H.] Good
Lt. & A.A.A.G.

* * * * * * * * * * * * *

Head Qurs Forces in Front
Aug 15th 1863

Special Ordr No

Lt Col B.W. [Benjamin W.] Watson Commanding 19th Texas Cav will turn over the command of his Regiment to Maj J J Dawes [Joel T. Daves] and assume command at once of Tex Cavly Brigade—

By ord
W.H. Parsons Col
Commandg
R.C.H. [Robert C.H.] Good A.A.A.G.

* * * * * * * * * * * * *

Head Quarters Texas Cavalry Brigade
August 16th 1863

Special Ord

Hereafter the Guards will be mounted at 8 oclock A.M. at which time all Furloughs, Papers, Communications must be forwarded to these Head Qrs, through the Adjutants of

[50] Harrisonburg is on the Louisiana side of the Mississippi River around thirty miles northwest of Natchez, Mississippi. Although this appears to be written G.W. Logan, it may be John L. Logan, who commanded the Eleventh Arkansas Cavalry and was in this region at the time. He operated with the Texans in late 1863 and 1864, and is certainly the man referred to in subsequent orders. See Report of Marcellus M. Crocker to William T. Clark, September 7, 1863, and Horace Randal to E. Surget, September 5, *OR* 26, pt.1, 273-76, 279-80.

the different Regiments, the times for transacting business, will be from 8 A.M. to 1 P.M. & at no other time will any business be attended to

By Order of
Lt Col [Benjamin W.] Watson Comandg Tex
Cavalry Brigade
R.C.H. [Robert C.H.] Good A.A.A.G-

* * * * * * * * * * * * *

Division Hd Qrs.
forces in front.
Hd. Qr. forces in front.
Aug 16th 63.

Special order No. 1-

(I) Lt. & A.D.C. J.E. [James E.] Terrell will proceed at once to the Hd. Qr. of Lt Col [Richard L.] Capers commanding the ~~forces in front~~ out Posts on ~~appe~~. Mason [Maçon] Bayou, ~~for~~ as inspecting officer.

(II) Lt Col Capers. Commanding out Posts will direct a commissioned officer of his Battalion ~~to~~ who is familiar with location & commanders of posts, to accompany Lt Terrell, A.D.C. and render him all the facilities necessary to further the object of his official visit.

(III) Lt Terrell A.D.C. will visit the outposts of the upper Mason [Maçon] above Delhi & then return & report to these Hd. Qrs. & afterwards proceed to visit the Posts below Delhi—

(IV) Lt Terrell A.D.C. will give such instructions in regard to location & position of Posts & pickets, & the duties of Post & picket commanders as may be necessary to insure the security of the line of out Posts, & Lt Terrell will be obeyed in these instructions.

By order
W.H. Parsons
Col Comdg forces in front
By [Robert C.H.] Good A.A.A.G.

* * * * * * * * * * * * *

Hd Qrs. Forces in Front.
Camp Dennis Aug. 16th 1863

Special Order No 2-[51]

All Property captured consisting of horses mules and negroes is Government property and all sales made by soldiers of such property or otherwise disposed of or used without the consent of Brigade or Regimental Commander will be regarded as a crime and severely punished.[52]

By order of
W.H. Parsons
Col. Commanding

* * * * * * * * * * * * *

Hd Qrs Forces in Front
Aug. 16th 1863.

Special Order No 3[53]

The commanding Grn. having delegated to the commander of the forces in front with special authority to use summary process and inflict summary punishment in certain cases of delinquincy, or violation of duty, and Whereas it has been proven to the satisfaction of the comdg. Officer that James Add. Calahan [Callahan] of Co.(A) 12th Texas Dragoons has been guilty of the crime of stealing a mule; it is therefore ordered that said James Ad. Calahan [Callahan] be dishonorably dismounted as no longer worthy to be a member of the cavalry arm of the Confederate army, and that his horse and cavalry equipments be turned over to the Q.M. of Brigade, the value thereof to be appraised and given to said Calahan [Callahan] and that said Calahan [Callahan] be sent under guard to the nearest conscript depot, to be enrolled into the infantry service. The comdg. officer is pained to take this course but the demoralizing results flowing out of the perpetration of such acts (growing he fears so frequent) has determined him to save the honor of the

[51] This order appears twice; the second order was signed by Lt. Col. Benjamin W. Watson, commanding the Nineteenth Texas.

[52] Confederate troopers often captured former slaves working on Federally-run plantations and used them as personal servants or sold them for personal gain. This practice became a source of friction and controversy between U.S. and Confederate authorities. Troopers also took animals off the plantations, which they frequently sold.

[53] This order appears twice with slight variations in each. The Confederate authorities constantly tried to stop stealing in order to keep the relationship between civilians and the military cordial. On April 8, J.C. Morriss had told his wife: "We arrested a man the other day at Powhattan who had a couple of negroes he had stolen and was taking them off to Texas to sell. There were two others engaged in the speculation and Col Giddings sent out to have them arrested." J.C. Morriss to Amanda Morriss, April 8, 1863, Weller, ed., *Civil War Letters*.

honest men of this command by inflicting summary and severe punishment on all such cases hereafter

By order of
W.H. Parsons
Col. Commanding
R.C.H. Good A.A.A.G.

* * * * * * * * * * * * *

Head Quarters Tex Cavalry Brigade
Aug 16th 1863

Special order No -

The commanding officer 12th Tex Drag will furnish the following detail to morrow morning viz 5 men to kill beeves report at Ferry daylight—4 men to report to Bg'd Comis at sun up mounted—

By Order-
Lt Col B.W. [Benjamin W.] Watson
R.C.H. [Robert C.H.] Good A.A.G.

* * * * * * * * * * * * *

Head Quarters 12th Texas Cavalry
Lake La Fourche August 17th, 1863

Special order No. -

Upon the reccomendation of Colonel Commanding Brigade W.G. Vardell[54] 1st Serg Company (F) 12th Regiment Texas Cavalry is hereby appointed Adjutant 12th Tex Cav with the rank of 1st Lieutenant and will enter upon the discharge of his duties immediately

By order of
(Signed) A.B. [A. Bell] Burleson
Comdg 12th Tex Cav

[54] William G. Vardell was eventually adjutant in the Twelfth Texas. This order appears twice with slight variations in each.

* * * * * * * * * * * * *

Head Quarters Tex Cavalry Brigade
Aug 17th 1863

Special order No

The commanding officer 12th Tex Drags will furnish 3 Commissioned officers to assist Mr W.A. Manly in assessing the damage done to his corn to report at these Head Quarters immediately

By order
Lt Col [Benjamin W.] Watson
R.C.H. [Robert C.H.] Good A.A.A.G-

* * * * * * * * * * * * *

Head Quarters Tex Cav Brigade
Camp Dennis Aug 17th 1863

Special Order No

The Commanding Officer 12th Tex Dgs will furnish the following detail for To morrow 1 Lt, 2 N.C. off and 8 pvts, Brigade Guard, 5 men to kill Beeves

By order of
Lt Col [Benjamin W.] Watson
R.C.H. [Robert C.H.] Good. A.A.A.G-
Mr L J Lindsey

* * * * * * * * * * * * *

Adjutant and Inspector Genl Office
Richmon[d] August 18- 1863

Genl order No 113

I Officer receiving volunteers from those liable to conscription will in no case grant furloughs for more than Ten days to such volunteers before entering on active Servise

II Every man liable to conscription volunteering before enrolement will report himself and the Company in which he volunteered and likewise be reported by his captain to the Commandant of Conscripts of the State with in ten days after his act of volunteering—otherwise he will be held Subject to enrolement and assignment

| | |
|---|---|
| Official | By Order of |
| J M Brandon | S [Samuel] Cooper |
| AAG | Adjt & Insp Genl |

* * * * * * * * * * * * *

Hd. Quarters Forces in Front
Aug 18- 1863-

Special order No. 4[55]

I The Texas Brigade will prepare to move at 3 O,Clock P.M. to day to their new camp at Jefferson Point

II The troops will cross at the Ford below the Ferry—The wagons cross at the Ferry—

III As Forage had been procured ~~fall~~ for the 19th ~~for to~~ Tex Cav. for to day it will not move till to-morrow morning

By order W.H. Parsons
Col. Commanding
R.C.H. [Robert C.H.] Good
Lt. & A.A.A.G

* * * * * * * * * * * * *

Head Quarters Sub Dist. North La
Monroe La Aug 19th 1863

General Order No 13

I. Officers throughout this "Military district" are enjoined to have more strict discipline than has hertofore existed. Incompetent or negligent officers must nesicarilly have ill disciplined & inefficient corps, and the officer in immediate command of him, so is generally the soldier—In a malarious country like this there must nesicarily be at this season of the year sickness among troops in the field much of this however can be pre-

[55] This order appears twice with slight variations in each.

vented if officers would enforce proper police regulations, and take care of the soldier, when he will not take care of himself—

II. Commands are, independent of sickness, much reduced in efficiency from desertion, absences without leave, unauthorized furloughs & c. Besides the usual penalties prescribed by the Regulations and Articles of War, mounted men, will as a preliminary be dismounted & placed on duty as infantry whenever their is an evidence of want of proper discipline, this will be done upon the report of the Major General & executed in all cases—

III. Commanders of Regiments, Battalions and Companies report upon paper large Aggregates and when called upon for duty, mere skeltons are ready for the field. All this must be changed and Officers must see to it—The incompetent or unwilling officer, in the discharge of the duties expected of him, shall go into the Ranks, and give place to another better & more efficient soldier—

A Law of Congress prescribes this remedy and it will be rigidly enforced—

By command of
Brig Gen P.O. Hebert [Paul O. Hébert]
Isaac Dennis A.A. & A Ins Gen

Col W.H. Parsons
Comdg & c Girard

Official
R.C.H. [Robert C.H.] Good
A.A.A.G

Official
J.M. Brandon
A.A.G.

True Copy
W.G. Vardell Adjt

* * * * * * * * * * * * *

Head Quarter Forces in Front
Aug 19th 1863

Special order No

The commanding officer 12th Texas Drags will furnish 6 men to kill beeves—report to these Head Qrs to [Benjamin] McKnight immediately—

By order
Lt Col W.B. [Benjamin W.] Watson
R.C.H. [Robert C.H.] Good A.A.A.G.

* * * * * * * * * * * * *

Head Quarters 12th Cavalry Brigade
Camp Davis [Daviess] Aug 19th 1863

Special Order No -

The commanding Officer 12th Texas Dragoons will furnish the following detail tomorrow morning 2 N.C. Officers, 10 privates Brigade Guard at 8. A.M. 4 men to report at Brigade Commissary at day light to kill beeves—

By order of
Lt Col B.W. [Benjamin W.] Watson
R.C.H. [Robert C.H.] Good A.A.A.G-

The Capt & 1st Lieuts will be detailed as off day & 2d Lieuts as off guard only

* * * * * * * * * * * * *

Head Qurs Tex Cavalry Drgs
Camp Daviess Aug 20th 1863

Special Order No -

The commanding officer 12th Tex Dgs will furnish the following detail for to-morrow morning—1 Lieut; 2 N.C. Off & 12 men Brigade Guard, "<u>mounted,</u>" 5 men to report to [Benjamin] McKnight at day break at church, to kill beeves, 5 men to report at Brigade Commissary at sun up—

By order
Lt Col B.W. [Benjamin W.] Watson
R.C.H. [Robert C.H.] Good A.A.A.G.

* * * * * * * * * * * * *

Hd. Qrs. Forces in Front
Jefferson Point La Aug. 20th 1863.

Special Order No -

Captain F.H. Ayers will settle up the business of the Commissary Department for the month of July 1863.

By order of
W.H. Parsons
Col. Commanding.
J.M. Brandon A.A. Genl.

* * * * * * * * * * * * *

Head Quarters 12th Tex Drag
Camp Daviess Aug 20th 1862

Special Order No -

Charles Taylor Company (B) 12th Tex Drags is hereby appointed orderly (Regimental) and will enter upon the discharge of his duties immediately—

By order
A.B. [A. Bell] Burleson Lt Col
W.G. Vardell Adjt
Commanding

* * * * * * * * * * * * *

Hd Qrs. Forces in Front
Aug. 21st 1863.[56]

Special Order No. 5[57]

Lt. Col. B.W. [Benjamin W.] Watson
Commanding Texas Cavalry Brigade

Sir—In obedience to orders from Hd Qrs. Sub Dist. No. La. the commanding officers of Co. H. 12th Texas Dragoons will be ready to march at an early hour in the morning with their baggage and equipment to report to Col. [Frank] Bartlett Commandant of the Post at Monroe La. without delay

By order of W H Parsons
Col Comdg
J M Brandon A.A.G.

[56] George Ingram wrote from Point Jefferson on August 21: "We have moved our camps to this place which is five miles distant from Lake La Fouche where I last wrote you. . . . The chills and Fever are increasing and if it continue[s] much longer thus but few will escape. In one company in Burfords Regt. evry man is reported sick and several in that Regiment have died. I believe but two have died in our Regt. as yet and they were killed by over doses of morphine administered by a numb scull of a doctor that was detailed from Capt. Veales Company while some of the regular Surgeons were sick." George W. Ingram to Martha F. Ingram, August 21, 1863, in Ingram, comp., *Civil War Letters*, 59.

[57] This order appears twice with slight variations in each.

* * * * * * * * * * * * *

Head Quarters Forces in Front
Camp Daviess Aug 21st 1863

General Order No 1

The Colonel Commanding announces the following "Staff Officers" to this command,

| | |
|---|---|
| Capt J.M. Brandon | A.A.G |
| Lieut R.C.H. [Robert C.H.] Good | Aid[e] de camp |
| " J.E. Terrell | Inspector Gen |
| " W.J. Mercer | Ordnance Officer |

Who will be obeyed and respected accordingly—

| | |
|---|---|
| "Official" | By Order of |
| R.C.H. [Robert C.H.] Good A.A.A.G- | W.H. Parsons |
| True Copy | Col Commanding |
| W G Vardell Adjt | "Signed" J.M. Brandon A.A.G. |

* * * * * * * * * * * * *

Head Quarters Cavalry Brig-
August 21st 1863

Special order No -

The Commanding officer 12th Tex Drags will furnish 2 men mounted & armed to report to Colonel W.H. Parsons immediately

By order
Lieut Col W.B. [Benjamin W.] Watson
R.C.H. [Robert C.H.] Good A.A.A.G-

* * * * * * * * * * * * *

Head Quarter Cav Brig
Camp Daviess Aug 21st 63

Special Order NO -

The Commanding officer 12th Tex Drag will furnish 3 N.C. Off & 14 privates for Brigade Guard to morrow morning at 8. o'clock, "mounted," also 3 men mounted & armed to Guard Negroes while killing beeves, to report at Brigade Commissary at day light—

By order of B.W. [Benjamin W.] Watson
Lt Col Commanding
R.C.H. [Robert C.H.] Good A.A.A.G

* * * * * * * * * * * * *

Head Quarters Tex Cavalry Brigade
August 22d 1863

Special Order No -

The comdg officer of 12th Texas Drags will furnish a Lieut and 1 man to report ~~to~~ at Col Parsons Head Quarters immediately to go after ordnance stores—

By order of
Lt Col W.B. [Benjamin W.] Watson
R.C.H. [Robert C.H.] Good A.A.A.G

* * * * * * * * * * * * *

Head Quarters Forces in Front
Camp Daviess Aug 22 1863

Special Order No 6[58]

Lt J.M. Noble of Company G-12th Texas Drags is hereby detailed as Ordnance Officer and will report for duty at this office at once—

By order
W.H. Parsons
Col commanding
J.M. Brandon A.A.G-

Official
R.C.H. [Robert C.H.] Good
AAAG

[58] This order appears twice with slight variations in each.

* * * * * * * * * * * * *

Head Quarters 12th Tex Cav Brigade
August 22d 1862

Special Order No -

The commanding officer of 12 Tex Dgs will furnish the following detail for to-morrow 1 Lieut, 2 N.C Officers & 14 men 'Brigade Guard' 2 men mounted & armed report at Brigade Commissary—

By order W.B. [Benjamin W.] Watson
Lt Col Comdg
R.C.H. [Robert C.H.] Good A.A.A.G-

* * * * * * * * * * * * *

Head Quarters Tex Cav Brig.
Camp Daviess Aug 22d 63

Special Order No -

The commanding officer of the 12th Texas Dragoons will have detailed from their command (2) Two Non Com Off Eleven privates, (11) for Brigade Guard and one private to guard negroes in killing beeves—

(Signed)
A.W. Dechman
A.A.A.G.

By order of
B.W. [Benjamin W.] Watson Lt Col Comdg
Tex Cav Brigade-

* * * * * * * * * * * * *

Hd Quarters Forces in Front
Camp Daviess August 22nd 1863

Special Order No. 6

Lieut. J.M. Noble (?) of Company G. 12th Texas Dragoons is hereby detailed as Ordnance Officer to this Command and will report for duty at this office at once.

By order of
W H Parsons
Col Commanding
J M Brandon A.A.G

* * * * * * * * * * * * *

Hd Qrs. Forces in Front Camp Daviess Aug 23rd

Special Order No. 7

Lt. Col. R.L. Capers commanding outpost will prefer charges against private Guilford Byles of Co. C. 13th Louisiana Battalion [Partisan Rangers] and send them through this office to be tried by General Court-Martial now in session at Monroe.

By order of
W.H. Parsons
Col Commanding
J.M. Brandon A.A.G.

* * * * * * * * * * * * *

Head Quarters Tex Cavalry Brigade
Camp Daviess Aug 23d 1863

Special Order No -

As the use of water melons, Peaches, Apples and Sugar Cane are by the chief Surgeon of this command considered detrimental to the health of the Troops, it is hereby strictly forbidden for any soldiers to bring any of the above mentioned fruits into camps—

By order of
(Signed) B.W. [Benjamin W.] Watson
Lt Col Comdg

A.W. Dechman
A.A.A.G.

* * * * * * * * * * * * *

Head Quarters Forces in Front
Vienna[59] August 30 1863

Special orders No. 8

Lieut. J.H. [John W.] Wright of Company F. 12th Texas Dragoons will rejoin his Company or Regiment at Vienna or wherever it may be without delay.

By order of
W.H. Parsons
Col. Commanding
J.M. Brandon A.A.G

* * * * * * * * * * * * *

Hd. Qrs. Forces in Front
Vienna August 30 1863[60]

Special Order No. 9

Maj Thos. [Thomas] Johns A.Q.M. will exchange a Govt mule for a troopers Horse

By order of
W.H. Parsons
Col Commg
J.M. Brandon A.A.G.

[59] Vienna is located halfway between Monroe and Minden. Henry Orr told his father on August 30 about skirmishing near Monroe. Federal troops under John D. Stevenson moved toward Monroe on August 22 and briefly took the town, but quickly retreated to the Mississippi River. Henry was appalled that the citizens of Monroe wanted to surrender the town to protect their homes rather than fight. See Henry Orr to "Father," August 30, 1863, in Anderson, ed., *Campaigning with Parsons' Brigade*, 116-17. George Ingram, writing from Vienna, told his wife: "This letter was lying in my trunk unfinished when we learned that a large number of Federals were advancing upon our position at Point Jefferson. This was on Sunday night 23d and our Squadron was ordered down to the crossing on Beouff River as a pickett. We remained there untill Tuesday the 25th when we were attacked by the Feds and driven from our position. . . . The Federals are now at Monroe and it is reported that they have started back towards Vicksburg. . . . Sickness still prevails in camp to such an extent that we have only about 500 fighting men out of three Regiments." On September 3 he added: "The amount of sickness that is prevailing in our command is enough to discourage any set of men in the world. You never saw a worse looking set in your life. Two thirds of them have not courage enough to fight an army of old women. We have not more than 25 men in our company that I could depend upon in a close place in their present condition. This swamp fever seems to make them indiferent to everything but eating and they have not life enough to cook that." George W. Ingram to Martha F. Ingram, August 30 and September 3, 1863, in Ingram, comp., *Civil War Letters*, 60-63.

[60] Writing from Vienna, which he said was "about thirty-five miles west of Monroe," Henry Orr told his father about the attack on Monroe: "Col. Parsons took position two miles east of Monroe to give them battle but they struck camp four miles back. While here, some citizens passed with flag of truce to the enemy, the character of which we have since learned was to surrender the place without a fight, provided they would guarantee not to destroy the town or interrupt private property. They (the citizens) had prevailed upon Gen. Hebert to let them do this. Col. Parsons, I have heard, was much displeased with this, but we fell back across the [Ouachita] River. The enemy came the next morning, and we continued to retreat. Near 1,000 of their cavalry crossed the river Friday evening. Our command arrived at this place last evening, and to our gratification we learned this morning that they had left Monroe, moving back [torn]. . . . The Fed Force, 7,000 infantry and 1,500 cavalry, [is] commanded by Gen. Stephenson; our force is about 600 all told." Henry Orr to "Father," August 30, 1863, in Anderson, ed., *Campaigning with Parsons' Brigade*, 116-17.

* * * * * * * * * * * * *

Adj & Inspt General Office
Richmond August 31 186_

General Order No 116-

I Generals or other officers Commanding Departments armies in the Field post or garrisons will cause all Deserters Stragglers or other absentees from duty and all persons liable to Military Servis found with in their lines and not belonging to their commands to be forthwith arrested and turned over to the nearest enrolling officer whose duty it Shall be to forward such absentees to their proper Commands or in case of conscription, to assign them to Service in the Army Nearest to his post according to his discretion

II Under instructions from the Bureau of Conscription an enroling officer will be attached to each military Department to cary out the purposes indicated in parag[rap]h

III Overseers intitled to exemption will be exempted from Military Service for one year when the overseer of the Slaves of whom the overseer has had charge Shall present to the enrolling officer the receipt of a QM for the amount of the tax imposed in Such cases By the act of Congress approved May 1st 1863 Officer of the Quartermaster department ar directed to receveive [*sic*] and recept [*sic*] for money thus paid

| | |
|---|---|
| Official | By Order of |
| J M Brandon | S Cooper |
| AAG | Adj & Inspt General |

* * * * * * * * * * * * *

Hd Qrs. Forces in Front
Vienna Sept 1st 1863.

Special Order No. 10

Captain M.B. Highsmith[61] commanding camps will release Guilford Byles private of Co. "C" Capers Battalion and order him to report to his company commander for duty at once.

By order of
W.H. Parsons
Col Commanding
J.M. Brandon A.A.G.

[61] Company D, Twelfth Texas.

* * * * * * * * * * * * *

Hd. Qrs. Forces in front
Vienna Sept. 1st 1863

Special Order No. 11

Maj. Thomas Johns A.Q.M. will pay over to Lt. Thos H. Killingsworth[62] money to buy forage for fifty Horses for ten days

By order of
W H Parsons
Col Comdg
J M Brandon A.A.G.

* * * * * * * * * * * * *

Hd. Qrs. forces in front
Vienna Sept 1st 1863

Special Order No. 12

(I) Lt. Thos H. Killingsworth is authorized to buy provisions for his men and give orders on the commissary of this division for pay

(II) In the event that provisions cannot be bought he is authorized and empowered hereby to impress supplies for his troops and give receipts therefore He will use no violence in procuring his supplies.[63]

By order of
W H Parsons
Col Comdg
J M Brandon A.A.G.

* * * * * * * * * * * * *

Head Qrs. Forces in Front
Vienna Sept 1st 1863

Special Order No. 13

Captains McNeil and Johnson will repair at once to Vienna and Report to these Hd Qrs. for instructions

By order of
W.H. Parsons
Col Commanding
J M Brandon A.A.G.

[62] Company H, Nineteenth Texas.

[63] Clearly such instructions were often overstepped, as Confederate cavalry often foraged with the same intensity as Union horsemen. This often hampered a friendly relationship between the military and local residents.

* * * * * * * * * * * * *

Sub. Dist. N. La Vienna
Hd Qrs. Forces in Front
[no date]

Special Order No. 14

(I) Maj L.J. [Lochlin J.] Farrar 12th Texas Dragoons is directed to make his Hd Qrs. at Monroe & take command at the out Posts patrols and Pickets East of the Washita [Ouachita] River.

(II) Major Farrar will at once issue orders to Capts. [John M.] Stone[64] and Brown[65] and Lt. [Thomas H.] Killingsworth[66] giving them notice of his assumption of command and call for such other forces as may be necessary to carry out the objects [he] had in view

(III) Major Farrar will place guards at River and detain all troopers and assign them to duty East of Washita [Ouachita] and render such aid as may be necessary to Col. Bartlett comdt. of Post at Monroe—in protecting the city.

(IV) He will cover by small scouts and parties the approaches to Monroe by the Winsboro [Winnsboro] Road: the Delhi: the Goodrich or Owen's ferry Road and the Ashton Road.

(V) He will by the line of couriers now established between Monroe and these Hd Qrs. make out a daily Report of the observations in front or any information of enemies movements.

(VI) He will draw on A.Q.M. [William] Oliver, A.C.S. Thomas [Johns] for forage and subsistence to sustain the outposts.

By order of
(signed) W H Parsons
Col Comdg
forces in front

[64] Company H, Nineteenth Texas. John M. Stone was twenty-six years old when he had enlisted in McLennan County. A native of Alabama, he gave his occupation as a farmer worth $759 in real estate and $1,900 in personal estate. Bailey, *Between the Enemy and Texas*, 224-25.

[65] Since there are two captains with the last name of Brown in the Twelfth Texas, it is impossible to know which one is indicated here.

[66] Company H, Nineteenth Texas.

* * * * * * * * * * * * *

Hd Qrs. Forces in Front
Vienna Sept. 3d 1863[67]

Special Order No. 15

(I) Surgeon T.M. [Thomas M.] Matthews as chief surgeon of Cavalry Division is relieved from Regimental duty. Asst. Surgeon R.P. Sweat [Sweatt] will assume control of the Medical Department of the 12th Texas Dragoons detailing such Physicians of the command as he may think proper to assist him.

(II) All Reports pertaining to the Medical Department must be made through Surgeon Matthews till further orders.

By order of
W H Parsons
Col. Commanding
J.M. Brandon A.A.G.

* * * * * * * * * * * * *

Hd. Qrs. Forces in Front
Vienna La. Sept. 3d 1863

Special Orde[r] No. 15a.

Captain Thomas Johns A.Q.M. will turn over to Lieut. H.B. Smith two Hundred Dollars to forage Horses of Pickets under his Comd.

By order of
W.H. Parsons
Col. Comdg
J M Brandon A.A.G.

[67] George Ingram told his wife on September 3 that he had begun a letter on August 21, but did not finish it because "the Federals made us skedadle from Point Jefferson." By early September, he was camped in the "Pine Hills 4 miles South [of] Vienna." He added, "I hope the health [of the men] will soon become better as we are now in the Pine Hills with no swamp or large Stream near us and as pure spring water as ever run out of the earth." There was no immediate Federal threat as the "Yankees have gone back to the Mississippi River." George W. Ingram to Martha F. Ingram, September 3, 1863, in Ingram, comp., *Civil War Letters*, 62-63.

* * * * * * * * * * * * *

Hd Qrs Forces in Front
Vienna Sept. 4th 1863

Special Order No. 16

The commanding officers in Camp will have consolidated Morning Reports of the La. Cavalry and the Texas Cav. Brigade made out every Tuesday Thursday and Saturday and forwarded through his Hd. Qrs. to this office.

By order of
W.H. Parsons
Col Commanding
R.C.H. [Robert C.H.] Good A.D.C.

* * * * * * * * * * * * *

Hd. Qrs. Sub Dist North La.
Vienna La. Sept. 4th 1863

(Extract)
Special Order No. 74

II 1st Col. Parsons will establish a regular line of Pickets toward the Miss. River as near as practicable to the enemies lines. The earliest and most reliable information of the movements of the enemy must be transmitted by the scouts and couriers properly posted in front.[68]

By order of
Brig. Genl. P.O. Hebert [Paul O. Hébert]
Isaac N. Dennis AA&A Ins. Genl.

"Official"
Robt C H Good (signed) A.D.C.

Major [Lochlin J.] Farrar will execute the above order

By order of
W.H. Parsons
Col Comdg forces in front
Robt. C.H. Good A.D.C.

[68] George Ingram wrote his wife on September 3, "I have charge of the Courrier line from Vienna to Monroe and ride up and down the line at my leisure and of course stop at the best houses on the route. The distance is 35 miles and couriers is posted evry 4 miles." Ibid. Dave Nance observed that the men of the Twelfth Texas spent time "conveying freight, scouting the banks of the Oauchita, and foraging for the Central Commissary and Rations depot in Shreveport." Gallaway, *The Ragged Rebel*, 74.

* * * * * * * * * * * * *

Hd. Qrs. Forces in Front.
Vienna Sept. 4th 1863

Special Order No. 17

Col Parsons having received orders from General Hd. Qrs. in reference to commands partially disorganized whose men are scattered about on East and West side of the Washita [Ouachita] River requiring them to be brought to Camp for duty & c. The commanding officers of Regiments and Companies on going to duty on East side of Washita [Ouachita] River use their utmost endeavors to get their command together in the enforcement of which order the General Commanding directs that officers will be held to strict accountability

By order of
W.H. Parsons
Col. Comdg & c.
Robt C.H. Good A.D.C.

* * * * * * * * * * * * *

Hd. Qrs. Forces in Front
Vienna Sept. 4th 1863

Special Order No. 18

I The 12th & 19th Texas will rendezvous at Vienna La.

II Major [Lochlin J.] Farrar will release the companies attachments and scouts of the 12th and 19th now on duty as soon as their places can be taken by the La. Cavalry.

III He will issue orders and have them inforced to bring in straglers, deserters and men absent without leave.

By order of
W.H. Parsons
Col. Comdg
Robt. C H Good A.D.C.

* * * * * * * * * * * * *

Hd. Qrs. Forces in Front
Vienna Sept. 4th 1863

Special Order No. 19

(I) The 3rd La. Partisan Rangers is hereby ordered to report to Major [Lochlin J.] Farrar at Monroe for duty.

(II) Camp of main body with train near Trinity West bank of the Washita [Ouachita] River adjacent to corn.

By order of
W H Parsons
Col Commanding & c.
Robt C H Good A.D.C.

* * * * * * * * * * * * *

Hd. Qrs. Forces in Front
Vienna Sept 4th 1863

Special Order No. 20

(I) The 13th Battalion of La. Cavalry is hereby ordered to report to Major [Lochlin J.] Farrar at Monroe for duty.

(II) Camp of main body with train near Trinity West bank of the Washita [Ouachita] River adjacent to corn.

By order of
W.H. Parsons
Col. Comdg.
Robt C H Good A.D.C.

* * * * * * * * * * * * *

Hd. Qrs 12th Texas Dragoons
Near Vienna Sept 4/63

Spl. Order No -

The position of Surgeon of the 12 Tex Dragoons being made vacant by the promotion of Surg Thomas M. Matthews to chief Surg Cav Division Assistant Surgeon R.P. Sweatt is hereby recommended and nominated for the position of Surgeon 12th Texas Drags and will enter immediately upon the discharge of his duties

By order of J C Brown, Capt, Comdg
12 Texas Dragoons

* * * * * * * * * * * * *

Hd. Qrs. Forces in Front
Vienna Sept. 4th 1863

Special Order No. 21

(I) Captain McNeil's Squadron of La Cavalry is hereby ordered to report to Major [Lochlin J.] Farrar for duty at Monroe.

(II) Camp as main body with train near Trinity West bank of the Washita [Ouachita] River adjacent to corn

By order of W.H. Parsons
Col. comdg
Robt. C H Good A.D.C.

* * * * * * * * * * * * *

Hd Qurs Tex Cav Brig
Sept 8 1863

The Comdg Officer of 12 Tex Drags will have detailed one man for Brigade wagoner to drive Ordnance wagon to report to Maj [Thomas] Johns, immediately

By Order
A B [A. Bell] Burleson Lt Col
Comdg Brigade

A M Dechman
AAAG

* * * * * * * * * * * * *

Adjutant & Inspector Genl Office
Richmond Va Sept 9th 1863

Genl Order NO 121

I Paragraph 1064 of the Army Regulations 1107 of the Regulations of the Quarter Masters Department is ammended to read as followes: Officers are entitled to pay from the date of the acceptance of their appointment and from the date of promotion provided that Distributing officers who are required to give official bonds Shall forward the sum always duly executed with their letters of acceptance, and that their acceptance Shall take affect only from the date of the approval of the bonds by the War Department Notifications of the receipt and approval of Sade bonds will be forwarded to officers through the Chief of the Bureau to which they belong

II All officers of the Quartermaster Generals and Commissary Genl Department (except Such as hold Commissions in the regular army of the Confederate State appointed prior to—Commencement of the present Session of Congress (January 12th 1863) and whose bonds prior to the date of their order have not been filed in and approved by the War Department are hereby dropped provided that On Satisfactory evidence that Such failure has no[t] been the result of gross neglect the Commanding Genl may grant the officers concerned a Short leave of absence to make and forward their bonds and Shall report this fact to the Quartermaster Generals

III As applications for the revocations of the above order in any individual case will be entertained by the War Department If a vacancy be occasioned in any Brigade or regiment or at a Post application will be made for a new appointment in conformity to General Order No 8—1863 and the appointee in accepting his position will be held strictly to the requirements of proceeding Paragraph I

IV Officers of the Quartermaster Generals department who[se] [torn] appointment bear date subsequently to the 12th of (Jan) [torn] and who hav not filed bonds duly executed will be allowed a furlough for Such time not exceding Sixty dayes as may be necessary to enable them to execute their bonds

V Commanding officers will be careful to recommend for appointment as disbursing officers only Such persons as furnish reasonable assurance of their ability to execute the bonds requiared by law

VI All letters of appointment hereafter isued [*sic*] will be accompanied by a notification of the appointment that his official bond must be returned with his acceptance and that the latter will take effect only from the date at which said bond is approved

| | |
|---|---|
| Official | By Order of |
| J M Brandon | S [Samuel] Cooper |
| AA General | Adj & Insp General |

* * * * * * * * * * * * *

Hd Qrs. Forces in Front
Vienna La. September 9th 1863

Special Order No. 21a

Captain Thomas Johns A.Q.M. will turn over to Captain H.W. Kyser[69] Two Hundred Dollars to forage Sixty-five Horses under his comd. on detached service.

By order of
W.H. Parsons
Col. Comdg
J M Brandon Asst. Adjt. Genl.

[69] Company G, Twelfth Texas.

* * * * * * * * * * * * *

Head Qrs Forces in front
Vienna Sept 10. 63

Special Order No. 22

I Major L.J. [Lochlin J.] Farrar is hereby relieved from command as Out Post and will report with detachments of 12th & 19th Tex Cavalry to these Hd Qrs. for duty.

II Upon the withdrawal of Major L.J. Farrar's command Major [Richard L.] Capers will assume immediate command of out Posts.

By Order of
B.W. [Benjamin W.] Watson
Lt Col Comdg Forces in front
Robert C H Good A.D.C.

* * * * * * * * * * * * *

Hd Qrs. Forces in front
Vienna Sept 10. 63

Special Order No. 23

Major [Richard L.] Capers will immediately upon assuming command of Out Post send a party of men under in the command of a Commissioned Officer to arrest the Couriers on the Monroe & Harrisburg [Hamburg?] road who have deserted their post and gone home, prefer charges and send them under guard to these Hd Qrs with a list of the witnesses names

By order of
B W [Benjamin W.] Watson
Lt. Col. Comdg forces in front
Robert C H Good A.D.C.

* * * * * * * * * * * * *

Hd. Qrs. Forces in Front
Vienna La. Sept. 11th 1863.

Special Order No. 24

Major Thomas Johns A.Q.M. C.S.A. will furnish Lt. Getzendanner [W.H. Getzendaner] with One Hundred (100) Dollars as Qt. Master's funds, to defray the expenses of couriers between his place and Monroe If Major Johns has no funds he will make a requisition on the Sub. Dist. Qt. M.

By order of
W.H Parsons
Col. Commanding
Robt. C.H. Good A.D.C.

* * * * * * * * * * * * *

Hd. Qrs. Forces in front
Vienna La. Sept 11th 1863.

Special Order No. 25

Captain J.J. [Jefferson J.] Mallard A.C.S. C.S.A. will furnish Lieutenant Getzendanner [W.H. Getzendaner] with One Hundred (100) Dollars as commissary funds to defray the expenses of couriers between his place and Monroe. If Captain Mallard has no funds he will make a Requisition on Sub. Dist. C.S.

By order of
W.H Parsons
Col. Comdg
Robt. C. H Good A.D.C.

* * * * * * * * * * * * *

Office
Hed Quarters A& I Genl
Richmond Va Sept 11 1863

Genl Order No 122

I Commanding officers of Regiments Battallions & c will immediately on receipt there of cause to be made out and forward through the proper channels to Col J S Preston[70] Chief of the Bureau of Conscription a complete list of all persons held as Substitutes in the army in their respective commands the list will imbrace the Regt Company & date of enlistment and age of each Substitute with the name and Post Office of the principal. They will also in the Same Manner furnish a monthly roll of all deserters and absent without leave; this will be arranged according to the County and Congressional district to which, the parties belong; and will Set forth the time an[d] place of desertion in each case

II All Officers charged by Commanding Gen's with the duty of arresting and returning deserters and absentees will report to the commandant of conscripts in the respective states to which such officers are sent and will co-operate generally with enrolling officers in the discharge of the duties assigned to them

III The following Act of Congress is published for the information of all concerned "Every person not subject to the Rules and Articles of War who Shall procure or entice a soldier of the confederate states to desert or who shall purchase from any soldier his arms, uniform, clothing, or any part there of Shall upon legal conviction be fined at the discretion of the court having cognizance of the same in any sum not exceeding three Hundred dollars and be imprisoned not exceeding one year"

By Order
Official J.M. Brandon A.A.G. S. [Samuel] Cooper adjt & Ins Genl.

[70] Preston served as the superintendent of conscription in Richmond, Virginia.

* * * * * * * * * * * * *

Hd. Qrs. Forces in Front
Vienna La. September 11th 1863.

Special Order No. 26

(I) Major [Richard L.] Capers will send a commissioned officer with Ten men to Ouachita City to picket at that place without delay.

(II) Major Capers will instruct Officers commanding party that if any thing specially occurs in front he will forward two couriers one to report to Hd. Qrs. Out Post and one to these Hd. Qrs.

By order of
W.H. Parsons
Col. Commanding
Robt. C.H. Good A.D.C.

* * * * * * * * * * * * *

Hd. Qrs. Forces in Front
Vienna La. Sept 11th 1863

Special Order No. 27

Lieut. [John I.] Richardson[71] is hereby relieved from Picket at Ouachita City. He will report forthwith to these Hd. Qrs.

By order of
W.H Parsons
Col. Comdg
Robt. C H Good A.D.C.

* * * * * * * * * * * * *

Hd. Qrs. Forces in Front
Vienna La. Sept. 11th 1863.

Special Order No. 28

The convalescent of the Texas Cavalry Brigade will proceed under the direction of Captain [Appleton M.] Maddox[72] to Pisgah camp ground

[71] Company F, Twelfth Texas.

[72] Company B, Twelfth Texas.

* * * * * * * * * * * * *

Hd. Qrs. Forces in front
Vienna Sept. 15- 1863.

Special Order No. 29

Capt. R.E. Sanders[73] will take charge of four wagons furnished by Capt [William] Oliver A.Q.M. and go to Princeton Ark. to bring off clothing belonging to the 19th Texas Cavalry

By order of
W H Parsons
Col. Comdg
J M Brandon A.A.G.

* * * * * * * * * * * * *

Hd Qrs Forces in front
Vienna La Sept 15. 63

Special Order No. 30

Capt J.J. [Jefferson J.] Mallard A.C.S. C.S. Army will furnish funds for the substance of 14 men, 12 days, if Capt Mallard has not funds he will make a requisition on Chief C.S. Sub Dist No La

By order of
W H Parsons
Col Comdg
J M Brandon A.A.G.

* * * * * * * * * * * * *

Hd Qrs forces in front
Vienna La Sept 15. 63

Special Order No. 31

Major Thomas Johns A.Q.M. C.S. Army will furnish Capt. R E [Reuben E.] Saunders with funds to forage 35 animals 12 days if Major Johns has not the funds he will make a requisition on the Chief Q.M. of Sub Dist No La

By order of
W.H. Parsons
Col. Comdg
J M Brandon A.A.G.

[73] Company F, Nineteenth Texas. Reuben E. Sanders (also seen spelled Saunders) was forty years old when he enlisted in 1862. Bailey, *Between the Enemy and Texas*, 224-25.

* * * * * * * * * * * * *

Hd Qrs. Forces in Front
Vienna La Sept. 13th 1863.

Special Order No. 32

(I) Lieutenant [John I.] Richardson[74] of 12th Texas Dragoons and Lt. [John J.] Greenwade[75] of 19th Texas Cav. and 60 men of Texas Cav. Brigade will report to Maj. I.W. [Isaac N.] Dennis A.A. & A. Ins. Genl. as body guards to Brig. Genl. Herbert [Paul O. Hébert], and remain in their present camp ground until further orders. The Lt. commanding body guard will report daily to Major Dennis for orders

(II) The Lieutenant commanding guard will furnish a courier to connect with couriers from Homer.[76]

(III) The first courier stand will be seven miles from Vienna at the first house beyond Bowdie Creek.

By order of
W.H. Parsons
Col. Comdg
J M Brandon A.A.G.

* * * * * * * * * * * * *

Hd Qrs. Forces in Front
Vienna La. Sept. 15th 1863

Special Order No. 32 a.

Captain Thomas Johns A.Q.M. will turn over to Captain R.E. Sanders[77] Ninety Dollars to forage thirty-five Horses ten days.

By order of
W H Parsons
Col. Comdg
J M Brandon A.A.G.

[74] Company F, Twelfth Texas.

[75] Company D, Nineteenth Texas.

[76] Homer is located northeast of Minden, less than twenty miles from the Arkansas border.

[77] Company E, Nineteenth Texas.

* * * * * * * * * * * * *

Adjutant & Inspector Gen'ls Office
Richmond Sept. 16. 1863.

Gen. Order. No. 123.

The following orders is published for the information of all concerned

Exchange Notice. No. 6.

The following Confederate Officers and men captured at Vicksburg Miss. July 4th 1863, and subsequently paroled have been duly exchanged and are hereby released

1st The officers and men of Genl C.L. [Carter L.] Stephensons division

2d The officers and men of Genl [John S.] Bowens division

3d The officers and men of Brig. Genl [John C.] Moores Brigade

4th The officers and men of the second Texas Regiment

5th The officers and men of Wauls Legion.

6th Also all confederate officers and men who have been at city point at any time previous to July the 25 1863 have been duly exchanged and ar[e] hereby So declaird

Ro Ould[78]
Agent of Exchange
Richmond Sept 12th 1863

Official
J M Brandon
AAG

By Order
S [Samuel] Cooper
Adj & Insp General

* * * * * * * * * * * * *

Hd. Qrs. Tex. Cav. Brig.
Homer La. Sept. 18, 1863

Special Order No. 1

Capt. J.P. Brown[79] will furnish one commissioned officer and 7 men to report to these Hd. Qrs. at Thompson's House immediately to act as couriers between his place and Camden Ark

By order of
W.H Parsons
Col. Comdg
Robt. C.H. Good A.D.C.

[78] Robert Ould served as the Confederate agent for the exchange of prisoners.

[79] Company K, Twelfth Texas.

* * * * * * * * * * * * *

Hd. Qrs. Texas Cav. Brigade
Homer La. Sept 18, 1863

Special Order No. 2

Captain [Appleton M.] Maddox[80] will forward all official communications he may have for these Hd Qrs by special courier direct.

By order of
W.H. Parsons
Col. Comdg.
Robt. C.H Good A.D.C.

* * * * * * * * * * * * *

Head Qrs. Tex. Cav. Brigade
Homer La. Sept. 19th 1863

Special Order No. 3

Lieutenant Isaac A. Clare Commanding Section Pratts' Battery will go at once to Shreveport La. to draw money to buy horses for his battery—Captain Wm. Oliver A.Q.M. & acting Dist. A.Q.M. has no funds on hand, and horses being actually necessary to move the guns.

By order of
W.H. Parsons
Col Commanding
J.M. Brandon A.A.G.

* * * * * * * * * * * * *

Head Qrs. Texas Cav. Brigade
Homer La. Sept 21st 1863

Special Order No. 4

Captain J.C. Brown[81] Comdg. at Camp will detail 8 select men and 2 comd. officers to report to these Hd. Qrs. early tomorrow morning to go on scout—also one special courier.

By order of
W H Parsons
Col. Comdg.
Robt. C H Good A.D.C.

[80] Company B, Twelfth Texas.

[81] Company E, Twelfth Texas.

* * * * * * * * * * * * *

Hd. Qrs. Texas Cavalry Brigade
Homer La. Sept 22d 1863

Special Order No. 5

Major L.J. [Lochlin J.] Farrar[82] will repair immediately to Reserve Camp and assume command of same—

By order of
W H Parsons
Col. Commanding
Robt. C H Good A.D.C.

* * * * * * * * * * * * *

Hd Qrs. Tex Cav Brigade
Homer La September 22. 63

Special Order No. 6

Major Thomas Johns A.Q.M. C.S. Army will proceed to Shreveport on official business

By order of
W.H. Parsons
Col. Comdg Tex Cav Brigade
Robert C H Good A.D.C.

* * * * * * * * * * * * *

Hd Qrs Tex Cav Brigade
Homer La Sept 22. 63

Special Order No. 7

Lt. R.B. Shaw[83] of 12th Tex Dgs is hereby ordered to repair to Monticello Ark for the purpose of establishing a picket of observation

By order of
W H Parsons
Col Comdg Tex Cav Brigade

Robert C H Good
A.D.C.

[82] Twelfth Texas.

[83] Company G.

* * * * * * * * * * * * *

Hd Qrs Tex Cav Brigade
Homer La Sept 22. 63

Special Order No. 8

Lt. Arch [Archibald] Graham[84] of 19th Texas Cav. is hereby ordered to repair to Harrisburg [Hamburg?] Ark.[85] for the purpose of establishing at picket of observation

By order of
Robert C H Good
A.D.C.

W H Parsons
Col. Comdg Tex Cav Brigade

* * * * * * * * * * * * *

Adjt. and Ins. Gen'ls Office
Richmond Va Sept. 22 1863

General. Order. No. 124

I Potatoes (sweet) gathered under the tax Law by Commissaries and Quartermasters at or within reach of places where hospitals are located will be transferred (Invoices and receipts being given) to the Medical Officers in charge of the hospitals to be cared for and secured against influences of frost & c for the use of the sick, Or for mess when the hospitals are more convenient of access than depot & may deliver their potatoes (tax in kind) to the Medical officers in charge taking receipts which will be acknowledged by the tax agents

II The pay of Surgeons (private physicians) employed under General Order No 82 adjt & Ins. Genls. Office of 1862 is increased to Six dollars per diem until further orders.

III "Assistant Medical directors" and assistant medical Inspectors not being authorized the titles will not be used,

IV The extra pay for soldiers detailed for duty as commissary Sergeants by the act of Congress approved May 1st 1863, will be paid upon the Muster and pay rolls of the companies to which they belong by the quartermasters charged with the duty of paying troops

By Order
Official
J M Brandon A.A.G.

S. [Samuel] Cooper
Adjt. & Ins. Gen'l

[84] Company B.

[85] Hamburg is in extreme southeast Arkansas in Ashley County.

* * * * * * * * * * * * *

Adjutant & Inspector Generals Office
Richmond September 186[3]

General Order No 125

I Information having been received of repeated misconstructions and violations of paragraph XII General Order No 85—1862 it is reiterated that no persons liable to conscription will be permitted under any circumstances to volunteer in regiment Battalion or Company's organized Since the 16th of Apprile [*sic*] 1862 except Such as were organized under the provisions of the Act of Congress of that date Entitled "An Act further to provide for the public defence"

II No authority exists for organizing new companies or portions of Companies now in Servis [*sic*]

III It Shall be the duty of Commandants of Conscripts on information of persons being recived [*sic*] in to Companies contrary to the provisions of this order to make immediate requisitions for Such persons on the officer Commanding and on failure of the officer to return the persons So received to the camp of instruction the Commandant Shall report the Matter with the facts of the case to the Bureau of Conscription, to be directed by the Department

IV No officer Commanding whose Company reaches the maximum allowed by Regulations Shall be permitted to receve [*sic*] recruits either as volanteers on in any other form

V No officer Commanding Shall accept or Muster in persons of conscript age unless Such persons Shall first exhibit a certificate approved by an enrolling officer Stating ~~first~~ that he has volenteered and Selected his Company which Company is allowed to receve [*sic*] recruit

VI The Bureau of Conscription is Charged with the establishment of Such regulations as will enforce the order

VII Paragraph I General Order No 122 September 1863 is so modified as to read as follows Commanding officers of regiments Battalions & c will immediatly on receipt heare of cause to be made out and forwared through proper channels to Col J S Best Cheaf of the Bureau of Conscription a completed list of all persons receved [*sic*] as Substitutes in the Army in their respective commands this list will embrace the regiment company date of enlistme[nt]and age of each Substitute with the name post office and date of enlistment of the principal It will allso [*sic*] State whether the Substitute is Now Serving or has died or been killed in action or or [*sic*] discharged from Servis or whether withe the date and circumstance of Such death discharge or desertion

They will allsoe [*sic*] in the Same Manner furnish a Monthly roll of all deserters an[d] absen without leave The roll will be arranged according to the county and Congressional district to which the persons be longs and will Set forth the time an place of desertion in Each Case

Hed Quarters Tex Cav Brig
Official
J M Brandon AAG

By Order of
S [Samuel] Cooper
Adjt & Insp General

* * * * * * * * * * * * *

Hd. Qrs. Tex. Cav. Brigade
Homer La. Sept. 23d 1863

Special Order No. 9

Maj. Samuel Boyer Davis is here for the purpose of inspecting the troops of this Brigade you will have your command prepared for inspection to morrow morning at 8 o'clock.

By order of
W H Parsons
Col. Comdg.
Robt C H Good A.D.C.

To Captain J.C. Brown
Comdg. Camp

* * * * * * * * * * * * *

Hd Qrs. Tex. Cav. Brigade
Homer La. Sept. 23d 1863

Special Order No. 10

As Maj. Samuel Boyer Davis is here for the purpose of inspecting the troops of this Brigade you will have your command prepared for inspection this evening at 5 o'clock.

By order of
W.H. Parsons
Col Commanding
Robt. C H Good A.D.C.

Major L.J. [Lochlin J.] Farrar
Comdg Reserve Camp

* * * * * * * * * * * * *

Head Qrs. Texas Cav Brigade
Homer La. Sept. 23d 1863

Special Order No. 11

Col. [Nathaniel M.] Burford will furnish an entire list of officers entitled to promotion according to seniority and in case a vacancy occurs in the rank of jr. 2d Lt. he will order an election and forward a list of those elected together with the list of other promotions to this office which the Brigade Commanders will publish sending one copy to Secretary of War and one to yourself.

By order of
W H Parsons
Col. Commanding
Robt. C H Good A.D.C.

* * * * * * * * * * * * *

Head Qrs. Texas Cav. Brigade
Sept. 23d 1863

Special Order No. 12

(I) Captain Brown will report with his command to Col. [Nathaniel M.] Burford at the camp at Pisgah

(II) Col. Burford will take command of the encampment and keep up the orders and regulations heretofore adopted.

(III) The Artillery will be encamped at or near the church and the men of the different companies of the well [convalescent] camp will join the companies at the encampment, and the officers will take charge of their respective companies

(IV) There will no longer be known a convalescent camp, Camp Pisgah will until removal, be known as the regular Brigade encampment.

By order of
W H Parsons
Col Commanding
Robt. C H Good A.D.C.

* * * * * * * * * * * * *

Head Qrs. Forces in Front
Homer La. Sept. 24th 1863

Special Order No. 13

Col. [Nathaniel M.] Burford will have a consolidated morning Report of the Brigade made out immediately and sent to these Head Qrs.

By order of
W.H Parsons
Col. Commanding
Robt. C.H. Good A.D.C.

* * * * * * * * * * * * *

Head Qrs. Forces Front
Homer La. Sept. 25th 1863

Special Order No. 14

Col. [Nathaniel M.] Burford will order the two Batteries back to the camp from which they came yesterday.

By order of
W H Parsons
Col. Commanding
Robt. C H Good A.D.C.

* * * * * * * * * * * * *

Hd. Qrs. Forces in Front
Northern La. Sept. 26th 1863

Special Order No. 15

Private J.G. Standard will report to Lieutenant Col. [Richard L.] Capers for duty.

By order of
W.H. Parsons
Col. Commanding
J.M. Brandon A.A.G.

* * * * * * * * * * * * *

Hd. Qrs. Forces in Front
Homer Sept. 26th 1863

Special Order No. 16

Lieutenant Isaac A. Claire Comdg 2nd Sec. Pratts Battery will remain at Camp Pisgah with his section of Battery.

By order of
W H Parsons
Col. Commanding
J M Brandon A.A.G.

* * * * * * * * * * * * *

Hd Qrs. Forces in front
Homer La Sept 26. 63

Special Order No. 17

Col. [Nathaniel M.] Burford will arrest and place under charge of Brigade Guard J.G. Smith under charges preferred against him by Col. [A. Bell] Burleson

By order of
(signed) W.H. Parsons
Col. Comdg

* * * * * * * * * * * * *

Hd. Qrs. forces in front No line La
Homer La. Sept 26. 63

Special Order No. 18

I Col. [Nathaniel M.] Burford Comdg Cav Brigade with detail of one commissioned 3 non-com,—and 15 privates, to guard the prisoners captured by Col [A. Bell] Burleson, and forward said prisoners under escort of said guard to therefore to be delivered over to the Post Commander with accompanying <u>report</u> [to] Col. Burleson

II Col Burleson will relieve Lt. Wilson and his men of further guard duty over the prisoners.

III Col Burford will direct Lt. Wilson to report to Col Burleson

By order of
(signed) W H Parsons
Col Comdg
forces in front N line La

* * * * * * * * * * * * *

Hd. Qrs. Forces in Front. North line La.
Homer La. Sept. 28th 1863

Special Order No. 19

Maj. A.J. Byrd C.S.P.A. C.S. will take charge of the Commissary Department of the Texas Cavalry Brigade.

By order of
W.H. Parsons
Col. Comdg.
J.M. Brandon A.A.G.

* * * * * * * * * * * * *

Adj & Inspt General Office
Richmond Va Spt 28th 1863

General Order No 126

In order to avoid all difficulty with respect to the payment of officers absent from their commands and who have not received Commissions or letters of appointmen[t] it is ordered that all Such officers Shall before leaving their companies be furnished with a transcript from the muster rolls of a certificate in leu their of may be convient Setting out the full name rank and date thereof of Such officers and that he is borne on the muster roll as such. These transcripts or certificates will be signed by the Commanding of the Regiments and Company and will be equivalent with the pay officer to the commission or letter of appointment referred to in Paragraph I General orders No 121 of 1863,

This provision however is not designed to dispense with the requirements of General orders No 28 Par II and III current series

II Paragraph I General orders No 116 Adjt. and Inspector Generals office is so modified as to read as follows "Generals or other officers Commanding departments armies in the field post or Garrisons will cause all deserters, straggler or other absentees from duty and all person liable to Military service found within their lines and not belonging to their commands to be forthwith arrested and turned over to the nearest enrolling officer whose duty it shall be to forward such absentee to their proper commands or in case of conscripts to assign them to service at the discretion of the commandant of conscripts of the state.

| | |
|---|---|
| Official | By Order |
| J M Brandon | S [Samuel] Cooper |
| asst. adjt. Gen'l | Adjutant & Ins. Genl. |

* * * * * * * * * * * * *

Head Qrtrs Forces in Front.
North Line La. Homer La. Oct 1st 1863

Special Order No. 20

Maj. A.J. Byrd C.S.A. will proceed to Shreveport on business for his Department.

By order of
W.H. Parsons
Col Comdg.
J.M. Brandon A.A. Genl.

* * * * * * * * * * * * *

Adj & Insp General's Office
Richmond Va Oct 2d 1863

General Order No 130

I The evils resulting from the prolonged absence of Soldiers who have obtained furloughs on account of sickness being greatly on the increase, the attention of officers of the Army is directed to the 7th paragraph of General Order No 69 of 1863 from this office and strict compliance their with is enjoined.

II Commanders of companies who _____ to the requirements of the aforesaid orders No 69 received from exam[an]ing bo[a]rds Notices of furloughs granted by them are requiared to make out and forward monthly to the Superintendents of the bureaus of Conscription (Col J S Preston at Richmond Va or Brigade General S J Pillow at Marietta Ga as the case may reqiuer) list of all men So furloughed and who do not promptly returne to their Companies at the expirations of the time granted them; and it ~~may~~ will be the duty of the Superientendent receving Such lists to direct the proper Enrolling officer to arrest and [have] returned to their Companies without delay all persons who are thus reported and found absent without proper authority

III Payment upon affidavit to Soldiers, Sick or Wounded in hospitals who ar[e] unprovided with discriptive lists will hereafter be limited to four Months pay

By Order of<br>
S [Samuel] Cooper<br>
Adjutant & Inspt General

Official<br>
J M Brandon

* * * * * * * * * * * * *

Hd. Qrs. Forces in Front North Line La.<br>
Homer Oct. 3d 1863

Special Order No. 21

Col [Nathaniel M.] Burford will have One Commissioned, three non commissioned officers and fifteen Privates detailed for Picket duty to report at these head qrs. at once.

By order of<br>
W.H. Parsons<br>
Col Commanding<br>
J.M. Brandon A.A. Genl.

* * * * * * * * * * * * *

Head Qrs. Forces in Front North Line La.<br>
Homer La Oct 3d 1863

Special Order No. 22

In obedience to instructions from Hd. Qrs. Sub. Dist. North La. Maj. Thomas Johns Quarter Master Texas Cav. Brigade will make requisition on Captain [William] Oliver Chf. Q.M. for transportation and cooking utensils to supply Brigade.

By order of W.H. Parsons<br>
Col. Commanding<br>
J.M. Brandon A.A. Genl..

* * * * * * * * * * * * *

Adj & Insp Genl Office<br>
Richmond Oct 5 1863

Genl Order No 132

I Cadets having been required by Genl Order 65 September 9 1862 to report to this office, those who have not complied with the terms of that order, and who fail to do So, either personly or by letter fo[r] the ensuing thirty dayes will be dropped from the rolls of the Army

II Officer of the Quartermaster Genl and Commisary Departments who are in charge of Depots will receive from officers collecting the tax in Kind and receipt for all product belonging [to] their respective Departments which may be invoiced to them and provide storehouses for the same

| | |
|---|---|
| Official | By Order of |
| J M Brandon | S [Samuel] Cooper |
| A A Genl | Adjt & Inspor Genl |

* * * * * * * * * * * * *

Hed Qrs Sub District North La
Vienna La Oct 6th 1863

Extract
Special Order No 103

I Private J Wheatstone of comp F 12th La Reg. Vols being seperated from his Command East of the Mississippi river and having reported for duty will report to the comdg officer of Co B. 12th Texas Dragoons for duty until further ordered

| | |
|---|---|
| | By Order of |
| Comdg Officer | Brig Genl P O Hebert [Paul O. Hébert] |
| Co B 12th Texas Dragoons | Isaac N Dennis A A & A Ins Genl |

* * * * * * * * * * * * *

Hd. Qrs. Forces in front & c
Homer La. Oct 9- 1863

Special Order No. 23

It having come to the knowledge of the Col. Commanding that men belonging to the Texas Cavalry Brigade in the swamps are now Committing depredations on the property of citizens and remaining absent from their commands without leave. Sergeant Thomas [H.] Patterson[86] will select from the Command Eight men and go into the swamps and arrest all men belonging to this Command and order them to Camps.

By order
W H Parsons
Col. Commanding
J M Brandon A.A.Gnl.

[86] Company F, Twelfth Texas.

* * * * * * * * * * * * *

Head Qrs. Forces in front
Homer October 9- 1863

"Extract"
Special Order No. 24

Leave of absence of ten days is granted Surgeon R.P. Sweat [Sweatt][87] of 12th Texas Dragoons at the expiration of which time he will report to his Regiment for duty

By order of
W H Parsons
Col. Comdg
J M Brandon AA Gnl.

* * * * * * * * * * * * *

Hd qrs. forces in Front N line La.
Homer Oct 9 1863

Special Order No. 25

Maj. A.J. Byrd C.S. will proceed to Alexandria La on business with his department

By order of
W H Parsons Col Comdg
J M Brandon A.A.G.

* * * * * * * * * * * * *

Hd. Qrs. Forces in Front North line La
Homer La. Oct. 10th 1863

Special Order No. 26

(I) Lieut. E.W. [Edward W.] Hunt,[88] 19th Texas Cavalry with four men and will proceed at once to Dallas Texas for the purpose of bringing Blankets for this Command.

(II) He will procure wagons at Dallas to bring back the Blankets

(III) In case he cannot hire wagon and teams he will impress them giving receipts for them and return to Camp with all possible dispatch.

By order of
W.H. Parsons
Col. Comdg.
J M Brandon A.A.G.

[87] Company H, Twelfth Texas.

[88] Company K, Nineteenth Texas.

* * * * * * * * * * * * *

Hd qrs. Forces in front North line La
Homer Oct 10- 1863

Special Order No. 27

Maj. Thos [Thomas] Johns Brigade Q.M. will turn over to Lieut. E.W. Hunt Two Hundred dollars to defray expenses in going after Blankets for the Command

By order of
W H Parsons
Col Comdg
J.M. Brandon A.A.Gnl

* * * * * * * * * * * * *

Hd Quarters 12th Texas Dragoons
Camp Pisgah La Oct 11th 63

Special Order No

A Board of survey will assem[ble] immediately at the wagon yard for the purpose of condemning some old harness.

The Board will be comprised of the following named officers

| | |
|---|---|
| Capt Jno. C. Brown | Co E 12th Tex |
| " J.P Brown | Co K " " |
| Lt J M Noble | " G " " |

A report will be made immediately to these Head Qurs by the Board in writing

By order of
L J [Lochlin J.] Farrar Major
Comdg 12th Tex Dragoons

We the under signed Commissioners appointed to examine harness & c belonging to the Quartermasters department of the 12th Regiment Texas Dragoons report the following list of Harness is absolutely worn out and unfit for service and we order the same dropped from the Roll of Quarter Mast Property and used for repairing other harnesses

(35) Thirty five Blind Bridles
(13) Thirteen Breeching
(26) Twenty six Back Straps
(27) Twenty seven Back Bands
(40) Forty Belly Bands
(9) Nine Lead Lines

Camp Pisgah Oct 11th 1863

| | |
|---|---|
| J C Brown | Capt Co E 12th T C |
| J P Brown | " " K |
| J.M. Noble | 1st Lieut Co G. |

* * * * * * * * * * * * *

Hd Qrs. Forces in front North line La
Homer La Oct. 12- 1863

Special Order No. 28

I Col. Nat M. Burford will detail a sufficient number of men and send to Rondo for Clothing and Bagage of the 19th Texas Cavalry.

II As the quarter master has no transportation a Commissioned Officer will be detailed to go with the men and hire wagons to transport the bagage

III In the event that wagons cannot be hired the officer in Command of the detail is hereby authorized to impress wagons and teams, complying with instructions in regard to impressments.

By order of
W H Parsons
Col. Comdg
J M Brandon Asst. adjt Genl

* * * * * * * * * * * * *

Hd. Qrs Forces North Front
Homer La October 15th 1863

Special Order No. 29

Major L.J. [Lochlin J.] Farrar Comdg. 12th Tex Dragoons will see that the ordnance report of his comd is sent up to these Hd Qrs weekly according to form herewith enclosed

By order of
W H Parsons Col. Comg
J M Brandon A.A.Genl

* * * * * * * * * * * * *

Hd. Qrs. forces North front La.
Homer La Oct 16- 1863

Special Order No. 30

In obedience to orders from Hd. qrs. Sub. Dist. north La the Q.M. of Tex Cav. Brigade will send purchasing agent at once to buy leather to mend briddles and saddles of Tex Cav. Brigade.

By order of
W H Parsons
Col. Commanding
J M Brandon asst. adjt. Genl.

* * * * * * * * * * * * *

Head Quarters 12th Tex Dragoons
Camp Pisgah Oct 19th 1863

Special order No -

Captain Hismith [M.B. Highsmith] Company (D) 12th Tex Drags will report to me tomorrow night 20th inst, on the most practible route towards Shreveport La, with Company Baggage & c.

By order
A.B. [A. Bell] Burleson Lt Col
Comdg & c
W.G. Vardell Adjt

* * * * * * * * * * * * *

Head Quarters 12th Texas Dragoons
Camp Pisgah Oct 19th 1863

Special Order No -

Lieut J.W. [John W.] Walden[89] 12th Reg Texas Drags is hereby appointed Quarter Master Tex Drags, date of Appointment to take place Oct 1st 1863

By Order of
L.J. [Lochlin J.] Farrar Maj Comdg
W.G. Vardell Adjt

[89] Company B.

* * * * * * * * * * * * *

Hd Qrs. Forces North front
Homer La Oct 21st. 63

Special Order No. 31

Major [A.J.] Byrd will furnish Lieutenant Getzendanner [W.H. Getzendaner] with Two hundred & fifty dollars for subsistance of the courier line between Homer & Camden

By order of
W.H. Parsons
Col. Commdg
Robert C H Good A.D.C.

* * * * * * * * * * * * *

Hd Qrs. Forces North front
Homer La. Oct 21st 63

Special Order No. 32

Col [Nathaniel M.] Burford will direct all officers in charge of courier lines to call on Major [A.J.] Byrd for funds to defray the expenses as subsistance

By order of
W.H. Parsons
Col. Comdg
Robert C H Good A.D.C.

* * * * * * * * * * * * *

Hd. Qrs. forces North front La.
Homer La. Oct. 22- 1863

Special Order No. 34

Private I. Nussbaum of 2nd Sec. Pratts Battery is hereby detailed to go to Shreveport to bring out ordnance Stores for his Sec. of Battery

By order of
W.H. Parsons
Col Commanding
J M Brandon asst adjt Genl

* * * * * * * * * * * * *

Hd Qrs. Forces North front La
Homer Oct. 26th 1863

Special Order No. 35

Maj. A.J. Byrd Brigade C.S. will pay over to [_____] Commanding courier line from Vienna to Homer money to pay board of couriers

By order of
W.H. Parsons
Col. Comdg
J M Brandon A.A. Genl

* * * * * * * * * * * * *

Hd. qrs North front La
Homer La. Oct. 26- 1863

Special Order No. 36

Corporal W.C. [William C.] McEntire[90] with privates [James T.] Wales and West[91] of Comp. (I) 12th Texas Dragoons are hereby detailed to go in pursuit of some men with stolen property who are going in the direction of Shreveport and will report back to their company for duty in five days for duty[92]

By order of
W.H. Parsons
Col. Commanding
J M Brandon A.A.Gnl

[90] Also spelled McIntire, Company I.

[91] Either David M. or James W. West, Company I.

[92] The inactivity for the troopers led to an increase in illegal activity. Henry Orr told his sister on November 8 that even the horsemen's "sport" often brought complaints from local residents. "Have to hunt hogs with dogs," he wrote, "and when we find them they seem to have a spirit akin to those we read about which you remember ran into the sea, but here they make for the worst thickets and sometimes into bayous and lakes. We get along very well with the people as a general thing, but sometimes the 'hog scout' catches fits from some old women who have not the proper control of their tongues. We are as sassy with them as our orders will admit." Henry Orr to "Sister," November 8, 1863, in Anderson, ed., *Campaigning with Parsons's Brigade*, 124-25.

* * * * * * * * * * * * *

Hd qrs. forces North front La
Homer La. Oct 27 63

Special Order No. 37

Maj. A.J. Byrd Brigade C.S. Tx Cav Brigade will pay Capt. John C. Brown[93] an acct of (624) Six Hundred and twenty four Dollars for commutation of Rations while acting under orders from Brig. Genl [James M.] Hawes for 52 men 16 days beginning on the 13th & ending on the 28th day of Dec. 1863

By order of
W H Parsons
Col Commanding
J M Brandon A.A.Gnl

* * * * * * * * * * * * *

Hd. Qrs. Forces North front La
Homer La. Nov. 5/63

Special Order No. 38

Private A.M. Walker of Co. "B" 12th Texas Dragoons & John Steen of Co "C" 12th Texas Dragoons will go forward and join their respective Companies now under Lt. Col. [A. Bell] Burleson at Marshal [Marshall] Texas or wherever they may be.

By order of
W H Parsons
Col. Comdg.
J M Brandon A.A. Genl.

* * * * * * * * * * * * *

Hd. Qrs. Forces North front La
Homer La. Nov. 5. 1863

Special Order No. 39

Sergt. Dennis in Comdg. Pickets will pay over to men under his comd. twenty-five dollars. Commutation money placed in his hands for that purpose.

By order of
W.H. Parsons
Col. Comdg.
J M Brandon A.A. Genl

[93] Company E, Twelfth Texas.

* * * * * * * * * * * * *

Hd. Qrs. Forces North front La.
Homer La. Nov. 6- 1863

Special Order No. 40

Maj. A.J. Byrd Brigade C.S. Tex. Cav. Brigade will send forward purchasing agent in the direction of Camden Ark. Via. Lisbon, to purchase supplies for the command.

The command will travel the road in which courier line is established.

By order of
W H Parsons
Col. Comdg.
J M Brandon

* * * * * * * * * * * * *

Hd. Qrs. Forces North Front La.
Homer, La. Nov. 6. 1863

Special Order No. 41

Captain Thomas Johns Brigade Q.M. Texas Cav. Brigade will send forage Master in the direction of Camden Ark. to procure forage for the command.

The road to be traveled is the one on which courier line has been established Via Lisbon.

By order of
W H Parsons
Col. Comdg.
J M Brandon A.A. Genl.

* * * * * * * * * * * * *

Hd. Qrs. Tex. Cav. Brigade
Camp Pisgah La. Nov. 6. 63

Special Order No. 42

Maj. John B Williams[94] of 19th Tex Cav and Capt. Jos. P. [Joseph P.] Weir of Company (A) & Capt. M B Highsmith Co D 12th Texas Dragoons will proceed at once to Shreveport on business for this command

By order of
W H Parsons
Col. Command
J M Brandon asst adj Genl

[94] Williams, a merchant from Hillsboro, had come to Texas from Georgia. He was twenty-eight years old when he enlisted as a captain in Company D; he proved to be a popular major in the Nineteenth Texas. Bailey, *Between the Enemy and Texas*, 41.

* * * * * * * * * * * * *

Hd. Qrs. Tex. Cav. Brigade
Camp Pisgah La Nov 6- 1863

Special Order No. 43

Lieut. Getzendanner [W.H. Getzendaner] with six men will proceed in advance of the command in the direction of Camden Ark. as a Picket of observation and report regularly to this command. The Col. Commanding not being fully appraised of the condition of things in that country enjoins upon Lieut. Getzendanner to use every exertion to keep himself posted and report to this office or on the march daily or oftener if necessary

By order of
W.H. Parsons
Col. Comdg.
J.M. Brandon A.A.G.

* * * * * * * * * * * * *

Hd. Qrs. Tex Cav Brigade
Camp Pisgah La Nov. 6, 63

Special Order, No. 44

Capt. M.B. Highsmith of Co (D) 12th Texas Dragoons will proceed at once to Shreveport La. on official business and by the consent of Lt. Genl. E Kirby Smith can go on to Bastrop Tex to get a horse and return without delay to his Regiment wherever it may be.

By Order of
W H. Parsons
Col. Commanding
Jas. M. Brandon asst. adj Genl

* * * * * * * * * * * * *

Head quarters Texas Cavalry Brigade
Camp Pisgah La. Nov 6. 1863

Special Order No. 45

Capt. Thomas Johns Brigade Quarter Master Tex Cavalry Brigade will remain at Camp Pisgah a few days to settle business of his department and will proceed to Shreveport La to get funds to pay the troops of this Command

By Order of
W H Parsons
Col. Comdg
J M Brandon asst adj Genl

* * * * * * * * * * * * *

Head Qrs forces North front
Homer La Nov 8- 1863

Special Order No. 46

Actg. asst Surgeon W G. McInnis will report to Lt. Col. A.B. [A. Bell] Burleson at Marshall Texas for duty

By Order of
W H Parsons
Col. Comdg.
J M Brandon asst adjt Genl

* * * * * * * * * * * * *

Hd Quarters Dept Trans Miss
Shreveport La Nov 10th 1863

General Order No 52

The following notice of Exchange is published for the information and guidance of all concerned

Exchange Notice 7—

The following Confe[de]rate officers and men are hereby declaired duly exchanged 1st All officers and men captured and paroled at any time previous to the 1st of September 1863 This Section however is not intended to include any officers or men captured at Vicksburge July 4th 1863 except Such as were declaired exchanged by Exchange Notice No 6 September 12th 1863 or are Specifically Named in this Notice. But it does embrase all deliveries made at City Point, or other places before Sept 1st 1863 and with the limitations above named all captures at Port Hudson or any other place where parties were released on Parole 2nd The Staff of General [John C.] Pemberton [Carter L.] Stevenson [John S.] Bowen [William E.] Baldwin [John C.] Moore [Seth M.] Barton S D [Stephen D.] Lee Cummings [Alfred Cumming] Han [Roger W. Hanson] and of Colonels [Daniel H.] Reynolds, [Francis M.] Cockrell and Dockray [Thomas P. Dockery] The officers are men belonging to the Engineer Corps and Sappers and Miners, and the 4th and 46th Mississippi Regiments all Captured at Vicksburg July 4th 1863 3rd The General officers captured a Vicksburg July 4th 1863 were declared duly exchanged July 13th 1863

Robrt Ould
Agent of Exchange
By Command of
Lieut General E Kirby Smith
S S Anderson AAG

Official
J M Brandon
AAG

## CHAPTER 5

# ARKANSAS

## November 12-December 31, 1863

During the last weeks of 1863 Parsons saw his regiments scattered all across the Trans-Mississippi. Several companies left for Texas prior to the brigade returning to Arkansas. Sending the horsemen home would alleviate two pressing problems: the shortage of forage for the animals and the rising number of civilians who complained about the men's behavior. In a more practical sense, state units serving on the West Texas frontier needed reinforcements. Not only did the governor have to deal with increased raids from Kiowas and Comanches, but the region had become a haven for dissidents avoiding Confederate service. Parsons's men had orders from the Bureau of Conscription to hunt for draft evaders and deserters. Several companies from the Twelfth Texas under captains Tom Haley, J. Em. Hawkins, H.W. Kyser, A.M. Maddux, and William G. Veal, as well as Captain Allen Beard's[1] company from the Nineteenth Texas, accompanied Lieutenant Colonel Bell Burleson to the Lone Star State around Halloween.[2]

While there was a lull in the fighting, the Confederate authorities tried once again to settle the command dispute between the two colonels, Carter and Parsons. Thomas J. Churchill, a brigadier general who ranked both, was placed over the Texans shortly before Christmas. George Ingram of the Twelfth Texas lamented, "It turns out that General Churchill superceeds Col.

[1] Beard was forty-two years old in 1862. He was a native of Tennessee who had enlisted in Dallas County. He gave his occupation as sheriff and claimed $1,200 in real estate and $1,500 in personal estate. Ibid.

[2] Henry Orr wrote on October 28 that six companies of the Twelfth and one from the Nineteenth had gone to Texas "to gather *conscripts* and *deserters*." Anderson, ed., *Campaigning with Parsons' Brigade*, 123. On the first of September General Kirby Smith had ordered the troopers to prepare to go to Texas to deal with bands of jayhawkers, deserters, and conscripts. See the *OR* 26, 1:194-95. See also, David Paul Smith, *Frontier Defense in the Civil War: Texas' Rangers and Rebels* (College Station: Texas A & M University, 1992).

Parsons in the command of this Brigade. I could weep like a child if it [would] do any good. Our Brigade is *ruined, ruined, ruined.* Last night the men slept but very little. The most intense excitement prevailed. They threaten to leave. It was all the officers could do to prevent them from going off by promising them that they would try to get the order countermanded and have Parsons restored." Frantic over recent events, Ingram worried, "I do not think that can be done and I fear the consequences to night." Another soldier moaned that Holmes "has taiken Col. Parsons away from us as Brg. Gen & put & Arkansawer over us." The men, he believed, were "dissatisfyed with it & say wee wont surve unde[r] him." Ingram described the chaos when he wrote: "The men now are shouting at the top of their voices 'Hurrah for Parsons, dam the Arkansaw General' and say they will have Parsons or no one. The Col. is absent, perhaps will be here to night. If he comes in time he may yet reconcile the men. No *other* man can. Old Holmes has done all he can against Parsons. . . . Heretofore there has been fewer desertions from this Brigade than any other but we cannot say so much longer."[3]

Many troopers saddled their horses, preparing to depart for Texas in protest. Only their officers' pleas convinced them to stay in camp while a delegation petitioned Holmes for Parsons's reinstatement. George Ingram thought Holmes would refuse while another soldier observed that it looked "mytey Bad." Trooper Archie Parks claimed that "the Texians all hate General Holms so bad that they want to kill him and some of them will do it if they get a chance at him. He dont like us ether he says that we are good fighters but he says we are a pack of damd theaves he givs us a bad name worse than we are."[4]

Demonstrations continued, and the troopers "called for Parsons or no one. When the colonel arrived in camp, the men ran toward his horse, throwing their hats in the air and shouting: 'Col. Parsons has come . . . here is the Champion of the West. . . . *He* is our commander, we want no other.'" George Ingram told his wife, "I never saw a man so much beloved as a commander as he." When the colonel began speaking he tried to calm the angry

[3] George W. Ingram to Martha F. Ingram, December 22, 1863, in ibid., 66-67; Robert F. Frazier to "Ma," December 23, 1863, Frazier Family Papers, Eugene C. Barker Texas History Collection, The Center for American History, Austin, Texas.

[4] George W. Ingram to Martha F. Ingram, December 22, 1863, in Ingram, comp., *Civil War Letters*, 66-67; A. Parks to "Mother," January 22, 1863, photocopy in the possession of the author.

men, and "implored them in the name of the honor of Texas, in the name of Fathers and Mothers and evrything that was sacred for them not to do anything today or at any time that they would be sorry for tomorrow, next year or when the final records of this war was made up. He spoke for about 25 or 30 minutes and rode out of the ring amid deafening shouts and hurrah for Col. Parsons."[5]

The troopers in the Twenty-first Texas felt differently. William P. Zuber said the men of Burford's and Parsons's regiments "were strangely attached to Colonel Parsons, and they treated General Churchill with scorn. Seeing that his assumption of command would cause a general mutiny of those two regiments, the General abandoned the command and did not visit our regiment." Even though the Twenty-first supported the change of command, Churchill asked Holmes to reinstate Parsons. "Consequently our command have cooled down and evrything glides on as quietly as usual except that it is Christmas times and some . . . have taken a little too much whiskey and are rather jolly."[6]

Although there were numerous attempts by Parsons's supporters to secure a promotion for the colonel, that never happened. The soldiers blamed this failure on General Holmes, noted George Ingram, and he concluded that the attempt to replace Parsons had been "to gratify his evil nature and agravate Parsons." Several officers wrote to friends in the Confederate Congress, as well as Nathaniel Burford and Brigadier General James F. Fagan, but to no avail. Burford noted: "Men and officers have expressed great astonishment at his not having been promoted." Fagan commented on his "intrepid daring" and his reputation as a "daring Cavalry Officer. . . . To treat Col Parsons much longer with indifference or neglect argues a poor return for the service he has done our State & South."[7]

Henry Merrell, an Arkansas industrialist who grew to know Parsons well, noted that when he heard the Twelfth Texas had arrived near Camden he rode out to meet the regiment. He found the soldiers camped in a river bottom near the Lone Pine Ferry. There was a "long, cold, soaking" rain falling and the roads and camps were "muddy & disagreeable in the highest

[5] George W. Ingram to Martha F. Ingram, December 22, 1863, in Ingram, comp., *Civil War Letters*, 66-67.

[6] William P. Zuber, *My Eighty Years in Texas*, edited by Janis Boyle Mayfield (Austin: University of Texas Press, 1971), 197; George W. Ingram to Martha F. Ingram, December 24, 1863, in Ingram, comp., *Civil War Letters*, 67-68.

[7] George W. Ingram to Martha F. Ingram, December 22, 1863, in Ingram, comp., *Civil War Letters*, 66-67; Letter of Nat M. Burford, November 27, 1863, photocopy in the collection of Joe and Ann Cerney, Wichita Falls, Texas; Petition to James A. Seddon for Parsons's promotion, signed by a number of soldiers, February 1, 1864, photocopy in the collection of Joe and Ann Cerney.

degree." The men had "but one tent, scarcely enough to shelter a dozen men" so the soldiers "were squatting or standing over fires that gave out little but smoke, & their poor horses, head down, draggled in mud & wet & cold with eyes shut, seemed to be dreaming of the warm sun & green waving prairies of their native Texas!" He said that "the men looked discouraged & as much disposed to go home as their mustangs themselves" for there were no sports going on, "not even card-playing." Colonel Parsons admitted that he had seven hundred men sick. Still, Merrell pointed out, the Twelfth was the elite of the cavalry as the "mounted men, with the exception of Parsons' 12th Texas, were not Cavalry in any sense, except that they moved on horse-back." He felt a special affinity for this regiment, as he noted how the men always made him feel like a "comrade." Yet with so many sick and disheartened, it was not surprising that morale suffered. Clearly the Texas soldiers needed a break. In two days before Christmas Kirby Smith instructed Holmes to place his men in winter quarters in order to instill "discipline and improve their *morale* for operations in the spring." But, he added: "The Texas Brigade goes directly to Texas."[8]

The following orders cover only two months. The inactivity and frustration following the surrender of Vicksburg and the resulting isolation of the Trans-Mississippi from the rest of the Confederacy took a toll on the men. The final weeks of 1863 saw organized discontent spread through the regiments and it quickly became apparent to the authorities that the only solution was to reassign the entire brigade to service in Texas. Included with the following orders are transcripts of the letters sent to Richmond requesting Parsons's promotion to brigadier general. In spite of these endorsements, the efforts proved unsuccessful.

[8] Henry Merrell, *The Autobiography of Henry Merrell: Industrial Missionary to the South*, edited by James L. Skinner III (Athens: University of Georgia Press, 1991), 351-52; E. Kirby Smith to Richard Taylor, December 23, 1863, *OR* 22, pt. 2, 1,110-11.

C H A P T E R 5

# DOCUMENTS

## Arkansas: November 12-December, 31 1863

Hd Qurt Camden Nov 1863[9]

Circular

All Port Hudson or Vicksburge paroled prisoners at present Serving with or Sojourning in any Company of this Command are ordered to report without delay to Brig General [Thomas P.] Dockery Comdg P and E prisoners at Washington Ark

| Official | By Order of |
|---|---|
| J M Brandon | Brig Genl [James F.] Fagan[10] |
| AA Genl | Wyatt C. Thomas A A Genl |

* * * * * * * * * * * * *

Hed Quarters Dept Trans Miss
Shreveport La Nov 12th 1863

General Order No 53

In accordance with instructions from the Secretary of War an auxileary branch of the Army Inteligence office Subsidiary to that in the City of Richmond is hereby established for the Department of Trans Miss at Shreveport La under the Superientendent of Mr R S Thomas Its object being to inform the friends and Relations of Sick and Wounded Soldiers of the whereabouts and conditions to facilitate communication with the Army;

[9] Henry Orr wrote from Black Bayou, Caldwell Parish, on November 8: "We have very agreeable times, however are getting along very slowly in our business. Hogs are very scarce indeed, so much so that we are getting but few except 'title hogs' which we received orders to gather as I came through Vienna. Several weeks will yet pass ere we get over the parish. . . . We have some rare sport sometimes. Have to hunt hogs with dogs, and when we find them they seem to have a spirit akin to those we read about which you remember ran into the sea, but here they make for the worst thickets and sometimes into bayous and lakes." On the thirteenth he added: "There are a great many of the Vicksburg soldiers in this parish who are marrying at the rate of two or three per week; parties are so numerous." Henry Orr to "Sister," November 8, 13, 1863, in Anderson, ed., *Campaigning with Parsons' Brigade*, 124-25.

[10] James F. Fagan was promoted to brigadier general after the fighting at Shiloh. He fought at Prairie Grove before taking part in the defense of Camden where he came to know Colonel Parsons well.

and to secure a correct list of the deathes which have occured or may hereafter occur among our troops whether within or out lines of those of the enemy

To the accomplishment of these ends all Surgeons will furnish to the Intelligence Office through the proper Channels and with the least possible delay a list of the sick and wounded now in Hospital and a list of the deathes among those who may have been under their charge—giving the name and rank Company and Regiment—whether the death was caused by sickness or wounds. In the case of a death in hospital the date of the admission of the deceased Should be given; Hereafter weekly reports embrasing the above spesified particulars must be forwarded promptly to the Inteligence Office through the proper Channels

Immediately after an engagement Commanding Officers are required to forward direct to the Intelligence Office without wating until their Official Report can be made a list of the casualties in their commands: giving in addition to the name the rank Company and Regiment, and the nature of the wound

Upon application of Mr Thomas accompanied by Surgeons cetificate of disability for field servis, the requisite number of men will be detailed for clerks in the Army Inteligence Office

The Quartermasters and Subsentance Department will furnish to Mr Thomas upon his requisition Such suplies as may [be] necessary

By Comd of
Lt Genl E Kirby Smith
(Sgn) S S Anderson A A Gnel

Hed Qurt & c
Camden Nov 17th 1863
Official (Sgd) Wyatt C Thomas A A G

Hed Quat Texas Cavalry Brg
Official
J M Brandon A A G

* * * * * * * * * * * * *

Head qrs. Texas Cav Brigade
Camden Ark. Nov 18- 1863[11]

Special Order No. 47

Maj. A.J. Byrd Brigade C.S. will furnish Lt. [J.K.] Jarman One Hundred and fifty (150) Dolls to subsist Thirty (30) men ten days

By order of
W H Parsons
Col. Commandg
J M Brandon asst adj Genl

[11] On November 15, George Ingram told his wife: "You see from the caption that we are at Camden. The Generals have been expecting a fight here but I think that there is no prospect at this time. I think from what I can learn that Gen. Price intends to attack the enemy at Little Rock. Maj. Williams and Capt. Wier have just started out on a scout towards Pine Bluff with 100 men." George W. Ingram to Martha Ingram, November 15, 1863, in Ingram, comp., *Civil War Letters*, 64.

* * * * * * * * * * * * *

Head quarters Tex Cav Brigade
Camden Nov. 19- 1863

Special Order No. 48

Maj. A.J. Byrd Brig. C.S. will pay over to Capt. J.B. [James B.] Doak[12] fifteen Hundred Dollars to subsist One Hundred and fifty men seventy days; now commanded by Maj. J B [John B.] Williams

By order of
W H Parsons
Col. Comdg
J M Brandon asst adjt Genl.

* * * * * * * * * * * * *

Hed Quarters 12th Texas Dragoons
Camden Arkansas Nov 20 1863[13]

Special Orders No -

By virtue of the authority in me vested by the 199th (?) Paragraph Art 25 of the Army Regulations There by constitute and appoint Henry Levy Sutler for the 12th Texas Dragoons with the priviledge and duties appertaining to that position

W H Parsons
Col Comdg 12 Tex Drg

Special order No -

Henry Levy Sutler 12th Texas will at once go to Hoston [Houston] Texas or Such point at which he can obtane [*sic*] supplies & lay in Such artical of mercantdise as will supply the present nesisity of the Command

W.H. Parsons
J M Brandon Col Comdg 12 T C

[12] Company D, Nineteenth Texas. Doak was twenty-nine years old when he had enlisted from Hill County. He was a native of Tennessee who gave his occupation as stock raiser with no real estate and $2,000 in personal estate. Bailey, *Between the Enemy and Texas*, 224-25.

[13] George Ingram wrote on November 20: "I am at this place [Arcadia, La.] in 8 miles of Mt. Lebanon." But on December 21 he told his wife: "I last wrote you from Mt. Lebanon which place I left on the 6th Inst. And arrived at this place [Camden, Ark.] on the 11th and on the 13th our command started for Lanes Fort on Red River. We went as far as Dooley's Ferry at which place orders came for us to return here and we have just struck camp. . . . It is hinted that Walkers Division will be here in a few days and then look out for a fight." George W. Ingram to Martha Ingram, in Ingram, comp., *Civil War Letters*, 65.

* * * * * * * * * * * * *

Hd Qurt Camden Nov 21st 1863

Circular

All persons at present Serving with or Sojourning [with] any Company of this Command who belongs properly to the 11th Ark Regiment (East Miss) will report with out delay to Maj Poe at this place (Camden)

Official
J M Brandon
A A Genl

By Order of
Brig Genl [James F.] Fagan
Wyatt C. Thomas A A Genl

* * * * * * * * * * * * *

Hd Quarters Tex. Cav. Brigade
Camden Ark Nov. 22d 1863

Special Order No. 49

Private Alonzo [L.] D'Spain detailed from Company "C" 12th Texas Dragoons as courier at these Hd Qrs is hereby ordered to go to Shreveport La. to bring up all letters belonging to this Command and will return without delay. The Post Master at Shreveport will please deliver to Mr. D'Spain all mail matters in his office for this command

By order of
W H Parsons
Col. Comdg
J M Brandon asst adjt. Genl.

* * * * * * * * * * * * *

Head Qrs. Tex. Cav. Brig
Camden Ark Nov. 22. 63

Special Order No. 50

Private J.H. Clemments [Joseph H. Clements] of Company (H) 12th Tx and Privates A.W. Ligon [Anderson W. Liggon] of Company (C) 12th Texas Dragoons will report at once to Capt. Jos. P. [Joseph P.] Weir of Company (A) 12th Tex Dragoons for duty near Princeton Ark.

By Order of
W H Parsons
Col. Comdg
J M Brandon asst adjt Genl.

* * * * * * * * * * * * *

Head qrs. Tex Cav Brig
Camden Ark Nov 22 1863

Special Order No. 51

Maj A.J. Byrd Brig C.S. Tex. Cav. Brig will turn over to Lt. Getzendanner [W.H. Getzendaner] One Hundred and sixty Eight Dollars to pay Commutation of Rations on Courier line from Camden Ark to Homer La.

By order of
W H Parsons
Col. Commandg
J.M. Brandon asst adjt Genl

* * * * * * * * * * * * *

Hd. qrs. Tex. Cav. Brigade
Camden Ark. Nov. 23d 1863

Special Order No. 52

I. Lieut. [Edward W.] Hunt[14] in charge of 20 men will place a picket of ten men and one Commissioned officer at Tates Bluff and relieve the officer in Command of that post.

II. He will place a picket of ten men at the junction of the Warren and Pine Bluff roads—

III. He will instruct his Pickets to arrest all negroes without proper passes, and all suspicious characters, and allow no one to pass without written permission from these Head Quarters or from the Head qrs. of Brig Genl [James F.] Fagan.

IV. The officer in Command of the Picket at Tates Bluff will report with his Command without delay to Captain McMurtry near Camden Arkansas.

By order of
W.H. Parsons
Col. Comdg.
J M Brandon Capt. & A.A. Genl.

[14] Company K, Nineteenth Texas.

* * * * * * * * * * * * *

Hd qrs. Tx Cav Brig
Camden Ark. Nov. 23. 63

Special Order No. 53

Capt. Thomas Johns A.Q.M. will turn over to Lt [Edward W.] Hunt funds to buy forage for twenty five horses ten days

By order of
W H Parsons
Col Comdg.
J M Brandon asst adjt Genl.

* * * * * * * * * * * * *

Head Qrs Tex Cav Brig
Camden Ark Nov 23, 63

Special Order No. 54

Maj A.J. Byrd Brigade C.S. will pay Lt [Edward W.] Hunt One Hundred and twenty Dollars commutation of Rations for twenty four men ten days

By order of
W H Parsons
Col. Comdg
J M Brandon asst adjt Genl

* * * * * * * * * * * * *

Head qrs. Tex Cav. Brig
Camden Ark. Nov. 23- 1863

Special Order No. 55[15]

Privates McClain [Argyle McLerran], [James] Wharton and McCurry [William Henry McCarley] of Johnsons Spy Company[16] will report to Maj L.J. [Lochlin J.] Farrar Command 12th Tex Dragoons for duty.

By order of
W H Parsons
Col Commsndg
J M Brandon asst adjt. Genl.

[15] This order appears twice with slight variations in each.

[16] Johnson's Spy Company became Company E, Morgan's Battalion.

* * * * * * * * * * * * *

Hd. Qurs. Tex. Cav. Brigade
Camden Ark Nov. 23d 1863

Special Order No. 56

Captain Thomas Johns A.Q.M. will turn over to Captain J.C.S. [James C.S.] Morrow[17] One Hundred Dollars to pay for foraging Couriers horses on line from Alabama Landing to Homer La.

By order of
W.H. Parsons
Col. Comdg.
J M Brandon A.A G.

* * * * * * * * * * * * *

Head Quarters Tex Cav Brigade
Camden Ark Nov 23-1863.

Special Order No. 57

Captain Thomas Johns Brigade A.Q.M. will pay over to Lieut. Getzendanner [W.H. Getzendaner] One Hundred and Thirty Seven Dollars to pay for forage on Courier line from Homer La. to Camden, Ark.

By order of
W H Parsons
Col. Commdg
J M Brandon asst adjt Genl.

* * * * * * * * * * * * *

Hd. qrs. Tex Cav. Brigade
Camden Ark. Nov. 23 1863.

Special Order No. 58

Capt. Robert A Terrell having been nominated for A.Q.M. 12th Texas Drags will proceed at once to Texas to make his Bond and return in Sixty days from this date report to his Regiment for duty

By order of
W H Parsons
Col. Command
J M Brandon asst adjt Gnl

[17] Company I, Twelfth Texas.

* * * * * * * * * * * * *

Head Quarters Texas Cav Brig
Camden Ark. Nov. 24- 1863

Special Order No. 59

Asst. surgeon R.P. Sweat [Sweatt][18] 12th Tx Dragoons having been nominated for promotion to the position of Surgeon 12th Tx Drags will report to Surgeon Cunningham Med. Director Dist. of Ark. for orders to appear before Board of Surgeons for Examination

By order of
W H Parsons
Col. Comdg
J M Brandon asst adjt Gnl

* * * * * * * * * * * * *

Head Quarters Tex Cav. Brig
Camden Ark. Nov 24 1863

Special Order No. 60

In compliance with above orders Jesse Cone and E.T. Killough are assigned to duty in Co. "I" 12th Tex Dragoons. Capt. J.C.S. [James C.S.] Morrow

By order of W H Parsons Col. Comg
J M Brandon AAG

* * * * * * * * * * * * *

Head qrs Tex Cav. Brigade
Camden Ark. Nov. 25- 1863

Special Order No. 61

Lieut. James E. Terrell acting Inspector General Texas Cavalry Brigade is hereby directed to proceed at once to Richmond Va for special purchase of securing duplicate (the original having been lost en route) of the appointment of Maj. [Thomas] Johns A.Q.M. of Texas Cav. Brig and other business connected with the interests of the Command[19]

Wm H. Parsons
Col. Commanding
Tx Cav Brigade

[18] Company H, Twelfth Texas.

[19] Terrell died at Jackson, Mississippi, on his way to Virginia.

* * * * * * * * * * * * *

Head Qrs. Texas Cav. Brigade
Camden Nov. 25th 1863

Special Order No. 62

George C. Pendleton is detailed to go to Clairbourn [Claiborne] and Bienville Parishes in Louisiana after Shoes for Captain [Car] Forrest's[20] Company and return in ten days.

By order of
W.H. Parsons
Col. Comdg.
J.M. Brandon
asst adjt. Genl

* * * * * * * * * * * * *

Hd. qrs. Texas Cav Brigade
Camden Ark. Nov. 25. 1863

Special Order No. 63

Privates McClain [Argyle McLerran], [William Henry] McCarley & Horton [James Wharton] of Johnson's "Spy Company"[21] will report without delay at or near Washington Ark

By order of
W H Parsons
Col. Comdg.
J M Brandon
asst adjt Gnl

* * * * * * * * * * * * *

Head qrs Tex Cav. Brig
Camden Ark Nov 26-1863

Special Order No. 64

Maj. A J Byrd Brig. C.S. Tex Cav Brig will proceed to the Hd. qrs. of Lt Genl [Theophilus H.] Holmes on business with his department

By order of
W H Parsons
Col. Commdg
J M Brandon asst adjt Gnl

[20] Company C, Nineteenth Texas. Car Forrest was thirty-three years old in 1862. He was a native of Tennessee who enlisted in Ellis County. He gave his occupation as a merchant with $4,000 in real estate and $7,000 in personal estate. Bailey, *Between the Enemy and Texas*, 224-25.

[21] Company E, Morgan's Battalion.

* * * * * * * * * * * * *

Hd. qrs Tex Cav Brig
Camden Nov 27 63

Special Order No. 65

Capt Thomas Johns Brigade A.Q.M. will pay over to Capt Forest [Car Forrest] funds to forage sixty-eight horses ten days.

By order of
W H Parsons
Col. Comdg
J M Brandon asst adjt Genl

* * * * * * * * * * * * *

Hd. qrs. Tex. Cav. Brigade
Camden Ark Nov 27, 63

Special Order No. 66

Maj A J Byrd CS Tex Cav Brigade will pay over to Capt Forest [Car Forrest] [_____] Dolls. commutation of rations for 68 men ten days

By order of
W H Parsons
Col Comdg
J M Brandon A A G

* * * * * * * * * * * * *

Hd Qrs
Camden Nov 27th, 1863

Hon C D. Mitchel, Richmond[22]
Dear Sir

I am now in command at this place. Col Parsons Texas Brigade Cavalry constitutes a portion of my command. With Col Parsons both of us have been long acquainted—his distinguished gallantry & eminent services as a cavalry officer having long since made him well known in this Dept. Since however I have been intimately associated with Col Parsons my previous notions of his personal daring & qualfications to command have not only been confirmed but elevated. He has long commanded a Brigade "in front" & dischaged with great success all the duties & responsibilities of a General Officer. And whilst his conduct has demonstrated his entire ability to discharge all the onerous &

[22] This letter, recommending promotion for Colonel Parsons, was written by Brigadier General James F. Fagan of Arkansas to Charles B. Mitchel, who represented Arkansas in the First and Second Sessions of the Confederate Senate (until November 1864). See the letter to Secretary of War James Seddon dated February 1, 1864, for a response. This correspondence is in the Records Division, War Department, National Archives.

responsible duties of a General Officer his servicess have, in my opinion, certainly won for him that position.

Would it be asking too much of you to request of you to interest yourself in Col Parsons' favor & endeavor to procure his promotion? In preferring this request I am as you, I know, will feel _______ actuated only by a desire to see merit rewarded. I can not think of Col Parsons' long service, his dash & gallantry, and the great good he has done for our state & [the] South without entertaining a desire to see him promoted.

I am sure nothing in Col Parsons' future, should you interest yourself for him, will ever cause you to regret such a step.

Will you then interest yourself in this matter & reward merit by procuring for Col Parsons a Brigadier Generals commission? I entrust the subject with hesitation to your own sense of justice & fairness.

Lt. Terrill [James E. Terrell], the Bearer hereof, will relate to you all the news.

Very Truly Yours
J F Fagan

* * * * * * * * * * * * *

Hd qrs
Camden
November 27th, 1863

Hon A. H Garland - Richmond[23]
My Dear friend

This will be handed to you by Lt. [James E.] Terrell of Col Parsons Texas Cavalry Brigade. This Brigade (Parsons) forms a part of my command at this place.

Of Col Parsons it is useless for me to speak to you as you are acquainted with his antecedents and gallant services. You recollect well not only what golden opinions he won for himself upon the lower Arkansas but in every section where he has been sent.

I send this merely to request your interest in obtaining Col Parsons promotion to the office of Brigadier General. He has long discharged all the duties & responsibilities of a General Officer and has fairly & honorably "won his spurs" on the field.

In preferring this request I am activated purely by a desire to see merit rewarded. It is only necessary for me to suggest this matter to you. I know, to secure your hearty aid & endeavors. I am satisfied that your own love of justice and senses of fairness will do the rest.

I have written also upon this subject to Hons R.W. Johnson[24] & C.B. Mitchell,[25] & more at length. You are too well acquainted with the length of service, the intrepid daring the ready resources & of Col Parsons as a dashing Cavalry officer to make it necessary to say more upon the subject.

[23] Augustus H. Garland succeeded Charles B. Mitchel as the Confederate senator from Arkansas in November 1864. See the letter to Secretary of War James Seddon dated February 1, 1864, for a response.

[24] Robert W. Johnson was a Confederate senator from Arkansas in both the First and Second sessions of the Confederate Congress.

[25] Charles B. Mitchel was a Confederate senator from Arkansas in both the First and Second sessions of the Confederate Congress (until November 1864).

To treat Col Parsons much longer with indifference or neglect argues a poor return for the service he has done our state & [the] South.

I leave the matter ________ in your hands. My only object in writing this must also be my excuse for troubling you at all. I desire to see justice done & merit properly rewarded. Lt. Terrill [James E. Terrell] will give you all the news. I wish you all possible happiness, healthy &

Very Truly Yours
J.F. Fagan

* * * * * * * * * * * *

Camden Arkansas
November 27, 1863

Gentlemen:[26]

My long personal acquaintance with each of you induces me to write you this note in regard to the promotion of Col W H Parsons—I know that you like myself have staked everything on the success of the revolution in which we are now engaged; this is a time when personal considerations should weigh nothing, but everything should be made to bend to the successfull accomplishment of the glorious enterprise in which we are engaged—Col Parsons belongs to that class of officers known to be usefull [hole] distinguished from its ornamental he has the capacity to command, he has the confidence of these soldiers placed under his command—men and officers have expressed great astonishment at his not having been promoted. The Texas Cavalry now doing service in Arkansas with one voice ask that he be promoted to a Brig General—I know this promotion would be advantageous to our cause In assisting to make him a Brig Genl you will ____ be of service to a meritorious officer, but at the same time be_______ the country valuable service. It is no personal predilection for the man that causes me to say this, but an honest desire to see our army well and effic[i]ently officered. Parsons has long commanded a Brigade of Cavalry consisting of the 12, 19 & 21 Rgts. Texas Cavalry and Pratts Battery. He enjoys the confidence of the men and officers of this Brigade—they have fought under him and prefer to fight under him in preference to any other officer I know of—

Please do what you can to procure him the appointment of Brig Genl.

Your Sincere friend,
Nat M. Burford

Hons W.S. Oldham[27]
M.D. Graham[28]
W.B. Wright[29]

[26] This letter recommending promotion for Colonel Parsons was written by Nathaniel M. Burford, who commanded the Nineteenth Texas Cavalry in Parsons's Brigade. He was also a former law partner of the Confederate Postmaster General John Reagan. The correspondence is found in the Records Division, War Department, National Archives. See the letter to Secretary of War James Seddon dated February 1, 1864, for a response.

[27] William Simpson Oldham served as senator from Texas in both sessions of the Confederate Congress.

[28] Malcolm Duncan Graham served as a representative from Texas in the first session of the Confederate Congress.

[29] William Bacon Wright served as a representative from Texas in the first session of the Confederate Congress.

* * * * * * * * * * * * *

Head qrs Texas Cav Brigade
Camp near Camden Ark. Nov. 28- 1863

Special Order No. 67

Capt. Thomas Johns Brigade Q.M. Texas Cavalry Brigade will divide equally between the 12th & 19th Texas Cavalry the horses captured by Capt. Commanding by Capt Jos. P. [Joseph P.] Weir[30] near Princeton Ark—Private John Young Company E 12th Texas Dragoons will be allowed to take one

By order of
W H Parsons
Col. Commandg
J M Brandon asst adjt Genl.

* * * * * * * * * * * * *

Head Quars Texas Cavalry Brigade
Camden Ark. Nov. 29th 1863

Special Order No. 68

Sergt. R.J. Oliphant of Pratts Battery is hereby detailed to go to Washington Ark. to bring clothing belonging to the men of his Company and return in ten days from this date

By order of
W H Parsons
Col. Comdg
J M Brandon A.A. & A Ins. Genl.

* * * * * * * * * * * * *

Hd. Quars. Texas Cav. Brigade
Camp near Camden
Ark. Nov. 30- 1863

Special Order No. 69

Maj. Thomas Johns Brigade Q.M. will pay over to Sergt. M.M. [Mat M.] Caldwell[31] money for forage Eleven horses ten days.

By order of
W H Parsons
Col. Commdg
J M Brandon asst adjt Genl.

[30] Company A, Twelfth Texas.

[31] Company I, Twelfth Texas.

* * * * * * * * * * * * *

Hd Qrs Tex Cav. Brigade
Camp Near Camden Ark
Nov. 30- 1863

Special Order No. 70

Maj A.J. Byrd Brigade C.S. Tx Cav. Brigade will pay over to Sergt. M.M. [Mat M.] Caldwell, [_____] Dollars Commutation of Rations for Eleven men ten days detailed as picket guard.

By order of
W H Parsons
Col. Comdg
J M Brandon asst adjt Genl.

* * * * * * * * * * * * *

Head Qurs. Tex Cav. Brigade
Camden Nov. 30th 1863

Special Order No. 71

Private I.D. Rodes [Isaac D. Rhodes] of Co. "A" 19th Tex. Cav. is hereby detailed as Blacksmith for the Tex. Cav. Brigade.

By order of
W.H. Parsons
Col. Comdg.
J.M. Brandon A A G

* * * * * * * * * * * * *

Head qrs. Parson's Tex Cav Brigade
Camp Near Camden Dec. 1st 1863

Special Order No. 72

Dr. John D. Parsons actg asst Surgeon 12th Texas Dragoon's will report without delay to Surgeon Cunningham Med. Purveyor District of Ark. for orders to appear before the Medical board for examination.

By order of
W H Parsons
Col. Commandg
J M Brandon asst adjt & actg Ins Genl

* * * * * * * * * * * * *

Hd qrs Tex Cav. Brigade
Camp near Camden Ark.
December 2nd 1863
Head Quarters Texas Cavalry Brigade
Camden Dec. 1st 1863

Special Order No. 73

Thomas Carter private in Co. "E" 12th Texas Dragoons is hereby detailed as nurse, to report early tomorrow morning to Dr. Burton Post Surgeon at Hospital in Camden.

By order of
W.H. Parsons
Col. Comdg.
J M Brandon A.A. Genl.

* * * * * * * * * * * * *

Head Quarters Tex. Cav. Brigade
Camden Dec. 2d 1863.

Special Order No. 74

Private Abe [Abraham S.] Wilson of Co. "D" 19th Texas Cav. is hereby detailed as Blacksmith for the Tex. Cav. Brigade.

By order of
W.H. Parsons
Col. Comdg.
J M Brandon Asst. Adjt. Genl.

* * * * * * * * * * * * *

Head qrs. Tex Cav. Brigade
Camp Near Camden Dec. 2- 1863

Special Order No. 75

It having been brought to the knowledge Lieut. Samuel Black of Company (H) 19th Texas Cavalry will relieve Lieut. [William A.] Buchanan of Company (G) 19th Texas Cavalry now in Command of guard at Mt Liban in La.

II. Lieut. Buchanan will report to his command at Camden Ark for duty.

By order of
W H Parsons
Col Comdg
J M Brandon A.A. & A. Genl

* * * * * * * * * * * * *

Hd qrs. Tex Cav Brigade
Dec 2- 1863

Special Order No. 76.

Capt James P. Brown[32] Commandg 12th Texas Dragoons will detail two men to saw plank for one week to report to Maj. [Thomas] Johns.

By order of
W H Parsons
Col Comdg
J M Brandon AA & A Ins Genl.

* * * * * * * * * * * * *

Head Qurs. Texas Cavalry Brigade
Camp Near Camden Dec. 10th 1863

Special Order No. 77

Captain Thomas Johns A.Q.M. of Texas Cavalry Brigade will pay Dr. John D. Parsons the amount due him as physician of the 12th Regiment Texas Dragoons pursuant to contract of April 18th 1863—He having been paid on said contract up to the 15th of June 1863.

By order of
W.H. Parsons
Col Commanding
J.M. Brandon asst adjt Genl

* * * * * * * * * * * * *

Head Quarters Texas Cavalry Brigade
Camp near Camden, Ark. Dec. 11th 1863

Special Order No. 78

Capt. Thomas Johns Brigade A.Q.M. will transfer to Lieut. J.W. Waldron Actg A.Q.M. 12th Texas Dragoons pay funds for his Regiment.

By order of
W.H. Parsons
Col. Comdg
J.M. Brandon Asst. Adjt. Genl.

[32] Company K.

* * * * * * * * * * * * *

Hd Qurs. Tex. Cav. Brigade
Camp Near Camden Ark.
December 11- 1863

Special Order No. 79

Captain Thomas Johns will turn over to Lieut. [James M.] Jackson[33] Funds to pay for forage for six horses nine days.

By order of
W.H. Parsons
Col Comdg.
J M Brandon A. A. Genl.

* * * * * * * * * * * * *

Head Qurs. Tex. Cav. Brigade
Camp Near Camden Ark. Dec. 11- 1863[34]

Special Order No. 80

Maj. A.J. Byrd will turn over to Lieutenant [James M.] Jackson [_____] Dollars, Commutation of Rations for six men six days detailed as guard to escort prisoners.

By order of
W.H. Parsons
Col. Comdg.
J M Brandon asst adjt Genl.

[33] Company A, Twelfth Texas.

[34] George Ingram told his wife on December 21: "Gen. Churchill is in command of the forces at this place. It was him that was in command at Arkansas Post. Gen. Churchill is to attack Pine Bluff in order to draw troops from Little Rock and Gen. Price and Walker will attack Little Rock immeadiately. From the best information that can be obtained there is about Twelve thousand Federals on the Arkansas River. If Gen. Walker comes up we will have 20,000. I think by the 1st of January we will have possession of the Arkansas River again." In a personal note, he added, "If you should be blessed with a boy, name him Robert Lee after the greatest man of the age and don't get in the habit of calling him 'Bob.'" George W. Ingram to Martha Ingram, in Ingram, comp., *Civil War Letters*, 65. Census records indicate that "Robert L. Ingram" was born in 1864.

* * * * * * * * * * * * *

Head Qurs: Texas Cav. Brigade
Camden Dec. 24th 1863[35]

Special Order No. 81

The following officers are constituted a Board of Survey to examine Horses of the 2d Section of Pratts Battery and report accordingly to these Hd: qurs:

| | |
|---|---|
| 1st Lieut. W.N. Kenner | Co. "E" 12th Texas Drags. |
| 1st " J.K. Jarman | " "C" 19th " Cavalry |
| Lieut. Thomas Killingsworth | Co "H" 19th Tex " |

By order of
W H Parsons
Col. Comdg.
J M Brandon asst adjt. Genl.

* * * * * * * * * * * * *

Hd. Qurs: Texas Cav. Brigade
Camp Near Camden Dec. 25th 1863

Special Order No. 82

Captain Thomas Johns A.Q.M. will turn over to Sergt. J.W. McGill [_____] Dollars to forage four horses for thirty days of men detailed to go after deserters.

By order of
W.H. Parsons
Col. Comdg
J M Brandon A.A. Genl

* * * * * * * * * * * * *

Head Qurs: Texas Cav. Brigade
Camp Near Camden Dec. 25th 1863

Special Order No. 83

Maj. A.J. Byrd Brigade Commissary, will turn over to Sergt. J.W. McGill [_____] Dollars to Ration four men thirty days, detailed to go after deserters.

By order of
W. H. Parsons
Col Comdg.
J M Brandon A A Genl

[35] On Christmas eve George Ingram wrote from Camden: "When Gen. Churchill learned of the general dissatisfaction prevailing in the command he asked to be relieved and that Col. Parsons be restored which old Holmes consented to. Consequently our command have cooled down and evrything glides on as quietly as usual except that it is Christmas times and some of the be-hogs [?] have taken a little too much whiskey and are rather jolly." George W. Ingram to Martha F. Ingram, December 24, 1863, ibid., 67-68.

* * * * * * * * * * * * *

Head Qrs: Tex Cavalry Brigade
Camp Near Camden Dec. 27- 1863

Special Order No. 84

Owing to the exigencies of the service the election of the following named officers of the 21st Tex Cavalry is hereby approved and they ordered to report to their Respective Captains for duty

| | | | |
|---|---|---|---|
| 2nd Lieutenant | A.P. [Arthur P.] Camp | Company | G |
| 2 " | " H McMillin [Hugh McMillan] | " | " |
| 2 " | " B.F. [Ben F.] Jackson | " | D |

To take effect from date of election

By order of
W H Parsons
Col. Commdg
J M Brandon A.A.G.

* * * * * * * * * * * * *

Hd. Qrs Tex Cav. Brigade
Camp Near Camden Ark Dec 28th 1863

Special Order No. 85

Private Dan [Daniel] Christman Co H 12th Tex. Dragoons is temporarily assigned to duty in Company D 12th Tx Dragoons his own Company being absent on detached service

By order of
W H Parsons
Col Commdg.
J M Brandon A.A. Genl

* * * * * * * * * * * * *

Hd: Qurs: Texas Cav. Brigade
Camp near Camden Dec 28th 1863

Special Order No. 86

I Sergt. James Brown, bugler 19th Texas Cavalry is hereby appointed chief musician of this Brigade.

II The Bugler of the Command will be subject to his order.

III A Bugler will be detailed each day by chief Bugler to report to these Hd: Qurs: at guard mounting

By order of
W.H. Parsons
Col. Commanding
J M Brandon A A Genl

* * * * * * * * * * * * *

Head Qurs. Texas Cav. Brigade
Camp Near Camden Dec. 28th 1863

Special Order No. 87.

Lieut. Col. B.W. [Benjamin W.] Watson, 19th Texas Cav, Captain James P. Brown[36] 12th Texas Cavalry, Captain Ed H. Vontress[37] Morgan's Battalion, and Captain G.R. [George R.] Freeman[38] of 21st Texas Cavalry, are hereby appointed a board to hear the excuse of all officers who remain away from their Comdg. a longer time than their leaves of absence grant.

It shall be the duty of each commanding officer of a Regiment or Battalion to order all officers who remain away from Camps to appear before said board after their leaves of absence expire.

Upon a hearing by the board of the officers charged with "absence without leave" the board will determine whether their excuse is a valid one, and if not he will be reported to these Hd: Qurs. for arrest and trial by Court Martial.

By order of
W.H. Parsons
Col. Commanding
J M Brandon A.A. Genl.

[36] Company K, Twelfth Texas.

[37] Company A, Morgan's Battalion.

[38] Company D, Twenty-first Texas.

* * * * * * * * * * * * *

Head Qurs: Texas Cav. Brigade
Camp near Camden Dec. 28th 1863.

Special Order No. 88

I Captain Joseph P. Weir of company "A" 12th Texas Dragoons is ordered to repair to Hempstead Austin County Texas and take command of Stragglers and recruits collected at that place under instructions from Lieut. Genl. E. Kirby Smith.

II Captain Weir will locate his camp at a place most convenient to wood and water and as near the Rail Road as practicable.

III He will apply to Lieut. Genl. Smith or Major Genl. [John B.] Magruder for orders and Q.M. for forage and Rations for his men.

IV He will put the officers and men who report to him through a thorough drill and have them in a condition to take the field on the arrival of the Brigade.[39]

By order of
W H Parsons
Col. Comdg.
J.M. Brandon asst. adjt. Genl.

* * * * * * * * * * * * *

Hd: Qurs: Texas Cav. Brigade
Camp Near Camden Ark Dec. 29th 1863

Special Order No. 89

Private Jacob [A.] Hesser Co. "H" 12th Texas Dragoons will report to his company now in Texas under Lt. Col. [A. Bell] Burleson or to Captain Joseph P. Weir[40] at Hempstead Austin County Texas comdg. Detachment of Tex. Cav. Brigade

By order of
W.H. Parsons
Col. Comdg.
J M Brandon asst adjt. Genl

[39] Dave Nance noted that the men in the brigade spent the coldest winter of the war while near Camden. Gallaway, *The Ragged Rebel*, 76.

[40] Company A, Twelfth Texas.

* * * * * * * * * * * * *

Hd qrs. Texas Cav Brigade
Camp Near Camden Dec. 29- 1863

Special Order No. 90

Private T.M. [Thomas M.] Carter Company "E" 12th Texas Dragoons detailed as nurse in the Genl. Hospital at Camden will report to his Company for duty

By order of
W H Parsons
Col Comdg
J M Brandon asst adjt Genl

* * * * * * * * * * * * *

Hd. Qrs. Tex Cav. Brigade
Camp near Camden Ark.
Dec 30- 1863

"Extract"
Special Order No. 91

The board appointed by Genl Order No. 87—to hear and consider the excuses of Officers who remain away from their Commands a longer time than their leaves of absence grant. Respectfully submit the following Capt. [William O.] Michaux[41] of Co. G. 19th Texas Cavalry having made a statement of his excuse for absence beyond the time granted him upon the honor of an officer & under oath the board are unanimously of opinion that the peculiar circumstances under which Capt. Michaux was placed made it his duty to prolong his absence and furnished a valid excuse."

Captain W.O. Michaux will therefore be relieved from arrest and resume the Command of his Company

By order of
W.H. Parsons
Col. Comdg.
J M Brandon asst adjt. Genl.

[41] William O. Michaux was a native of Florida who had enlisted in Kaufman County at age twenty-eight. He gave his occupation as merchant and his worth as $500 in real estate and $8,000 in personal estate. Bailey, *Between the Enemy and Texas*, 224-25.

* * * * * * * * * * * * *

Head Qurs: Tex. Cav. Brigade
Camp Near Camden Dec 31st 1863

Special Orders No. 92

I Captain [Car] Forrest Co. ( )[42] 19th Texas Cav. will take command of the wagon train and sick which will be left behind.

II The sick will be required to remain in camps and not allowed to straggle about the country.

III A forage master and commissary agent will accompany the command to the place here after to be designated.

By order of
W.H. Parsons
Col. Comdg.
J M Brandon A.A. Genl.

* * * * * * * * * * * * *

Head Qurs: Tex. Cav. Brigade
Camp Near Camden Dec. 31st 1863.

Special Order No. 93

Under no circumstances whatsoever will the Brigade Staff wagon, containing the effects of the adjunct General's office, be used for other transportation.

By order of
W.H. Parsons
Col. Comdg.
J M Brandon A.A. General.

[42] Company C.

CHAPTER 6

# ARKANSAS AND LOUISIANA

## 1864

By the third year of the war most of the Texians in Parsons's brigade had never participated in a real battle. Although the Twelfth Texas had arrived in Arkansas in time to fight in the summer campaign against Samuel Curtis's invading army in 1862, the men of the Nineteenth and Twenty-first did not join Parsons until autumn; their only real action had come during Marmaduke's Missouri raid in the spring of 1863. These troopers were now veterans, having endured many hardships in the past two years while scouting in Arkansas and Louisiana, but they had never faced a truly organized or determined enemy army. While they spent a relaxing intermission from the reality of war with their families in late 1863 and early 1864, the Texians had no idea that they were destined to experience war firsthand in the swampy lowlands of Louisiana's Red River Valley.

In the spring of 1864, Union authorities planned massive coordinated movements all across the Confederacy. Grant, who replaced Halleck as general-in-chief, would attack Lee's Army of Northern Virginia with George G. Meade's Army of the Potomac, while Sherman would attack Joseph E. Johnston's Army of Tennessee in Georgia. Grant also ordered Major Generals Franz Sigel in the Shenandoah Valley and Benjamin Butler on the Yorktown Peninsula to advance at the same time. Since both President Lincoln and Henry Halleck had long supported a Union offensive against Texas, there would be a march toward Shreveport. While there had been limited action in southern Louisiana and along the Texas coast in the previous two years, the result was Federal occupation of only a few barrier islands in the Gulf of Mexico. New England mill owners clamored for raw cotton, and that increased the pressure to move into the East Texas cotton fields.[1]

Major General Nathaniel P. Banks, a former governor of Massachusetts, saw the advantages for his postwar political career by providing this coveted cotton to his home state's mills, and he wanted to be the man to lead the Louisiana expedition. The Trans-Mississippi operation would originate from two different states: Arkansas and Louisiana, with the objective being Shreveport on the Red River in northeastern Louisiana. Frederick Steele would march south across Arkansas while Banks, in command of the Department of the Gulf, would advance up the Red River. Admiral Porter would furnish naval support and Sherman promised to lend ten thousand soldiers, although the bulk of his command was at Chattanooga readying to move on Atlanta.[2]

While Union authorities debated the spring strategy during the winter of 1864, most of Parsons's men finally headed home to Texas. The long-awaited orders did not come soon enough to prevent some of the troopers from having to join in an attack on Union-held Pine Bluff, however, and this, and other repeated delays, only increased frustration. "The boys are very impatient and in great suspense," wrote George Ingram in early February. "They have their heads set homewards and many are determined to go orders or no orders. I hope that we may be ordered to go very soon and that no one will disgrace themselves."[3]

By early March, numerous companies had returned to Texas. Edmund Kirby Smith, fearing a strike along the Rio Grande, decided to transfer the Texans to John B. Magruder, commanding the District of Texas. But Magruder did not want to provide food for the troopers and forage their hungry mounts either, and he sent each company to its home county to hunt for conscripts and deserters. Smith promised that if an attack developed in Louisiana or Arkansas, he would immediately order the cavalrymen to return to duty.[4]

[1] The standard history is Ludwell H. Johnson, *Red River Campaign: Politics and Cotton in the Civil War* (Baltimore: The John Hopkins Press, 1958). For a newer version of events, see Michael J. Forsyth, *The Red River Campaign and the Loss by the Confederacy of the Civil War* (Jefferson, N.C., and London: McFarland & Company, Inc., 2002).

[2] For the Arkansas campaign, see Michael J. Forsyth, *The Camden Expedition of 1864 and the Opportunity Lost by the Confederacy to Change the Civil War* (Jefferson, N.C., and London: McFarland & Company, Inc., 2003).

[3] George W. Ingram to Martha F. Ingram, February 6, 1864, in Ingram, comp., *Civil War Letters*, 68-69.

[4] E. Kirby Smith to Jefferson Davis, January 20, 1864, *OR* 34, pt. 2, 895-96; Richard Taylor to E. Kirby Smith, January 4, 1864, *ORN* 26:162-63; John G. Meem, Jr., to W.H. Parsons, April 9, 1864, *OR* 34, pt. 3, 754.

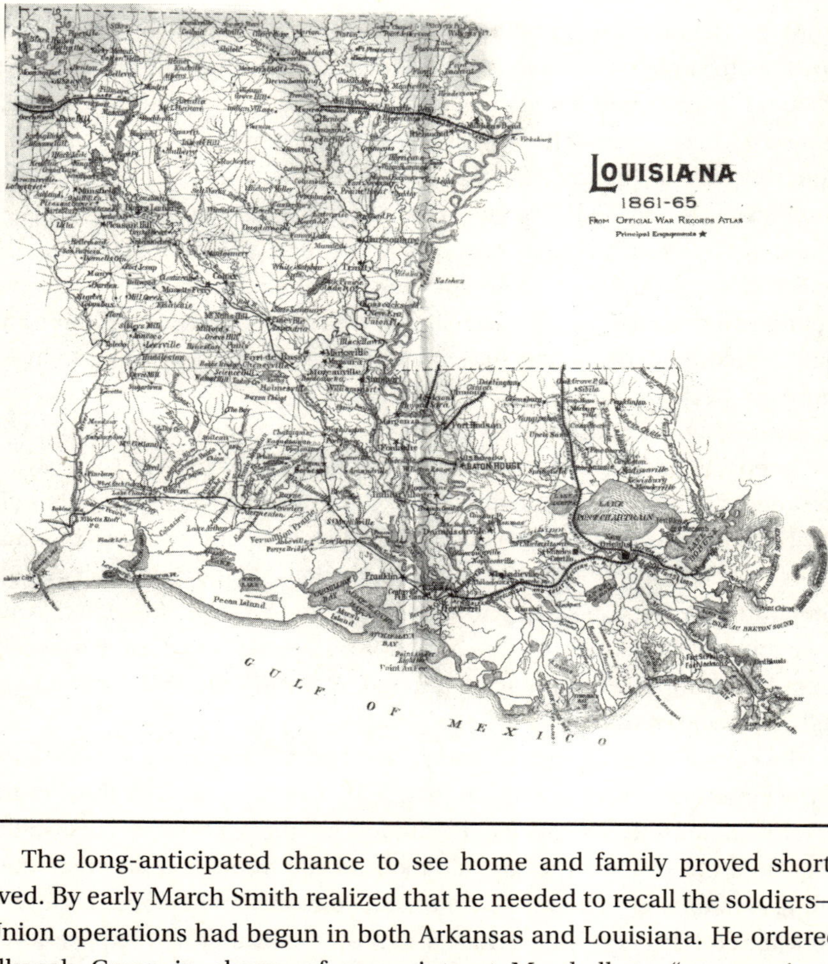


The long-anticipated chance to see home and family proved short-lived. By early March Smith realized that he needed to recall the soldiers—Union operations had begun in both Arkansas and Louisiana. He ordered Elkanah Greer, in charge of conscripts at Marshall, to "communicate immediately with Colonel Parsons, and direct him to hurry up as fast as possible the assembling of his brigade." Speed was essential, and a few days later Smith telegraphed: "Push forward as rapidly as possible the concentration of Parsons' brigade." Some of the units gathered at Shreveport, but Smith held them in reserve while he decided which state needed reinforcements the most.[5]

[5] S.S. Anderson to E. Greer, March 12, 1864, *OR* 34, pt. 2, 1,038; E. Cunningham to T.H. Holmes, March 7, 1864, ibid., 1,026; E. Cunningham to E. Greer, March 24, 1864, ibid., 1,077-78. See also, *Condensed History of Parsons Texas Cavalry Brigade.* Not all of the men were at Shreveport; some of the companies gathered at Nacogdoches.

Banks's advance up the Red River began in March. Brigadier Generals Joseph A. Mower and Thomas Kilby Smith each led divisions and Alfred W. Ellet sent one thousand men from his Marine Brigade (an army unit despite the name). In addition, Admiral Porter offered numerous armed vessels and transports. His fleet would join Banks for the attack on Shreveport where the two commanders planned to link with Steele's army coming from Arkansas. Once united, Federal soldiers could easily march into East Texas, and the coveted cotton would be theirs for the taking.

Confederate General Richard Taylor, in command in Louisiana, quickly gathered all the available cavalry and infantry. Greatly outnumbered, Taylor won a stunning victory at the Battle at Sabine Crossroads near the little town of Mansfield on April 8. A second battle followed the next day at Pleasant Hill. Even though Banks prevailed, he decided not to pursue his victory; he chose to withdraw to Alexandria instead. Porter, however, continued to move upriver unaware of Banks's decision to call off the expedition.

On the day of the Battle of Mansfield Parsons's received instructions to join Taylor's army although about seven hundred men, still waiting for the wagon trains in Texas, had not arrived. As soon as Smith heard of the Taylor's victory at Sabine Crossroads, he instructed Parsons to move with the troopers on hand. Lieutenant George Ingram noted that the soldiers were "to assist in the great battle that is now going on."[6]

Parsons joined the cavalry under Texan Tom Green, and participated in a daring attack on the Porter's fleet at Blair's Landing on April 12. Parsons later reported that the "valor of the officers and men" was so obvious that even Admiral Porter acknowledged the rebels' "*desperate courage baffled description*." Although Green was killed, Porter turned his vessels around and retreated down the river to join Banks at Alexandria. The Confederates had succeeded in thwarting another invasion of Texas.[7]

For the next several weeks the cavalry harassed Porter and Banks both night and day, as the Federal forces slowly retreated through Louisiana.

[6] E. Kirby Smith to Richard Taylor, April 8, 1864, *OR* 34, pt. 1, 528; John G. Meem, Jr., to W.H. Parsons, April 9, 1864, *OR* 34, pt. 3, 754; George W. Ingram to Martha F. Ingram, April 9, 1864, in Ingram, comp., *Civil War Letters*, 71.

[7] These quotations come from the original copy of W.H. Parsons to W. Steele, June 3, 1864, *Houston News Bulletin*, July 9, 1864. The letter, edited by Bryce Suderow, was reprinted in *Civil War Times Illustrated* in September 1988.

There were two important changes in command. Major General John A. Wharton filled Tom Green's place as Taylor's cavalry commander, and Brigadier William Steele, who had arrived from Texas, took over command of a division that in reality included only one brigade, that of Colonel Parsons. It was the cavalry under Wharton and Steele that pushed Banks toward the Mississippi River (most of the infantry having been sent to Arkansas to stop the Union advance on Camden). The Battle at Yellow Bayou on May 18 was the final engagement of the Red River Campaign and, for many of the Texans, the most intense fighting they saw in the entire war.[8]

Andrew Jackson Smith ordered General Mower to clear out the rebels trailing the retreating Federal army down the Red River. In the battle that followed many of the Texans had to abandon their mounts and charge the enemy on foot. Parsons was hesitant to ask his men to undertake such an unfamiliar maneuver, for the horsemen seldom fought well as infantry, and when he finally ordered the line of dismounted cavalry forward, enemy volleys decimated the ranks. Yet a Union colonel noted, "the line advanced as steadily as infantry veteran[s] over an open field," took position, and "held it until ordered to retire." At one point men of the Sixteenth Corps engaged the Confederates at a distance of less than thirty paces. The Texans could hear voices yelling "surrender you damned Rebels or we'l [*sic*] Kill you all." Overpowered, the Southerners fell back, and under the cover of darkness, retired.[9]

The Red River Campaign ended with a Confederate defeat. Lieutenant Buck Walton of the Twenty-first recalled that the Battle at Yellow Bayou "was one of the bloodiest battles fought West of the Mississippi River—in which we got decently licked. The battle continued about six hours and was fiercely fought on both sides and there was great slaughter to both—I did not think" that the "battle ought to have been fought." Moreover, many agreed. Colonel Parsons concluded however: "It is unnecessary, therefore, for me to speak of the patient endurance, of long and continued privations, the oft recuring night watch, the incessant, never ending days fight, and the cool

[8] Wharton, as the commander of all the cavalry in the Red River Campaign, was popular with the men, as his family was from Texas. Moreover, he had commanded cavalry in the Confederate Army of Tennessee and had earned a respected reputation. Steele, however, was a New Yorker. An 1840 graduate of West Point, he had served in the Seminole and Mexican wars before assignment with the Second U.S. Dragoons. When the war came he joined the Seventh Texas Cavalry and fought in the New Mexico Campaign. His most recent assignment had been the defense of Galveston. He would, however, gain the confidence of the Texans.

[9] W.H. Parsons to W. Steele, June 3, 1864; Alwyn Barr, *Polignac's Texas Brigade* (1964; rpt., College Station: Texas A&M University Press, 1998), 45-47.

and unflinching courage which, always against ten and often twenty times their number, bore them up against every apparent reverse and wrung from both the U.S. Army and Navy officers (as we learn from interviews with flag of truce parties) the tribute that *the world never witnessed such fights as those rebel troops who hung with such dogged valor upon their rear in this pursuit.* To state the above fact of acknowledgement of the enemy is the highest tribute I can pay the noble and deserving men who compose this brigade."[10]

Still, the cost was high. An incomplete list from Parsons's brigade indicates twelve killed, sixty-seven wounded, and two missing. The Twelfth Texas suffered the greatest number of casualties with ten killed, sixty-one wounded, and two missing. The Nineteenth Texas reported only one wounded, the Twenty-first counted four wounded, and Morgan's battalion reported two killed and one wounded. Obviously many casualties went unreported since letters home indicate the loss in the brigade was much greater.[11]

Because of the almost constant fighting in April and May, there were few orders issued, and even fewer survived. After the campaign ended, the brigade remained in Louisiana between the Red and Mississippi rivers while Confederate authorities tried to decide what to do next. The men disliked the muddy bayous, and in June Henry Orr wrote that everyone was "tired of [the] Red River." George Ingram said he preferred anywhere "to this Swampy country." Another soldier noted with anticipation: "We are certainly off for Arkansas, or perhaps Missouri; we hope to the latter, at any rate we will take Arkansas in preference to Louisiana." In mid-June Wharton said that he had been instructed to forward the brigade to Texas, as it was "the largest . . . under my command, and is equal to any to be found here or elsewhere in gallantry and soldierly qualities."[12]

But while the Texans languished in the Louisiana swamps waiting for orders, Kirby Smith changed his mind. There was concern for an "advance

[10] William M. [Buck] Walton, *An Epitome of My Life: Civil War Reminiscences* (Austin: The Waterloo Press, 1965), 83; W.H. Parsons to W. Steele, June 3, 1864.

[11] The list of Texans appeared in the *Houston Daily Telegraph* on June 8, 1864. A count is also found in Alwyn Barr, "Texas Losses in the Red River Campaign, 1864," *Texas Military History* 3 (Summer 1963): 103-10.

[12] John A. Wharton to J. Bankhead Magruder, June 17, 1864, *OR* 34, pt. 4, 680-81; J.G. Walker to E. Kirby Smith, August 13, 1864, ibid., 41, pt. 1, 106; Richard Taylor to E. Kirby Smith, August 18, 1864, ibid., 110-11; W.R. Boggs to S.B. Buckner, August 22, 1864, ibid., 118; Henry Orr to Mary Orr, June 11, 1864, in Anderson, ed., *Campaigning with Parsons' Brigade*, 141-42; George W. Ingram to Martha F. Ingram, June 12, 1864, in Ingram, comp., *Civil War Letters*, 75-76; Heartsill, *Fourteen Hundred and 91 Days in the Confederate Army*, 196, 209, 212-13.

of the enemy from the lower Arkansas." He decided to send the men north, and Wharton wrote in early August that "Parsons' brigade (with Carter's regiment, now in Texas, which can reach Arkansas almost as soon as troops from here) is very full, and having operated in Arkansas [before] would be more efficient there than any other troops of my command." To the relief of the men who hated the humid Louisiana heat, they would return to their old location southeast of Pine Bluff. Pratt's battery was no longer with the cavalry, however, having been sent on a raid into Missouri with General Sterling Price. Joseph Pratt would die from wounds sustained in that campaign.[13]

Most of the Texans had become weary of the war. October 28, 1864, was a significant date, as it was the anniversary of the day that the men of the Twelfth Texas had sworn their allegiance to the Confederate States of America. "Nearly all of the men in some of the companies say the[y] are going home after the 28th of the month," George Ingram wrote his wife. Still, Ingram, now a captain, confidently observed, "I think they boys in this company will behave themselves as becometh good soldiers." Nonetheless, another trooper wrote: "I think I will get to be of no account as a soldier for when a soldier sets his head to go home, I have noticed, that they are no account until they do get to go, and I have got my head set homeward and I will never be satisfied until I get there."[14]

By late 1864, Trans-Mississippi soldiers suffered shortages of almost everything. William Steele noted that he needed provisions for man and beast as well as weapons and ammunition. To complicate matters, the veterans with Parsons did not know if they would stay in southeastern Arkansas, return to the Red River Valley, or be ordered across the Mississippi River to reinforce John Bell Hood's Army of Tennessee. There was even talk of being sent to Fort Smith in far western Arkansas. By November, Kirby Smith decided to transfer the cavalry to East Texas where food and forage was more plentiful, a decision that proved popular. From there the troops could move either back to Louisiana or the Texas coast if there was a threat

[13] John A. Wharton to E. Kirby Smith, August 9, 1864, *OR* 41, pt. 2, 1,049-50; J.W. Lewis to W.H Parsons, September 11, 1864, ibid., 41, pt. 3, 923.

[14] George W. Ingram to Martha F. Ingram, October 20, 1864, in Ingram, comp., *Civil War Letters*, 77-78; J.C. Morriss to Amanda Morriss, November 6, 1862 [4], in Pruett and Black, eds., *Civil War Letters*, 47-49.

in either direction. Another year of war was drawing to a close, but the fighting was not yet over.[15]

The following orders cover all of 1864, twelve months that ranged from dreary inactivity to intensely active fighting. The Red River Campaign was for many troopers the only real combat they saw, and for others, it was the only fighting they wanted to see. Since few orders for the weeks during the actual campaigning survived, Parsons's official report, as published in the *Houston News Bulletin* on July 9 is included.

[15] E.K. Smith to S.B. Buckner, November 29, 1864, *OR* 41, pt. 4, 1,082-83; George Williamson to J.B. Magruder, November 30, 1864, ibid., 1,084; J.F. Belton to J.B. Magruder, December 1, 1864, ibid., 1,090-91; J.F. Belton to J.G. Walker, December 2, 1864, ibid., 1,092; W.R. Boggs to J.B. Magruder, December 3, 1864, ibid., 1,096; J.B. Magruder to W.R. Boggs, December 9, 1864, ibid., 1,104; J.B. Magruder to W.R. Boggs, December 12, 1864, ibid., 1,107-108; E.K. Smith to J.B. Magruder, December 21, 1864, ibid., 1,120; J.B. Magruder to W.R. Boggs, December 28, 1864, ibid., 1,131; W.R. Boggs to J.G. Walker, December 28, 1864, ibid., 1,131.

CHAPTER 6

# DOCUMENTS

## Arkansas and Louisiana: 1864

Hd: Qurs: Texas Cav. Brigade
Chambersville Ark. Jan. 8th 1864.

Special Order No. 1

Maj. A.J. Byrd C.S. Tex. Cav. Brig. will turn over to Captain John M. Stone[16] funds to Subsist sixty men ten days.

(signed) W.H. Parsons
Col. Comdg. Brigade

* * * * * * * * * * * * *

Hd: Qurs: Texas Cavalry Brigade
Camp near Camden Ark. Jan. 1st 1864.

Special Order No. 1a

Captain R.A. Terrell is hereby ordered to duty as Quarter Master of the 12th Texas Dragoons.

(signed) W H Parsons
Col Comdg. 12th Tex. Dragoons

[16] Company H, Nineteenth Texas.

* * * * * * * * * * * * *

Hd: Qurs: Texas Cav. Brigade
Chambersville Jan. 8th 1864.

Special Order No. 2.

Maj. A.J. Byrd Brig. C.S. will turn over to Captain John R. [John Rutledge Smith] Alston[17] funds to Subsist forty-nine men ten days.

(signed) W.H. Parsons
Col. Comdg. Brigade

* * * * * * * * * * * * *

Hd: Qurs: Texas Cav. Brigade
Chambersville Ark. Jan 7th 1864.

Special Order No. 3.

Captain Thomas Johns A.Q.M. will turn over to Capt. John R. Alston funds to forage fifty-two horses ten days.

(signed) W.H. Parsons
Col. Comdg. Brigade

* * * * * * * * * * * * *

Hd: Qurs: Texas Cav. Brigade
Chambersville Jan. 8th 1864.

Special Order No. 4.

Captain Thomas Johns A.Q.M. will turn over to Captain John M. Stone[18] funds to forage sixty-two horses ten days.

(signed) W.H. Parsons
Col. Comdg. Brigade

* * * * * * * * * * * * *

Hd. Qrs. Texas Cav. Brigade
Chambersville Jan. 8th 1864.

Special Order No. 5

Lt. Col. [Benjamin W.] Watson, 19th Tex. Cav. is directed to go at once to the reserve Camp of the Texas Cav. Brigade at or near El Dorado Union Co. Ark. and bring with him

[17] Company H, Twenty-first Texas.

[18] Company H, Nineteenth Texas.

to Warren, or to whatever point the Brigade may be at, all men belonging to the Brigade able to ride: horses that may need shoeing will be brought to Warren for that purpose. Sufficient men will be left at El Dorado merely to guard the train and they must consist of the super numeraries who are actually unable to do any other duty.

(signed) W.H. Parsons
Col. Comdg. Brigade

* * * * * * * * * * * * *

Camp Eldorado Jany 27th 1863[4]

Special Order No

Maj ~~L J Farrar~~ A J Byrd will turn over to Lieut J W [John W.] Walden 12th Tex Cav enough money to subsist two men for twelve 12 Days

By order Maj L J [Lochlin J.] Farrar
12th Tex Drg Comdg Reserve Camp Brig

* * * * * * * * * * * * *

Camp Eldorado Jany 27th 1863[4]

Special Order No

Capt Thomas Johns will turn over to Lieut J. W [John W.] Walden 12th Tex Dragoons enough money to forage three horses for twelve (12) Days

By order Maj L J [Lochlin J.] Farrar
12th Tex Comdg Reserve Camp Brig

* * * * * * * * * * * * *

Camp Eldorado Ark
Jany 27th 1863[4]

Special Order No

Lieut J W [John W.] Walden Co H 12th Tex Drag having been ordered to report to his company in Texas by Col W H Parsons will take with him two of his men who have been detained with this part of the command

By order of
Maj L J [Lochlin J.] Farrar
Comdg the Tex Cav
Comdg Reserve Tex Cav Brig Camp

* * * * * * * * * * * * *

Camp Eldorado
Jany 27th 1864

Special order No -

Capt [Car] Forrest 19th Tex Cav will furnish one wagon & team to report early in the morning at the Commissary Department in town. He will also furnish a detail of one man mounted to report to the Commissary Dept & provided with rations for one day.

By order of
L J [Lochlin J.] Farrar Major 12th Tex
Drg
Comdg Brig Reserve Camp-

* * * * * * * * * * * * *

Camp Eldorado Head Quarters
Jan 27th 1864

Special order No -

Lieut W J Forster [W.J. Foster] of Col Morgan's Battalion will proceed at once with the wagons belonging to the Brigade to a point designated by James Shropshire[19] and impress corn at the Government price for the use of the Brigade for one day

By order of
L J [Lochlin J.] Farrar Major 12th Tex
Drag
Comdg Brigade Reserve Camps

May
Resumed Dates encumbent as Adjutant
April 8th 1864
W.G. Vardell

* * * * * * * * * * * * *

Richmond
February 1, 1864

Honl James A. Seddon[20]
Secy. of War

Sir,

We respectfully present for your consideration, and that of the President, the name of Col William H. Parsons of the Regt. of Texas Cavalry, for appointment as a Brigadier General.

[19] Company C, Twelfth Texas.

[20] Colonel Parsons was recommended for promotion in February 1864 but the promotion was never confirmed, although his men called him "General Parsons" following the war. This correspondence is in the Records Division, War Department, National Archives; photocopy in the collection of Joe and Ann Cerney. The xerox does not include all of the signatures, therefore some are missing.

He has served faithfully for nearly three years—and had been actively engaged during the whole period. He has rendered efficient service and distinguished himself as a gallant and skilful officer and merits promotion, as we learn from various sources—We submit the accompanying papers recommending him, and refer to the reports of his Commanding officers in the Trans-Mississippi Department

W.B. Wright[21] P.W. Gray[22]
F.B. Sexton[23] M.D. Graham[24]
John R. Wilcox[25]

* * * * * * * * * * * * *

Head Quarters Texas Cavalry Brigade
Camp near Shreveport La., Febry 7th 1864[26]

Special Order No. 6

1st Lieutenant A.G. Hervey[27] of Co. "F" Morgan's Batt. is promoted Captain of the same, vice B.D. McKie elected to the Majority.

Snr 2nd Lieutant L.T. [Lucius T.] Wheeler to be 1st Lieut. vice Hervey promoted

Snr 2nd Lieutenant H.A. Tate to be Snr. 2nd Lieut. vice Wheeler promoted

The Comdg Officer of Morgan's Batt. will cause an election to be held in Co. "F" to fill the vacancy of Jnr 2nd Lieut

The above promotions to take effect from the date of Major [B.D.] McKie's elections

By order of
W.H. Parsons
Col. Comdg
Robt. C.H. Good A.D.C. & A.A.A. Genl.

[21] William B. Wright was a Confederate representative from Texas in the first session of the Confederate Congress.

[22] P.W. Gray was a Confederate representative from Texas in the first session of the Confederate Congress.

[23] Frank B. Sexton was one of only two Texans elected as representative for both terms of the Confederate Congress.

[24] Malcolm D. Graham was a Confederate representative from Texas in the first session of the Confederate Congress.

[25] John R. Wilcox, representative from Texas in the first session of the Confederate Congress, was elected to the second session but died of "apoplexy" on February 7, just days before taking office and just six days after signing this letter.

[26] Henry Orr wrote from San Augustine, Texas, on February 8: "The brigade was expected to be at Shreveport in a few days. 'Tis believed here it will go to southwest Louisiana to Taylor, in Green's place whose command has gone farther down the [Red] River." Yet his journal indicates that he remained at San Augustine until the twenty-first when the company left for Huntsville. The men remained there until March 4, when they disbanded and started to their individual counties. He arrived home on March 8. On March 22 he wrote: "My departure is again near at hand. . . . Oh! That war did not curse our land, and that peace and prosperity were ours." Henry Orr to "Sister," February 8, 1864, and journal entries dated March 12 and March 22, 1864, in Anderson, ed., *Campaigning with Parsons' Brigade*, 129-30.

[27] A.G. Hervey, a native of Tennessee, had enlisted in Navarro County. He was thirty-four years old in 1860 and gave his occupation as a farmer with $3,000 in real estate and $12,000 in personal estate. Bailey, *Between the Enemy and Texas*, 228-29.

* * * * * * * * * * * * *

Hd Quarters 12th Texas
Dragoons February 12th/64

Special Order NO 25-

The following named officers are appointed as a bord [*sic*] of Servey to condemn some spoiled salt-pork & c

Capt J J [Jefferson J.] Mallard A.C.S. to the 12th Tex Dragoons

Board

| | |
|---|---|
| 1st Lieut J.F. Morris | Co I 12 Tex |
| " " J.W. Reese | Co D " " |
| 2nd " J.W. Burgess | Co E " " |

The bord [*sic*] will report immediately—

By order of
L J [Lochlin J.] Farrar
Comdg 12 Tex Drag-

* * * * * * * * * * * * *

Camp near Shreveport
Feb 12 1864

In obedience to Special Order No 25 signed by Major L J [Lochlin J.] Farrar 12 Tex Drag we the undersigned board of survey appointed to condemn some spoiled salt pork issued to the 12th Tex Dragoons, have to report that there are ninety-eight pounds of Salt-pork issued to Said Regiment to day that is totally unfit for use & we recommend it to be thrown away as useless—

| | |
|---|---|
| 1st Lieut John F. Morris | Co I |
| " " J.W. Reese | Co D |
| 2nd " J.W. Burgess | Co E |

* * * * * * * * * * * * *

Orders from Regimental Head Quarters
Head Quarters 12th Texas Dragoons
Camp Near Marshall Tex February [torn]

Special Order No 26

The following named officers are appointed as a Board of Servay to examine Some Beefe issued by Capt J J [Jefferson J.] Mallard ACS to the 12th Texas Dragoons

Board

| | |
|---|---|
| 1st Lt J W [John W.] Reese | Co "D" 12th Tex Drag |
| 2d Lt W J [William J.] Montgomery | Co "I" 12th Tex Drag |
| 2d Lt W H Getzandanner [Getzandaner] | Co "E" 12th Tex Drag |

The Board will report immediately

By Order of
J C Brown Capt-
Comdg 12th Texas Dragoons
H H Highsmith
Sergt Maj

* * * * * * * * * * * * *

Head Quarters Texas Cavalry Brigade
Camp near Marshall Febry 15th 1864

General Order No. 2

The commanding Officers of Regts & Batt[alions will] cause to be made out and sent to these Hd. Qurs a full list of the <u>extra</u> <u>duty</u> men in their respective commands, giving new Company & Regiment and description of duty each man is assigned.

By order of
W.H. Parsons
Col. Comdg.
J.M. Brandon A.A.G.

* * * * * * * * * * * * *

Camps Near Marshall Tex February 17th 1864

In obedience to Special Order No 26 issued by Capt J C Brown comdg 12th Texas Dragoons we the undersigned as a board of Survey appointed by the Order aforesade to Examine a lot of beefe—Sixty three pounds—issued by Capt J J [Jefferson J.] Mallard ACS to the 12th Tex Dragoons to Day. We hereby Certify that wee have Carefully examined the Said lot of beef that it is almost too poor to be fed to the dogs—and that on account of its extreme poverty it would not turn & cut more than an third of its weight in meat! If it not edible—we therefore most respectfully condemn the said lot of beef as wholey unfit to be fed to the men.

Board of Survey

| | | |
|---|---|---|
| J.W. [John W.] Reese | 1st Lt Co D | 12th Tex |
| W.J. [William J.] Montgomery | 2nd Lt Co I | 12th Tex |
| W.H. Getzendaner | 2nd Lt Co. E | 12th Tex |

* * * * * * * * * * * * *

Camp Near Marshall Texas
February 22d 1864

[S]pecial order No 27

Capt R.A. Terrell asst A.Q.M 12th Tex Dragoons is ordered to turn over to the commanders of companies present the Sum of five hundred dollars each as Quarter Master funds, an[d] the Sum of four hundred dollars to each commander of company present as a commissary fund The Regiment is composed of five companies present; and the distribution will have reference to this number ~~of companies~~

By order of
L J [Lochlin J.] Farrar Major
Comdg 12th Tex Drag

* * * * * * * * * * * * *

Hd Qrs. Parsons Cavalry Brigade
Camp in Marshall Tx Feby 22 1864

____ Order No 3

I The companies composing this Brigade will move forward at 8 o'Clock in the direction of home.

II Companies will be marched by commanding officers to the counties the members live and there be furloughed for ten days the expiration of which they will report for duty to [their] Captains at the County Sites of counties where the Captains [may] direct.

III At the expiration of the ten days Captains will spend ____ week in their own counties in gathering up Conscripts, deserters and all men liable to Military duty between the ages of 18 and 45 years

IV Comdg officers of companies will rendezvous as [torn] The companies 2 from Kaufman, 2 from Parker, 2 [from] Dallas, 6 from Ellis, 1 from Johnson, & 1 from Collin will rendezvous at Chatfield Point, Navarro Co. The (2) companies from McClennan, 2 from Hill, 2 from Navarro, 1 from Limestone [torn] from Freestone county will rendezvous at Waco. Companies in Burnett & Travis one, one Company from Bell & Milam; & (2) from Williamson & one (1) from Bastrop will rendezvous near Austin, & one Co. from Walker, one (1) from La. [torn] one (1) from Orange, one (1) from Washington, one

(1) from [torn] one (1) from Grimes, one (1) from Goliad, & one (1) from _____ County will rendezvous at Hempstead.

V The Col. Comdg enjoins upon company Comd's to [enforce] rigid discipline and prevent by every means pos[sible any] depredations upon the property of private citizens. [Officers] responsible for any outrage or depredations caused by their men & will be immediately placed in arrest & [transferred when a] depredation is committed it shall be punished

* * * * * * * * * * * * *

Head Quarters Parsons Brigade
Waco Tex. March 1864

General Order No 4

I Paragraph XII General Order No 3 from these Head quarters is revoked

II That part of Paragraph (III) which directs the gathering of Conscripts, deserters, and all men liable to Military duty between the ages of 18 and 45 is hereby explained for the guidance of Officers engaged in the work; as to the class or classes of men subject to arrest All valid and legal exemptions, Leaves of absence furloughs and details must be respected. A legal furlough, leave of absence, or detail is granted only by Department or Dist. Commanders. Officers and Soldiers absent without the proper authority will be arrested and their papers sent to Brig. Genl. E Greer at Marshall Texas

III Under an agreement between Lt. Genl [E. Kirby] Smith, Major Genl. [John B.] Magruder & the Governor of Texas, the militia who have been in the service of the state during the past six months are at this time "legally exempted" from arrest as Conscripts, provided they volunteer into Confederate service or reorganize into state service, by the 15 day of March. Those between the ages of 18 & 45 who were actually in the state service and who volunteered or reorganized by the 15th of March will not be subject to arrest [torn] and men of this.

IV. No details for teamsters or other wise are valid unless by authority of Department or District Commanders and military organizations of minute men between conscript ages; are recognized confederate or state authority

V. All deserters from the army, who have failed to report to the proper [enroll]ing officers, or to the camp of instruct[ion] after enrollment, and all detailed who have not been detailed by Dep[t] or Dist. Commanders, or if detailed proper authority and not actually engag[ed] in the service for which the detail [was] made—will be arrested—The Col Com[dg.] is directed by Brig. Genl E Greer, Conscription to require the officers enga[ged] in gathering conscripts & c, to call upon enrolling officers of the different counties cause them to accompany them thru their respective counties for the purpose of furnishing information and facilitate the service and the enrolling officers required to report to Brig Genl E Gre[er] at Marshall Texas the names of all detailed men not in the regular [discharge] of their duties to the end that other details may be revoked

VI. Field officers in command of different Districts will require Weekly report from company commanders of the districts and [torn]

* * * * * * * * * * * * *

Head qrs Parsons Brigade
Jonesville April 1 1864

General Order No 6

Company Commanders who have enlisted men in their companies, subject to conscription, will make out a Discriptive list of all such men and send up to these Head quarters at once, so that they can be transfered by Brig. General [Elkanah B.] Greer from conscript serv[ic]e to the companies in which they have enlisted.

By order of
W.H. Parsons
Col Comdg
J M Brandon A A Genl

* * * * * * * * * * * * *

Head Quarters Parsons Brigade
Jonesville April 2d 1864.

General Orders No 7

I The colonel commanding regrets to learn that the men of this command are straggling all over the country, and annoying citizens; hereafter no men will be allowed to leave the limits of the camp with out written permission from the commanding officer of the Brigade

II Commanding officers of Regiments are required to have Roll call at revillee, Twelve o'clock and retreat and all men absent without proper leave will be punished

III Special attention is called to Guard officer from Department Head Quarters dismounting men for committing depredations on the property of citizens These orders will be strictly enforced on any man in this brigade caught committing depredations.

IV We are soon expected to take the field, and in order to get the command in an efficient state of drill, a field will be selected adjacent to the encampment. The drill will be commenced Monday evening, and Regimental and company drill will be kept up every evening thereafter while remaining in camps. The drill will be confined to the actual movements expected to [be] used in the field—thereby preparing the Brigade to win new laurels in addition to those which already crown it.

V Dress Parade will be held at the usual hour, (1/2 hour before Sunset) every evening; all guns must be brought out on dress Parade.

By Order of
W.H. Parsons
Col. Commanding
J.M. Brandon
A.A. Genl.

* * * * * * * * * * * * *

Head Quarters Texas Cavalry Briga[de]
Jonesville, April 3rd, 1864

General Order No. 8

I All officers of this command are required to wear a sword when on duty, except when going into a fight it then being the best left to the discretion of the officer.

II Any private wishing to turn over his sword to an officer can do so by taking his receipt for the same which receipt will then be given to the Ordnance Officer of the Brigade.

By order of
W.H. Parsons Col. Com.
J.M. Brandon A.A.G.

* * * * * * * * * * * * *

Head Quarters 12th Texas Cav
Camp near Jonesville April 6th 1864

Special[28]

Agreeable to orders emenating from Head Quarters Dept and Headquarters Cav Brigade to furnish Pratt's Battery with ten (10) men from the 12th Texas Cav, Comdg officer will proceed to furnish one (1) man each—

By order of Major [Lochlin J.] Farrar
Comdg
[W.G.] Vardell Adjt

Copy of endorsement on above order
Head Quarters & c

We the undersigned Captains of the 12th Texas Cav have used our influence with our companies to fill above orders, but have failed to get them—Our men are volunteers, and have fitted themselves out as Cavalry men at a great expense and we know of no legal way that we could force or compel them to take a different service

Therfore we respectfully decline obeying above order

| | | | |
|---|---|---|---|
| (Signed) | M.B. Hismith [Highsmith] | Co D | 12th Tex Cav |
| " | W.G. [William G.] Veal | " F | " " " |
| " | J.E. Hawkins | " H | " " " |

true copy to W.G. Vardell
Adjt.

[28] Even as the Texans headed for battle they declined to give up their horses. This had been a point of pride the entire war, and the troopers were not going to relinquish their horses willingly, even if doing so aided the war effort.

* * * * * * * * * * * * *

Head Quarters 12th Texas Cav
Jonesville April 6th 64

Special[29]

Captains Hismith [M.B. Highsmith],[30] [William G.] Veal[31] and [J. Em.] Hawkins[32] are placed under arrest for disobedience of orders until further orders—

By orders of
"Maj [Lochlin J.] Farrar" comdg
[W.G.] Vardell Adjt-

* * * * * * * * * * * * *

Head quarters Dist of La
Office of Chief Ordnance-
In the field April 7th, 1864[33]

[C]ircular -[34]

The attention of all Ord. officers of the command is [torn] to the fact that cartridges without caps, have been issued from the Depots to the Troops of the Army—Unless the utmost diligence and care are used, in giving information of the fact, grave disasters may overtake us in the presence of the Enemy in issuing cat. [cartridges] without caps. Ord. offcs. will always in form the parties even then of the fact and will accompany the issue with caps in proportion of (13) thirteen caps to each package of (10) ten catrdg [cartridges]. In issueing all cartridges the 'invoices' will be carefull to specify the cartridges, as with, or without caps, ord officers will in all cases, when practicable open & examine the ammunition boxes received by them so that a personal inspection, may show, whether they are properly invoiced or not, and whether the ammunition be recievable in each case of issue by the off. It implies assurance on his part that he has examined the ammunition, that it is what it is represented to be & that it is servicable. The attention of offc's Comd Regts, will see in all cases that caps accompany the cartridges issue them, & that the car, are suitable to the calibre of the gun[s] of the Regt—More than ordinary care

[29] As result of this incident, the three captains were placed under arrest.

[30] Company D, Twelfth Texas.

[31] Company F, Twelfth Texas.

[32] Company H, Twelfth Texas.

[33] On April 27 Henry Orr wrote from Rapides Parish, Louisiana. He told his parents that the brigade had been constantly fighting, noting that "Captain Veal is one of the bravest men I ever saw." After one encounter he proudly announced: "Gen. Wharton said of our charge (though on a small scale) that he never saw it equaled on the other side of the River." Henry Orr to "Father, Mother, and Family," April 27, 1864, in Anderson, ed., *Campaigning with Parsons' Brigade*, 131-34.

[34] This circular appears twice with slight variation in each.

is required owing to the fact that so many 'Calibres' of arms are found in the Army, requiring different size cartridges,

Division Commanders will cause this order to be read to every Reg Commander-

By Command of
Maj Gen [Richard] Taylor
(Signed) J.L. Brent Major
Chief Ordnance
Dist West La

B.H. Davis
A.A.G.
J M Brandon
A.A.G.

* * * * * * * * * * * * *

May—resumed Duties encumbent as Adjutant

April 8, 1864
W.G. Vardell

* * * * * * * * * * * * *

Head Quarters Trans Mississippi Dept
Shreveport La, May 17th 1864[35]

Special order No 121

Private Jas T Scott Co G—12th Tex Cav is detailed as a miller at the Flemming Mill of Mr A.B. Johnson in Kaufman Co Texas, and will report accordingly

By command of
General E. Kirby Smith
S.S. Anderson Asst Adjt Genl

True Copy
W.G. Vardell adjt

[35] On May 11, J.C. Morriss of Carter's Regiment wrote: "We have been fighting for 18 days, one excepted, without intermission up to last Sunday since which time we have been picketing in sight of the enemy. Our company is just off of picket this morning where we have been in sight of them for the last 24 hours. They shot at us several times yesterday morning, but as they were on the opposite side of a large plantation about three quarters of a mile from us, they could not reach us." J.C. Morriss to Amanda Morriss, May 11, 1864, Weller, ed., *Civil War Letters.*

* * * * * * * * * * * * *

Head Quarters Trans Miss Dept
Shreveport La May 24th 64[36]

Special Orders No 127

I Private P.L. Lusk Co 'D' Goulds Texas Battalion Infantry is transfered to Co C 12th Texas Cav & will report for duty accordingly

II Private E. Boykin Co 'C' 12th Tex Cav is transfered to Co 'D' Goulds Batt Tex Inft & will report for duty accordingly

By command of
Gen E.K. Smith
S.S. Anderson Asst. Adjt General

True Copies
[W.G.] Vardell Adjt

* * * * * * * * * * * * *

Pursuit of Banks' Army on Red River—Official Report.[37]
Headquarters Parsons' Brig. Tex.
Near Fort DeRussy, Red River, June 3d, 1864.

Brig. Gen. W. Steele, Commanding Division,

GENERAL:—Having just received the reports of the commanding officers of the regiments composing this Brigade, consisting of the 12th, 19th, 21st and Morgan's Battalion, in reference to the series of engagements with the Federal army on and near Red River, during its retreat from Grand Ecore to Simsport, near the mouth of the river; I have the honor to present the following resume of its operations:

The Brigade (with the exception of a detachment from each regiment sent to the interior of Texas for arms,) immediately after the battles of Mansfield and Pleasant Hill, were thrown forward by Maj. Gen. Taylor to attack the fleet of gunboats and transports, then descending Red River to join Banks' retreating army at Grand Ecore. As this is the commencement of the pursuit of the retreating enemy by the Brigade, I deam [*sic*] it due to the command here briefly to record the fact of its participation, with [Peter C.] Wood's

[36] Henry Orr of Parsons's Regiment wrote from near Keatchie, Louisiana, on May 14: "Had I opportunity I could write a little volume of interesting incidents connected with our first month's life in the valley of Red River, but one event crowds so fast upon the heels of another that they appear stale or out of date in a week from the time they transpired. . . . Our troops are mainly on this side of the River and below." On May 17 he added that he was not with the main body of the regiment, but still near Mansfield. He arrived to the command, some thirty odd miles below the Atchafalaya River on May 25, where he noted the death of his messmate, Johnny Morgan, in the Battle at Yellow Bayou. He later indicated the camp as being near the battlefield, four miles from Simmesport and six miles from the mouth of the Red River. Henry Orr to "Sister," May 14, 17, 25, 29, 1864, in Anderson, ed., *Campaigning with Parsons' Brigade*, 138-41. J.C. Morriss of Carter's regiment added on May 11: "We have had one of the hardest campaigns that any one has had since the war commenced. With our briggade [*sic*] of 1200 or 1500 men we have been hanging on the rear of a retreating army of 20,000 or 30,000 men and fought them for seventeen days out of 18." J.C. Morriss to Amanda Morriss, May 11, 1864, Weller, ed., *Civil War Letters*.

[37] Colonel Parsons official report appeared in the *Houston News Bulletin* on July 9, 1864, and provides an account of the brigade's service in the Red River Campaign. Although this report is out of chronological order, it is inserted here before Wharton's statement of congratulations to the army on May 24. The campaign had ended on May 18.

and [Nicholas C.] Gould's regiments, in the boat-fight at Blair's Landing, on the 12th of April, 1864. So conspicious was the valor of the officers and men in this encounter with seven gunboats, exposed upon an open plantation for two hours without shelter, to a front and enfilading fire, as to extort from Rear Admiral [David D.] Porter, U.S.N. in his official report, the acknowledgement that "*their desperate courage baffled description.*" Three boats (one gunboat and two transports), hoisted the white flag, but six gunboats coming to their relief, from above and below, kept up the unequal contest until dark, and we could not take possession of our prize, but retired in good order, having to mourn the loss of our Chief, Maj. Gen. [Tom] Green, and several of our bravest men and officers. Capt. Jno. C. Brown, of the 12th Texas Dragoons, was severely wounded by a canister shot. The Brigade moved to once to aid in the investment of Grand Ecore, where Banks' army had halted after its retreat from Pleasant Hill. The Brigade was thrown forward on the direct road to Nachitoches, the enemy's southern line extending from Grand Encore to that town. From the 14th to the 22d, the different regiments of the Brigade were engaged in daily heavy skirmishing with the enemy's cavalry, in sight of Nachitoches. The remainder of the cavalry corps having been withdrawn from the upper, or Grand Ecore road, the task was assigned to the Brigade of covering all the approaches to the enemy, and you were placed in command of the front, including this Brigade, with other troops under your immediate orders. On the 19th, 20th, and 21st April the enemy made heavy demonstrations upon our right to conceal and cover the evacuation of Grand Encore. The fighting was heavy on the 20th and 21st on the lower, or Nachitoches road, in which the whole of the 12th Battalion and the 5th Squadron of the 21st participated, the 19th being in position on the upper, or Grand Ecore road. Lieut. Fred Cox, of the 12th Texas Dragoons, was wounded in the affair of the 21st. On the morning of the 2nd, the 19th regiment, under the immediate command of Brig. Gen. [Frederick] Steele, drove in the enemy's pickets, following up the enemy, and drove a brigade of Federal cavalry, composing their rear guard, through the town, occupying the northside. Almost simui-taneously the remainder of the Brigade drove the enemy's pickets on Old River, and the town was in our full possession. After concentrating the entire Brigade, I received orders to pursue the enemy, and moved promptly down the Valley of Old River, which I discovered was the line of retreat for the whole Federal army About 1 1/2 P.M., on the evening, (22d April) I suddenly came upon the enemy's rear guard, seven miles below Nachitoches, at the "Prudham's" place. The enemy, in strong force of infantry, artillery and cavalry, had taken position on the opposite bank of the crossing of the Cane River, to check our pursuit. I at once made disposition for an engagement. Threw the Battalion on the left, 21st and two squadrons of the 12th in the centre, the 19th on the right—all dismounted, holding the remainder of the 12th mounted as a reserve. Our line advanced to the river bank, when the enemy, in largely superior force, opened with small arms and artillery. A hot fight of three hours ensued, our left and centre most heavily engaged. Lieut. Col. [Charles] Morgan, commanding Battalion on the left and Maj. [L.J.] Farrar and Col. [G.W.] Carter in centre, being the whole time under very heavy fire. They and their men displayed conspicuous courage. Maj. [B.D.] Chenowith, with two squadrons of the 21st, here gallantly waded the river in face of the enemy's fire and attempted a flank movement on the open plan[t]ation on the opposite bank. Capt. [J.R.S.] Alston, of the 21st, was here severely wounded in the head. The enemy in the meantime recalled troops from their line of march and had heavily reinforced, when I remounted the command to make new dispositions to meet the increased odds against us. At this moment

Maj. Gen. [John] Wharton and myself, together, came up from Nachitoches. The enemy shortly withdrew, and the Brigade encamped on the battle ground. Took up the pursuit the next morning, 23d of April, and encountered the enemy's rear, 16th army corps, 12,000 strong, under Federal General [A.J.] Smith, at LeCompte place, one mile North of Cloutersville.[38] In the pursuit of the morning, Maj. [John B.] Williams, of the 19th, commanding advance, captured 43 prisoners, with their arms and several horses. On the northern suburb of Cloutersville the enemy had taken position and opened with artillery on our advance. The battalion and 21st were thrown into the woods on our left, and soon became engaged with enemy's infantry, the 12th was held in the centre, and the 19th on the right—both in open ground. Capt. Barnes' battery, of three pieces, during the engagement came up and opened with effect in reply to the enemy's guns, which had been furiously shelling our right and centre. A detachment of Wood's regiment, 130 strong, had joined us after the fight of the evening previous, and I assigned it to duty with the 21st. The detachment under Maj. Chenowith, together with the 21st, under Lieut. Col. [D.C.] Giddings, and the battalion under Lieut. Col. Morgan, pressed the enemy back in the wood on the reserve. You, yourself, with a squadron of the 12th, moved down to the left, and here the fight became very severe, again driving the enemy. They threw forward their infantry in force, and pressed our men (whose ammunition was completely exhaus[t]ed) back to our line on open ground. Here the 12th dismounted to cover the retrograde movement of our left. When the enemy had turned our left, the 12th, under command of Lieut. Col. Burleson, remounted, changed front to the enemy's flank movement, whilst I directed the fire of Capt. Barnes' Napoleon gun upon the enemy's rapid advance—the steadiness with which the 12th held their ground, under Lieut. Col. Burleson, aided by Barnes' artillery, checked the enemy's advance, and the fight terminated. The enemy retired from Cloutersville, and we occupied the place.

At 2 o'clock the following morning, 24th April, Maj. Gen. Wharton directed me to move forward with two regiments and one piece of artillery, find the enemy's position, and shell their camp in the night. The order was executed. The column moving silently in the darkness on the sandy bank of Cane river, until my advance, two miles below Cloutersville, was fired upon by the enemy's pickets, which disclosed their position. Their camp-fires being plainly seen, I ordered the artillery to open, which threw shells into their sleeping camps, producing visible confusion and consternation. Daylight found the pursuing and pursued under arms and in position, when the skirmishing commenced. The fight raged until the evening. Our whole force of cavalry, in the open field, confronted an overwhelming force of the enemy of all arms, sheltered and covered from view by woods, buildings and fences. This (the battle of Cloutersville) was characterized by a stubborn courage, reckless daring, and acts of heroism, upon the part of the officers and men of this brigade, which, as the last of the three days pursuit upon Cane river, Major General [Richard] Taylor has already pronounced in General Orders that "*In daring, vigor, and soldier ship, will compare with any operation of the war.*"

The enemy occupied an advanced position, in front of their main body, covered by the ruins, walls and fences of a residence destroyed by them the day previous. I was directed by Maj. Gen. Wharton to order up a regiment of the brigade to charge. I directed Col. Carter to move forward with the 21st; Lieut. Col. Giddings had been assigned by me to command the advance skirmishers, consisting of the first squadron of the 21st, and

[38] Cloutierville is about halfway between Natchitoches and Alexandria. Parsons's misspelling will be retained throughout the report.

Capt. [William G.] Veal's company of sharpshooters of the 12th. With these companies, Lieut. Col. Giddings led the charge, one of the most brilliant and daring of the war, took and held the position, which commanded the enemy's main line, upon which, supported promptly by the 21st, they opened such a well directed fire as to force back their advance and compel the enemy to unmask his strength. This movement was aided by the battalion on the left, which skirting the field on edge of the timber, gained position on the enemy's right, and Capt. Peavy's [William W. Peevy] company, of the 19th, sent over the river on the enemy's left; the 12th and 19th being held in reserve to cover the movement, drawn up in parallel lines of battle a few hundred yards to the rear, in open field. The enemy, upon the loss of this position, brought up large bodies of infantry, and unmasked seven pieces of artillery, directing a concentrated fire upon the devoted heroes who had wrested it from them. The fire was terrific, and what passed through and over those occupying it, plunged and whistled through the ranks of the 12th and 19th to the rear. Having developed such immensely superior strength on the part of the enemy, Maj. Gen. Wharton and yourself ordered our advance to fall back, which they did, covered by a charge of the 12th, under Lieut. Col. Burelson, to prevent the enemy from taking advantage of the retrograde movement. The battalion which had performed such distinguished service upon the left, fell back with the movement. The enemy attempted an advance with cavalry and infantry. Our men, having rallied and formed by regiments in parallel lines of battle impatiently awaited the anticipated charge of the enemy when our artillery, by a well directed fire, threw their shells into the head of the advancing columns, which broke and fled in confusion, in full view of our whole force, amid their shouts of exultation. This closed the battle. The enemy retired rapidly upon their main body, closely followed by our pressing column—our advance constantly skirmishing with their rear. The enemy's force reached the Cotile Bayou, at its junction with Red River, that night. The following day, the 25th, the brigade came up with their rear, then under cover of their gunboats.

Col. Brent, of Major-General Taylor's staff, with a battery, supported by four companies of the 19th, under Maj. Williams, made an attack on the gunboats above the mouth of the Cotile. The battalion was left at that point, and was engaged on the 27th and 28th, in sharpshooting at the gunboats, and then joined the brigade, which, on the 28th, commenced active operations with the main body of the Cavalry Corps, under Brig Gen [James] Major, against the enemy's lines north of Alexandria, in the valley of Bayou Rapides. The main body of the brigade was held in reserve, during the engagement, with the exception of the 19th, which was thrown across on the east side of the Rapides, with orders to move parallel with Gen Major's division. This regiment was engaged for several hours with a largely superior force, gallantly holding its position until driven back by superior numbers. I sent the 21st to support it, and followed it shortly after with the 12th, crossing to the east side of the Bayou late in the evening. Here a most gallant fight ensued. I sent forward the fourth squadron of the 12th, under Capt. Veal, to aid in driving the enemy from the wood on the left. The charge of the 21st and Veal's squadron, dismounted, was eminently successful in driving the enemy from the timber, then from a ditch, and finally from a breastwork of rails, and putting the enemy, greatly superior in numbers, to flight, holding the ground—the 21st camping on the battle-field. Colonel Wood's regiment participated in the movement. Colonels Carter and Wood greatly distinguished themselves in this affair.

I retired the main body at dark. That night the brigade relieved Gen. Major's pickets along the enemy's lines on both sides Bayou Rapides, and from that date to until the 7th

May, the entire brigade was engaged in picketing by regiment, two on each side of the bayou, within four miles of Alexandria and in sight of the enemy's main infantry camps. From daylight until dark the skirmishing was almost incessant, each day, between the pickets of both parties. During four days of the period, being prostrated with fever, I turned over the command of the brigade to Col. Carter. On the 5th the enemy, exasperated by the audacity of shelling their camp the evening previous by yourself in person came out in force to drive us from the valley. I assumed command of the brigade in the morning, shortly before you came upon the field at Middle bayou. The fight was very hot throughout the day, the enemy forcing the 12th battalion, on east side, from position to position, which was stubbornly held until forced to retire by overwhelming numbers. On this field Lieut. Geo. Hall, of the 12th, was killed, a most gallant officer. On the 6th, the enemy having fallen back to their original camp, the whole command resumed their old position within a few hundred yards of enemy's main body. That evening I was again taken sick and turned over the command to Col. Carter, who had command the following day, the 7th, when the enemy, exasperated at the temerity of such a small force menacing their army, threw out army corps and forced the command out of the valley. In this moment Lieut. John Haley, of the 12th Texas, an officer of great gallantry, was severely wounded. The 21st remained after the fight of the 7th and resumed picketing and skirmishing in the Rapides valley on our old ground. The remainder of the brigade moved below south of Alexandria, to Bayou Boeuff on the enemy's lines, thus performing the arduous task of picketing all the outlets of Alexandria around the enemy's camps. I assumed command of the brigade on the 13th, and on the night of the 14th pickets reported an unusual commotion in the enemy's lines. I visited they videttes at daylight and discovering that the Federal army were in full retreat from Alexandria I at once commenced the attack on the enemy's flank in open field. Major [John B.] Williams, commanding skirmishers distinguished himself by one of the most brillant and successful charges in line and cavalry skirmish, supported by the 19th, under the command of Col. [N.M.] Burford. As the enemy's rear retreated from Gov. Moore's place into the timber, the advance, under Maj. Williams, followed in pursuit and soon became hotly engaged: the enemy in force taking position and stubbornly holding their ground, to enable the Federal column, moving from Alexandria by the river bank, to pass the point of junction, This column, throughout the day, was closely and successfully pressed by Lieut. Col. Giddings with 21st Texas, who had followed the retreating army through Alexandria and down the river bank. The engagement of the advance, under Major Williams, soon became one of the hotest of the pursuit. I reinforced with the whole of the 19th, under Col. Burford, and with one squadron of the 12th under Capt. [Thomas] Haley, and Capt. Vontrees' [Edward H. Vontress] squadron of the battalion. The command dismounted, engaged at very close quarters in the dense undergrowth of the swamp, and with cheers steadily drove the enemy. Capt. John M. Stone, of the 19th, was here wounded and is deservedly mentioned in the regimental report for conspicuous gallantry. The pursuit was taken up the following morning, the 15th, and ten miles below at the Wilson plantation on Red River, the whole brigade was engaged with the enemy's rear in position at a point where the Chaneyville road strikes Red River. The enemy's artillery having opened my line of attack, I ordered forward two rifle guns of the Valverde battery, under Lieut. Holmes, which silenced the enemy's fire. Resumed pursuit on the morning of the 16th in hearing of Gen. Wharton's artillery attack at Mansura on the enemy's front pressed forward and struck the enemy's column on the flank on Marksville prairie, one mile above

Marksville—attacked with artillery and dismounted cavalry. Capt Bogges, of the battalion, captured several wagons and prisoners. On the 17th we joined the other Division of General Wharton's cavalry corps, and this brigade was placed by Gen. Wharton in the advance in the rear of the enemy's column, fighting the entire evening and driving them before us. The enemy's advance had reached their gunboats at Simsport, and the 18th of May was signalized by their last desperate stand at Norwood plantation six miles from Simsport. Lieut. [Ed. J.] Gardner, of the 12th, an officer of high merit, was here killed. This battle, in which my brigade bore such a conspicuous part closed the series of the most protracted, continuous, brilliant and successful cavalry affairs which has characterized this war.[39]

The battalion picketed up to enemy's line the night of the 19th, and began skirmishing at daylight; the whole brigade was ordered forward to bring on the attack, supported by the other divisions of the cavalry corps, and by 11 o'clock A.M. sustained by Maj. Gen. [Camille] Polignac's division of infantry, Gen. A.J. Smith U.S.A. with the XIXth army corps, reinforced by fresh troops from New Orleans, confronted us. The 19th and 21st were ordered to charge and feel the enemy, the 12th dismounted to support the movement. The enemy advanced in force, the 12th occupied a line of fence and hedge on lower side of the plantation, where I had directed the construction of rail breastworks. Col. [Peter] Hardeman's brigade of cavalry, dismounted, was on the right of the 12th Texas, the other regiments of the brigade acted as cavalry throughout the day on the extreme right, the 19th as reserve and support to artillery under heavy fire, and 21st and one squadron of battalion participating in supporting the infantry and dismounted troops on extreme right. The 21st and battalion under Lieut. Col. [D.C.] Giddings drove the enemy's left and continued the fight an hour after the left and centre of Polignac's infantry had fallen back; on our extreme left resting on bayou, De Glacie the 12th dismounted, occupied position with Hardeman's brigade, dismounted on the right as before stated. The line was ordered to fall back to ditches in the centre of the field on the enemy's advance, and the enemy occupied the defenses our men had constructed. The enemy had massed upon their right, supporting their artillery in position, with heavy bodies of infantry and heavy reserves. After a furious cannonade, in which our artillery had silenced their fire, the line of dismounted cavalry were ordered forward to charge. The 12th being upon the extreme left, confronted the position where the enemy had massed his greater strength; amid a storm of grade and minnie balls the line advanced as steadily as infantry veteran over an open field upon the enemy masked in a strong position. The 12th, of whom as a part of my brigade, in this charge I am alone privileged to speak, went through the storm which met them, took the position and held it until ordered to retire. Capt. Jos. P. Weir, an officer of unusually distinguished merit, who commanded this regiment fell at his post; Captain [Thomas] Haley, Lieut. [J.B.] Abbott, and Lieut. [W.H.] Getzendaner wounded; here we have to mourn the loss in this gallant regiment alone, of ten killed and sixty wounded of its brave spirits; the principle loss sustained was on retiring over open ground, and here I must pay a tribute to McMahan's battery and the section of the Velverde [Valverde], under Lieut. Hume, for their timely and well directed fire, which effectually checked the enemy's advance as our line retired. It is proper for me also to mention the valuable services of Capt. Mosby's battery on bayou Rapids It is not proper for me to describe a battle in which so many other troops

[39] The last several sentences of this paragraph were typeset out of order and had to be reconstructed to make sense.

participated; but of the heavy loss of 600 admitted by the enemy—my men so cool and brave, cut down their share of the hated invader. Throughout this unexampled pursuit the brigade, which I have the honor to command, has fought almost the whole period under your own eye and supervision as Division Commander, and during the pursuit on Cane river; and the battles and skirmishes on bayou De Glacie, under the eye of Maj. Gen'l, commanding cavalry corps. It is unnecessary, therefore, for me to speak of the patient endurance, of long and continued privations, the oft recurring night watch, the incessant, never ending days fight, and the cool and unflinching courage which, always against ten and often twenty times their number, bore them up against every apparent reverse and wrung from both the U.S. Army and Navy officers (as we learn from interviews with flag of truce parties) the tribute that *the world never witnessed such fights as those rebel troops who hung with such dogged valor upon their rear in this pursuit.* To state the above fact of acknowledgement of the enemy is the highest tribute I can pay the noble and deserving men who compose this brigade.

To the regimental commanders and field officers of the 12th, 19th, 21st and Morgan's Battalion, I am indebted for the promptness and coolness in action, and the patient example of fortitude and endurance with which they have shared the privations of their gallant men. Among the conspicuous for gallantry and ability (where so many are entitled to a place on the roll) mentioned by regimental and detachment commanders, are Maj. Williams and Capt. J.M. Stone, of the 19th; Capts. Ed. H. Vontress and M.M. Boggess and Capt. Nunn, of Morgan's Battalion, and Capt. W.G. Veal, of the 12th, who was wounded in the 25th fight of the pursuit. Capt. Haley and Lieut. Abbott, of the 12th also, and Capt. Alston, of the 21st, wounded on the 22d April; also private James A. Nelms, of Co. B. Morgan's Battalion, which endorsement for ability and courage I take pleasure in presenting to the attention of division and corps commanders. I also deem it my duty to mention the conspicuous gallantry of Capt. J.M. Brandon, A.A.G., and Lieut. Mercer (W.J.) Of my personal staff, upon every field. The whole loss of the Brigade during the entire pursuit of Banks' army from Blair's Landing, near Pleasant Hill, to the last battle field near Simsport, is 29 killed and 189 wounded, total, 218; of which the 12th Texas Dragoons had 14 killed and 93 wounded; the 19th Texas, 7 killed and 21 wounded; 21st Texas, 3 killed and 23 wounded; Morgan's Battalion, 5 killed and 22 wounded. Our casualties, though heavy and demonstrating the fiery ordeal of shot and shell through which we have passed during the 36 days of pursuit, is slight compared to the damage we know we inflicted upon the enemy. It was inappropriate to mention the results in casualties and successes of each days fight. The grand total of (4,000) four thousand killed, wounded and captured of the enemy, reported by the Maj. Gen. Commanding Cavalry Corps, as the result of the labors of his command, and the position in the rear of Banks' army assigned to this Brigade, is evidence that to it belongs some share of the glory in common with its gallant comrades in the other brigades of this corps, of inflicting such terrible and merited chastisement upon the once arrogant, but not humbled, mercenaries of the "Grand Army of the Gulf."

With great respect, your obt. Servt.

W.H. Parsons

* * * * * * * * * * * * * *

To the Officers & Soldiers of
Wharton's Cavy Army of Western La.
In the field May 24/64

General Orders No. 7[40]

Soldiers

For forty Six days you have daily engaged the enemy always superior in numbers When the beaten foe (4 Army Corps of Infantry and 5000 Cavalry) began his retreat, you were formed in battle array in his front & hung upon his flank & rear only to destroy. In his retreat from Grand Ecore to Atchafalaya,[41] you killed, wounded and captured 4000 men destroyed 5 transports & 3 Gun boats. All this was accomplished with a loss to you of 400 men, 2/3 of whom will report for duty again in forty days

The history of no other campaign will present the spectacle of a cavalry force capturing and killing more of the enemy than <u>their own numbers</u>. This you have done and in so doing have immortalised yourselves and added new luster to Texas. The Gallantry of whose Sons has been illustrated on every battle field from Gettysburg to Glorietta—Had a portion of our force been where I was informed they were an hour and a half before the engagement at Norwoods Plantation[42] the rear guard of the enemy would have been entirely destroyed, as it was 30 of his dead left upon the field 65 graves iscribed "killed in action on the 18th of May" besides his wounded carried away by him testify to the slaughter you inflicted upon him Federal Prisoners recently captured announce their loss as 800 men killed and wounded at the battle of Norwood Plantation

Your advance guard are now watering their horses in the Miss River while you will soon follow on short rations and with scarcity of forage and in the saddle day and night you have neither murmured nor complained—In all your trials and dangers the veteran 2nd La Cav have been by your side They have shared your dangers & are participants in your glory. During the entire retreat the different Batteries of Artillery either acting separately or under Col Brent or Maj. Semmers displayed the most marked skill & gallantry. They were particularly distinguished in the engagement at Mansura[43] and Norwoods Plantation I as your Commander honor you for your deed and thus acknowledge my

[40] This congratulatory order was issued in the field following the Battle at Yellow Bayou at the end of the Red River Campaign. J.C. Morriss wrote his wife nine months later that the reason his regiment was not to be dismounted in early 1865 was "owing to our good character as a regt. We were complimented by Gen Wharton in La by a special complimentary order for galant [*sic*] conduct in La. And the order was ordered to be read before every regt. In the army on dress parade: and the general says that it is not only on account of the gallantry of the men but on account of the gallantry of our Lt. Col. Giddings in leading the charge at Cloutierville where we drove the enemy from a very strong position that they had taken from which they annoyed us very much." J.C. Morriss to Amanda Morriss, February 17, 1864[5], Weller, ed., *Civil War Letters*.

[41] Banks began his retreat from Grand Ecore toward Alexandria on April 21. He finally crossed the Atchafalaya at Simmesport on May 19.

[42] Yellow Bayou, the final battle in the Red River Campaign, was also known as Norwood's Plantation.

[43] The fighting at Mansura was on May 16, when Taylor made a final effort to stop the Union army.

appreciation of your services. Genl Taylor cheerfully accords to you the need of his approbation and in his time and way will signify his admiration

A grateful people will cherish the record of your gallantry.

(Signed) John A. Wharton
Maj. Genl

Official
(Signed) Thos C. Howard[44]
Lieut & A.A.A.Gnl
Hd Qrs Parsons Brigade
Hornesville[45] May 28/ 1864
Official J M Brandon A.A.Genl
Copy

* * * * * * * * * * * * * *

Head quarters Whartons Cav Corps
In the field May 24th 1864

[C]ircular No 4-

Complaints from citizens and Dist Head qua[r]ters are continually made to these Head quarters of the depredations commited throughout the country by stragglers from the Cavalry. This evil must be corrected at once, Division Commanders will through Division and Brigade Provost Guards and by detail under good officers for this purpose have the county patroled [blacked out] All men absent without leave, will be taken to their respective 'Div Head qrs' where they will be dismounted, the men sent to 'Div head qrs,' for assignment to infantry or such other dispositions as it is deemed best should be made. Their horses will be turned over to the Quarter Master of the Regiment to which they belong, who will issue them to dismounted men of the same command—giving owners certificates of their value. Div Commanders are enjoined to take the matter in hand, and check an evil that cannot longer be endured—These stragglers pillage & destroy the subsistence of the people whilst their brave comrades, are in the front battling with the Enemy. A few bad men of this kind blast the reputation for gallantry and discipline that Regts' Brigs' and Divs'establish by their soldierly conduct—They are a disgrace to their comrades, and each private in the ranks who does his duty, should feel an interest in seeing them brought to justice

(Signed) Maj Gen John A. Wharton
Official (Signed) F.B. Lubbock
Lieut Col & A.A.G
L.W. Moore A.A.G
J.M. Brandon A.A.G

True Copy
W.G. Vardell Adjut

[44] Howard had been with the Seventh Texas Cavalry (Seventh Regiment Texas Mounted Volunteers, Third Regiment, Sibley's Brigade).

[45] Although this is clearly written as Hornesville, the location has not been determined. The brigade was probably still near Simmesport on this date. Following the battle at Yellow Bayou the men spent the next few days burying the dead "in an enclosed graveyard at a church" on the Coco Plantation. Both this place and the Norwood Plantation served as hospitals. Gallaway, *The Ragged Rebel*, 122.

* * * * * * * * * * * * *

Head Quarters Whartons Cav Corps
In the field May 24th 1864

General Order No 6

There will be established in the [torn] a general system of furloughs at the rate of four men for every forty enlisted mounted men present for duty—

The men to be furloughed will be selected by the commanding officers of the respective companies for meriterous conduct and their names sent up to these Head Quarters through the regular channels

The furloughs shall state the residence of the applicants, so that twenty days be allowed to soldiers to stay at home, exclusive of the time consumed in traveling.

After the furloughs of the first four have been expired and they return to duty, <u>and not</u> <u>before</u>, the comdg officer will select four other names and send them to these Head Quarters, who will be furloughed on the same condition and they will continue to select and send up the names in ______ untill all the men in their respective command shall have been furloughed—

In every case the officers sending up the names of persons desiring furloughs shall certify the number of men in their commands absent on furlough and the number present for duty

In no cases shall furloughs be granted to stragglers and skulkers from the field of honor but to those brave men who are always ready at the sound of the bugle—

By order of
Maj Gen [John A.] Wharton
B.H. Davis (Signed)

off signed: Couches A.A.G — True copy
Brandon A.A.G — [W.G.] Vardell- adjt

* * * * * * * * * * * * *

Head Quarters Whartons Cav Corps
In the Field May 24th 1864

[Gen]eral Order No 8

The Major General comdg takes pleasure in calling the attention of the troops under his command to the gallant conduct of Lt Col D.C. [DeWitt Clinton] Giddings and four companies of the 21st Texas Cav, under his command on 21st April 1864. Two miles this side of Courtierville [Cloutierville] La—

On this occasion four companies, made a desperate charge against the Enemy greatly superior to him in force, driving them from their position, and holding it until reinforcement was sent him—

Not only on this, but on several other occassions has the chivalry of Lieut Col Giddings been personally marked with pleasure by the Maj Gen. Comdg

By order of
Maj Genl John A. Wharton
(Signed) B.H. Davis
[W.J.] Cowles[46] A.A. General
Brandon A.A. General

Official (Signed)
True Copy
[W.G.] Vardell adjt

* * * * * * * * * * * * *

Head Quarters 12th Tex Cav Brigade
In the field May 28th 1864

Special Order No 30

Commanding Officers 12th Texas Cav will order an election to fill vacancy in companies A, C, G & K—He will also appoint a Board of Officers of his Reg to examine applicants for promotion and send up to These Head quarters a report of the same that they may be assigned to duty.

By order of
Col W.H. Parsons Comdg Brig
J.M. Brandon A.A.G-

* * * * * * * * * * * * *

Head Quarters Steeles Div June 4th 64

Col-

The Brig General Comd'g directs me to say to you that he has received instructions from Maj Gen [John A.] Wharton, that letters be tied up in packages with the names of the Reg\marked "Army Mail" To be mailed at Shreveport or Beaumont. They will then be sent up to these Head Quarters Tri-weekly. Each letter should be franked or prepaid, so that the mail will take them.

Respectfully
(Signed) L.W. Moore A.A.G-
(Signed) J M Brandon A.A.G-

True Copy
[W.G.] Vardell adjt

[46] W.J. Cowles (also seen as Coroles) was an adjutant in the Twenty-first Texas.

* * * * * * * * * * * * * *

Head Qrs. Parsons Brig
David's Landing[47] June 4th 1864

Col

In obedience to your orders I have investigated the charges against the prisoners arrested by Captain M.B. Highsmith[48] as straglers and and have the honor to report as follows:

Sergt. E.B. Brister Co. "C" 21st Texas Cavalry was found by Captain [M.B.] Highsmith about fifteen miles from the command at Smiths Mills in company with P.A. [Peter H.] Joiner of same Co. & Regt. They were ordered by Capt Highsmith to their command and they promised to go, but about four days afterwards were found in Anacoco prairie about fifteen miles from Sabine, traveling on the Burr Ferry road going in the direction of Texas. There appears to be no mittigating circumstances in their case except in the case of Joiner who is very nearby blind and who has a surgeons Certificate for Discharge. Sergt. Brister was wounded on Bayou Rappides and sent to the Hospital at McNutts hill, and when the Hospital was abandoned he left. His wound was well when first ordered by Captain H to camp.

Private J.A. Berry Co "I" 19th Texas Cavalry was arrested on Anacoco prairie about fifteen miles from Sabine on Burr Ferry road. He had an order from Lieut [Robert J.] Wright of his company to go back to Natchitoches to wait on a sick brother, his brother had got well and returned to his command, but in the mean time private Berry had taken sick and in trying to get some place to stay had wandered off to the place where arrested. Henry Dawson Co. "I" same Regt was found in company with private Berry. He had no papers: says he had been detailed to go to Natchitoches for meal with a wagon. says he was taken sick and met with private Berry and remained with him, till he (Dawson) got well and Berry being so sick he remained to take care of him. Sergt W.J. Wright Co "I" 19th Texas Cavalry was arrested at Paul's(?) on his return to his command. He had Surgeons Certificate ordering him to the Hospital at McNutts Hill on his arrival at the Hospital, he was ordered to do the best he could. He went to Anacoco prairie being the only place he could obtain anything for himself or horse. Capt. W [Samuel Wright][49] did not arrest him but thought it his duty to report his case; Corpl T.J. [Thomas J.] Moore of same Co. & Regt was with him and had a similar order and was badly afflicted with absess's. D.A. Lindsey and Wiley Voss Privates Co "C" 12th Texas Cavalry went with the train on the retreat from McNutts Hill to Hynson. They had certificate from Dr. [Thomas D.] Lorance[50] permitting them to go to the country to recover their health. They were found about six miles from Hynston both in ill health The gentlemen with with whom they were stopping informed Capt. H [Highsmith] that they intended to go to their command the next day after their arrest. J.M. [John M.] Loyd and H [Henry N.] Moore Co "H" 12th Texas Cavalry were arrested in Anacoco prairie with an order to go to the rear with

[47] David's Ferry or Madam David's was near Marksville on the lower Red River.

[48] Company D, Twelfth Texas.

[49] Company I, Nineteenth Texas. Wright was forty-six years old when he had enlisted in Navarro County in 1862. He was a native of Tennessee who gave his occupation as farmer and his worth as $1,800 in real estate and $1,440 in personal estate. Bailey, *Between the Enemy and Texas*, 224-25.

[50] Thomas D. Lorance was assistant surgeon in the Twelfth Texas.

their horses on account of their backs being too sore to ride. They exchanged their horses for others after they were arrested and brought by Capt H [Highsmith] to camps

Wm [William W.] Baldridge and Jo. [Joseph L.] Matt Co "B" 21st Tex Cav were found on the Calcasieu River about four miles from Hyston. private Matt was very sick and died while Capt H- was absent and private Baldridge who was attending him returned promptly to camp. Baldridge was not arrested and his name Capt H. says was was [*sic*] on the list by mistake. W.H. Gorman Co. "D" 12th Texas Cavalry was found on his return from Anacoco prairie to Camps in company with private [William] Dixon of same Co. who had been wounded. They were not arrested by sent forward and arrived at camps several days before Capt H. did.

J.S. McBride Co "E" 19th Texas Cavalry was detailed by a Lieutenant in his company to take care of horses belonging to company officers, he was found in Anacoco prairie and permitted by Capt H- to remain there one day to await the arrival of his Lieut. on his (the Lieuts.) failure to arrive with a furlough for him, he was to furnish private W.H. Davis Co. K 19th Tex Cav who was wounded and dismounted a horse to come to Camps. McBride returned to the command promptly private Davis was severely wounded in the shoulder and has not yet returned. Private T D Lanes name is on list by mistake. Private Sam'l Campbell Co F 12th Texas Cavalry whose name is not on the list was found near Calcasieu on his return to camp. He had a certificate from Dr. Mathews [Thomas M. Matthews] for "five" days which had been changed to "fifteen" days. He explains the changing of the certificate—The La. state guards were out arresting all men who were out without proper authority and sending them to Natchitoches. He had remained six days and for fear of being sent to Natchitoches he says he changed the pass to fifteen days—He was arrested on his way to camps the seventh day after date of his pass—There are some and indeed most of these cases, appear to have been absent on the authority of some officer or other. And I would respectfully suggest that in most of the cases, the men ought not to be punished for the errors of officers. The practice of subaltern officers ordering men to the rear or to any other place without authority, frequently misleads men and the officers ought to be held responsible and not the men.

Col W.H. Parsons<br>Comdg Brigade

Very Resply Your Obdt svt.<br>B.F. Jackson A.A.I. Genl.

* * * * * * * * * * * * *

Head Quarters Parsons Cav Brigade
June 5th 1864

General Orders No -

Lieut B.F. [Ben F.] Jackson[51] is assigned to duty as inspector General of this Brigade and will be obeyed and respected accordingly

By order of
W.H. Parsons Col Comdg Brig
J.M. Brandon A.A.G.

* * * * * * * * * * * * *

Head Quarters Steele's Div
Madam Davids' June 6th 1864

[Gene]ral Order No 7

I. Serg E.B. Brister & P.E. Joiner Co 'D' 21st Texas Cav, J.H. Dawson & Henry Berry Co 'I' 19th Texas Cav & W.B. Darnell of Co 'H' Morgans Batt having been arrested during the late pursuit of the Enemy, Straggling a long distance from their comdg;—are hereby dismounted and will be forwarded to Maj Gen [Richard] Taylor for assignment to Infantry.

II. Their horses wil be turned over to the Q.M. of their respective regiments, who will give them proper vouchers therefore.

III. The Brig Genl Comdg Div announces that a like prompt cause will be pursued towards all stragglers until the evil is effectivally & permanently cured—

By command of
Brig Gen [William] Steele Comdg Div
(Signed) Moore A.A. G-

Signed
J.M. Brandon A. A. Genl
True Copy
[W.G.] Vardell adjt

* * * * * * * * * * * * *

Head Quarters Steeles Division Cavalry
Madam Davids Ferry June 6th 64

Circular No 6

Several cases having come to the notice of the Brig Gen Comdg Division, in which men excuse themselves for absence from their commands, it is announced that no authority

[51] Company D, Twenty-first Texas.

exists for Sending or permitting officers or men to absent themselves from Camp without the authority of the Division Commander and any authorising of such is forbidden

Signed
J.M. Brandon A.A. Genl
True copies
[W.G.] Vardells adjt

By command of
Brig Gen [William] Steele
Signed L.W. Moore A.A.G

* * * * * * * * * * * * *

Hd Qrs Parsons Brigade
June 6th 1864

Special Orders No. 1

I The commanding officers of the 19th Tex Cav & Morgan's Battalion will cause to be sent to these Hd Qrs at once the horses and riging of private J.H. Berry & Henry Dawson Co "I" 19th T.C. and of W.N. Darnell Morgan's Battalion

II The commanding officers of the 12th, 19th, 21st & Morgan's Battalion Texas Cavalry will cause to be made out a list of all the names of the men who have been dismounted by casualties and forward the same to these Head Quarters

III Persuant to instruction of the Genl Commanding relative to the complaints of private W. [William] Debusk against Capt L.J. Wilson[52] Co. "I" 21st Regiment Texas Cavalry The commanding officer of the 21st Tex. Cav. will cause due notice to be given the parties concerned and they [are] ordered to Report at these Hd Qrs tomorrow at 6 O'clock A.M. for the purpose of an investigation of the complaints.

By order of
W.H. Parsons
Col. Comdg
B.F. Jackson A.A.I. Genl

* * * * * * * * * * * * *

Head quarters Steeles Division
In the field June 7th, 1864

General Order No -

Commanders of Reg will grant passes to their men for one (1) day, not excusing them from stated roll calls, or regular details.

official
Brandon A.A.G.

By order of B. Gen [William] Steele Comd'g
Moore A.A.G

[52] Wilson was forty-eight years old in 1862. The 1862 tax rolls of Bryan City indicate he owned a town lot, three slaves, and a few cattle for a net worth of $2,360. In 1867 he was elected Bryan's mayor but there is no evidence he ever served. Bailey, *Between the Enemy and Texas*, 220-21.

* * * * * * * * * * * * *

Head Quarters Parsons Brigade
David's landing June 7th 1864

Col.

In obedience to your instruction the commanding officers of the 19th Tex. Cav. and Morgans Battalion have been ordered to send the horses of privates [J.A.] Berry & [Henry] Dawson Co "I" 19th T.C. and W.N. Darnell Co. "H" Morgan's Batt to these Head Quarters and do most respectfully submit the following:

Lt. R D [Robert D.] Bills comdg Co "I" 19th T.C. states that it is impossible to execute your order; that Henry Dawsons horse has been sold some time, and J.H. Berry's horse cannot be found or accounted for.

Lt. J.D. Moore comdg Co "H" Morgan's Batt says that the horse and riging of private Darnell has not been in his camp, neither has he ~~had~~ received any official information of the same since the arrest of the said Darnell and therefore is unable to give any information of them unless they are in the hands of the guard who arrested him.

Col.
W.H. Parsons
Comdg Brig

Your Obdt. Svt.
B.F. Jackson
A.A.I. Genl

* * * * * * * * * * * * *

Head Quarters Trans Mississippi Dept
Shreveport 8th June 1864

Special Order No. 143

The following named men are relieved from duty with the 'Ord. Dept'—The soldiers will report to their commands and the conscripts to Brig General [Elkanah B.] Greer Commandant of Conscripts T.M.D.

Private '<u>W.A. Martin</u>' Co A; 12th Tex Cav

By command off
General E. Kirby Smith
S.S. Anderson
Asst Adjt General

* * * * * * * * * * * * *

Head Quarters Trans Mississippi Dept
Shreveport La June 11th 1864

Special order No 146

Upon certificate of examining board, the following named men are detailed for duty on post guard at Shreveport La, and will report to Colonel <u>W.B. Shivers</u> Comdg Post

Private <u>J.B. Byrd</u> Co H, 12th Tex Cav

By command of
Gen E. Kirby Smith
S.S. Anderson Aist. Adjt. Gen

* * * * * * * * * * * * *

Head Quarters Parsons Brigade
Compton Place, June 12th [1864]

General Order No 14

I Grazing will be done at Regular hours each day, regulated by the regimental comdrs

II All the horses of each co will be grazed the horses of details & cooks will be taken out at the same by some of the Co. One com. off[icer] will go out [with] their Co. & keep the men from pasture ground

III Regimental Comdrs. will prevent the men roaming the country

IV Dress Parade will be held regularly at evening & roll call twice each day at Revielle & Retreat

[I and II partially marked out; a variation of the following order]

By order of
Col. W.H. Parsons
J.M. Brandon A.A.

* * * * * * * * * * * * *

Head Quarters Parsons Brigade
Compton Place June 12th 1864

General Order No -

Grazing will be done at regular hours twice each day, regulated by Regimental commanders at bugle stable call All the horses of each company will be grazed together, the horses of details & cooks will be taken out at the same time by some of the company—One coms officer from each company will go out with their company & keep the men from straggling from pasture ground—Regimental comds will prevent the men from the country—Dress Parade will [be held] regularly each evening & roll call twice each day at Revielle & Retreat. Regt. comds will instruct co. comdes to require their men to attend more strictly to policing their co. camps—to burn all refuse meat, bones & c to prevent drawing flies, to require their men to go well to the rear for "sink" purposes The health of the Troops in the valley, will depend much upon the observance of the order.

By order of, W.H. Parsons Comdg Brig
True Copy - [W.G.] Vardell Adjt J.M. Brandon A.A.General

* * * * * * * * * * * * *

Head Quarters Steeles Div. Cav.
In the field June 12th 1864

[torn] Order No 8

The attention of officers is called to the 2nd paragraph Genl orders 104 of the servis 1062 from Richmond which reads as follows: "Arms must not be carried from Camp, nor will mounted men in camp be allowed to ride their horses except on duty Cavalry horses having been hired to Govt. the owners has no legal right to use them as many are constantly tiring to the detriment of their efficiency for Service

By command of Brig Gen [William] Steele
L.W. Moore A.A.G- Comdg Div

* * * * * * * * * * * * *

Head quarters 12th Tex Cav
Camp 3/4 miles Alex[andria] June 13th/64

Special

Dress parade will be held this evening at 5 o'clock—Prompt attendance required—

By order of
Colonel [A. Bell] Burleson Comdg & c
[W.G.] Vardell Adjt

* * * * * * * * * * * * *

Head Quarters Tex Cav Brigade
Compton Place June 13th 1864

Special Order No -

The following named officers of 12th Tex Cav having been examined by a board of officers & pronounced proficient will enter upon their duties in their respective companies with the rank set opposite their names

| | | | | |
|---|---|---|---|---|
| 1st Lieut | G.W. [George W.] Ingram | Co A | Capt | 18th May 1864 |
| 2d " | H.B. Smith | " " | | 1st Lieut " " " |
| " " | [James M.] Jackson | " " | | Sr 2d " " " " |
| Srgt | [Robert W.] Calhoun | " " | | Jr " " Date of election |
| Srgt | S.E. [Samuel] Killough | " 'C' | | " " " " " " |
| | [J.W.] Spikes | " G | | " " " " " " |
| Sr 2d Lieut | R.C.H. Good | " K | | 1st " " Date of vacancy |
| | V [Vance] Walling | " | Jr 2d | " " " election |

By order of
W.H. Parsons Comdg Cav Brgd
J.M. Brandon A.A.G-

True Copy
W.G. Vardell Adjt

* * * * * * * * * * * * *

Head Quarters Parsons Cav Brigade
Compton Place June 13th 1864

Special order No 36

Commanding officers 12th Tex Dragoons will cause an election to be held in Co H 12th Texas Dragoons to fill vacancy occasioned by the promotion of Lieut Smith [J. Levi Smith, Jr.]

True Copy
W.G. Vardell
Adjt

By order of
Colonel W.H. Parsons Comdg
J.M. Brandon A.A.G

* * * * * * * * * * * * *

Head Quartes Steele Division
June 14 1864

General Order No 10-

Surgeon J.L. Estorge (?) having reported with orders from Maj Gen [Richard] Taylor as chief Surgeon of this Division is accordingly announced

Official
J.M. Brandon A.A.G.

By command of Brig Gen
[William] Steele
L.W. Moore A.A.G

* * * * * * * * * * * * *

Head Qrs Steeles Division
In the field June 14th 1864

Circular -

By reports received at these Head quarters it appears that Quartermaster, Commissaries & other Staff officers have been in the habit of making Details for their own Dept. Such a course is at variance with the proper custom of Service—Details are made only by the authority of the Commander to whom application is made for his consideration & order—Thus the commander of a Regt is to make all details for Service in the Regt. Commanders of Brigades for Service in Brigades—& the orders for such details should be on the files of the special orders of their respective officers, wherever the duty is other than of daily routine—Surgeons of Regts & c have no power to give leaves of absences for <u>any</u> length of time—Their authority is limited to giving a certificate of the facts for the action of the Commander—

Off.
Brandon A.A.G-
True Copy
[W.G.] Vardell Adjt

By order of
Brig Gen [William] Steele
Comdg Div
Moore A.A.G

* * * * * * * * * * * * *

Head quarters 12th Tex Cav
Camp Wier[53] June 15th 1864

Special Order No -

Lieut R.B. Shaw Company G—12th Tex Cav. is hereby appointed acting A.Q.M 12th Tex Cav. and will report at once to these Head quarters

By command of
W.G. Vardell Adjt — Lieut Col [A. Bell] Burleson Comdg

* * * * * * * * * * * * *

Quarter Masters office Parsons Brig
June 15th/64

Commanding officers[54]
12th Tex Cav

You will please inform the commanders of Companies that I wish them to make out a list of all the horses killed in action, prior to the first day of June 1864 & then mustered into service and forward the same with as little delay is possible

Your Obdient Servant
R.A. Terryl [Terrell]
A.A.Q.M Parsons Brig

True Copy
W.G. Vardell

* * * * * * * * * * * * *

Head Qrs Parsons Brigade
June 17th 1864

Special Order No 40

Private E Weygand of Co 'C' 12th Tex Cav is detailed as Wheelwright for this Brigade and will report to Capt R.A. Terryl [Terrell] and M for duty at once

By order of
W.H. Parsons
Col Comdg

J.M. Brandon
A.A.G

[53] Joseph Wier, who had died at Yellow Bayou, had briefly commanded the Twelfth Texas after Colonel Burleson received a slight wound at Blair's Landing.

[54] Since horses were the personal property of the soldiers and their value was assessed by a board before being used in the service, the men expected reimbursement for animals killed in battle.

* * * * * * * * * * * * *

Head Quarters Steeles Div
June 18th 1864

General Order No 11

The increase of the number of unarmed men leads to the belief that proper care is not been taken with the arms that have been issued, it is therefore ordered that every company immed—take a report of the number of arms he has in his Co. which report shall be kept by the Reg comdr from times—when there is a change in the number of arms on hand in the Company, the commander will be required to explain the change in writing, and whenever it appears that arms have been lost or disposed of, the name of the man so losing or disposing will be exposed and an examination had for the purpose of dismounting such men as dispose of their arms, or fail to take the proper care of them—

By order of Gen [William] Steele Comdg
Colonel Parsons
Comdg Drags

Signed Moore
Capt & A.A G-

* * * * * * * * * * * * *

Head Qurs Parsons Brigade
Compton Plantation La. June 18th 1864.

General Order No 15

I. The order of march for this Brigade to Texas will be as follows—21st Tex on the 19th, the 12th on the 20th, the Battalion on the 21st and the 19th on the 22d instance II. Each regimental commander will keep a rear and advance guard and keep his column closed up in the line of march, and also have roll call three times a day. III. Each regimental commander will keep a memorandum of the point from which [he] starts on the march each day, and the point at which he camps at night with the correct date, so that depredations—should any be committed—may be located upon the proper parties. Company commanders will be held responsible to regimental, and regimental to the brigade commander for the conduct of their respective commands—Marches will be twenty (20) miles each day, grazing at intervals on the route.

By order of Col W.H. Parsons
Commanding Brigade
J.M. Brandon A.A. Genl

* * * * * * * * * * * * *

Head Quarters Parsons Brigade
Near Red Fork September 27th 64[55]

[torn] order No 16

Comdg officers of Regiments battalion & Battery will furnish at the earliest possible moment Monthly returns of their commands giving in addition to their regular [hole] the number horses[,] no and kind [of] arms [marked out]

* * * * * * * * * * * * *

Head quarters Parsons Brig
Near Red Fork Septr 27/64

Genl order No 16

Comdg officers of Regiments Battallion and Battery will make out monthly returns and forward by 30th inst being careful to include the number of Horses Return receipts for Blanks transmitted herewith

By order of
Col W H Parsons
Comdg Brigade
J.W. [John W.] Walden A A A Genl

* * * * * * * * * * * * *

Head Qrs Parsons Brigade
Near Red Fork Spt 28th 64

Genl order No 17

Commanding officers will not allow horses to run at large but will keep them tied up and have grass pulled for the horses from fields in the vicinity

By order of
W H Parsons Col Com Brg
J M Brandon

[55] In the weeks between June 18 and September 27, Parsons's men remained the the Red River Valley. A religious revival swept through the regiments and Henry Orr observed: "There is a protracted meeting going on in our brigade. It is generally well attended, though there has been no professions yet. For the last several days there has been a good many seekers. It is likely to continue several days yet. A soldier church or rather an association was formed on Sunday evening." He also noted that the brigade had been ordered to Houston, destined for the Rio Grande, but had barely moved into Texas before being returned to the Red River where it remained. Rumors of crossing the Mississippi River met with resistance among the soldiers. Henry Orr to "Sammie," August 4, and Henry Orr to "My Dear Brothers," August 26, 1864, in Anderson, ed., *Campaigning with Parsons' Brigade*, 144-47.

* * * * * * * * * * * * *

Hd qrs Steeles Brigade
Warren Oct 19- 64[56]

1/
Capt-

I have the honor to report my arrival at this place and that I have assumed command as directed

I find Watsons Regiment and Morgan's Batt, at Mount Elba[57] crossing of Saline[58] & Parsons Regt is in this vicinity picketing, the crossing of the Saline except one company detached with train, bringing arms from Missippi. Some small parties are out one with Capt. McNelly, one with Lieut Nelson, one with Major Runnels, and twenty men, & Lieut. sent to establish communication with the river and bring out news, and one party of observation on Ark & White Rivers.

(signed) Wm. [William] Steele
Brig. Genl

* * * * * * * * * * * * *

Hdqrs Steeles Brig
Warren Oct 19- 64

2/
Capt

I am directed by the Brig Genl Commandg to ask if you have received any information or report has been received from the parties sent out to ascertain what amount of forage was in your vicinity. You will report as soon as you ascertain the amount.

Resly yr obt sevt.
J M Brandon AA& I Gnl.
Capt Geo W. [George W.] Ingram
Comd Picketts Bradleys Ferry

[56] Upon his return to Arkansas, General Steele made his headquarters at Warren, some forty miles south of Pine Bluff and around fifty miles from the Mississippi River.

[57] Mt. Elba is on the Saline River about twenty-five miles southwest of Pine Bluff between the road from Pine Bluff to Princeton and the road from Pine Bluff to Warren.

[58] The Saline River flows from near Little Rock east of Warren and eventually empties into the Ouachita River.

* * * * * * * * * * * * *

Hd Qrs. 1st Brigade
Warren Oct 20. 1864

3/
Capt

I am directed by the Brigadier General Comdg to say you will send, under the guidance of Mr. [T.J.] Curry, as many men as you can spare to arrest Gray Buckin(?)

I am Capt very Respfy
your obt servt.
J M Brandon A.A. Genl.

Capt. G.W. [George W.] Ingram[59]
Comdg. at Bradley's Ferry

* * * * * * * * * * * * *

Hdqrs Steeles Brig.
Warren Oct 21- 1864

4/
Col

I enclose an open letter to Genl Wharton's Hdqrs. for Genl [John B.] Magruder's ~~Hd qrs~~; perusal after which please forward to its destination

Resly your obt. Svt
Wm [William] Steele
Brig Genl

Col E.P. Turner
A A Gnl

* * * * * * * * * * * * *

Hd qrs Steeles Brigade
Warren Oct 21st 64

5/
Capt.

From reports of agents sent out to examine the country for forage it appears that the supply within reach will be exhausted in five days.

Resly yr obt svt
Wm [William] Steele
Brig Genl

Capt. B.F. Weems
A.A.G.

[59] Company A, Twelfth Texas.

An inquiry has just been made of me if a planter wishing to move to Texas can turn over his corn here to the govt. and have it returned in Texas.

W Steele
Brig. Genl

* * * * * * * * * * * * *

Hd qrs Steeles Brig
Warren Oct 21- 64

6/
Capt.

I send a note from an officer sent on to the lower Arkansas for the purpose of obtaining information Col [Charles L.] Morgan returned to Mt Elba day before yesterday from a scout near Pine Bluff. The enemy's lines around that place are closed no one being to go in or come out—This information taken in connection with the landing of troops at Napoleon indicates a move into this country from the lower Arkansas.

Respectfully
yr obt sevt,
Wm [William] Steele
Brig Genl

Capt B.F. Weems
A.A.G.

The arms are by time at Moro.[60] I hope no time will be lost in supplying some of unarmed men of my command.

* * * * * * * * * * * * *

Hed qurs Brigade
Warren Oct. 21- 64

7/
Col.

Your report of yesterday has been received. You will be well upon your guard and keep out small parties of observation The closing of the enemy's lines is indicative of preparation for a movement of some kind. Use every exertion to get the earliest information of what it is.

Resly your obt sevt
Wm [William] Steele
Brig Genl

Col. [Benjamin W.] Watson
Mt. Elba

[60] Moro, on the Ouachita River, was about thirty miles southwest of Warren.

* * * * * * * * * * * * *

Head Qrs. Warren
Oct 21st 1864

8/
Colonel

I find no instructions for your command. I think it will be dangerous to leave your present position any great distance. You will therefore not go to Col. [John W.] Logan's assistance unless he is compelled to fall back to your vicinity. In the mean time keep well advised of what is doing in the direction of Pine Bluff—The closed lines at that place indicate a movement and this move via Benton may be in connection with it.

Communicate with Col Logan and advise me of the nature and strength of his force if you have or can get the information. Also keep advised of Colonel Logans movements and let me know all you learn.

Respectfully
Your Obt Servt
(signed) Wm [William] Steele
Brig. Genl.

Colonel [Benjamin W.] Watson
Mt. Elba

* * * * * * * * * * * * *

Hd qrs 1st Cav Brig
Warren Oct 22, 64

9/
Col.

The Brig Genl comdg directs me to say you will send one company with the wagon which goes to Monticello[61] for bayonets as an escort.

Very Respectfully
Yr obt servt
J M Brandon
A.A. Genl Cav

Col W H Parsons
Comdg 12th Tex Cav

[61] Monticello was less than twenty miles east of Warren.

* * * * * * * * * * * * *

Hd. qrs. Steeles Brigade
Warren Oct 22- 64

10/
Col.

In answer to your letter dated Oct 21st in reference to arms I have the honor to State these arms passed Longview safely on the 18 Inst. Information was forwarded by Col. Parsons that the enemy had abandoned the pursuit under date of Oct 16th and again under date of Oct 19th he reported the fact ~~of~~ that the "arms train" had reached Longview on the day previous. On the 21st I wrote to Genl Wharton sending the letter Open & under Cover to Genl [John B.] Magruders Hd qrs that the arms by that time reached Moro. In reply to the question, "have you wagons to send the arms to Camden" I will answer that I believe that this Brigade has less transportation than any other Brig In the Trans-Miss Department. Having no quartermaster commissary or ordnance train, company bagage wagons being used for these purposes.

Respectfully your
obt servt.
(sgd) Wm [William] Steele Brig Genl

Col. E.P. Turner
A A Genl

* * * * * * * * * * * * *

Head Qrs Brigade
Warren Oct 22nd 1864

11/
Colonel

The enclosed letters are sent for your information though I suppose you have probably received this intelligence direct from Col. [John W.] Logan. It will be become necessary to keep a close watch in the direction of Princeton as well as of Pine Bluff from which latter place a column starting in the after noon would reach your position before day light next morning. You must fall back should reinforcements be necessary as I do not wish to move the troops from here until I have further [information] from some movements on the lower Arkansas. It is not necessary to impress [on] you the necessity of great vigilance

Col. [Benjamin W.] Watson
Mt. Elba

Your Obt. Servt.
Wm [William] Steele Brig Genl

* * * * * * * * * * * * *

Hd. qrs. 1st Brigade Cavalry
Warren Oct 22, 64

12/
Col.

I am directed by the Brig. Genl commanding to instruct you to move with your Regiment as rapidly as possible to this place, leaving your Bagage at the Camp near Hillsboro. The enemy are reported advancing from Princeton and Dispatch is necessary. If the Pontoon Brigade is not down at Moro you will cross at the Eldorado Ford if the River can be forded at that place.

Very Respectfully
your obt servt
J.M. Brandon A.A.G.

Lt. Col. [DeWitt Clinton] Giddings
Comdg 21st Tx Cav.

* * * * * * * * * * * * *

Hd Qrs. Steeles Brigade
Warren Oct 22/64

13/
Col.

I yesterday received notice from Col. [John W.] Logan through Col. [Benjamin W.] Watson at Mt. Elba that the Enemy 600 strong were moving down the Saline. I sent your communication to Col. Watson for his information and guidance. I directed last night that Col. Watson should not leave his position any great distance as there is evident preparation for some move from Pine Bluff and from near the mouth of the Arkansas river.

Col. [Isaac F.] Harrison left Monticello on the 15th inst. I shall order Col. [DeWitt Clinton] Giddings in the direction from El Dorado.

Respectfully
Your Obt Servt
Wm [William] Steele
Brig Genl

Col. E.P. Turner
A.A. Genl

* * * * * * * * * * * * *

Hd qrs 1st Cav Brig
Warren Oct. 22, 64

14/
Capt.

The Brig Genl directs me to say that you will please send him all the late papers you can get and any information you may get of the movements of the enemy or any other items of interest.

Capt. A.R. Tibbetts (?)
______ lake, Ark.

Very Resly & c
J.M. Brandon A.A.G.

* * * * * * * * * * * * *

Head Quarters 1st Cav Brig
Warren Oct 22 8 oclock P.M. 64

15/
Col.

I am directed by the Brig Genl Comdg to say that the enemy, having been driven back and the necessity has ceased for it at this place you will resume your former position on the River and carry [out] the orders given you by Genl. [William] Steele.

Lt. Col. D.C. [DeWitt Clinton] Giddings
Comdg 21st T.C.

Very Respectfully Your Obt. Servt.
J.M. Brandon A.A.G.

* * * * * * * * * * * * *

Hd qrs 1st Cav Brigade
Warren. Oct 23-64

16/
Col

Brig Genl [William] Steele directs me to endor[se] for your information, the communications from Col [John W.] Logan & District Hd. qrs. and to say that you will keep out four scouts & as to ascertain any movement of the enemy from Pine Bluff in the direction of Princeton & give information of the same (should any move be made) to the train of Col Logan

Very Resplly & c
J M Brandon A.A.G.

* * * * * * * * * * * * *

Head Qurs 1st Cavalry Brigade
Warren Oct 24th 1864

17/
Colonel,

Your letter addressed to Col. Parsons was received last night. Lieut [J.B.] Abbot[62] will be instructed to forward any matter you may wish to send. Should the line you now depend upon be broken up, it is of more importance that information should come through, than that it should be received by any particular party—

Genl. [John B.] Magruder complains that papers and perhaps other documents are opened on the route, & some do not come at all. As these things hitherto have not passed through my office, I cannot tell with whom the fault lies—Perhaps it would be better to send under cover to me, and forward by my line to Genl Magruder—I think safety and dispatch would be gained by such a course, and in the event that information should be of importance to out posts, open to my perusal—

I should be obliged if you could send me papers, periodicals & c.

Your Obt Servt
(Signed) Wm [William] Steele
Brig Genl

Col. White

* * * * * * * * * * * * *

Hd Qrs 1st Cavalry Brig.
Warren Ark Oct 24/64

18/
Lt.

Your letter to Col. Parsons was received last night. There is no money here in the hands of either Quarter Master or Commissary. I hope for some on the return of Capt [Jefferson J.] Mallard from Camden or Maj [Thomas] Johns from Shreveport, [on news] when you shall be supplied—

I wish you to afford every facility to Col White in the transmission of mail either to Genl [John B.] Magruder or myself. He is employed by Genl Magruder. It is not of so much importance that I should get the news, as that it should come through rapidly,

Get information if you can of what is doing on White River, Whether boats are going up with troops or supplies or empty, or if coming down either way—

Request your agents to note such matters in detail If a diary of boats passing and how freighted could be obtained it would be of value—

Your Obt Servt
Wm [William] Steele
Brig Genl

Lieut Abbot

[62] Company B, Twelfth Texas.

* * * * * * * * * * * * *

Head Quarters 1st Cavalry Brig
Warren Ark Oct 24 1864

19/
Captain

I desire that my position be a little more clearly defined of what does my command consist, and to whom I am expected to report? Orders and instructions are sent me direct. Orders are also sent direct to the commanding Officer at Mt Elba—Within what limits are movements of my Brigade, or portions of it to be discretionary? I think it would be well to send a strong scout to the lower Arkansas and Miss Rivers occasionally—

Respectfully
Your Obt Servt
(signed) Wm [William] Steele
Brig Genl & c

Capt. B.F. Weems
A A Genl

* * * * * * * * * * * * *

Hd Qurs 1st Cavalry Brigade
Warren Ark. Oct 24th 1864

20/
Colonel,

The Brig. Genl Comdg directs me to call your attention to Genl Orders No 18 from Corps H'd: Qrs:, and to say your Certificate has not been received for the week ending Oct 22nd 1864—

You will see that returns required by Circular from Corps H'd Qurs 10th and 25 of each month are forwarded promptly—

Very Respectfully
Your Obt Servt
J M Brandon
A.A. Genl.

Col B W Watson
Marks Mill
and Lieut Col C.L. Morgan
Comdg Battn

* * * * * * * * * * * * *

Hd qrs 1st Cav Brigade
Warren Oct 24. 1864

21/
Colonel

The Brig. Genl commandg directs me to say that you will send up to these Hd qrs a morning report of your Command and also a report of arms giving numbers & kind and amount of ammunition on hand

Very Respectfully
Your Obt Servt
J M Brandon
A.A. Genl.

Lieut Col D.C. [DeWitt Clinton] Giddings
Comdg 21st Tx Cav.

* * * * * * * * * * * * *

Head Quars 1st Cav Brig.
Warren Ark Oct. 25, 1864

22/
Col

In reply to your Communication of yesterday the Brigadier Genl Commandg instructs me to say that Capt. [William M.] Harper's Company[63] at Longview can be ordered by you to return to the Regiment as there can be no use for it at that place and it is believed there will be none for any at any place; You will however keep your pickets on the river for any emergency which might arise

Very Respectfully
Your obt Servt
J M Brandon
A A Genl

Lieut Col D.C. Giddings
Commandg 21st T.C.
New Longview Ark

* * * * * * * * * * * * *

Head Qurs 1st Cavalry Brig
Warren Ark Oct 25 1864

23/
General

I hereby have the honor to recommend Lieut. Thos C. Howard Adjt 7th Regt Texas Cavalry for Asst Adjt Genl for my Brigade—

[63] Company E, Twenty-first Texas. Harper, a native of Tennessee, had enlisted in Lavaca County. He was a thirty-seven year old farmer in 1862, and claimed $3,000 in real estate and $10,000 in personal estate.

Lieut Howard was born in Virginia, is now a resident of Texas, and is twenty five years of age He has served as adjt or acting Asst adjut Genl since the 9th of October 1861.

I am Sir
Very Respectfy
Your Obt Servt.
(Signed) Wm [William] Steele
Brig Genl & c

Genl. S. [Samuel] Cooper
Agt & Inpt Genl
Richmond Va.

* * * * * * * * * * * * *

Head Qurs 1st Cavalry Brig
Warren Ark Oct 25th 1864

24/
General

I hereby have the honor to recommend for Asst Inspt Genl of my Brigade Lieut W.J. Cowles Adjt. 21st Regt Texas Cavalry—

Lieut Cowles is 21 years of age, was born in Virginia, ~~an~~ is now a resident of Texas and has served as Adjt since the [_____] of April 1862.

I am Sir
Very Respectfly
Your Obt Servt
Wm [William] Steele
Brig Genl Comdg

Genl S. [Samuel] Cooper
Adjt & Inspt Genl
Richmond Va

* * * * * * * * * * * * *

Head Qurs Steele's Brigade
Warren Ark Oct 25 1864

25/
Colonel,

I have the honor to enclose herewith communications of Staff Officers for my Brigade and to request that they be forwarded and that these Officers may be assigned to duty in the positions to which they have been recomended

Respectfully
Your Obt Servt
Wm [William] Steele
Brig Genl Cav Brig

Lt Col E P Turner
A A Genl
Dist of Ark
Not Sent

* * * * * * * * * * * * *

Head Quars. 1st Cav. Brig
Warren Oct 26 1864

26/

The following endorsement is upon my application of Major L.J. [Lochlin J.] Farrar 12th Tx Cav. to have two men sent to their Company (D) of his Regiment who are detained by Capt Flemming 17th Tex Infty & Enrolling officer of Bastrop County—The application was forwarded and returned and this endorsement is made & all the papers again sent up

I have the honor to request that these papers be refered to Departmental Hd qrs for the purpose of having the men of Captain [M.B.] Highsmiths Co[64] arrested. The effort made in this Regiment (12th) to force a reorganization demands that more than ordinary means be taken to bring these deserters to trial. It would appear as if there was a combination on the part of citizens and officers to encourage desertion by the use of every subterfuge to give a color of right to their absence or to get them a detail after they have exhausted all other excuses. Capt Flemmings conduct should not be passed over in silence. The leniency shown those who remaining absent are in fact deserters are excused on every frivolous pretext is a fruitful source of discont. amongst those who remain true to their obligation

(Sgd) Wm [William] Steele Brig Genl

* * * * * * * * * * * * *

Head Quarters Steeles Brig
Warren Ark Oct 26. 64

27/
Capt,

Your letter (413) arrived this morning. I do not anticipate trouble with the 12th Regt, from all that I can learn the matter is completely at rest.

The portion of the Brigade at this place is getting but about half forage and that has to be hauled fifteen miles and then picked up in small lots. The Regiments at Mt Elba Col. [Benjamin W.] Watson reports can get forage but two days longer

Perhaps by moving about they can remain and forage in that vicinity some longer. All the corn that Mr Martin could spare was used before I came here. A portion by the Post QM before the Brigade came

[64] Company D, Twelfth Texas.

I sent copy of a note from Lieut [J.B.] Abbott[65] who is on the lower Arks for the purpose of getting information. I get little news and few papers the latest being mailed through to Genl [John B.] Magruder I have sent several papers to Genl [John A.] Wharton, the latest being of the 21st inst.

Yr obt Srvt
(Sgd) Wm [William] Steele
Brig Genl

Capt B F Weems
A.A.G.

* * * * * * * * * * * * *

Hed Qurs 1st Cavalry Brigade
Warren Ark Oct 26th 1864

28/
Colonel,

I have the honor to request that the following named Officers Lieut Thos C Howard [marked out] Adjt 7th Regt Texas Cavalry and Lieut W.J. Cowles Adjt 21 Regt Texas Cavalry who have been recomended for the positions of Asst Adjt Genl and Inspector on my Staff, be assigned to duty in the positions to which they have been nominated

I am Sir
Very Respectfully
Your Obt Servt
Wm [William] Steele
Brig Genl Comdg & c

Col S S Anderson
A.A. Genl

* * * * * * * * * * * * *

Head Qurs 1st Cav Brigade
Warren Oct 27- 1864

29/
Lieut

Genl [William] Steele directs me to say he wishes you to direct your attention particularly to the movements of the enemy on the Island on White river and anywhere else as it is of the utmost importance that such information should be known as speedily as possible

yr obt srvt
J M Brandon
A A Genl

Lieut Jo Abbott
on Arks river

[65] Company B, Twelfth Texas.

* * * * * * * * * * * * *

Head Qurs Steeles Brigade
Warren Oct 27th 1864

30/
Colonel,

A letter was received last night directed to Col Parsons ordering a party sent in pursuit of Officers of Genl [Thomas C.] Hindman's Staff who it is supposed have pressed Col [Isaac F.] Harrisons train and taken a lot of tobacco which had been ordered to be impressed & c

The letter also stated that those officers had been ordered to be arrested, and sent to ~~Colonel~~ Camden—

This letter purports to be from Dist Head Quarters at Washington, is signed by a Surgeon and sent to Col Parsons which irregularity taken in connection with the extravagant supposition that the [t]rain of a Brigade could be impressed by a few officers leads me to doubt the authority of the order; the party will however be sent—Instructions from Dist head Qurs under Date of Oct 17th required assistance to be given to Lieut Nelson who was to receive or impress the tobacco A party was sent with Lieut Nelson in accordance with these instructions from which no report has been received

The same letter desired the Officers named to be ordered to report at Dist Hd Qurs—an order was sent for them to report by Lieut Nelson—

Col Harrison left Monticello on the 15th inst If the tobacco went in his train there is but little prospect of taking it—

Respectfully
Your Obt Servt
Wm [William] Steele
Brig Genl

Col E.P. Turner
A.A. Genl.

* * * * * * * * * * * * *

Headquarters 1st Cavalry Brigade
Warren, Ark Oct 27th 1864

31/
Captain,

Supplies as all kinds are becoming very scarce, particularly forage. Half rations of corn is all that can be given to animals now, and the difficulty is increasing. I have sent out agents and have made deligent inquiry and can learn of no forage except a small supply which may be in the Saline some ten or twelve miles below long view [Longview].

Respectfully
Your Obt Servt
Wm [William] Steele
Brig Genl

Capt. B.F. Weems
A.A. Genl

* * * * * * * * * * * * *

Head Qurtrs 1st Cavalry Brigade
Warren, Ark Oct. 27th 1864

32/
Lieut.

Enclosed please find a letter for Col. White which please cause to be delivered to him.

I wish you would devote yourself more particularly to getting information of the Enemy's movements on the Arkansas and White rivers & on the Islands it is rumored that a Brigade of negroes were at the Post [Arkansas Post] a few days ago in route to Pine Bluff. I have no authority for spending money for news papers even if I had the funds that would pass

Your Obt. Servt.
Lt. J. Abbott — Wm Steele Brig Genl

* * * * * * * * * * * * *

Head Qurs Steeles Brigade
Warren, Ark. Oct 27th 1864

33/
Colonel,

I have represented to both Genl [John A.] Wharton & [John B.] Magruder the prospect that you would be out of forage in a few days. I have received no answer. Can you not get some forage by moving a few miles one Regt at a time. Perhaps you can by moving 10 or 15 miles, feed and bring back enough to last one or two days. Your Regt and the Battalion alternating—

I do not think it will be necessary to keep picketts constantly at the fords if you have small squads on scout towards Pine Bluff, nor do I think it essential that you should keep your command at one particular place.

Col [Charles L.] Morgan has I am afraid interfered with your leaving your present position by stating to the Officers who lately inspected your command that there was sufficient forage to last six weeks.

Write daily on this subject. I shall forward your letters note to Hd Qrs of the Dist.

Your Obt Servt
Col. [Benjamin W.] Watson — Wm Steele
Mt. Elba — Brig Genl

* * * * * * * * * * * * *

Head Quarters Steele's Brigade
Warren Ark. Oct 28. 1864

34/
Col.

I am instructed by General [John A.] Wharton to move your Regiment on the 1st of Nov. to Princeton to report temporarily to Col. [John W.] Logan.

I am surprised at your report of arms. I was under the impression you had at least 500 since drawing the 200 at Shreveport.

In moving to Princeton it will be necessary to have as much corn as you can. I doubt if you get any on the Road.

Lt. Col. [DeWitt Clinton] Giddings
Comdg. 21 st Tx. Cav.
official
J.M. Brandon A.A.G. (sgd)

Your Obt. Servt
Wm Steele Brig Genl

* * * * * * * * * * * * *

Hd Qrs Steele's Brigade
Warren Oct 28. 1864

35/
Col.

Capt. [Jefferson J.] Mallard will send you a small supply of beef Cattle. He has just returned from Camden and reports the supply of Beef Cattle at that place very small. He is doubtful if he can get any more at present I have no authority to remove you, as the stationing of two Regiments at that point was ordered by higher authority. Capt. [R.A.] Terrell has sent you some wagons which will relieve your wants.

Send Mrs. Reaves home & send send [*sic*] some one with her to see if things are as she represents and to learn if possible what her character is for loyalty.

Arrest all men belonging to the Army who have not regular passes an[d] all who are Conscripts and not in the service.

Your Obt Srvt
Wm Steele
Brig Genl

All regimental papers should be signed by yourself as well as leaves of absence going up. The command you have does not relieve you of command of your Regt.

(sgnd)W [William] Steele Brig Genl

* * * * * * * * * * * * * *

Hd. Quarters Steeles Brig
Warren Oct. 28 1864

36/
Genl.

Your letter of 25th Inst was received this morning I intended to have ordered [Lt. Col. DeWitt Clinton] Giddings to a point on the Saline below Longview if my information regarding forage at that point should turn out correct, with about four Cos. at this place to be foraged by hauling and to send Col. Parsons with his regiment on a scout to the lower Arkansas and Mississippi Rivers. Capt. Polk who is charged with the care and disposal of govt. cotton writes me that he wishes assistance and Col. Parsons thinks he can subsist both men and horses in that region—the force that landed at Napoleon remained but a short time A scout of about one hundred of enemys Cavalry went about 40 miles in the direction of Red Fork and returned after robbing several citizens.

I do not know how much corn I can get by exchange for Texas corn. The question was asked for the benefit of a gentlemen who had about 200 bushels. I thought it probable if it was given in one case that more could be obtained on the same terms. Col. Parsons (who has just come into my office) tells me that the same question has been asked him in several cases in regard not only to corn but Bacon also.

Whilst writing I have received a letter from Capt. Polk which I send you. I will send Col. Parsons and will bring up a squadron of the 21st which is at Longview, which with a company of Morgan's Battalion now here, will, I think be sufficient as the scouts from Elba cover the front in the direction of Pine Bluff. There is no forage that I can hear of between this place and Camden. The only places where Corn is reported are a point 10 or 15 miles below Longview. Of the truth of the report I have sent to ascertain and the country below Hamburg on the Bartholomew.

Respectfully
yr obt svrt
(sgd) Wm Steele
Brig Genl

Col. [Benjamin W.] Watson wrote yesterday that he was entirely out of corn. I sent the letter direct to Dist. Hd Qrs. He will be obliged to move about the country and scatter his command still more.

Maj. Genl. J.A. [John A.] Wharton
Official J.M.B.

* * * * * * * * * * * * *

Hd Qrs Steeles Brigade
Warren Oct 29- 64

37/
Col.

I am directed by the Brig Genl Comdg to enclose for your information communications from Dist. Hd Qrs. which you will read & return by courier.

Very Resly
Your obt servt
J.M. Brandon
A.A. Genl

* * * * * * * * * * * * *

Head Quarters 1st Cavalry Brig
Warren Ark. Oct. 29- 1864

38/
Col.

I am directed by the Brig Genl Commanding to say that when the order was given to Cunningham for the mule and horse nothing was known of the Character of Cunningham for loyalty. You will retain the mule and horse till further orders ~~from~~ In the community it is difficult to tell whom to trust

I am Col. Very Resly
your obt servt.
J.M. Brandon
A.A. Gnl

Col. B.W. [Benjamin W.] Watson
Comdg at Mt Elba

* * * * * * * * * * * * *

Warren Oct 29th 1864

39/
General,

Since writing this morning I have received a report of the corn on the Saline below Long View. I can get at least 3000 bushels in a neighborhood some 10 or twelve miles below Longview. Col. [Benjamin W.] Watson wrote that he has succeeded in getting half rations for today It will be impossible to keep him there much longer Some of the Animals here have no corn today, part less than half rations.

I think it would be better to concentrate the brigade in the vicinity of Longview (a little below, and from that point send out small parties of observation If the Enemy advance we can have timely notice, and and [*sic*] can let them come far enough to trap them, or punish them severely before they can get back. There is little (as far is any observation goes) to protect between the Saline and Camden, and Camden of course is not exposed to a raid.

Respectfully
Your Obt Servt
(signed) Wm. Steele
Brig. Genl.

Maj. Genl. [John A.] Wharton

P.S. A battery could be supported at that point I cannot supply my command by hauling to this point. I have two few wagons and the mules are too poor

(signed) W.S.

* * * * * * * * * * * * * *

Head Qurs 1st Cavalry Brig
Warren Ark Oct 29th 1864

40/
Col.

I am directed by the Brig Genl Comdng to call your attention to the last paragraph of Genl Order No. 58, from H'd Qur's Dist. Ark 14th Oct 1864, which has not been complied with by your own Regt & Col. [Charles L.] Morgan's Bttn. Please send up Certificates

Very Respectfully
Your Obt Servt
J.M. Brandon
A.A. Genl

Col.
B.W. [Benjamin W.] Watson
Comdg at Mt. Elba

* * * * * * * * * * * * * *

Head quarters Steele's Brigade
Warren Arks. Oct 29. 64

41/
Col.

In reply to your communication of this date Genl. [William] Steele instructs me to say you can withdraw your scouts from Pine Bluff & Princeton road as they are not necessary since the return of Col. [John W.] Logan to the latter place.

I am Col.
Your Obt Servt
J.M. Brandon A.A. Genl

Col. B.W. [Benjamin W.] Watson
Commanding at Mt Elba

* * * * * * * * * * * * * *

Head Qrs. Steeles Brigade
Warren Arks Oct. 30- 64

42/
Col.

I am directed by the Brig. Genl. Commandg to say if private Arrowood Co "C" 12th Tex Cavalry can establish his ownership to the horse specified in affidavit of Bennett & Epps you will cause the horse to be delivered to him.

Lieut. Col.
D.C. [DeWitt Clinton] Giddings
Comdg 21st T.C.

I am Col Very Respectfully
Your obt servt
J.M. Brandon A.A. Genl

* * * * * * * * * * * * * *

43/
Lieut.

Genl. [William] Steele directs that you move the whole Reserve Camp, leaving only a guard sufficient to guard the Baggage which cannot be hauled to some point in the vicinity of and below Longview where he has been informed forage can be had, say ten miles below Longview.

yr obt servt
J.M. Brandon A.A. Genl

* * * * * * * * * * * * * *

Head Qurs Steeles Brigade
Warren Ark. Oct 30th 1864

44/
Col.

I have ordered Capt. [William M.] Harper[66] with his squadron to this place. I wish you to move at once to the vicinity of Longview and send at once a small party of observation to the vicinity of Hamburg. Let the party go by the way of Marie Saline & join you near Longview. There is more Corn on the Saline below Longview than any place I have heard

It is reported to me that a force of Federal Cavalry 1500 strong landed at Ashton & would move via Hamburg to Monticello Instruct the party you send to find out the truth by going as far as Bartholomew if necessary and communicate with you as speedily as possible.

If you find it necessary to Camp below Longview for convenience to forage you must keep a picket at the Bridge See that corn is not wasted, as I am trying to get the authority

[66] Company E, Twenty-first Texas.

to concentrate the Brigade in that region as it is the only place I can hear of any corn. Report your arrival at Longview by the line of couriers passing that place.

Lt. Col. [DeWitt Clinton] Giddings
Comdg 21st Tx Cav.

your obt servt
Wm Steele Brig Genl.

* * * * * * * * * * * * *

Head Qurs 1st Cavalry Brigade
Warren, Ark. Oct 31st 1864

45/
Captain,

I have the honor to state in reply to your letter No. 444, that Lieut. [Thomas C.] Howard is at present detailed upon my Staff, but has been nominated for appointment, and application made to Dept. HQ for his assignment, until such time as his nomination may be heard from

I am Sir Very Respectfully
Your Obt. Servt.
Wm Steele
Brig. Genl & c

Capt. B.F. Weems
A A Genl

* * * * * * * * * * * * *

Head Qurs. Steele's Brig
Warren, Ark. Oct. 31st 1864

46/
Col,

I have the honor to inform you that circular from Inspection Genl. Officer Dist. Of Ark. Camden October 11th 1864 has this day reached this office. The Regts of my command are so much scattered that it cannot be distributed in time to reach them until this evening and tomorrow, and I have no muster Rolls (blanks) to send out.

Respectfully
Your Obt. Servt.
Wm Steele
Brig. Genl.

Col. E P Turner
A A Genl
Dist. Ark

* * * * * * * * * * * * *

Head Qurs Steele's Brig.
Warren Oct. 31st 1864

47/
Col.

An order received today through Genl. [John A.] Wharton's Hd Qurs. requires that all trains be so employed in the collection of Quarter Master and Commissary stores, as to enable you to move in two days in any direction.

This Brigade has so little transportation, and what it has is so indifferent that it is insufficient for the daily supply. More than a year since the transportation was turned over to the Quarter Master Dept during the movement that was being made into Misouri [*sic*] under [John S.] Marmaduke [in the spring of 1863], and never returned. What they now have is utterly inadequate.

The order above referred to was signed by N.S. Hill, C.S.

Respectfully
Your Obt. Servt.
Wm Steele
Brig. Genl.

Col. E.P. Turner
A A Genl

* * * * * * * * * * * * *

Head Qurs Steele's Brigade
Warren Ark Nov 1st 1864

48/
Col.

Yours of Oct. 31st is at hand and I must say that I do not approve of their arrangements, as it scatters your command so much that it is not much [in] your control for any emergency and placing them at the mercy of the enemy.

You will please change this at once. For the main body under your immediate control and detach small parties as moveable pickets each within certain limits.

With your present arrangements the troops from one marine boat could take your whole Regt without the loss of scarcely a man.

Your Obt Servt
Wm Steele
Brig Genl
Com Cavl Brigade

Col. W.H. Parsons
Comdg Regt

* * * * * * * * * * * * *

Head Qurs. Steele's Brigade
Warren Ark Nov 1st 1864

49/
Col.

In making inquiries concerning roads it appears to me that the direct road from this place to Pine Bluff must pass not very far from you, if such is the case. Keep it under your observation. the force here is so small that it would be no obstacle to a force passing below you and to your rear. I wish you would give me as complete a sketch as you can get of the roads leading out of Pine Bluff.

Your obt Servt.
Wm Steele
Brig. Genl.
Comdg & c.

Col. B.W. [Benjamin W.] Watson
Comdg at Mt. Elba

* * * * * * * * * * * * *

Head Qurs. Steele's Brigade
Warren Ark Nov 1st 1864

50/
Capt.

I have the honor to enclose a letter from Col. Parsons and its enclosures. I sent Col. Parsons as reported upon the application of Capt Polk, (who was authorized by Special Order from Dist. He'd Qurs to call upon me for assistance), and for the purpose of checking the movements of the enemy from Island and their Gun Boats in small force.

The arrangements as stated in Col. Parsons letter I have disapproved and have instructed him to keep the main body of his Regiment together under his immediate command and to cover the different points by small movable pickets.

I have now at this place only three companies one of [Charles L.] Morgan's and two from the 21st and it is a matter of great difficulty to supply the small force with a small and insufficient ration of corn for their horses. Some nights they get none and this whilst using the company wagons of the 12th and all other available transportation. I have ordered Col. [DeWitt Clinton] Giddings to halt for further instructions, near Longview, hoping that Genl. [John A.] Wharton would authorize his remaining there, as well as the collection of the other portion of my Brigade at the same point. By such arrangements the horses could be foraged, the men fed and the movements of the enemy could be known, by means of small parties a system that I depend more upon now than in pickets and stations, which soon become known and are easily avoided. The command at Mt Elba is now much strained for forage, only getting in small quantities from long distance. They cannot remain where they are, nor can troops be kept at this place without soon sending their animals totally unfit for service.

The Saline River is so easily crossed in the present stage of water that pickets at the regular crossings or anything less than a cordon along its whole length, only serves to embarrass legitimate travel without giving security against spies or even portions of Cavalry without wagons—the line is however much protected by the force at Mt Elba which is in almost a direct line with this place and Pine Bluff and the parties in the directions of the Miss. will give ample notice of any force on that front—

Your obt. Servt
Wm Steele
Brig. Genl.

Capt. B.F. Weems
A.A.G.

* * * * * * * * * * * * *

Head Qurs. Steele's Brigade
Warren Ark. Nov 1st 1864

51/
Capt.

It would be of much advantage to my office if I could be furnished with a copy of the first inspection reports. In investigating the cases of some men reported delinquents in the late inspections it is asserted in some cases that the men reported did not have arms. I cannot ascertain if the Inspectors have made an error. Many arms have been taken from one and given to another on these and many other accounts it is desirable that I should have a copy of the organized reports.

We are very deficient in Blanks and indeed in stationery of all kinds. I am even obliged to beg a little ink for my office. Some of the clothing reports have come in, but differing (?) so much from the requirements of the order that they were sent back. As soon as I can assertain [*sic*] who are clearly not delinquents in regard to missing arms & accurtrements [*sic*] I will send the others reported so to your H. Qurs.

Your obt servt
Wm Steele
Brig Genl.

Capt. B.F. Weems

* * * * * * * * * * * * *

Head Qurs Steele's Brigade
Warren Ark Nov 1st 1864

52/
Capt.

On the 29th ult several boats landed troops at Napoleon who went down to the mouth of Cypress by land and embarked.

Respectfully
Your Obt Servt
Wm Steele
Brig. Genl.

A copy to each
Capt. B.F. Weems
Col. E.P. Turner
A.A. Genl's

* * * * * * * * * * * * *

Head Qurs Steele's Brigade
Warren Ark Nov 2nd 1864

53/
Col.

I sent down a day or two since a party of prisoners with among them one youth named Sutton. The father of Sutton has since called upon me and expressed the wish that his son might be put into the service. He says he has been enticed from home by the band of horse thieves, he was taken with some five weeks since and has remained with them and the old prisoner Smith, who is considered as the recipient and disposer of stolen horses.

Respectfully
Your Obt Servt.
Wm Steele
Brig Genl.

Col. E.P. Turner
A.A.G.

* * * * * * * * * * * * *

Head Qurs Steele's Brigade
Warren Ark Nov 2nd 1864

54/
Capt.

I have the honor to inform you that Special Order No. 260 Paragraph XII Trans Miss Dept Assigning Surgeon Dashield [William Bond Dashiell] Medical Officer with the 19th Regt. Surgeon [D.] Fontress[67] of Morgan's Batt. serving immediately with the 19th was taken for the same duty. This leaves the two commands with but one very young & sickly Medical Officer. I earnestly request that measures be taken to supply the deficiency.

Your Obt Servt
Wm Steele

Capt. B.F. Weems A.A.G.

* * * * * * * * * * * * *

Head Qurs Steeles Brigade
Warren, Nov 3rd 1864

55/
Col.

Your letter of yesterday is just received. Some beef Will be sent down at once, about 10 head, which is all that can be sent until more are received, which it is expected will be in a few days.

[67] Fentress (Fontress) was an assistant surgeon in Morgan's regiment.

We are out of forage here, and I can hear of none except on the Saline below Long View. I hope you will use it with economy, and use from the East side of the River if practicable. I have heard nothing from my application to keep you at Long View. I had no orders to send you there, but took the authority for a few days If I get no favorable reply soon you will move on to Princeton. Get your returns and reports in as soon as possible whilst you remain.

Your Obt Servt<br>
Wm Steele<br>
Brig Genl.

Lt. Col. [DeWitt Clinton] Giddings<br>
Comdg 21st Tex Cav.

* * * * * * * * * * * * *

Head Qurs Steele's Brigade<br>
Warren Ark ~~Oct~~ Nov 3rd 1864

56/<br>
Capt.

I have the honor to report that it is impossible to forage the animals at this place any longer

The Quarter Master has only been able to furnish an inadequate supply for the present week. Now the distance is so much increased, and the roads in such condition that the teams can scarcely haul more than enough for themselves.

Very Respectfully<br>
Your Obt Servt<br>
Wm Steele<br>
Brig Genl

Capt. B.F. Weems<br>
A.A. Genl

* * * * * * * * * * * * *

Head Qurs Steele's Brigade<br>
Warren Nov 3rd 1864

57/<br>
General

Your letter of the 28th ult has been received. My letter (to which it was an answer) was written from no desire to find fault—I found that Colonel [Benjamin W.] Watson had instructions of which I had no copy. There was a letter from your H'd Qurs, which I recolect to have read at your head qurs, but supposed was sent through Colonel Parsons, and instructions from Dist. Head Qurs in reference to covering roads leading to Princeton. Letters from and documents were, and still are coming to me without passing through your office, some requiring answers, which renders me liable to a rebuke, as was the case with Colonel Parsons, whose letter direct to Dist. Head Quarters (he informs me) was an answer to one sent direct him. The orders to Col. [DeWitt Clinton] Giddings I had no reference to.

The ford spoken of by Maj. Runnels was unguarded as well as others still lower down, but the approaches to these fords from any point occupied by the Enemy were closely observed. To guard the line of the Saline River would require more force than I have or have had at my disposal, or than could be maintained if I had them.

Respectfully
Your Obt Servt
Wm Steele
Brig. Genl.

Maj. Genl. J.A. [John A.] Wharton
Comdg Cav.

P.S. Have you heard whether corn and bacon could be exchanged. Inquiry has been made in behalf of a planter east of Saline who has supplies for his stock and fifty negroes, and has 6000 lbs. of pork, which he is willing to drive to Camden on to sell, if it can be returned to him in Texas. Precise amount of corn not stated.

Wm Steele
Brig Genl

* * * * * * * * * * * * *

Head Qurs Steele's Brigade
Warrren Ark Novr 3rd 1864

58/
Colonel

I have ordered Acting Chief Q.M. of my Brigade to Camden, to procure if possible some stationery and other necessary stores. All of the Regts as well as my Head Quarters are out of paper and stationery of all kinds. I found myself this morning reduced to the last half quire. I hope this state of affairs will excuse the irregularity of sending to Camden instead of to the distant Head Qurs of Cavalry.

Respectfully
Your Obt Servt
Wm Steele
Brig. Genl.

Col. E.P. Turner
A.A. Genl

* * * * * * * * * * * * *

Head Quars Steeles Brigade
Warren Ark Nov 4th 1864

59/
Genl

Your letter of the 1st inst containing instructions withdrawing my brigade & c was received this morning I have expressed repeatedly to Col. Parsons who is with his

Regiment near the Lower Arkansas, and to Col. [DeWitt Clinton] Giddings who is at Longview, as soon as possible I will give them their instructions and report at your Head Qurs.

There is I think more forage where the 21st now is than in the vicinity of El Dorado. I would advise them remaining there.

Respectfully
Your Obt Servt.
Wm Steele
Brig. Genl.

Maj. Genl. John A. Wharton
Comdg Cavalry

P.S. An order was this morning received from Trans Miss Dept placing Col. Parsons upon a board to examine incompetent officers which I have not sent to him.

Wm Steele
Brig Genl.

* * * * * * * * * * * * *

Head Qurs Steeles Brigade
Warren Ark Nov 4th 1864

60/
Col.

Your letter (No. 440) received this morning. I think you have made a mistake in the name you intended to use. The instructions received at the same time from Genl [John A.] Wharton placed these squadrons one on the road from Camden to Pine Bluff via Mt. Elba and the other on the Road from Camden via Warren. Whereas your arrangements puts both on the same Road from Camden via Mt. Elba upon the insertion of Camden instead of Warren. I will make it right as I think it was intended.

Respectfully
Your Obt Servt
Wm Steele
Brig. Genl.

Col. E.P. Turner
A.A. Genl

* * * * * * * * * * * * *

Hd qrs. Steeles Brigade
Warren Ark Nov. 5. 1864

61/
Capt.

I enclose a note from Lt. [J.B.] Abbott who has been getting information. Lieut. Col. [John B.] Williams who has just returned from a scout close to Pine Bluff reports information derived, from a lady, that the force at that place (Pine Bluff) is 3000 Infty & 2000 Cavalry General [Powell] Clayton returned to his command a few days since. I leave to day for your Hd qrs

Your obt servt.
Wm Steele
Brig. Genl.

Capt. B.F. Weems
A.A. Genl.

* * * * * * * * * * * * *

Head qrs Steeles Brigade
Warren Ark Nov. 5. 1864

62/
Col.

I am directed by Brig Genl [William] Steele to say, that you will withdraw your out posts as quickly as possible and move with your own Regt. and Morgans Battalion across the Saline and down on the East side of the Saline via Monticello, re-crossing the Saline at Longview, where you will send your train from your present camp, moving by Moro Landing. you will report to these Head Quarters at Eldorado Ark The Genl. desires that you will let no one know that you are leaving but wishes you to make the impression on the people that you have gone on a scout. The Genl. Suggests that it would be advisable to say nothing to any of your officers of the destination of your command but make the impression that it is a scout.

I am Col.
Very Respectfully
Your obt Servt
J M Brandon
AA Genl

Col. B.W. [Benjamin W.] Watson
Commandg at Mt Elba
Ark.

* * * * * * * * * * * * *

Walnut Hill, Ark
Novr 26th 1864

63/
Genl.

I send this direct, hearing that you are in Louisville, and perhaps have no Staff Officer.

I arrived here today having traveled daily since I left Camden, having been forced many miles out of the direct road by high water and ruined bridges—I first found the 12th Regt (Parsons) which is now en route for the east of the Washita [Ouachita] River—The 19th and Morgans Battalion are at this place, and will soon move in the same direction as the 12th. The whole will of necessity be compelled to travel very slowly—The transportation of my Brigade which was inadequate to its necessities under the most favorable circumstances, is now much more so from the bad state of the roads and the condition of the mules, broken down as they are by constant marching and scarcity of forage—I have also a number of dismounted men who could remount themselves if permitted to be sent home for that purpose—These men are unarmed and are only an incumbrance.

I have applications for short leaves to go to points in this district for clothing, which has been sent to friends or relations in other commands. In one case in Forney's Division which is now but a short distance from my line of march—Can I not have some discretion in this matter.

Is Col. Parsons to join his Regt for the duty to which it has been assigned, under your verbal order—

I hope my Brigade will be soon relieved as Genl [John A.] Wharton writes me you promised to do, in order that I may have some time to put it in condition for the next campaign, which you are aware cannot be done whilst on picket duty

Respectfully
Your Obt Servt
Wm Steele
Brig Genl.

Maj. Genl. J.B. [John B.] Magruder
Comdng Dist. Ark. (Signed)

* * * * * * * * * * * * *

Hd Qrs. Steeles Brigade
Near Walnut Hill Nov 29. 64

64/
Major

I am directed by Genl. [William] Steele to enclose copy of instructions from Dept. Hd. Qrs. and to say you will not make its contents public, but find out where all the cotton is, and be ready to execute the order should the exigencies of the case demand it.

I am Maj.
Your obt Servt
J.M. Brandon A A Genl

Maj. L.J. [Lochlin J.] Farrar
Comdg. 12th T.C.

* * * * * * * * * * * * *

Head Qurs. Steeles Brigade
Walnut Hill, Ark. Novr 29 1864

65/
Colonel,

I am much embarrassed in the effort to move this Command, by the want of transportation and supplies—The mules having been worked hard at Mt. Elba in hauling forage with insufficient food there and on the march, are reduced in flesh and strength until some of the teams can scarcely haul an empty wagon.

I have no Quarter Master or Commissary train with the exception of two four mule wagons, and only one ordnance wagon—I have but about two days beef that is fit for issue, and here I would remark upon the unnecessary loss of which is inflicted upon the Govt. By this issue at Camden of beef so poor that troops will not eat it, and the refusal of Dept. Commissaries to receive it when condemned—The issue of such beef only results in its being thrown away and gives an excuse for depredations. I can get bacon at Washington and but have no means of transporting it. I can get, as I am informed some mules, probably ten or twelve if authorized to impress—They are unbroken, and running with the mares in a cane brake, where they have been kept to prevent impressment—I can also get some beef by this same means. I request that I may be authorized to impress these animals. The mules are not used for planting purposes, but are entirely unbroken. I have tried in vain to get transportation for this Brigade from the time it was under my Command in Louisiana last Spring to the present time. Inspections have been made several times, and all agree that it is very deficient on transportation, and has less than any other Brigade, yet the difficulty has not been remedied—

All orders on the subject of transportation appear to be made for large Infantry Commands. No allowance is made for Commands like mine, which is now scattered over a large extent of country in not less than five different bodies, each of which must have a wagon at least, even if it does not number one hundred men.

In moving from here I shall be compelled to subsist upon the Country, and to do so will frequently necessitate impressment, there being an indisposition to sell for Confederate money. As an example I will state that for two days before my arrival at Magnolia, coming from Three Creeks. I tried and vain for two days to buy meat of any kind, sufficient for my small party of five, (which was out of provisions owing to delay from high water).

Some of the Company wagons are absent for a small supply of Quarter Master stores to be turned over by the Q.M. at Cav. H'd Qurs; when they return I will move as rapidly as I can, to the position assigned me below Hamburg.

I am Sir
Very Respectfully
Your Obt Servt
Wm Steele
Brig Genl.

Lt. Col. E.P. Turner
A.A. Genl
Dist. Ark

* * * * * * * * * * * * *

Head Quarters Steele's Brigade
Camp near Walnut Hill Novr 30/64[68]

66/
Colonel

I am directed by Brig Genl [William] Steele to say that the Provost Guard of this Brigade frequently come in contact with men riding over the country, who say they are the Provost Guard of your Brigade. If you will give your Provost Guard a written certificate, or have it done by the officer comdng Guard, it will prevent deceptions. The Provost

[68] Walnut Hill is near the location where Arkanasas, Louisiana, and Texas touch.

Guard of this Brigade will be given the same by Lieut. I.F. Mulkey who commands it—Men are not allowed to be absent from this camp except on passes signed by Regimental Commanders, and not more than two from a company[69]

I am Col
Very Respectfully
Your Obt Servt
J.M. Brandon A A Genl

Col. [John W.] Logan
Comdng Cav
Near Walnut Hill

* * * * * * * * * * * * *

Head Qurs Steeles Brig
Near Walnut Hill Decr [1864]

General Orders
No 27

The Brig Genl Comdg having ascertained that in some instances men have been enlisted into one company, by officers of his command, while actually belong[ing] to another, attention is called to the 22nd Art of War where the criminality of such conduct is set forth.

By Command of
Brig. Genl. Wm Steele
Thos C Howard A.A.A. Genl

[order cancelled out and rewritten]

* * * * * * * * * * * * *

Head Qurs Steeles Brigade
Near Walnut Hill Decr 1/64

Genl Orders
No 27

The attention of all officers of this Brigade is especially called to the 22nd Art. Of War

By Command of
Brig Genl Wm Steele
Thos C Howard A.A.A.Genl

[69] On November 6, J.C. Morriss had told his wife: "Our officers are getting very tight. They are trying, by Court Martial every one who has over staid his time and has been reported absent without leave. I hope it will have a salutary efect upon the army, and that it will cause all the absenttees to come up, which President Davis says will increse our army two thirds." J.C. Morriss to Amanda Morriss, November 6, 1862[4], Pruett and Black, eds., *Civil War Letters*, 46-49.

* * * * * * * * * * * * *

[beginning missing]

committing other depredations, therby bringing [the] name of the Brigade in disrepute, every [man] must be invoked by comdg officer to protect the character and reputation of the good men who conduct themselves in an orderly manner.[70]

By command of
Brig Genl [William] Steele
J M Brandon A.A.G.

* * * * * * * * * * * * *

Hd Qrs Steeles Brigade
Near Walnut Hill Ark Dec 1/64

67/
Col.

Your letter of inquiry as to the position of the diferent portions of my command I have the honor to state that I have with me at this place the 19th Regt and Morgan's Batt. The 12th is enroute for the duty assigned it on the lower Arkansas & Miss rivers it was two days since at Homer La traveling via Washita [Ouachita] City the more direct routes being destitute of forage.

The 12th is at present commanded by Maj. L J [Lochlin J.] Farrar The Col (Parsons) being on examining board and the Lieut. Col. ([A. Bell] Burleson) in arrest.[71] The 21st Regt Lt. Col. [DeWitt Clinton] Giddings Commanding has its Hd Qurs near Longview with two squadrons detached to report to yourself to pickets in front of Camden A detachment leaves to day under command of Lieut. Smith to guard prisoners from Camden to Shreveport This detail could have been made from troops at this place who are not enroute for a distant position as my commands is.

Lt Col. Giddings is scouting on the Arkansas River from near Pine Bluff down around the Miss River as far down as Gainses landing until the 12th Regt arrives. I shall leave for the vicinity of Hamburg as soon as some wagons return which have been sent to Dooly ferry for Quarter Master's stores, probably by Monday next at the latest. My progress will be slow on account of the small amount of transportation and the broken down condition of the mules. My route will be via Homer, Farmersville & Washita [Ouachita] City. I have no means of hauling supplies with me and consequently must travel through a

[70] Perhaps in an effort to raise the morale and improve the behavior of the men, churches became a popular destination. J.C. Morriss noted: "Since I stoped writing this morning I have been to church and heard a very excelant [*sic*] serman by a Presbeterian minister. The church was crowded, mostly with soldiers—some fifteen or twenty ladies and as many gentlemen, citizens and the balance of the congregation made up of soldiers of our Regt." J.C. Morriss to Amanda Morriss, November 6, 1862[4], Pruett and Black, eds., *Civil War Letters*, 46-49.

[71] Burleson, along with some of the officers, had presented a petition first to Wharton and then to Magruder requesting that the men of the Twelfth Texas be allowed to go home at the end of their three-year commitment on October 28. Apparently Magruder was so annoyed that he ordered Burleson's arrest. Henry Orr wrote in late November: "Report says that Burleson has gone to Yankeedom. He was over towards Monticello sick, when he was ordered by an officer direct from Gen. Magruder to report under arrest." Henry Orr to "Father," November 24, 1864, in Anderson, ed., *Campaigning with Parsons' Brigade*, 151.

country where they can be obtained I would again call your attention to the fact that I have as yet been unable to get wagon sheets for even the wagons used to transport ammunition

Respectfully
Your Obt Servt
Wm Steele
Brig Gnl

Lt. Col E.P. Turner
A Genl

* * * * * * * * * * * * *

Head Qurs. Steele's Brigade
Camp near Walnut Hill, Dec 1- 1864

68/
Colonel

I have received a letter of which the following is an extract. "I desire you to send a suitable man to some point in the vicinity of the mouth of White River, to watch the movements in that quarter, and on to the vicinity of Napoleon for observation at that point. Instruct them to obtain as many newspapers of late date as possible The expenses which they incur both in Confederate and Federal money will be promptly paid upon my receipt of proper (ordinary) vouchers. Let the men report to you, and forward their information & c & c.

Please make the arrangement required above as soon as possible, and until I arrive, send your information to Maj. H.M. Clark A.A.G. Chief of S.S. Dist. Ark. Mark every communication of importance "confidential". I shall leave here in a day or two to travel via Homer and Washita [Ouachita] City. The 12th is already some days en route on the same line.

Send one by special courier the furloughs as allowed by Genl Order No 81. One in 15 for those present, will I imagine be the allowance to your Regt.

Your Obt Servt
Wm Steele Brig Genl

Lt Col. D.C. [DeWitt Clinton] Giddings

* * * * * * * * * * * * *

Head Qurs Steeles Brigade
Camp near Walnut Hill Decr 2nd 1864

69/
Major

Your letter of the 25th on the subject of Monthly returns has been today received without the returns.

Please forward another supply at once, as it will require the whole of this month to get them properly distributed. Send for three Regts and a battalion of nine companies Viz: 12th or Parsons Regt 19th or Watson's, 21st or Carter's, now commanded by Lieut Colonel [DeWitt Clinton] Giddings and Morgan's Battalion. Four companies of the 21st are picketing on the roads leading from Camden in the direction of Pine Bluff and Warren, and Lieut Col. Giddings with the remainder of the regiment is at Long View. If you will send returns direct to these commands you will facilitate the distribution. I am also desirous of being furnished in time with muster rolls. I am desirous too that there should be a complete and acurate muster of my Brigade on the last day of this month, after which I hope to get returns & c regularly. All orders on this subject have come too late, not sufficient allowance being made for irregularities and for and for [*sic*] the time requisite for commands like mine; scattered over several hundred miles. This portion of my Brigade will move in two days for a point near Hamburg, to which the quickest channel of communication will be via Long View

Your Obt Servt
Wm Steele
Brig Genl.

Maj. J.T. OBrien
A.A. & I Genl

* * * * * * * * * * * * *

Head Quarters Steeles Brig.
Walnut Hill Ark Dec. 4. 1864

70

I am directed by Brig Genl [William] Steele to order you to halt your command and collect it together as much as possible. Find a good place for forage and await further orders. Orders have been issued by Genl Smith to General [John B.] Magruder to send this Brigade to Nachogdoches Texas; as soon as the order can be sent from Genl Magruder you will receive Orders. In the mean time Genl Steele desires you to collect all your men together if possible

Your obt servt
J.M. Brandon
A A Genl

Major L.J. [Lochlin J.] Farrar
Comdg 12th TC

* * * * * * * * * * * * *

Head qrs. Steeles Brigade
Near Walnut Hill Dec 5. 64

71
Col.

I am directed by the Brig. Genl. Commdg to send you the enclosed copies of communications from District Hd qrs. and to say he has received no information as to the extent of Capt. Polks power but supposes he has complete controll of the cotton in that section of country as he is recognized by Department Hd qrs. and you will so consider him unless further instructed

I am Col. very Resly
your obt servt
J M Brandon A.A. Genl

* * * * * * * * * * * * *

Head Qurs Steeles Brigade
Walnut Hills Dec 6th 1864

Capt.

I have received two letters from you within the last few days directed to me at Monticello, the first letter I acted upon by sending an extract to Lt. Col. [DeWitt Clinton] Giddings commanding 21st Tex Cavalry whose Hd Qurs are near Longview, directing him to carry out your instructions. I am surprised it should not be supposed at Dist. Hd Qurs that I was at Monticello. I have not been ordered to that place and have been in daily correspondence with Col Turner from this. I am now informed that I am ordered in an other direction with all my Brigade except the 21st under Lt Col Giddings, you will do well to correspond directly with him. I did not communicate the cipher.

Capt. H.M. Clark
A.A. Genl
Camden Arkansas

Your obt servt
Wm Steele
Brig Genl.

## CHAPTER 7

# TEXAS

## 1865

Relocating the soldiers to Texas did not solve all the problems. As the concentration of men and horses increased around Nacogdoches, providing forage for the animals became a burden. By January Kirby Smith decided "to reduce their number by at least one-half." The reorganization resulted in General Steele taking command of a cavalry corps under Wharton comprised of Parsons's brigade, which now included the Twelfth and Nineteenth Texas, Morgan's regiment, and the Thirtieth Texas cavalry (Carter's Twenty-first Texas having been reassigned to Walter P. Lane's brigade). By March, however, even the veterans under Parsons feared losing their mounts. Philip Frazier of the Thirtieth Texas wrote that his messmates received the news that their horses might go home without them with a huge "uproar." W.W. Heartsill believed that if the authorities dismounted the troopers that "a great many will desert rather than walk."[1]

Although the veterans did not lose their horses, they did lose their commander when Colonel George W. Baylor murdered General Wharton on April 6 after a personal altercation. The men's sorrow was short-lived however, because much to their delight, Colonel Parsons returned to take command of the brigade. When he arrived in camp, the men "raised a yell," recalled George Ingram, "and about twelve or fifteen hundred went out to

[1] J.F. Belton to John A. Wharton, January 25, 1865, *OR* 41, pt. 4, 1,344; Organization of Wharton's Cavalry Corps, commanded by Maj. Gen. John A. Wharton, C.S. Army, for March 1865, ibid., 1,458; Philip D. Frazier to "Mother, Brother, & Sisters," March 2, 1865, Frazier Family Papers; Heartsill, *Fourteen Hundred and 91 Days*, 235.

the house and called for him. He came out, got up into a buggy and made the best speech I have heard from him."[2]

Yet the end was near and after rumors of Robert E. Lee's surrender reached Texas, the brigade assembled at Camp Walker in Robertson County on May 2. By late May, Parsons announced that military officials intended to disband the army. He gave the companies permission to take their wagons home and "bade his Brigade an affectionate farewell."[3]

These final orders cover the first months of 1865, the last weeks of service for the rebel troopers. These Texas Confederates had served loyally for four years. Throughout March and April, commanders tried to maintain a sense of continuity and authority as disarray appeared all around, but it was clear that the Confederacy had reached its final days. Lee's surrender of the Army of Northern Virginia in early April, while symbolic, was only the beginning of a wave of despair that spread across the South in the weeks that followed. Joseph E. Johnston capitulated to Sherman in North Carolina in late April, and Richard Taylor relinquished his command in Mississippi and Alabama in early May. The end finally came when Kirby Smith formally surrendered the remaining fragments of the Army of the Trans-Mississippi on May 26.[4]

[2] Brigadier General Hamilton P. Bee replaced Wharton as cavalry commander. See for the quote, George W. Ingram to Martha F. Ingram, April 7, 1865, in Ingram, comp., *Civil War Letters*, 78-79.

[3] Heartsill, *Fourteen Hundred and 91 Days*, 244-45.

[4] Robert L. Kerby, *Kirby Smith's Confederacy: The Trans-Mississippi South, 1863-1865* (New York: Columbia University Press, 1972), 424.

C H A P T E R 7

# DOCUMENTS

## Texas: 1865

Head qrs. Steeles Brigade
Camp Bonaparte Jany 11, 65

1/
Col

I am directed by Col. [Benjamin W.] Watson to say that you will cause commanders of companies to require all men who go out on passes to return them immediately on their return to Camp to be destroyed

Very Respectfully
Your obt servt
Col. C.S. Morrow J.M. Brandon A.A.G.

* * * * * * * * * * * * *

Head Quarters Steele's Brigade
Camp Bonaparte Jany 18. 65

2/
Capt.

A letter from J. Douglass Bruner of 17th inst. is at hand and I am directed by Col. [Benjamin W.] Watson to say that a General Order from Shreveport (QMD) directs that "all army guns in the hands of citizens and not in the service be taken by the soldiers and officers of the army." No orders have been issued to impress arms from these Hd Qrs. The Col. has written to the Commd'g General Cavalry Corps for instructions in regard to receipting you for the arms. Our command is very deficient in arms (never having drawn any from the Government) and as it will no doubt add materially to the service. Trust an arrangement can be made by which the arms can be turned over to the troops in the field before the campaign opens in the spring.

Capt. G.H. Mitchell
Enrolling Officer
Polk County

Very Respectfully
Your obt Servt
J.M. Brandon A.A.G.

* * * * * * * * * * * * *

Head Quarters Steele's Brigade
Camp Bonaparte Jany 18. 1865

3/
Genl

I have just received a letter from the Enrolling Officer of this County stating that the Reserved Corps of this County had Army guns turned over to them, and the guns receipted for. I have collected a good many of those guns, the citizen or Reserved Corps sold their guns to the troops or gave them to them. I have given but one order to impress and that was a case where a soldier had left the gun at a citizens house. Shall I give those guns up or shall I keep them and receipt for same? I think the guns should be kept in the Army, they are all fine arms and I am loth to give them up

Brig. Genl. Wm Steele
Comdg. Cav. Corps

Very Respectfully
Your Obt Servt
B.W. [Benjamin W.] Watson

* * * * * * * * * * * * *

Head Quarters Steele's Brigade
Camp Bonaparte Jany 19th 1865

4/
Genl.

The acting Quarter Master informs me that we can remain at this camp but eight days longer an account of scarcity of forage. The Commissary tells me it is with difficulty that he can subsist the Command at this time. When the (12) Twelfth arrives it will reduce the time several days; and I would respectfully ask for permission to move the Com'd about thirty miles from this point on <u>Trinity River.</u> Maj [Thomas] Johns will be in Waco in a few days; he has an order from General Walker to impress One Hundred-twenty mules for this Brigade

Genl Wm Steele
Comdg Cav. Corps
Nacogdoches

Very Respectfully
Yr Obt Serv't
B.W. [Benjamin W.] Watson
Col. Comdg Brigade

* * * * * * * * * * * * *

Head Quars Steeles Brig
Camp Bonaparte Jany 26. 65

Maj.

I am directed by Col. [Benjamin W.] Watson to call your attention to Par. V Genl Order No. 31 from Corps Head Qrs Series of 64, and to say it is necessary to carry out that Par to the letter.

Your obt servt.
J.M. Brandon A.A. Genl

* * * * * * * * * * * * *

Hd Quars Steeles Brig.
Camp Bonaparte Jany 28- 1865

7/
Genl

We are now reduced to the necessity of impressing forage for the command and to take all in this county on this side of Trinity River. Will not be more than enough to last two days—In this county there are three hundred indigent families and two hundred on this side of the river—I have had to take the responsibility of impressing myself, as we have no bonded Qr. Master, and the officer spoken of in your letter having not yet arrived. I have put off moving to the last moment and will leave for the Trinity the day after to morrow and hope it will meet your approval. I will not cross the river if I can impress wagons on the other side to haul to the river. I dislike very much to move without orders but necessity compells me to do so

Respectfully your obt srvt
B.W. [Benjamin W.] Watson
Col. Comdg Brigade

* * * * * * * * * * * * *

Head Quarters Steeles Brigade
Camp Bonaparte Jany 31- 1865

8/
Col.

Orders from Corp Hd Quarters require from your Regiment the following returns lists—

1st List. of imcompetent, Inefficient & disabled Officers to go before the Ex-board

2nd List. of detached (not including extra duty) men in accordance with circular from Corps Hd. Oct 24-64.

3d Report of Qr. Masters under G.O. 43 from Corps Hd qrs. 1864

4th Date of Organization of your Regiment

6th List of deserters

7th Quarterly Return of deceased soldiers

8th Annual Return of Changes

Col. [Benjamin W.] Watson directs that these lists be made out as speedily as possible & forwarded

Very Respectfully
Col. C.S. Morrow Your obt servt
Comdg. Regt. J.M. Brandon A.A.G.

* * * * * * * * * * * * *

Hd Qrs. Steeles Brigade
Cold Springs Tex Feby 14. 1865

Major Genl. [John G.] Walker,

I have the honor to report that in obedience to instructions from Brig Genl [William] Steele Comdg Major Genl. [John A.] Wharton's Cavalry Corps Nacogdoches Texas Feby 9th 1865 a Courier line is now in position from these Head quarters to West Liberty on Trinity River Texas.

I have the honor to be
Very Respectfully
Your Obt Servt
Col. Comdg Steeles Brig.

* * * * * * * * * * * * *

Head Quarters Steeles Brigade
Cold Springs Tex. Feby 16. 1865

Capt.

Herewith I forward to you, within charges. I desire to know whether you wish me (at this date) to forward the prisoner for trial and witness to Alexandria La in compliance with order from Maj. Genl Buckner[5]

Capt. B.F. Weems Very respectfully
A.A.G. Your obt Servt

[5] Although the cause of this arrest is unknown, J.C. Morriss wrote on February 26 that the authorities were "getting very struck in discipline" if a soldier "overstays his time [on furlough] one day he will be held to account. Col. Giddings is still at Nacogdoches attending the Court Martial" J.C. Morriss to Amanda Morriss, February 26, 1865, Weller, ed., *Civil War Letters.*

* * * * * * * * * * * * *

Hd Qrs Steele Brigade
Near Waverly Tex March 22. 1865

Capt.

I am desirous through you to see the decision of the Maj. Gen. Comdg on the following point; many of the officers and men of this Brigade are from the remote West and distant from the location of any examining board of Surgeons, they are some time sent home wounded & allowed to go there on leave or on furlough sick, and are afterward unable to get discharged, retired, or extention of time. They frequently send certificates from private physicians vouched for by enrolling officers and this is all they can do. Should they be reported absent without leave and dropped as deserters on the next return as in case of those who remain over their time? There are other cases in which the men are unable to get even this evidence of their disability and many certificates sent never reach the command when the men are known to be unable to move. What report should be made on such extreme cases?

Capt. B.F. Weems
A.A.G.

I am sir
very resfy

* * * * * * * * * * * * *

Head Quarters Steele's Brigade
Camp Waverly Tex March 27th 1865

Genl

I would respectfully ask for information on Par III Genl. Orders No. 34 Adjutant and Inspectors Genl's office at Richmond. Shall the Medical Examining Board in case of retirement or discharge have final action or should the action of the Board be subject to the approval or disapproval of the Brigade and Corp Commanders and should papers for retirement be approved by Company and Regimental Commanders.

I would also call your attention to the fact that the Regiment has no Major. Capt. J.M. Stone [John M. Stone] and Capt R.E. [Reuben E.] Saunders were ordered before an Examining Board and were examined and I have heard nothing from the result. For the good of the Regiment Genl. I would most respectfully ask that you have this matter attended to at your earliest convenience. Every thing considered Capt. Stone should be the Major. Capt. Saunders is old and has been in bad health for at least ten months.

I am occasionally genl catching up men subject to conscription or belonging to other commands without passes. What shall I do with them?

I have the honor to be Genl
Your Obt Sevt
B.W. [Benjamin W.] Watson
Col. Comdg. Brigade

* * * * * * * * * * * * *

Head Quarters Steeles Brigade
April 3rd 1865

Capt. B.F. Weems

I have the honor to report that the Brigade has arrived at the place designated by the Maj. Genl. Comdg near John Cross Jones'. I found a large quantity of corn in the neighborhood but the citizens claim to have paid the tithe and that they have no more to spare. The Commissaries reports no Beef in the Country and but little Bacon to be had. I shall have to impress if I remain here longer than two days. Be pleased to give me orders in the premises.

Very Respectfully
Yr Obt Serv't
B.W. [Benjamin W.] Watson
Col. Comdg Brigade

* * * * * * * * * * * * *

Hd Qrs Parsons' Brigade
Wallace Prairie April 9th 1865

Brig. Genl. [William] Steele

Gurley's Regt[6] having arrived as I have notified you. I find they have a surplus of seven wagons. These were the Regimental quota of the Brig. train to which Gurley's Regt has been heretofore attached. The Regt Q.M. has not receipted to the Brig Q.M. Capt. Ware, now at Hempstead.

You are aware of the necessities of this Brig. for Commissary train. Capt. [Jefferson J.] Mallard informs me that the teams are nearly pulled down, and that the points of supply are so remote, that his transportation is utterly inadequate. I state the facts in regard to the surplus wagons (which are very fine although teams inferior) in order that you may, if you see proper, avail yourself of this perhaps favorable opportunity of suppling the pressing wants of the portion of your Division.

Capt. Ware was Genl. Bee's Brig Q.M. and the Genl knows all the facts in reference to the train as the Regimental quota of [James] Duff's Regt is in the other Division Vis may be permitted to remain in yours I hope it can be consumated.

Very Respectfully Yrs.
W.H. Parsons
Col. Comdg

Hd Q

Since closing the foraging letter I have received a communication. Lt. Duvall (as official) enclosing copy Special Order No. 65 April 2d 65. Corps Hd. Qrs. in which Genl. [John A.] Wharton authorizes you to order the impressments of forage & c.

[6] The Thirtieth Texas Cavalry was commanded by Edward J. Gurley.

As this is an order to yourself as Division Commander to order "impressment of forage," I cannot without special authority from you make or direct the impressments of forage.

Lt. Duvall has wisely sent me the copy of your authority. Is it not necessary that you should confer the authority upon me to direct Maj. [A.J.] Byrd Q.M. to make the impressments now so much needed?

Very Respectfully
W.H. Parsons
Genl. & c

* * * * * * * * * * * * * *

Hd Qrs Parsons Brigade
Wallace's Prairie Tex April 10th 1865

Lt. Duval
A.A.A.G.

I send enclosed the report of my Brig. Q.M. relative to field transportation.

As I stated in communication of 9th there are seven-6 mule teams and wagons now in possession of the A.A.Q.M. of the 30th Tex. Formerly belonging to Gano's Brig. not reported in the within report.[7]

8 days rations for 3000 men (our aggregate Brig strength) is 48480 lbs requiring 10 wagons to transport.

100 rounds ammunition each for aggregate strength Brig is 30000 lbs on the calculations of 10 lbs to 100 rounds. This requires 10 wagons.

This estimate is based upon the allowance under orders from Richmond and apportionment of 3000 lbs to the wagon, whilst there is no team we have on march in this country [that] can haul our 2000 lbs.

Very respectfully
W.H. Parsons
Col. Comd'g Brig

[7] The Thirtieth Texas joined Parsons's brigade, Steele's corps, in March 1865, arriving in Parsons's camp in April. It had been raised and commanded by Waco lawyer Edward J. Gurley, and served in Texas until the summer of 1863 when it transferred to the Indian Territory. For the next two years the regiment fought in engagements there and in Arkansas, taking part in the Camden Expedition of 1864, in particular, the Battle of Poison Spring. See Bailey, *Between the Enemy and Texas*, 234-38.

* * * * * * * * * * * * *

Hd. Qrs. Parsons Brigade
Wallace Prairie April 12th 1865

Capt. Duval
A.A.A.G.

No copies of the Special field returns called for have been attained, and with the papers sent up to your office to day. The last of the Regimental Field returns are transmitted some having been sent up by yesterday's courier, the balance having come in this morning. The Genl desired in letter of last evening a synopsis of the returns as he could not wait for the arrival of the complete.

They are now all in your office and you can make the desired estimate of our aggregate

The surplus wagons of [Edward J.] Gurley's [Thirtieth Texas cavalry] Regt have been ordered up to Corps Hd qrs. and have gone.

I shall execute instructions in reference to use of transportation contained in letter S.O. 3

Very Respt Yrs
W.H. Parsons
Col. Comdg Brig.

* * * * * * * * * * * * *

Hd. Qrs. Parson's Brigade
Wallace Prairie April 13th 1865

Brig. Genl. [William] Steele

Your letter in reference to arms has been received. I have taken steps to execute your wishes.

This section is very peculiar; notwithstanding the rains, it is principally watered by wet weather branches and drains; exceedingly difficult to get near our corn, and find Sandy Camp ground, grass and water.

In this locality the Regiments had to camp apart to get water; no one spot within half mile of each had water for two Regiments. The ground became so messy, that Regimental Commanders requested permission to move, and the parties I sent out, found it difficult to obtain ground, grass, and water near the corn.

The Regiments moved day before yesterday and yesterday. As we have no fodder and our corn was reduced to 8 lbs. grass is a consideration and I gave permission to Regimental Commanders to select their own camp having these qualities in view. Hence we are separated on a line of three miles for the whole Brig. Encampment, the flanks within 15 minutes of my Hd Qrs. I had sent out the Insp Genl to look for encampment and he reported no spot, with water sufficient for two Regiments together, at all convenient to our corn.

There are no longer Creeks between Navasota River and Wallace Creek, the camp as before remarked, watered by wet weather branches.

I hope we will not have to leave the vicinity of these Prairies, as I have been exceedingly anxious to take the Brig through the evaluations of the line and you are aware of the almost indispensable advantages of ample open ground. There has been no day since I have been here but what it has rained and the ground on prairie has been impossible for cavalry evaluations

I have ordered the troops out for maneuvers, but had to send them back to camp and countermand the order

I shall spend this day, in hunting for a Camp to get this Brig in a body in pursuance to your order No. 5

The weather has been very distressing on the troops yet every thing is cheerful and contented, perfect order prevails, and not a single deprivation has been committed

Very Respectfully Yrs
W.H. Parsons
Col. Comdg

* * * * * * * * * * * *

Hd Qrs Parsons Brigade
Grimes Prairie April 16th 1865

Maj. Brandon
AAG

The orders given to Maj. [B.D.] Chenoweth,[8] were to picket all the roads from Brazos River to Trinity, and down Trinity to West Liberty, establishing himself at some central point in communication with his chain of pickets. To guard all roads leading north and arrest all soldiers without proper authority, especially charging him that he was placed on this duty to intercept Gould's men who had deserted below. I gave him these verbally relying upon his experience and promptness for their execution.

I spent the day yesterday in looking for a camp. I had to be governed by the only locality from which we were drawing forage, near Grimes Prairie accompanied by Capt [William G.] Veal[9] and a citizen thoroughly familiar with the topography of the country. I report that I could find no spot with water for four Regiments suitable for a Brig Encampment, and that governed by the necessities of our situation I encamped two regiments each together, one mile apart, which gives all water and grass and intermediate drill grounds. My Hd. Qrs. with one of the wings. Command moved to day. If fair tomorrow commence Cav drill. Our drinking water is wet weather branches and will not last long. Every thing is moving as it should in this command

Very Respectfully
W.H. Parsons
Col. Comdg Brig

[8] Twenty-first Texas.

[9] Company F, Twelfth Texas.

* * * * * * * * * * * * *

Hd Qrs. Parsons Brigade
Grimes Prairie April 23rd 1865

Col Matheson

Sir

Pursuant to instructions from Dist Hd. Qrs. and which received to day from Genl. [Walter P.] Lane. I send Ordnance wagon for (150) One Hundred & fifty enfield rifles, which I was informed were in your Regiment for me

My ordnance officer is directed to receipt & c

Yours Respectfully
W.H. Parsons
Col. Comdg Brig

* * * * * * * * * * * * *

Hd Qrs. Parsons Brigade
Grimes Prairie April 23rd 1865

Maj. Brandon
A.A.G.

Co I Morgan's Regt was ordered to take position on Trinity by Genl [John A.] Wharton before my assignment to Brig duty.

The purpose was to arrest straglers and deserters They are still on duty. Maj. [B.D.] Chenoweth was directed by me to take charge of them and assign river position in connection with his detachment from 21st Cav. Hd Qrs. knows their locality. I not knowing where he placed them, as he has been ordered to report to Genl. [Walter P.] Lane and I have had no communication since with him

Very Respectfully
W.H. Parsons
Col. Comdg

* * * * * * * * * * * * *

Hd Qrs Parsons Brigade
Grimes Prairie April 24th 65

B.F. Weems
A A G

In reply to circular of 21st Inst I find by reference to Special Order Book of Brig March 28th 65 Order No. 40 prior to my resumption of Command, that Privates J.M. Weaver Co B 19th Tex. Cav. and G.R. [Green R.] Williams Co. D. 19th Tex Cav were ordered to report without delay for duty to Maj. Busby at Mound Prairie, Anderson County Tex. These men thus detailed were actually sent with Special from these Head Quarters.

In reply to circular April 21st I would reply that the letter came for these dismounted men prior to my assuming command. The adjutant states, the order came whilst on the March from Waverly and he has no record of it. The men are sent up to day. The clerk, Mr. Felton, informs me the men were actually sent by Col. [Benjamin W.] Watson

Very Respectfully Yrs & c
W.H. Parsons
Col Comdg

* * * * * * * * * * * * *

Hd. Qrs. Parsons' Brigade
Camp Walker, Little Brazos May 1st 1865

Maj. J.M. Brandon
A.A.G

I arrived at this camp ground designated by Div Q.M. early this morning.

The camp is sizible, near corn in abundance, plenty of good water and grass to last I hope some weeks.

The Commissary Dept. is inconvenienced in being compeled to haul bread corn, eight miles to mill.

All things considered the camp is very good. More prairie would be advantageous for abundant grass and room for Cav. drill.

This I am reliably informed can be obtained a few miles above here near Sterling, where there is abundance of forage, water extensive prairie and of course grass inexhaustible. This last is a great item as we are getting no fodder and the horses have commenced improving and will fatten with plenty of fine spring grass; our ration of 8 lbs. corn being abundant where we can get grass.

Yesterday I had all the Regiments mustered, two before leaving camp on march and two on reaching camp. Upon all prairies I marched the command in column of squadrons, close and open, and Reg in line, loosing no time on march and training horses and accustoming troops to perform the most difficult of all movements for regularity the "march in line."

If duty in the field does not demand our services soon, this Brig of your Div shall be the best drilled, as I believe it already is the best ordered in this Dept.

Very Respectfully
W.H. Parsons
Col. Comdg & c

* * * * * * * * * * * * *

Hd qrs. Parsons Brigade
Camp Walker, Little Brazos May 1st 65

Maj. Brandon
A.A.G.

Capt. [John W.] Posey[10] Morgan's Regt and Capt. [Fauntleroy R.] Ball[11] of the 19th Tex Cav. who were assigned to duty on Gen Court Martial for Brig were permitted leaves of absence prior to reception of Special Order

Consequently we lack the minimum number to constitute a court.

The numbers present with Brig. Commd to day are ordered there to await the appointment of others to constitute the necessary compliment

I forward the names of

| | |
|---|---|
| Capt. W.R. [J.L.] Smith | Co I 30th Tex Cav. |
| " C Murray Lea | " K " " " |
| Lt. L.T. [Lucius T.] Wheeler | " F Morgan's Regt |

Lt. [J.B.] Abbott appointed on the list has had a leave of absence in his pocket for some weeks, and remain'd for the interest of his Co. until now. He is entitled to go home and if Lt. Wheeler can be appointed Judge Advocate should go. Can I relieve him?

Very Respectfully
W.H. Parsons
Col Comdg Brig

* * * * * * * * * * * * *

Hd Qrs Parsons Brigade
Camp Walker Texas May 1. 1865

General order No 4

I On account of the proximity of many of this command to their homes, 10 per cent of each company estimating those actually present will be allowed passes from one to seven days. Company officers will in case of necessity only grant for the longest term and confine it to those to procure horses or attend to business of importance. Attention is again called to G.O. No 1 from these Hd Qrs which restricts all applicants for indulgence to the regular channels and regular office hours. Personal applications will in no case be entertained, the practice of applying to Brig Comdr in person by applicants is irregular and cannot be allowed.

10 Company A, Morgan's Regiment. Posey replaced Captain Vontress, after the latter was killed by lightning in 1864. Posey was only nineteen years old in 1860. A native of South Carolina, he had enlisted in Williamson County. When the war began he was a student with no money nor land. Bailey, *Between the Enemy and Texas*, 228-29.

11 Company F, Nineteenth Texas. Ball was twenty-seven years old when he joined the army in 1862. He was a native of Kentucky who had enlisted in Parker County. He gave his occupation as a grocer who had $75 in real estate and $1,360 in personal estate. Ibid., 224-25.

II The whole command will muster on foot under arms and repair to Brig Hd Qrs tomorrow at 4 1/2 P.M.

By order of
Col W.H. Parsons

* * * * * * * * * * * * *

Head Quarters Parsons
Camp Walker May [1865]

Circular

Owing to the large number [of] loose Horses, in and around the Enc[amp]ment, the attention of Regimental Com[manders] is called to G.O. No 5 Div Hd Qrs; who [will] be held strictly responsible for the no[n] compliance with the requirements of Paragraphs 2, 3, 4 & 6 of said order.

II. Capt W G [William G.] Veal[12] 12th Texas Cavalr[y] is detailed as "Field Officer of the Day," a[nd] will be ordered to report to these Hd Qrs immediately.

By order of
Col W H Parsons
J C S [James C.S.] Morrow A.A.A.G.

* * * * * * * * * * * * *

Head Quarters, Parsons Brigade
May 6th 1865.

Brig Genl Steel[e],

I am in receipt of a subpoena by courier from G.R. [George R.] Freeman.[13] Captain and Judge Advocate of the G.C.M. now in session in Hempstead Texas, on the [A. Bell] Burleson case.[14] Summoning me to, "be and appear personally, before the Gen. Court Martial, now in session" & c "to testify as a witness for the accused" & c "until you are released from attendance."

This subpoena is endorsed as follows: "Respectfully forwarded to to [*sic*] Hd Qrs Cav Corps, with request it be served. the party ordered accordingly, and evidence of these facts returned to Judge Advocate." (Signed) G.R. Freeman Capt & c. I have received this paper by courier without any endorsement by Corps or Div. Commander, & as Capt. Freeman evidently and I think properly contemplated, that I should be officially relieved & ordered by my immediate commanders: and as I have received no notice from them; I feel at a loss, as to the proper course to pursue.

This will be readily appreciated by you, with your knowledge of the condition of my command, as to officers. There not being a Field Officer present for duty in the whole

[12] Company F, Twelfth Texas.

[13] Company D, Twenty-first Texas.

[14] The inquiry into Burleson's arrest in the autumn continued for several months.

Brigade and I seriously question the power of a Judge Advocate, to summons; a Brigade Commander, without notice to, and action by, immediate superiors; which latter has not been taken in this case.

The interests of this large command would certainly be prejudiced by such a summary course. The law on Courts Martial giving the Judge Advocate power to summons, directs he shall, "not summon any officer of the army without the order of the Court unless satisfied that his testimony is material, and necessary to the ends of justice."

The subpoena addressed to me is not by order of the Court, nor does it state that "my testimony is material and necessary to the ends of justice."

I do not raise these exceptions, to the informality or illegality of the summons, to avoid prompt compliance; but state these facts in connection with my doubts, as to the propriety, or my duty to summarily leave my command, situated, as you are aware I am, so differently from any other officer in it.

I write this to ask your advice or orders.

I think Lieut. Col. [A. Bell] Burleson should be required to state, that my testimony in his behalf "is material and necessary to the ends of justice," and not be compelled on frivolous grounds to absent myself, unnecessarily, during a protracted trial, where I feel and know, that my presence is [so] much needed, for the good of the service with my Brigade.

The Judge Advocate as law officer of the Court, while he is prosecutor, is so far the advisor of the Prisoner, that he may suggest to him what defense to make and it is clearly his province and right to know, the materiality of such facts, as, the accused may desire to prove by me. Hence the importance of his knowledge of the fact, and his statement or allegation of its materiality in the subpoena, to prevent frivolous grounds, upon which to base a summons for "any officer of the army" whose services may be deemed of importance to the command.

I would state that I have many officers, much needed with their companies, some companies being utterly destitute, on account of their indefinite detention upon this languishing case. I do not wish to swell the list of those, who have been detained months from their command. I am more than willing to go down when my testimony is wanted, to be dismissed when it is taken. But I ask you Gen'l for the welfare of my command at this juncture; that I be protected against any efforts, on part of accused, to hold me up on this trail, away from my Brigade, perhaps, until the termination of the war.

I learn reliably, the Court adjourned a few days since for 15 days, on Surgeons Certificate of inability on part of accused to attend. These adjournments have been numerous, and I don't wish to be forced to be a hanger on the Court subjected to such an indefinite protraction of its labors.

Very Respectfully Yours
W H Parsons

* * * * * * * * * * * * *

Head Quarters, Parsons Brigade
Little Brazos May 6. 1865

Maj. J.M. Brandon
A.A.G.

I have issued a Special Order, assigning Capt. J C S [James C.S.] Morrow Co I 12th Texas Cavalry, to temporary duty, as A.A.A.G. of my Brigade. He has three (3) officers present for duty, and he has the smallest company in the Regiment. This officer would be far more serviceable to the command and myself, in this capacity than in the line. I need him, and ver[y] much want him personally, both from his tried competency for the duties, and his personal qualities that fit him for the position. I must respectfully ask that Gen Steel approve my action.

Very Truly yours
W H Parsons
Col. Comd'g & c

* * * * * * * * * * * * *

Head Quarters, Parsons Brig
Camp Walker May 7. 1865

Gen'l orders No 5

Owing to the non-compliance on the part of many of the company com'crs with the requirements of G.O. No 17 Dept Hd Qrs, and G.O. No 4 Brig Hd Qrs, and the irregular form in which Furloughs and Passes are presented at these Hd Qrs; the attention of the Field and Company officers of this Brig is called to the orders above Specified.

II. Hereafter the Forms herewith encased [rest missing]

* * * * * * * * * * * * *

Head Quarters, Parsons Brigade
Camp Walker, Texas May 8. 1865

Hon. John C. Breckenridge [Breckinridge]
Secretary of War

Sir,

I hereby respectfully recommend and nominate for promotion, Abraham A. Kemble; a Private of Co. "C" of the 19th Regiment of Texas Cavalry as Assistant Commissary of Subsistence of my Brigade, with the Rank of Major

I. The vacancy is not an original one, but, was caused by the resignation of Major A.J. Byrd, the former incumbent.

II. Abraham A. Kemble, is 38 years of age was born in Warren County in the State of Kentucky, and now resides in Ellis Co in the State of Texas.

III. Although he has never acted in the capacity for which he is recommended, he has for the past three years, been an agent in the Quarters Masters Dept, connected with this Brigade, in the active field.

IV. His ability, energy and tact, have reccommended him to my notice; and much needing a man of his capacity, to supply the commissariat of such a large body of Troops, acting as they most always have been, in independent fields of operation, I respectfully urge his appointment. He can furnish the Bond required by law.

Colonel.
Comd'g Brigade, Texas Cav.

* * * * * * * * * * * * *

Head Quarters Parsons Brigade
May 9. 1865. 5 oclock P.M.

Major Brandon
A.A.G.

A courier left here at 1 P.M. precisely with the Regimental reports. It was the same courier you sent up in the morning who informed me, he had orders to return to Redtop & then follow your route wherever you had gone.

This may account for the delay, to day. Your note was received last night ordering them, and it was acted on with great promptness.

Hope you will have received them before this hour.

Yours Respectfully
[blank]
Col. Comdg Brig

* * * * * * * * * * * * *

Head Quarters, Parsons Brigade
Camp Walker, May 13th 1865.

Capt.

I am directed by the Col. Comd'g to say to you, that he has been reliably informed, that several officers with squads of men, have been ordered to impress unbroke Horses, for the use of the army, and desires that you should be very cautious, and allow no improper conduct on the part of your men towards officers or men, who are properly authorized to impress, but demand their authority. I herewith enclose you a copy of G.O. 5 Dept. Hd Qrs. (series of 1864.)

I am Captain
Very Respectfully
Your Obt Sv't,
J C S [James C. S.] Morrow A.A.A. Gen.

* * * * * * * * * * * * *

Head Quarters Parson's Brigade
Camp Walker, May 16th, 1865

General Orders No. 9

The comd'g officers of Regiments and Detachments, will have forwarded to these Head Quarters, with as little delay as posible, applications for for [*sic*] furloughs, for men to harvest their wheat—

II One man out of every few, in each company, present [rest of order torn off]

# APPENDIX I

## Miscellaneous Orders

South Bend Hed Qrs Texas Out Post
February 5 1862-

Genl Order[1]

For, the preservation of Military discipline and [for the use of] officers the following regulations are published for the government of the troops constituting Cavalry outposts

I No private or officer will go further than one mile from the Hed Qrs of this comdg without a pass from the proper office to wit in passing from one squadron or battalion to another belonging to the same Regim[ent] the pass off the officer comdg the squadron or battalion is required

II In passing from one regiment to another or to any other point than the one designated above the pass of the officer comdg must be countersigned by the Brigade Comder.

III All details or business or duty must have the proper passes duly required an[d] countersigned

IV The Regts will be subsisted and foraged by the staff officer of same subject to order from these hed Qrs the officers of the Staff will see that the rations, an[d] such a_____ allow & that due care is taken to prevent waste of rations

[1] This order is the only one in the Order Book to date from the time that Parsons's Regiment was in Texas at the beginning of the war. By late 1861 the men of the Twelfth Texas were in camps of instruction outside Hempstead near Houston. They remained there until the late spring of 1862. The right side of the order is torn below item IV and not incluede here.

* * * * * * * * * * * * *

*Captured Orders of the First Wisconsin Cavalry Regiment*[2]

Head Quarters 1st Regt Wis Cav
Bloomfield Mo. July 8 1862

General Order No 1

Lieut. Owen with Squadron "M" will act as an escort to the train, and will march at 4 oclock A.M.

The 2d Battalion will march at 6 oclock A.M. The march will be conducted slowly and the men will walk at least one mile in _____.

By Order of
Col. Edward Daniels
Comdg. 1st Wis Cavalry

Geo. O. Clinton
Regt. Adjutant

* * * * * * * * * * * * *

Head Quarters 1st Regt Wis Cavalry
Camp Scatterville Ark July 10 1862

General Order No 2

The attention of the officers of 1st Wis Cavalry is directed to ........ Chapter 2 Volume Cooks Tactics (on the march) the rules there laid down will be strictly conformed to by all.

2nd No Soldier will sit upon his horse at a halt except when required to do so under orders form his superior officers, when halting even for a few moments every soldier will dismount and the utmost care will be taken to releive the horses of their Saddles as soon as possible after the march is concluded.

3d There will be Roll Call as follows: at Revillee and the beginning and end of each march, and at Tatoo.

4d The Bugler from each Squadron will repeat all calls of Chief Bugler from Head Quarters

By Order of
Col. Edward Daniels
Comdg 1st Regt Wis Cavalry

Geo. O. Clinton
Adjutant

[2] This, and subsequent correspondence of the First Wisconsin Cavalry, was captured by Colonel Parsons at the skirmish at L'Anguille Ferry, Arkansas, on August 3, 1862. See Bailey, *Between the Enemy and Texas*, pages 75-81.

* * * * * * * * * * * * *

Head Quarters 1st Regt Wis Cav.
Gainesville Ark. July 11d 1862

General Order No 3

There will be a meeting of all the commissioned officers of the 1st Regt Wis Cavalry at Head Quarters at 6 A.M. July 12 1862

By Order of
Col. Edward Daniels
Comdg. 1st Wis Cavalry

Geo. O. Clinton
Adjutant

* * * * * * * * * * * * *

Head Quarters 1st Regt Wis Cavalry
Gainesville Ark July 11 1862

General order No 4

Orders of the Day

Revillee .........$5^{30}$ A.M.
Surgeons Call ...$5^{30}$ " "
Breakfast .......7 " "
Guard Mounting 8 " "
Grazing .........$5^{30}$ " "
Recall ..........7 " "
Orderlys Call ....$8^{30}$ " "
Dinner .........12 M
Grazing .........3 P.M.
Recall ..........$4^{30}$ " "
Supper .........6 " "
Retreat .........Sundown
Tattoo ..........$8^{30}$ " "
Taps ............$8^{45}$ " "

Squadron Buglers will follow the calls at Head Quarters.

By Order of
Col. Edward Daniels
Comdg. 1st Wis Cavalry

Geo. O. Clinton
Adjutant

* * * * * * * * * * * * *

Head Quarters 1st Regt Wis Cavalry
Jonesboro Ark July 14 1862

General orders No 5

1st Buglers will meet and practice on call

2nd Signal guns will be fired to call in all detachments. Two guns or more will indicate danger, and all detachments will return to camp, observing every caution in approaching it so [not] to be cut off

3d Major H.S. Eggleston is hereby appointed Provost Marshal of the district in N.E. Arkansas now occupied and hereafter to be occupied by the Federal Forces under my command

4d The Chiefs of Squadrons will see to it that their horses are kept in the shade, and fed

5d At the close of the march, after the Camp is established and horses cared for, the officers call will be sounded, after which the Field Officers and Squadron Chiefs will report at Head Quarters to receive orders.

| | |
|---|---|
| 40 | By Order of |
| G.O. Clinton | Col. Edward Daniels |
| Adjutant | Comdg 1st Wis Cavalry |

* * * * * * * * * * * * *

Head Quarters 1st Regt Wis. Cav.
Madison, Ark, July 19 1862

General Order No 6

1st No Officer will be permitted to ride a Government horse unless he has already in service the number actually required by the Regulations, all of which are disabled. In any case he shall give his receipt and either pay for the horse or return it in good condition

2nd Officers on detachments will immediately on their return present themselves at Head Quarters sending their men to Quarters in charge of some subordinate

3d They will take full and accurate notes of the roads forage provisions &c or whatever they saw or heard of importance they will deliver promptly to the Provost Marshal or in his absence to the commanding officer all captured property

| | |
|---|---|
| | By Order of |
| Geo. O. Clinton | Col. Edward Daniels |
| Adjuta[nt] | Comdg. 1st Wis Cavalry |

# APPENDIX II

## Officers of Parsons's Texas Cavalry Brigade

Twelfth Texas Cavalry Regiment

| | |
|---|---|
| William H. Parsons | colonel |
| John W. Mullen | lieutenant colonel |
| A. Bell Burleson | lieutenant colonel |
| Emory W. Rogers | major |
| Lochlin J. Farrar | major |
| William G. Vardell | adjutant |
| A. Bell Burleson | adjutant |
| William M. Daviess | adjutant |
| T.G.A. Willis | quartermaster & commissary |
| Henry L. Rankin | quartermaster & commissary |
| R.A. Terrell | quartermaster |
| F.H. Ayres | commissary |
| J.R. Grover | quartermaster |
| John D. Hogan | surgeon |
| Thomas M. Matthews | surgeon |
| W.H.B. Goodwin | surgeon |
| Thomas D. Lorance | assistant surgeon |
| A.J. Embree | assistant surgeon |
| William Bethell | detailed surgeon |
| W.F. Compton | chaplain |
| J. Fred Cox | chaplain |
| Elisah Terry | chaplain |
| Joseph Weir | captain, Company A |
| George W. Ingram | captain, Company A |
| Appleton M. Maddux | captain, Company B |
| William Jeff Neal | captain, Company C |
| Thomas F. Haley | captain, Company C |
| Benjamin Barnes | captain, Company C |
| M.B. Highsmith | captain, Company D |
| John C. Brown | captain, Company E |
| William G. Veal | captain, Company F |
| H.W. Kyser | captain, Company G |
| W.J. Stokes | captain, Company H |
| J. Em Hawkins | captain, Company H |
| William M. Campbell | captain, Company H |

| | |
|---|---|
| J.W. Mullen | captain, Company I |
| Wiley Peace | captain, Company I |
| James C.S. Morrow | captain, Company I |
| A.F. Moss | captain, Company K |
| James P. Brown | captain, Company K |

Nineteenth Texas Cavalry Regiment

| | |
|---|---|
| Nathaniel M. Burford | colonel |
| Benjamin Watson | lieutenant colonel |
| Joel T. Daves | major |
| John B. Williams | major |
| James E. Terrell | adjutant |
| Scott Whitfield | adjutant |
| Alex Harwood | quartermaster |
| Jefferson J. Mallord | commissary |
| William H. Pyle | surgeon |
| John W. Knight | assistant surgeon |
| W.B. Dashiell | assistant surgeon |
| William H. Hughs | chaplain |
| Fountain P. Ray | chaplain |
| William W. Parks[1] | captain, Company A |
| William W. Peevy[2] | captain, Company A |
| Allen Beard | captain, Company B |
| James T. Hasbrook[3] | captain, Company B |
| Benjamin Watson | captain, Company C |
| Car Forrest | captain, Company C |
| John B. Williams | captain, Company D |
| James B. Doak | captain, Company D |
| Reuben E. Sanders | captain, Company E |
| Patrick H. Saunders[4] | captain, Company F |
| Fauntleroy R. Ball | captain, Company F |
| Dubart Murphy[5] | captain, Company G |
| William O. Michaux | captain, Company G |
| John M. Stone | captain, Company H |
| Samuel Wright | captain, Company I |
| Nicholas T. Sneed | captain, Company I |
| James Thomas[6] | captain, Company K |

[1] Parks was forty-two years old in 1862. A native of Tennessee, he had enlisted from Ellis County where he was court clerk. He claimed $2,500 in real estate and $6,200 in personal estate. Bailey, *Between the Enemy and Texas*, 224-25.

[2] Peevy was thirty-eight years old in 1862. He was a native of Alabama and had enlisted from Ellis County. A farmer, he claimed $1,950 in real estate and $2,550 in personal estate. Ibid.

[3] Hasbrook was thirty-one years old when he enlisted in 1862. Ibid.

[4] Saunders was twenty-eight years old when he enlisted in 1862. Ibid.

[5] Murphy was a native of Missouri who had enlisted in Kaufman County. He was fifty six years old and gave his occupation as farmer worth $1,720 in real estate and $6,382 in personal estate. Ibid.

[6] Thomas was thirty-nine years old when he enlisted in Dallas County. He was a native of Tennessee who gave his occupation as farmer and his worth as $3,000 in real estate and $4,000 in personal estate. Ibid., 224-25.

Twenty-first Texas Cavalry Regiment

| | |
|---|---|
| George W. Carter | colonel |
| DeWitt Clinton Giddings | lieutenant colonel |
| B.D. Chenoweth | major |
| S.G. Ward | adjutant |
| W.J. [ I.] Cowles (Coroles) | adjutant |
| B.F. Cockson | adjutant |
| Robert Graham | quartermaster |
| Wellington Triplett | quartermaster |
| P.W. Connell | quartermaster |
| J.J. Lyons | commissary |
| A.H. McCleish | commissary |
| J.T. Norris | surgeon |
| Thomas Norris | surgeon |
| T.J. Petty | assistant surgeon |
| D.C. Hewson | assistant surgeon |
| Anthony Martin Branch[7] | captain, Company A |
| G.W. Farris | captain, Company A |
| William M. Rust | captain, Company B |
| William M. Walton | captain, Company B |
| Thomas B. Shannon[8] | captain, Company C |
| R. Sample Howard[9] | captain, Company C |
| G.R. Freeman | captain, Company D |
| W. Hess Jones[10] | captain, Company E |
| William M. Harper | captain, Company E |
| D.C. Giddings | captain, Company F |
| John C. Lusk | captain, Company F |
| J.H. Hannah | captain, Company G |
| John R.S. Alston | captain, Company H |
| L.J. Wilson | captain, Company I |
| Martin M. Kenney | captain, Company K |
| J.B. Rocke[11] | captain, Company L |

[7] Branch, elected to the second session of the Confederate Congress in 1863, was unable to use his influence to obtain a promotion for Colonel Parsons. It is unknown if he sided with Carter, his regiment's colonel in the dispute between Parsons and Carter over command of the brigade.

[8] Shannon was a native of Alabama who at thirty years old had enlisted from Montgomery County. He gave his occupation as a miller with $14,000 in real estate and $5,600 in personal estate. Most of his men came from Montgomery and Grimes counties. He resigned after barely a year, claiming medical reasons. Bailey, *Between the Enemy and Texas*, 220-23.

[9] Howard was a native of Mississippi who at twenty-seven years old had enlisted from Anderson County. He gave his occupation as farmer with no real estate and $500 in personal estate. Ibid.

[10] Jones was a native of Tennessee who at thirty-eight years old had enlisted from Gonzales County. He gave his occupation as a farmer with $3,000 in real estate and $300 in personal estate. By the summer of 1862 he was diagnosed with tuberculosis. After an operation he returned home. Ibid., 220-22.

[11] Rocke was twenty-nine years old in 1862. He was a native of Virginia and lived in McLennan County. A doctor, he had no real estate and $3,500 in personal estate. He commanded recruits from the frontier towns of Gatesville and Lampasas. He resigned in 1863 after a long illness. It is possible the small company was consolidated with another at that time. Ibid., 220-23.

Morgan's Regiment

| Charles L. Morgan | lieutenant colonel |
|---|---|
| Benjamin D. McKie | major |
| W.H. Carl | adjutant |
| D. Fentress | assistant surgeon |
| Edward H. Vontress | captain, Company A |
| John W. Posey | captain, Company A |
| Milton M. Boggess | captain, Company B |
| David Alexander Nunn[12] | captain, Company C |
| Franklin L. Farrar | captain, Company D |
| William Ivy Coggins | captain, Company D |
| Alf Johnson | captain, Company E |
| Thomas James | captain, Company E |
| R.B. Carr | captain, Company E |
| Benjamin D. McKie | captain, Company F |
| A.G. Hervey | captain, Company F |
| F.G. Lemmon[13] | captain, Company G |
| James N.Scott[14] | captain, Company G |
| Drury Field[15] | captain, Company H |
| Samuel Richardson | captain, Company I |
| William Herbert Beazley[16] | captain, Company K |

Tenth Texas Field Artillery

| Joseph H. Pratt | captain/major |
|---|---|
| A.J. Simons | lieutenant |
| H.C. Hynson[17] | lieutenant |
| Isaac A. Clare | lieutenant |

[12] Nunn was twenty-three years old in 1860. A native of Mississippi, he had enlisted in Houston County. He was a lawyer with no real estate and $2,000 in personal estate. He had raised the "Crockett Boys" after serving as the town of Crockett's first mayor. The unit subsequently joined the Twenty-eighth Texas Cavalry but eventually became independent. This was the second company that Nunn headed called the "Crockett Boys"; the first had taken part in the New Mexico campaign, but Nunn had returned home after the Battle of Glorieta Pass. Ibid., 228-32.

[13] Lemmon was a native of Kentucky who had enlisted in Cass County. He was forty-three years old in 1860, and claimed to be a farmer with $3,000 in real estate and $7,705 in personal estate. Ibid.

[14] Scott was a native of Kentucky who had enlisted in Marion County. He was twenty-three years old in 1860 and claimed to be a farmer with $2,800 in real estate and $15,500 in personal estate. Ibid.

[15] Field was a native of Tennessee who had enlisted in Panola County. He was thirty-two years old in 1860 and was a lawyer with $2,000 in real estate and $13,000 in personal estate. He owned twelve slaves. Company H appears to have been organized in 1864 from former Texas State troops. Ibid., 228-33.

[16] Beazley was a native of Mississippi who had enlisted in Harris County. He was twenty-two years old in 1860 and a trader (later a doctor). He claimed no real estate and only $650 in personal estate. His company was attached to Morgan only two days before the end of the war, and was composed of pardoned deserters from other Texas organizations along with Indians from the Alabama and Coushatta tribes living in Polk County as well as one or two from the Muscogee tribe. Ibid., 228-34.

[17] Hynson, who was eighteen years old when he joined, had been associated with the Jefferson Ice Manufacturing Company, although he gave his home as Marshall. Ibid., 256.

# INDEX